The Power of Negativity

The Power of Negativity

Selected Writings on the Dialectic in Hegel and Marx

By Raya Dunayevskaya

Edited by Peter Hudis and Kevin B. Anderson

LEXINGTON BOOKS
Lanham • Boulder • New York • Oxford

LEXINGTON BOOKS

Published in the United States of America
by Lexington Books
4720 Boston Way, Lanham, Maryland 20706

12 Hid's Copse Road
Cumnor Hill, Oxford OX2 9JJ, England

British Library Cataloguing in Publication Information Available

Library of Congress Cataloging-in-Publication Data

Dunayevskaya, Raya.
    The power of negativity : selected writings on the dialectic in Hegel and Marx /
  Raya Dunayevskaya.
      p. cm.
    Includes bibliographical references and index.
    ISBN: 978-0-7931-0267-1
    1. Dialectic. 2. Political science—Philosophy. 3. Hegel, Georg Wilhelm Friedrich,
  1770–1831. 4. Marx, Karl, 1818–1883. I. Title.

B2949.D5 D86 2002
110—dc21

                                                                                          2001029456

Printed in the United States of America

♾™ The paper used in this publication meets the minimum requirements of
American National Standard for Information Sciences—Permanence of Paper for
Printed Library Materials, ANSI/NISO Z39.48—1992.

~

Contents

Part III: Theory and Practice at a Turning Point, 1964–71

~

Acknowledgments

The editors would like to thank the following people for helpful comments and criticisms during the preparation of this manuscript, particularly the introduction and notes: Stephen Eric Bronner, Douglas Kellner, Joel Kovel, Bertell Ollman, and Tom Rockmore. We are also grateful to dozens of other friends, students, and colleagues, who made suggestions or who helped in other ways. Finally, we would like to acknowledge support from Northern Illinois University, including assistance with wordprocessing and photocopying.

Abbreviations

CHD	Critique of the Hegelian Dialectic (1844), RD translation
EL	*Encyclopedia Logic*
LCW	Lenin, *Collected Works*
LSW	Lenin, *Selected Works*
MCIF	*Capital*, Vol. I, Fowkes trans.
MCIK	*Capital*, Vol. I, Kerr edition
M&F	*Marxism and Freedom*
MECW	Marx and Engels, *Collected Works*
P&R	*Philosophy and Revolution*
PhGB	*Phenomenology*, Baillie trans.
PhGM	*Phenomenology*, Miller trans.
PhGH	*Phenomenology*, Hoffmeister German edition
PPC	Private Property and Communism (1844), RD translation
PM	*Philosophy of Mind*
SLI	*Science of Logic*, Johnson and Struthers trans., Vol. I
SLII	*Science of Logic*, Johnson and Struthers trans., Vol. II
SLM	*Science of Logic*, Miller trans.
RLWLKM	*Rosa Luxemburg, Women's Liberation, and Marx's Philosophy of Revolution*
WLDR	*Women's Liberation and the Dialectics of Revolution*

Editors' Note

Some of the texts in the following writings have been shortened, or were slightly edited and amended for clarity; all additions are indicated by the use of brackets. All endnotes to the chapters have been supplied by the editors; those by the author are at the bottom of the page.

We have also added page references to works cited in the text, in brackets. Quotations from Hegel's *Phenomenology of Mind* are usually from the translation by Baillie and quotations from the *Science of Logic* are usually from the translation by Johnston and Struthers, as these were the editions most often used by the author. We have provided cross-references for each quote to Miller's translation of the *Phenomenology* and his translation of the *Science of Logic*. For in-text citations from Marx, we have usually referred to Marx and Engels, *Collected Works*, and for those by Lenin, to his *Collected Works*. We have done so for the sake of brevity, even when the text actually being quoted is from a different translation.

~

Raya Dunayevskaya's Concept of Dialectic

Peter Hudis and Kevin Anderson

The Present Moment

Marx's *oeuvre*, which many had declared obsolete, has taken on new life at the dawn of the twenty-first century because the strength of his critique of the destructive power of capital is so missed. Today's unprecedented inequities in wealth and power, accompanied by wrenching technological changes and environmental havoc, as well as monopolization and social fragmentation, are increasingly begetting the sense that the time has come to return to Marx. In a process that conjures up the spirit of the dialectic itself, the very fact which had been heralded as proving the death of Marx—the universalization of capital, as it invades every corner of the earth and all spheres of everyday life—has led workers as well as intellectuals, activists as well as academics, to look anew at what Marx's work means for today. This is reflected in everything from journalistic discourses on the need to face "the specter of Marx," to theoretical analyses on the cogency of the Marxian critique of globalized capitalism.[1] The more the globalization of capital spurs social dislocation and impoverishment, the more we can expect such appraisals of Marx in the coming period.

One surprising feature of much of the current return to Marx, however, is the relative silence on Hegel and the dialectic. This attitude has developed despite Marx's insistence in *Capital* and other works that his method was at its core dialectical and that Hegel's dialectic was for him "the source of all dialectics."[2]

For example, in his *Specters of Marx*, Jacques Derrida terms Marx's writings "urgent" for an understanding of today's globalized capitalism on the one hand, while on the other he distances himself from the Hegelian dialectic, which he calls an "onto-theology" and "anthropo-theology."[3] From the vantage point of the Frankfurt School, a tradition once rooted in a form of Hegelian Marxism, Jürgen Habermas rejects the Hegelian dialectic as the remnant of a romantic idealist philosophy of consciousness, and attacks Marx for remaining "tied to Hegelian logic."[4] Even Moishe Postone, a Frankfurt-trained critical theorist who has urged a return to Marx's critique of capital in order to comprehend the present crisis, considers the Hegelian dialectic as little more than a philosophical expression of the logic of capital.[5]

At the same time, the present moment is rife with serious studies of Hegel by non-Marxists. The past decade has experienced a veritable explosion of new works on Hegel in the Anglo-American world, as seen in such recent books as H. S. Harris's *Hegel's Ladder*, a 1,600-page study of Hegel's *Phenomenology of Mind*. On a more modest, yet significant level, new studies on Hegel by feminists, especially those from a postmodernist background, have emerged.[6] The ongoing discussions of Hegel and Marx often appear, however, as two trains passing each other in the dead of night, very nearly unnoticed by one another.

Fredric Jameson has spoken to this problem:

> This is a time when people no longer understand what dialectical thinking is or why the dialectic came into being in the first place, when they have abandoned the dialectical for less rewarding Nietzschean positions. So there is certainly a need today for a revitalized vision of the dialectic. There I would certainly not abandon Marx, but I would want to go back to Hegel for an enlargement of the way we have normally understood Marx. This is not any particularly new idea with me. Lenin had already said that no one could understand *Das Kapital* who had not already worked his way through Hegel's logic. . . . I think the coming years will show an unconscious need for the dialectic which some of us on the left ought to have the mission to satisfy.[7]

The writings in this volume will, we hope, take us toward satisfying this need. At each stage in the history of Marxism, revolutionaries and theorists have felt the need to transcend the seemingly insurmountable barriers facing the radical movement by turning anew to Hegel. This was true of Lenin in 1914, when he responded to the collapse of established Marxism with the outbreak of World War I by delving into Hegel's *Science of Logic*. It was true of such diverse tendencies as the Frankfurt School and French neo-Marxists in the 1930s and 1940s, who turned to Hegel in a period defined by fascism and the rise of Stalinism. Likewise, in the 1950s, in the face of the new challenges posed by the freedom struggles of the post–World War II era, Raya Dunayevskaya (1910–87) developed the philosophy of Marxist-Humanism through a direct encounter with Hegel's dialectic.

Dunayevskaya's life and work represent a rare combination of passionate involvement in freedom struggles and intense philosophical exploration. Born in Ukraine in 1910, she immigrated to the United States as a teenager, and by the mid-1920s became involved in labor, socialist, and Black liberation movements. After serving as secretary to Leon Trotsky in 1937–38, she broke with him at the time of the Hitler-Stalin Pact in 1939, and subsequently developed a theory of state-capitalism. She argued that Roosevelt's New Deal, Hitler's Germany, and especially Stalin's Russia, represented varieties of a new stage of global capitalism, one in which the fetishism of state planning was paramount.[8] This work soon brought her into a period of close collaboration with the Trinidadian Marxist and cultural critic C. L. R. James, author of *The Black Jacobins*. During the 1940s, she also engaged in dialogue with a number of intellectuals of the anti-Stalinist left, such as Meyer Schapiro, and became a sharp critic of those, such as the pragmatist Sidney Hook, who strongly rejected Hegel as a reactionary thinker.

In the mid-1950s, Dunayevskaya moved in a different direction from James, as she developed a new philosophical perspective through a reexamination of the Hegelian underpinnings of Marx's thought, which she soon termed Marxist-Humanism. In the late 1950s, she engaged in an extensive correspondence on dialectics with the Critical Theorist, Herbert Marcuse, and, a bit later, with Erich Fromm, another former Frankfurt School member.[9] In her *Marxism and Freedom* (1958), to which Marcuse contributed a critical preface, she included as appendices the first English translations of major parts of Marx's 1844 *Economic and Philosophical Manuscripts* and of Lenin's *Philosophical Notebooks*. In rethinking and extending Marx's humanist conceptions in light of the contemporary struggles of rank-and-file labor, women's liberation, African Americans, and youth from the 1950s to the 1980s, she developed an original philosophy of liberation through a continuous return to the Hegelian dialectic. On the one hand, this entailed scathing critiques of anti-Hegelian Marxists such as Louis Althusser, and on the other, more sympathetic but nonetheless probing critiques of leading dialecticians, many of them Hegelian Marxists, including Marcuse, Georg Lukács, Karl Korsch, and Theodor Adorno. In her later discussions of dialectics, she also gave prominence to what she regarded as the highly original contributions of the African liberation theorist, Frantz Fanon, and dissident East European Marxist humanists, as can especially be seen in her *Philosophy and Revolution* (1973) and *Rosa Luxemburg, Women's Liberation, and Marx's Philosophy of Revolution* (1982).

Contemporary Issues in
Dialectical Philosophy

The need to return to the Hegelian dialectic with new eyes is no less urgent today, in light of the crisis confronting all liberation movements, whether of workers, Blacks and other minorities, women, lesbians and gays, or youth. This crisis is disclosed by the aborted and unfinished revolutions that marked the twentieth century, from Russia 1917 to Spain 1936, China 1949, and Cuba 1959, and from Iran to Nicaragua to Grenada in the 1970s and 1980s. In particular, the experience of the Russian Revolution after 1917 suggests that even to *begin* to address this crisis means confronting such questions as, what happens *after* the revolution? How can we ensure that a new form of totalitarianism or bureaucracy will not once again take over after the collapse of the old order? How can ending the division between mental and manual labor move from underlying concept to social practice?

Here is where Dunayevskaya's work as founder of Marxist-Humanism in the United States takes on special importance. Few thinkers in the revolutionary tradition have focused as exhaustively on these issues as Dunayevskaya, especially on the need to confront philosophically the question of what happens *after* the revolution. And even fewer have done so by means of a new interpretation of Hegelian dialectics. On the whole, radical interpreters of Hegel in this century have emphasized such aspects of his thought as the master-slave dialectic and the unhappy consciousness in the *Phenomenology of Mind*, or the concepts of essence, negativity, and contradiction in the *Science of Logic*. While Dunayevskaya also addresses these issues, we believe that her core contribution to dialectics centers on what many other Marxists have ignored or rejected—Hegel's concept of *absolute* negativity.[10] In Hegel, absolute negativity signifies not only the negation of external obstacles, but also the negation of the earlier negation. The power of negativity gets turned back upon the self, upon the internal as well as external barriers to self-movement. Such a negation of the negation is no mere nullity, for the positive is contained in the negative, which is the path to a new beginning.

One of Hegel's first references to absolute negativity in the *Science of Logic* occurs during a critique of Spinoza's notion that "every determination is a negation." Hegel considers such a stress on negativity to be a great advance over previous positions. However, this advance is not without contradiction and in Hegel's view falls short by dissolving into a "formless abstraction," because this type of bare negativity lacks determinateness.[11] At this point, Hegel goes beyond bare or first negativity to what he calls second or absolute negativity, with the latter containing not only a rejection of the old, but also the basis for a forward movement: "But in all this, care must be taken to distinguish between the *first* negation as negation *in general*, and the second negation, the negation of the negation: the latter is concrete, absolute negativity, just as the former on the contrary is only *abstract* negativity" (pp. 115–16).

If the question of absolute negativity were exhausted here, in a more or less formal process of the negation of the negation, there would be far less controversy among radical interpreters of Hegel. For example, writing more than a century ago, Friedrich Engels, whose studies of dialectics have formed the basis of most orthodox Marxist discussions of the topic ever since, did at least mention the negation of the negation. However, while extolling a formalized and sometimes scientistic notion of negation of the negation, Engels also attacks Hegel's Absolute Idea, which, he maintains, includes a notion of "the end of history" in which "the whole dogmatic content of the Hegelian system is declared to be absolute truth, in contradiction to his dialectical method, which dissolves all that is dogmatic."[12] Thus, Engels mentions the negation of the negation as a principle of the dialectic, while attacking the Absolute Idea as dogmatic and even reactionary.

In contrast to Engels and most subsequent interpreters within the Marxist tradition, Dunayevskaya finds extremely important insights for dialectics of liberation in Hegel's Absolutes, which Hegel develops in the concluding chapters of his major works. In so doing, she focuses on the chapters on Absolute Knowledge in the *Phenomenology*, the Absolute Idea in the *Science of Logic*, and the Absolute Mind in the *Philosophy of Mind*.

Hegel's Absolutes have been frequently dismissed not only as dogmatic, but also as a closed ontology. These are interpretations which, as Dunayevskaya argues in many of the selections in this volume, are hard to maintain once one examines Hegel's actual texts. This can be seen from a few representative passages from the chapter on the Absolute Idea, which concludes Hegel's *Science of Logic*. Hegel begins his discussion by stating that the Absolute Idea is "the identity of the theoretical and the practical idea," thereby holding to a notion of practice as well as of theory at the very point where some have seen only a flight into an abstract universal. A few lines further in this same passage, Hegel also writes that "the Absolute Idea . . . contains within itself the highest degree of opposition" (p. 824). Here, at least, Hegel rejects the notion of an oppositionless totality which has absorbed all negativity and particularity, as is so often charged. Some pages later, at the conclusion of the chapter, Hegel writes of the Absolute Idea as an "absolute liberation," as a dialectic of freedom in which "no transition takes place" (p. 843). The human spirit now moves toward liberation, having already worked through the myriad obstacles which lay in wait for freedom in the previous 800 pages of his work.

Dunayevskaya's focus on Hegel's Absolutes countered the traditional Marxist view of them as a "closed ontology" in which all particularities and difference are effaced in the name of an abstract unity. As early as her initial studies on dialectics in the late 1940s, she emphasized "the sheer genius of [Hegel's] language which defines identity as 'unseparated difference'" (see the appendix to this volume, p. 350). Nor was she attracted to Hegel's Absolutes out of an affinity with Lukács' emphasis on totality. Throughout her work, from her "Letters on Hegel's Absolutes" of 1953 through *Marxism and Freedom* (1958), *Philosophy and Revolution* (1973) and *Rosa Luxemburg, Women's Liberation and Marx's Philosophy of Revolution* (1982), she saw in Hegel's Absolutes "the categories of freedom, of subjectivity, of reason, the logic of a movement by which humanity makes itself free."[13] As she put it in chapter 1 of *Philosophy and Revolution*, her most sustained and important discussion of Hegel:

> Precisely where Hegel sounds most abstract, seems to close the shutters tight against the whole movement of history, there he lets the lifeblood of the dialectic—absolute negativity—pour in. It is true that Hegel writes as if the resolution of opposing live forces can be overcome by a mere thought transcendence. But he has, by bringing oppositions to their most logical extreme, opened new paths, a new relationship of theory to practice, which Marx worked out as a totally new relationship of philosophy to revolution. Today's revolutionaries turn their backs on this at their peril (pp. 31–32).

This interpretation diverges in important ways from those of other Hegelian Marxists, such as Lukács and Marcuse. As seen in chapter 12 of the present volume, Dunayevskaya applauds Lukács' argument in *History and Class Consciousness* (1923) that the dialectic is the core of Marxism, but she also critiques his theory of reification. In *The Young Hegel* (1948), Lukács, like Dunayevskaya, writes that "it would be quite mistaken to see the 'absolute spirit' as nothing but mysticism."[14] Here, as elsewhere in his work, Lukács connects Hegel's writings to the historical and social reality of his time. However, Lukács in the end dismisses Absolute Knowledge as a flight from objective reality which cannot serve as a source for the further development of Marxist dialectics: "Absolute Knowledge, Hegel's designation for the highest stage of human knowledge, has a definite idealistic significance: the reintegration of 'externalized' reality into the subject, i.e. the total supersession of the objective world."[15]

In his *Reason and Revolution* (1941), Frankfurt School member Herbert Marcuse, also like Dunayevskaya, stresses the revolutionary character of

Hegel's dialectic, especially the concept of negativity: "Hegel's philosophy is indeed what the subsequent reaction termed it, a negative philosophy. It is originally motivated by the conviction that the given facts that appear to common sense as the positive index of truth are in reality the negation of truth, so that truth can only be established by their destruction."[16] At the level of the Absolute Idea, which Marcuse holds to be a "totality," he concedes that the Absolute is also "dialectical thought and thus contains its negation, it is not a harmonious and stable form but a process of unification of opposites." However, what he ultimately stresses concerning the Absolute is what he sees as its totalizing moment, wherein "all negativity is overcome."[17] Dunayevskaya's debates with Marcuse on these issues can be found in a number of the selections in this volume, which include several letters from the extensive Dunayevskaya-Marcuse correspondence.

Dunayevskaya's emphasis on the liberatory dimension of Hegel's dialectic also underlines her similarities and differences with other thinkers, such as the Frankfurt School philosopher Theodor Adorno. Adorno affirmed the liberatory character of Hegel's overall philosophy, writing in his "Aspects of Hegel's Philosophy" (1957), "In Hegel reason finds itself constellated with freedom. Freedom and reason are nonsense without one another. The real can be considered rational only insofar as the idea of freedom, that is, human beings' genuine self-determination, shines through it."[18] As against those who contend that Hegel's dialectic ignores the actual and leaves it as mere notion of freedom, Adorno argued that Hegel "accomplishes the opposite as well, an insight into the subject as a self-manifesting objectivity" (p. 7). Yet Adorno parted company with Hegel when it came to the concept of absolute negativity. Adorno, who sought to expunge the affirmative character of Hegel's dialectic, went so far as to link absolute negativity to Nazi genocide! In the midst of a discussion of the horrors of Auschwitz and its implications for philosophy in *Negative Dialectics* (1966), Adorno writes: "Absolute negativity is in plain sight and ceased to surprise anyone."[19] On the basis of her own reading of Hegel's *Science of Logic*, Dunayevskaya attacks this view, terming it a "vulgar reduction of absolute negativity" (see this volume, Part 4, p. 187).

Adorno contended in "Aspects of Hegel's Philosophy" that Hegel's Absolutes "dissolve anything not proper to consciousness" by reducing all existence to the self-movement of the absolute subject. By holding fast to idealism, he said, Hegel's Absolutes invoke a totalizing subject which swallows up the actual. This, Adorno argued, bears a striking resemblance to what Marx conceptualizes as alienated labor. Just as Reason in Hegel subsumes all otherness into the self-movement of the concept, so the labor process in capitalism subsumes all human and natural contingency into the movement of mechanized, abstract labor. According to Adorno, "In Hegel, abstract labor takes on magical form. . . . The self-forgetfulness of production, the insatiable and destructive expansive principle of the exchange society, is reflected in Hegelian metaphysics. It describes the way the world actually is" (p. 44)—but not, as in Marx, the way it can be transformed. This notion that Hegel's Absolutes provide, at best, a philosophical gloss for the self-expansive power of the capitalist production process, rather than, as Dunayevskaya contends, the ground for a philosophy of human emancipation, is shared in different ways by a wide variety of contemporary thinkers, including Jürgen Habermas, Gilles Deleuze, Tony Negri, Moishe Postone, and István Mészáros.[20]

Another challenge to the concept of absolute negativity has come from Jacques Derrida's deconstructionism. To be sure, Derrida has acknowledged Hegel's creation of an "immense revolution" in philosophy "in taking the negative seriously," and has even tried to ground his concept of *différance* in Hegel's affirmation of the inseparability of identity and difference in the *Science of Logic*.[21] Yet Derrida argues that the self-activating power of absolute negativity means that "the concept of a general heterogeneity is impossible" in Hegel. As Derrida sees it, Hegel's Absolutes "determine difference as contradiction, only in order to resolve it, to interiorize it, to lift it up . . . into the self-presence of an onto-theological or onto-teleological synthesis."[22] He therefore calls for a total "break with the system of *Aufhebung* [transcendence] and with speculative dialectics." Even more problematically, he has argued that such an "absolute break" with Hegel also characterizes Marx: "Marx [in his 1844 critique of Hegel] then sets out the critical moment of Feuerbach and in its most operative stance: the questioning of the *Aufhebung* and of the negation of the negation. The absolute positive . . . hence must not pass through the negation of the negation, the Hegelian *Aufhebung*. . . . "[23]

We need to underscore that Adorno's and Derrida's characterizations of Hegel's concept of negativity, especially absolute negativity, seem to diverge from those of Marx. It is true that Marx took sharp exception to Hegel in his 1844 "Critique of the Hegelian Dialectic" and elsewhere for dehumanizing the development of Idea by treating it as stages of disembodied consciousness instead of the creation of live men and women. As a result, Marx argued, Hegel's philosophy ends in a series of absolutes which elevate the abstract at the expense of life itself. For this reason he called Hegel's *Logic* "the money of the Spirit."[24] Yet this did not mean that he followed Feuerbach in rejecting "the negation of the negation" and Hegel's Absolutes as a mere idealist delusion.

Nor, like Adorno, did he view Hegel's concept of dialectical self-movement as simply expressing the self-expansive power of capitalism. It is true that Marx critiqued the way capital takes on a life of its own and becomes self-determining. He did not, however, view the actuality of Hegel's concept of self-determination as limited to that of capital. Quite the contrary. For Marx the subjective struggle of the workers is capable of attaining a liberatory, *human* self-determination by experiencing the dialectic of absolute negativity. Marx broke this down concretely in his 1844 *Economic and Philosophical Manuscripts* by showing that the abolition of private property is merely the first negation. To reach the goal of a truly new society, he writes, it is necessary to negate this negation. In contrast to what he called "vulgar communism," which stops at the mere abolition of private property, he stressed that only through the "transcendence of this mediation" is it possible to reach "*positive* humanism, beginning from itself." This "thoroughgoing Naturalism or Humanism," Marx continues, is the result of the negation of the negation. This is why he writes, in commenting on the chapter on "Absolute Knowledge" in Hegel's *Phenomenology of Mind:* "The greatness of Hegel's *Phenomenology,* and of its final result—the dialectic of negativity as the moving and creative principle—lies in this, that Hegel comprehends the self-production of the human being as a process. . . ."[25]

Two decades later, in the closing pages of *Capital,* Vol. I, Marx makes recourse once again to Hegel's concept of absolute negativity, here also discussing the negation of the negation. In his discussion of "the absolute general law of capitalist accumulation," Marx refers to the brutal expropriation of the peasants from their land during the sixteenth century agricultural revolution in England as "the first negation of private property," in which the peasants lose their property. Over the next centuries, capitalism develops and eventually "begets its own negation," the working class which it has called into existence. Marx concludes:

> This is the negation of the negation. It does not reestablish private property, but it does indeed establish individual property on the basis of the achievements of the capitalist era: namely, cooperation and the possession in common of the land and the means of production produced by labor itself.[26]

Thus, Marx sees Hegel's concept of negativity and of the first and second negation neither as purely destructive nor as limiting us to an overly affirmative stance toward existing society. In addition, contrary to the claims of Louis Althusser and others, Marx's critical appropriation of Hegel's dialectic was continuous, even in his late writings, as seen in his reference to the negation of the negation in his Mathematical Manuscripts.[27]

Since Marx's death in 1883 the emergence of new objective crises has again and again stirred interest in this dialectic of negativity, no matter how often Hegel was declared dead and buried. This is reflected not only in the work of such Western Marxists as Lukács, Gramsci, and Adorno, but also in the dialectical humanism of Frantz Fanon. Fanon's profound return to Hegel in light of what he considered to be the additive of color in the contemporary freedom struggles demonstrates the importance of dialectical philosophy in meeting the challenges posed by new forces of liberation. This is no less true when it comes to today. The collapse of statist communism in the former Soviet Union and Eastern Europe has given new meaning to Marx's critique of the tendency to stop at first negation, the mere abolition of private property, without moving on to the negation of the negation, and the creation of new humanist social relations. As the power of capital continues to expand and globalize, bringing with it ever-greater social dislocations and inequities, the search for new alternatives rooted in the dialectic of second negativity is sure to show itself.

This can already be seen on one level in the appearance of a number of studies of Hegel over the past decade, such as those by Daniel Berthold-Bond and John Hoffmeyer, which sharply contest the notion that Hegel's Absolutes are a "closed ontology" signifying "the end of history."[28] As Berthold-Bond put it in his discussion of the final pages of Hegel's *Phenomenology*:

> Absolute Knowledge is not the End of history, but the sort of knowledge which is possible only at the end of an epoch of history, and which is required to comprehend the development of the world-spirit within that epoch, so as to prepare the rebirth and transformation of the world into a new shape, a new existence. . . . Recollection [is] not only a sort of memorial of the past but an anticipation of the future, a redemption or resurrection of spirit into a new birth in historical time (p. 136).

As Dunayevskaya noted in *Philosophy and Revolution*, "Hegel's Absolutes have ever exerted a simultaneous force of attraction and repulsion" (p. 4).

We believe that Dunayevskaya's specific interpretation of Hegel, in emphasizing the cogency of the dialectic of absolute negativity for today's freedom struggles, takes on new life at the present moment. As this collection will make clear, she views Hegel's Absolutes *as new beginnings*. Central to this is her belief that the concept of absolute negativity expresses, at a philosophical level, the quest by masses of people, not simply to negate existing economic and political structures, but to create *totally new human relations* as well. As Louis Dupré put it in his Preface to *Philosophy and Revolution*:

> A notable difference separates Raya Dunayevskaya's from the earlier positions of [Lukács and Karl Korsch]. Their interpretation had limited the revolutionary impact of Hegel's philosophy to the sociopolitical order. Dunayevskaya aims for a total liberation of the human person—not only from the ills of a capitalist society but also from the equally oppressive State capitalism of established communist governments. (p. xv)

In situating the concept of absolute negativity in the struggles of workers, women, youth, Blacks, and other minorities, Dunayevskaya opened new ways of concretizing and projecting this concept *philosophically*. Once the dialectic of second negativity is seen as intrinsic to the human subject, it becomes possible to grasp and project the idea of second negativity as a veritable force of liberation. Dunayevskaya's writings on Hegel and dialectics provide a new basis for working out a vision of the future—of totally new human relations, of an end to the division between mental and manual labor and of alienated gender relations—which can animate and give direction to the emerging freedom struggles of today.

Our time is burdened by the absence of a vision of a future which transcends the horizon of existing society. Everywhere, we are confronted with the assertion that we must accept the limits of actually existing capitalism as our sole alternative. The profound crisis of the socialist movement over the past decades has made this crisis of the imagination all the more overwhelming. The failure to project an alternative to both existing capitalism and statist communism is a more important facet of today's social crises than is generally recognized. Unless we rethink the meaning of Marx's Marxism in light of *this* problem, *this* reality, *this* contradiction, it is hard to see how it is possible to break through the many-sided retrogression that has engulfed the world ever since the Reagan-Thatcher era of the 1980s. For this reason, we believe, Dunayevskaya's studies of Hegel's dialectic and his Absolutes, in which she saw the vision of a liberatory future that post-Marx Marxists had failed to articulate, is more timely than ever.

Dunayevskaya's Writings on Dialectics

Although Dunayevskaya founded the philosophy of Marxist-Humanism in the mid-1950s, the work which preceded this is of considerable importance. Foremost here is her theory of state-capitalism. As mentioned earlier, Dunayevskaya served as Russian-language secretary to Leon Trotsky in Mexico, in 1937–38. Her break from Trotsky at the time of the Hitler-Stalin Pact in 1939 over his insistence that Russia remained a "workers' state, though degenerate" led to her birth as a theoretician. She contended that Russia had transformed into a state-capitalist society, and set out to prove it through a series of articles and essays analyzing the Russian economy.

In 1941 she joined forces with C. L. R. James, who had independently come to a state-capitalist position, also from within the Trotskyist movement. The two formed what became known as the Johnson-Forest Tendency or State-Capitalist Tendency within the American Trotskyist movement, from the early 1940s to the early 1950s (Johnson was James' pseudonym; Forest was Dunayevskaya's). A third key member was the Chinese-American Grace Lee (Boggs). Dunayevskaya authored most of the Tendency's analyses of state-capitalism in Stalinist Russia.

A number of theories of state-capitalism had arisen on the anti-Stalinist Left by the 1940s. Dunayevskaya's was distinctive among them in seeing state-capitalism not just as a Russian phenomenon, but as part of a new world stage of capitalism emerging from the Great Depression. Moreover, from the start her theory of state-capitalism was no mere social and economic theory, for it reached for something more, for new forces and a new vision with which to oppose the horrors of totalitarian state-capitalism as well as the bureaucratic state-capitalism of the welfare state. Central to this was the discernment and theoretical analysis of new revolutionary forces, such as rank-and-file workers opposed to the emergent labor bureaucracy, anti-colonial movements, independent struggles of the Black masses in the United States, and new struggles of women and youth. No less central was the way she began to carve out a form of dialectical philosophy with which to critique and oppose the crude and scientistic materialism found, not only in Stalinist ideology, but also in Trotsky's work, as well as in that of other Marxist intellectuals of the period. Her engagement with the dialectic in the 1940s took varying forms, such as exposing Stalinist distortions of the law of value in *The American Economic Review*, attacking their deletion of chapter one of *Capital* with its section on commodity fetishism from the teaching of *Capital*,[29] and critiquing Trotskyists for failing to "keep their fingers on the pulse of human relations."[30] Most importantly, she wrote one of the first discussions in the United States of Marx's *1844 Manuscripts*, her 1942 essay "Labor and Society."[31] In this period she also studied Lenin's 1914–15 *Philosophical Notebooks* on Hegel, which she was the first to translate into English in the late 1940s.

James, Dunayevskaya, and Lee debated Hegelian dialectics intensely in this period. In the face of the phenomenon of counter-revolution from *within* the revolution, which they viewed as the "absolute contradiction" of the age, they began to speak of the need to explore a dimension of Hegel that Marxists had tended to shy away from—the last book of Hegel's *Science of Logic*, "Subjective Logic, or the Doctrine of the Notion," and especially its final chapter "The Absolute Idea." At the same time, they began to speak of the need to relate dialectics to questions of organization within the revolutionary movements. By the late 1940s, the Johnson-Forest Tendency was moving away from the Leninist concept of the vanguard party to lead and had begun to pose the need for a new relation of spontaneity to organization. Working out such a new relation, they held, required a direct encounter with dialectics. As James put it in his *Notes on Dialectics* (1948), "We have to get hold of the Notion, of the Absolute Idea before we can see this relation between organization and spontaneity in its concrete truth."[32]

By 1949, however, underlying differences between James and Lee on the one hand, and Dunayevskaya on the other, began to surface. Some of this can be seen in the extensive three-way correspondence between James, Dunayevskaya, and Lee in 1949–51, the period in which Dunayevskaya completed her translation of Lenin's "Abstract of Hegel's *Science of Logic.*" As she suggested in a letter to James, included in the appendix to this volume, James did not actually fulfill his stated aim of delving into the Doctrine of the Notion, in which Hegel most fully develops the concept of absolute negativity. In his *Notes on Dialectics*, she writes, James had much less to say about the Doctrine of the Notion than did Lenin in his 1914–15 Hegel Notebooks. Instead of delving into the Absolute Idea, she writes to James, "the thing you chose to stop at and say, *hic Rhodus, hic salta* to, was the Law of Contradiction in [the Doctrine of] Essence."[33]

When James finally responded to her letter, he equivocated on the issue of Hegelianism and idealism altogether, at one point defending even so crude and mechanistic a work as Lenin's early *Materialism and Empirio-Criticism* (1908) with its notion that theory should be a photocopy of reality. James declared that, "reading the book now I find no inadequacy" in it.[34] Though important dialogue between them on the dialectic continued until the mid-1950s, James never explored in depth the contemporary significance of Hegel's Absolutes. Nor, in Dunayevskaya's view, did he ever deal seriously with the young Marx. As she later put it, he "stopped dead" before reaching either Hegel's Absolutes or Marx's Humanism, thereby failing to project a full *philosophical* break from Trotskyism (see this volume, pp. 165). This led, in 1955, to a political and theoretical break between Dunayevskaya and James.

In the years preceding that break, far from deterring her from a journey into Hegel's Absolutes, these differences spurred Dunayevskaya to continue to work out their meaning. New impulses for liberation arising from ongoing social struggles also helped to focus her journey. For example, at the time she was translating Lenin's 1914–15 notes on Hegel, with their strong emphasis on subjectivity, she was also active with coal miners in West Virginia, who in 1949–50 conducted a massive wildcat strike against the introduction of automation. The strike was motivated not primarily by issues of wages and benefits, but by the nature of the labor process and the degree of worker control of production. Dunayevskaya saw that in asking questions such as "what *kind* of labor should man perform?" the workers were seeking to go beyond the traditional framework of leftist and trade union politics.[35] New questions were being raised about *what it means to be human* in the very course of the struggle against dehumanizing working conditions. The abstract question of second negativity became newly concrete to her, as in her view workers were attempting to go beyond the mere negation of the immediate structures of oppression by posing what *kind* of human relations they are *for*. Dunayevskaya remained closely attuned to the emergence of such sentiments from workers, women, Blacks, and youth throughout the late 1940s and early 1950s, as seen in her extensive writings on the independent character of the Black struggle in the United States and her singling out of women as a force of liberation, as early as 1950 in an essay on "The Miners' Wives."[36] In the same period, as she later acknowledged, the new type of worker-peasant revolution in Bolivia in 1952 became especially important to her.[37]

The most critical moment in this search for new revolutionary forces came with the death of Stalin in March 1953. The long-awaited death of this tyrant, she felt, was bound to lift an incubus from the minds of the Russian and East European masses. She was seeking to anticipate the kinds of revolts that might follow Stalin's death and the new thinking they would require from revolutionary theoreticians.

This helped motivate her direct exploration of Hegel's Absolutes in two letters written to Grace Lee in May 1953. Both letters, which are included in this volume, explore the relation of spontaneity to organization in light of Hegelian categories. The first letter, written on May 12, 1953, focuses on the final chapter of Hegel's *Science of Logic*, "The Absolute Idea." A number of dialectical categories are discussed here, from the limits of the concept of causality, to the concept of the subject as "personal and free," to Hegel's notion of the "free release" of the Idea of absolute negativity as constituting an "absolute liberation." In the second letter, written on May 20, 1953, Dunayevskaya moves from Hegel's *Logic* to his *Philosophy of Mind*, a work which had not been explored before by Marxists. She takes up such issues as Hegel's concept of freedom, the relation of "will" to the dialectics of freedom, and most important of all, the final three paragraphs of the *Philosophy of Mind*, which represent a summation of Hegel's philosophy as a whole. Here, she develops her own distinctive version of the dialectic, seeing Hegel's Absolute Mind not as a mere logical abstraction but as the expression of a *dual* movement—a "movement from practice that is itself a form of theory and a movement from theory that is itself a form of philosophy and revolution."[38]

Hegel's statement, made near the end of his *Philosophy of Mind*, that "nature implicitly contains the Idea" becomes her jumping off point for developing the view that mass practice from below in the grassroots freedom movements *is itself a form of theory*.[39] In this way, she disclosed a new vantage point for a total opposition to existing society, one which does not stop at a first or bare negation, but which moves on to the second negation, to the positive within the negative, to express philosophically the yearning of women, children, and men to be whole human beings. Dunayevskaya developed these new interpretations of the dialectic on the eve of two major revolts against totalitarian communism, the East German uprising of June 17, 1953 and the 1956 Hungarian Revolution, which in opposing both capitalism and existing communism placed the *humanism* of Marx, especially his *1844 Manuscripts*, onto the historic stage. This was also the period of the historic Montgomery Bus Boycott of 1955–56. To Dunayevskaya, these new freedom movements were inseparable from the new stage of dialectical cognition she was attempting to work out.

In anticipating these new movements from practice, Dunayevskaya in her breakthrough on Hegel's Absolutes also discerned a new *movement from theory reaching for philosophy*. Once the Idea of absolute negativity was seen as intrinsic to the subject, it no longer became necessary (as with an older generation of historical materialists) to "fear" the self-determination of the Idea as some mystical abstraction. The Idea itself could now be *philosophically* developed in order to give revolutionary action its *direction*. (We will return to this point, below.)

In the 1980s, when Dunayevskaya was reviewing the 50-year development of the philosophy that she had termed Marxist-Humanism in 1957, she discovered that the 1953 letters represented nothing less than its philosophical moment.[40] Each stage of her development of this body of ideas constituted a further fleshing out and concretization of the new points of departure contained in the 1953 letters. But all of their ramifications were not evident from the start, even to herself. It took repeated returns to them on her part, in response to objective world events and developments in Marxist-Humanism, for the full meaning of these letters to show itself.

This can be seen in her changing assessment of Lenin. Lenin was a crucial figure for her, not only because of 1917, but also because he was the one major Marxist leader after Marx to turn directly to Hegel. He did so in 1914–15, in response to the collapse of the Second International at the outbreak of World War I. Moreover, his "Abstract of Hegel's *Science of Logic*" delved deeper into the dialectic than many Marxists who followed him, in that he engaged in a materialist reading of the most idealistic part of Hegel's *Logic*, the "Doctrine of the Notion." However, the 1953 letters also represent a philosophical departure from Lenin. As Dunayevskaya notes in her letter of May 12, 1953, Lenin stopped short of the "free release" of the Idea in his encounter with Hegel and never went into Hegel's *Philosophy of Mind*—the work in which he most fully developed the concept of absolute negativity. By holding fast to "materialism," "objective world connections," and "practice," Dunayevskaya argued, Lenin failed to develop his own insight in his Hegel Notebooks that "cognition not only reflects the objective world, but also creates it" (see chapters 1 and 17 of this volume). Yet although a philosophical critique of Lenin is already central to Dunayevskaya's 1953 letters, its full ramifications became clear to her only near the end of her life. These writings from the 1980s make more explicit the distinctiveness of her overall approach to dialectics.[41]

The Structure of This Volume

The texts which comprise this volume vary greatly with regard to style, length, and intended audience. Some are essays and articles that were edited and published by Dunayevskaya. Others, of a more fragmentary nature, are letters, transcripts of lectures, and works in progress. We have chosen to include many of the latter, because we believe that they make an important contribution to ongoing discussions and debates on dialectical philosophy. It will also be clear from this collection that Dunayevskaya did not write in conventional academic prose, being a "a philosopher of the barricades" who worked out her ideas in close contact and dialogue with activists and theorists in the grassroots movements. Her unconventional style will no doubt seem jarring to some, although others will find it captivating and provocative, as we do.

Dunayevskaya's "Letters on Hegel's Absolutes" of May 12 and 20, 1953 serve as the anchor of this collection. Never published in book form during her lifetime, they represent two of her most important, albeit difficult, writings on dialectical philosophy. To facilitate comprehension of their content, especially in light of contemporary issues in radical theory, we begin the collection with one of her last writings, which discusses the 1953 letters at length—the "Presentation on the Dialectics of Organization and Philosophy" (June 1, 1987). As Marx put it in the Preface to Vol. I of *Capital*, "Beginnings are always difficult in all sciences. The understanding of the first chapter . . . will therefore present the greatest difficulty." This is no less true when it comes to the content of the first two chapters of this volume. Yet centering Part I on the birth of her concept of Marxist-Humanism, will, we hope, illuminate the significance of Dunayevskaya's interpretation of the dialectic of *absolute* negativity in the ensuing four parts. This collection will also flesh out themes from her major philosophical works, which she sometimes referred to as her "trilogy of revolution"—*Marxism and Freedom* (1958), *Philosophy and Revolution* (1973) and *Rosa Luxemburg, Women's Liberation, and Marx's Philosophy of Revolution* (1982)—as well as her *Women's Liberation and the Dialectics of Revolution* (1985). In addition, it will include texts related to "Dialectics of Organization and Philosophy," a book project left unfinished at the time of her death in 1987. At the same time, we have included essays on Hegel and the Black dimension, Hegel and feminism, outlines of Hegel's major works, and other texts that will present her original interpretations of the dialectic in Hegel and Marx.

After the break with James and her founding of a new organization, News and Letters Committees, in 1955, Dunayevskaya set out to complete a work which would reestablish the American roots and world humanist concepts of Marx's thought. The result was *Marxism and Freedom, from 1776 until Today*, first published in 1958. It took up Hegel's Absolutes as well as Marx's Humanism, and, as mentioned earlier, included the first English translation of two of the main essays of Marx's *1844 Manuscripts*, "Private Property and Communism" and "Critique of the Hegelian Dialectic." It also explored the dialectical structure of Marx's *Capital*, Lenin's legacy, including his debt to Hegel, the fate of the Russian Revolution, and the rise of state-capitalism in Stalinist Russia. As a whole, *Marxism and Freedom* can be seen as a direct concretization of the 1953 "Letters on Hegel's Absolutes," in that it was structured on the concept developed in those letters, that the movement from practice is itself a form of theory. In chapters such as "The Humanism and Dialectic of *Capital*, Vol. I" and "Automation and the New Humanism," she also elaborated her concept of Marxist-Humanism.

No sooner was *Marxism and Freedom* off the press than Dunayevskaya turned to develop what she termed the movement from theory that is itself a form of philosophy, by writing *Nationalism, Communism, Marxist-Humanism and the Afro-Asian Revolutions* (1959) and beginning work on a new book probing more directly into the Hegelian dialectic. It ultimately became *Philosophy and Revolution, from Hegel to Sartre and from Marx to Mao* (1973). Her turn to the dialectic proper in the period following the publication of *Marxism and Freedom* is reflected in her 1960–61 summaries of Hegel's *Phenomenology of Mind, Science of Logic*, and *Smaller Logic*, which are contained in part 2. These summaries offer a wealth of discussion on crucial dimensions of Hegel, including some that have received scant commentary by Marxists. One example is the section on the "Three Attitudes Toward Objectivity" in the *Smaller Logic*, which contains a critique of intuitionism and romanticism. Anticipating more recent critiques of unilinear evolutionism, Dunayevskaya argues that this section shows retrogression as integral to the dialectic of history as progression.

Throughout her life, Dunayevskaya worked out her ideas in dialogue with theoreticians and activists. This is reflected in her philosophical correspondence of the early 1960s with such figures as Marcuse and Fromm, included in part 2.[42] Her letters to Marcuse, to whom she sent an early draft of *Philosophy and Revolution*, deal with questions he asked, such as, "why do you need the Absolute Idea" to express the subjectivity of self-liberation? In a somewhat different vein, Dunayevskaya's 1961 letter to the China scholar Jonathan Spence suggests: "For our epoch, we needn't prove the materialism of Hegel, but rather the idealism (materialistic idealism, but idealism none the less) of Marx which has been so perverted by the Stalins, Maos and Khrushchevs" (see this volume, p. 117). In this period, as throughout her life, she involved workers as well as intellectuals in her discussions on and development of philosophy. In this regard we include here as well a 1960 letter to Charles Denby, the Black autoworker who was the editor of *News & Letters*, on the French philosopher Maurice Merleau-Ponty; it is a remarkable example of how she conducted philosophical dialogue with worker colleagues.

Dunayevskaya was active in many freedom struggles of the 1960s, from the Civil Rights Movement to the Berkeley Free Speech Movement, on which she co-authored a pamphlet with student leader Mario Savio.[43] As she kept her ears attuned to new developments in the freedom struggles, she became aware that a new situation had emerged by the middle and late 1960s. In her view, although many creative mass revolts had emerged in that exciting decade, the needed new stage of dialectical *cognition* had not. This problem was reflected in the prevailing attitude in the New Left that activism was sufficient to make the revolution and that theory could wait. In addition, the link to Marx's Humanism was not being reestablished in a fundamental way. What predominated instead were such alternatives to Marx's Humanism as Maoism, Trotskyism, and Existentialism, each of which in her view fell far short of the concept of absolute negativity. Dunayevskaya's conclusion that a new stage of cognition did not emerge in the 1960s meant that the demands facing the movement from theory became that much greater. It led her to a shift of emphasis in the development of her concept of Marxist-Humanism. She now stressed the need to openly engage the movements from practice more directly, by discussing publicly with them the dialectic of absolute negativity. As Dunayevskaya put it in the 1964 letter to Marcuse, which opens part 3 of this collection, "We certainly can no longer, as Lenin did, keep 'our' philosophical notebooks private. We live in the age of absolutes, and freedom as the innermost dynamic of both life and thought demands the unity of philosophy and revolution." This perspective of discussing philosophy directly with members of grassroots movements in order to challenge them is strikingly illustrated by her 1966 lecture on Hegel to a large audience of workers and anti-nuclear activists in Japan, in which she delves into each of Hegel's major works. At the same time, the resistance that this dive into the dialectic proper evinced even from some of her closest associates compelled her to write a series of reflections on the meaning of dialectics, such as "The Newness of Our Philosophic-Historic Contribution," which is also found in part 3.

As the late 1960s approached, Dunayevskaya further concretized this shift of emphasis in the development of Marxist-Humanism by changing the form of *Philosophy and Revolution*, which was to appear in 1973. The book's form now better reflected the development of a new philosophical category, "Absolute Negativity as New Beginning." She had earlier intended to begin with an economic and political analysis of contemporary capitalist world reality in light of the revolts in Africa, Eastern Europe, and the developed capitalist lands, and end with a chapter on Hegel's Absolutes. She now decided to turn the structure of the book around, by having as its first part, "Why Hegel? Why Now?" The first chapter was entitled "Absolute Negativity as New Beginning," thus restructuring the book on the movement *from theory*.

This new point of departure was also worked out through discussions with workers and intellectuals, as seen in her presentation to a Black/Red Conference in Detroit in 1969. Dunayevskaya had long been active in the Black movement, as far back as the 1920s, when she worked with the American Negro Labor Congress, an organization that sought to span the divide between Garveyism and Marxism. Her attentiveness to new developments in the Black Dimension proved of critical importance in her development of Marxist-Humanism, as seen in such works as *American Civilization on Trial: Black Masses as Vanguard* (1963). The 1969 speech to the Black/Red Conference, included in part 3, sought to involve activists in the ongoing Civil Rights and Black Power movements in the development of *Philosophy and Revolution* itself. This is likewise reflected in a speech given later that year, also included in part 3, entitled "Logic as Stages of Freedom, Freedom as Stages of Logic."

A crucial expression of Dunayevskaya's determination to create a new kind of philosophical dialogue, in which the most difficult and concentrated aspects of Hegelian and Marxian philosophy are worked out in conjunction with living forces of liberation, is seen in her emphasis on ensuring the public full access to the *process* of her philosophic labor captured in her Archives. As early as 1969, she donated an extensive collection of her writings, both published and unpublished, to Wayne State University's Walter Reuther Archives of Labor and Urban Affairs in Detroit. The collection has been updated several times since then, and in 1986 she entitled the 15,000-page collection *The Raya Dunayevskaya Collection: Marxist-Humanism—A Half-Century of Its World Development*. It is available on microfilm. Most of the texts published here are drawn from these Archives.[44]

Philosophy and Revolution, published in 1973, contains the most extended presentation of Dunayevskaya's concept of "Absolute Negativity as New Beginning." Dunayevskaya further developed its meaning in several presentations and essays after the book came off the press, the most important of which is a paper presented to the Hegel Society of America in 1974. Here, in a discussion of the Absolute Idea in Hegel's *Science of Logic*, she critiques Adorno, finding more affinity with the Czech Marxist humanist Karel Kosík and Fanon. This lecture, as well as a 1976 talk on "Hegel, Marx, Lenin, Fanon and the Dialectics of Liberation Today," which contrasts "Absolute Negativity as New Beginning" to the contributions of thinkers such as Lukács, Sartre and Adorno and discusses the contributions of Fanon, is found in Part 4. In this part we have also included Dunayevskaya's brief critique of Lukács, whom many consider the foremost Marxist philosopher of the twentieth century.

Throughout her work, Dunayevskaya's explorations of Hegel were closely linked with the reexamination of Marx. As far back as the 1940s, she called attention to the humanist writings of the young Marx, and was among the first to analyze them in *Marxism and Freedom*. In *Marxism and Freedom* and *Philosophy and Revolution* she also discusses the dialectical foundation of the economic categories of Marx's *Capital*, seeing them not as a break from his early writings, but as the fullest expression of a reconstituted, recreated dialectic of the concrete. The standard interpretation of Marx was that he shifted from a philosophical approach in his early writings to an economic one with *Capital*. Dunayevskaya challenged this view while working on *Rosa Luxemburg, Women's Liberation, and Marx's Philosophy of Revolution* (1982) in the late 1970s and early 1980s. In this book, she reevaluated post-Marx Marxism in light of Marx's entire legacy. With the concept of "Absolute Negativity as New Beginning" in hand, she probed anew into Marx's *oeuvre*, especially what she viewed as the new moments of his last decade (1872–83), when he penned the French edition of *Capital*, the drafts of a letter to Vera Zasulich on the Russian village commune, and most importantly, his *Ethnological Notebooks* on tribal and non-Western societies. In *Rosa Luxemburg, Women's Liberation, and Marx's Philosophy of Revolution*, she showed that in his last decade Marx returned to many of his concerns of the 1840s, only on a new, higher ground provided by his work of the intervening thirty years. Instead of moving from philosophy to political economy, she held that the whole of Marx's development, including *Capital*, constituted a philosophy of "revolution in permanence." This is what post-Marx Marxists had failed to build on, she argued. The final section of Part 4, which includes a letter to the Scottish labor activist and Marxist-Humanist

Harry McShane and an essay on the 150th anniversary of Hegel's death, addresses Marx's transformation of Hegel's revolution in philosophy into a philosophy of revolution.

The most important new category which emerged from this work on *Rosa Luxemburg, Women's Liberation, and Marx's Philosophy of Revolution* was what Dunayevskaya termed "post-Marx Marxism, beginning with Engels, as pejorative."[45] The need to achieve continuity with Marx's new continent of thought by transcending the limitations of post-Marx Marxism became a central theme in her writings of the 1980s, which contain some of her most intense and creative work. Part 5 includes a selection of these from the period after *Rosa Luxemburg, Women's Liberation, and Marx's Philosophy of Revolution* was finished. Her 1982 letter "On the Battle of Ideas" explores the category of "post-Marx Marxism" by looking anew at Hegel's work and its reception by the Johnson-Forest Tendency of the late 1940s. Her 1983 letter on Karl Korsch extends the category of "post-Marx Marxism" to Western Marxists. And her "Marxist-Humanism, the Summation That Is a New Beginning," surveys Marx's development in light of the concept of "revolution in permanence." Part 5 also contains essays and lectures on the relationship of philosophy to forces of revolt, as well as on philosophy as itself a force of revolt.

As previously mentioned, Dunayevskaya is one of the few thinkers to seriously explore the Hegelian and Marxian dialectic in terms of women's liberation. As against the prevailing tendency among Marxists to elevate issues of class above those of gender, she rooted herself in Marx's contention, voiced already in his *1844 Manuscripts*, that the man/woman relation is the most fundamental relation in society and the measure of whether a revolutionary transformation has reached second negativity. On this basis she worked out a new approach to women's liberation, in which the striving for second negation was seen as integral to women's critique of the male chauvinism *within* the Left as well as in the dominant classes. In 1985, a collection of her extensive writings on feminism over the course of more than three decades appeared, entitled *Women's Liberation and the Dialectics of Revolution*. Part 5 contains a speech delivered shortly after this book first went to press.

Dunayevskaya likewise placed great emphasis on youth as a subject of revolution, seeing the idealism often found in youth movements as a material force for social transformation. Included in Part 5 is a letter which addresses this issue, and which also includes a brief critique of Claude Lévi-Strauss' structuralism. Her view of the living human subject as not only force, but also as *reason*, is likewise developed in "Not by Practice Alone: The Movement from Theory," an essay which takes issue with those who fail to see that the unique contribution of Marxist-Humanism lies in its core philosophical notions. This movement from theory is further articulated in "The Power of Abstraction," an essay which argues that the Hegelian dialectic gave Marx his philosophical cutting edge and his vision of how a new human society could be born. To Dunayevskaya, the thought comes before the act. Revolutionary thought becomes key to the transformation of reality.

Dunayevskaya's category "post-Marx Marxism as pejorative" illuminates her view that the missing link in the Marxist movement was the relation of dialectics and organization. In *Rosa Luxemburg, Women's Liberation, and Marx's Philosophy of Revolution* Dunayevskaya argued that this separation characterized even the greatest Marxists. It was true of Lenin, who dug deeply into Hegelian dialectics in his 1914–15 *Philosophic Notebooks*, but who never connected dialectics to organization. Even after his philosophical reorganization of 1914, he continued to espouse, albeit with some changes, the elitist vanguard party form. This is not without importance for the future emergence of what Dunayevskaya called the single-party totalitarian state. Yet the separation of dialectics from organization also characterized the thinking of such critics of Lenin as Rosa Luxemburg, who dug deeply into spontaneous forms of mass self-organization, especially in 1905–96, and raised the question of revolutionary democracy again after the 1917 Russian Revolution, but who kept clear of Hegelian philosophy. Even the greatest revolutionaries, then and later, failed to assume organizational responsibility for the dialectic of *second* negativity.

By the mid-1980s, this led to an impasse. New revolutions, from Iran to Grenada, had arisen in the 1970s, only to fall prey by the 1980s to counterrevolution from *within*. In 1979–83, Dunayevskaya wrote a number of analyses of the takeover of the Iranian revolution by reactionary and anti-feminist ayatollahs, and of the internal coup which killed Grenadian revolutionary leader Maurice Bishop in 1983, paving the way for Reagan's invasion. On a global scale, Dunayevskaya held, the conceptual basis of an array of revolutions and freedom struggles had been proved insufficient, because a new relation between theory and practice that could *realize* the idea of freedom was not concretized. This was not only because so many continued to adhere to the elitist vanguard party and narrowed the vision of a new society to nationalized property. It was also because those who opposed Stalinism from the Left had failed to unfurl a new banner of liberation, as if a liberating vision of the future could be left to spontaneous action alone. Each of the mass movements of the post-World War II era—be it feminism or the Black Dimension, youth struggles or the labor movement—faced a new retrogressive political climate by the 1980s, in large part, she argued, because they were left bereft of a philosophy of revolution which could answer their quest for universality.

In response to the retrogression which engulfed the radical movement in the Reagan-Thatcher 1980s, Dunayevskaya held that it had become necessary to delve anew into the dialectic of negativity, this time in direct relation to the problem of organization. She therefore began work in 1986–87 on a new book entitled "Dialectics of Organization and Philosophy: The 'Party' and Forms of Organization Born out of Spontaneity." Although she died before completing a draft of this work, Part 5 contains a number of writings which she considered of central importance to it.[46] As part of her exploration of the dialectics of organization, she once again reexamined Hegel's writings, especially the *Phenomenology of Mind*, the final paragraph of which speaks of an "intellectually comprehended organization." She delved once more into the section on "Third Attitude toward Objectivity" in the Smaller Logic, where Hegel writes of the difference between a "copious body of objective truth" and mere faith born from intuition. She also took up once again Lenin's philosophical ambivalence, this time showing that he became so enamored of practice as the resolution of contradiction in his *Philosophic Notebooks* that he cut short his own journey through Hegel's Absolutes. And she reviewed her own 1953 "Letters on Hegel's Absolutes," this time to see what these texts had to say about the need to work out a new relation between philosophy and organization.

These issues are expressed most fully in one of her last writings, just before her death on June 9, 1987, the "Presentation on the Dialectics of Organization and Philosophy" of June 1, 1987, already mentioned above and with which this volume begins. Here, the whole question of the dialectic of absolute negativity, in terms of its importance, its urgency, and its meaning, comes into full view when explored in light of the central problem of the radical movements, the relation of philosophy to organization. Because the Presentation of June 1, 1987 looks anew at the 1953 letters in light of this problematic, it serves as the first piece in Part I and can be seen as a sort of introduction to the 1953 letters themselves. Despite the rough form of this oral presentation, it might without too much exaggeration be viewed, as Dunayevskaya once said in a different context of the Preface to Hegel's *Phenomenology*, as the kind of "serious Introduction which is really always written at the end and is at the same time an Overview" of the whole.[47]

Dunayevskaya's determination to work out a new relation between philosophy and revolution is expressed in the very nature of her writing. Neither an academic nor a mere political polemicist, she writes passionately without being dismissive of abstract thought. To cite Adrienne Rich's Foreword to *Rosa Luxemburg, Women's Liberation, and Marx's Philosophy of Revolution*: "Raya Dunayevskaya caught fire from Marx, met it with her own fire, brought to the events of her lifetime a revitalized, refocused Marxism. Her writings, with all their passion, energy, wit, and learning, may read awkwardly at times because she is really writing against the grain of how many readers have learned to think: to separate disciplines and genres, theory from practice. She's trying to think, and write, the revolution in the revolution."[48]

If Dunayevskaya is correct that the "Absolute" is no closed ontology, no pinnacle, no endpoint of development, then the task that awaits a new generation, we would argue, is to work out these points of departure as a new beginning. At a time when even Marxists are jettisoning the dialectic in favor of pragmatism and what they often term non-totalizing modes of thinking, Dunayevskaya's confidence in the dialectic of Hegel, Marx, and Marxist-Humanism is the type of perspective that can help us to navigate through a period like ours. Yet developing that is never easy. For at great revolutionary turning points, as in the 1960s when the pragmatic radicals of the New Left rejected philosophy, and even in 1914–17 when Lenin tried so valiantly, especially in his Hegel studies, to fill the philosophical void after Marx's death, the overemphasis on practice has tended to overwhelm and muffle the dialectic even for revolutionary thinkers and activists.

The need to transcend this historical legacy has never been greater than now, when the renewal of the Marxian project itself may depend upon our willingness to work out the unresolved question of the past century—what happens *after* the revolution? For this reason, the content of these texts by Dunayevskaya on the dialectic in Hegel, Marx, and today can be seen as a letter to the future.

In 1987, the year of her death, Dunayevskaya focused on Marx's *Critique of the Gotha Program* (1875), where he outlined a perspective on revolutionary organization, one which never became the basis for the large Marxist parties of the twentieth century, who instead opted for either Social Democratic reformism or Leninist vanguardism. We close with a passage from that essay:

> The burning question of the day remains: What happens the day after [the revolution]? How can we continue Marx's unchaining of the dialectic organizationally, with the principles he outlined in his *Critique of the Gotha Program*? The question of "what happens after" gains crucial importance because of what it signals in self-development and self-flowering—"revolution in permanence." No one knows what it is, or can touch it, before it appears. It is not the task that can be fulfilled in just one generation. That is why it remains so elusive, and why the abolition of the division between mental and manual labor sounds utopian. It has the future written all over it. The fact that we cannot give a blueprint does not absolve us from the task. It only makes it more difficult.[49]

June 1, 2001

NOTES

1. The protests against the World Trade Organization in Seattle at the end of 1999, and the demonstrations in Washington, D.C., Sao Paulo, and Quebec in 2000 and 2001, have proved of special importance in turning a new generation to Marx's critique of capital.

2. Karl Marx, *Capital*, Vol. I, trans. by Ben Fowkes (London: Pelican, 1976), pp. 102, 744.

3. Jacques Derrida, *Specters of Marx*, trans. by Peggy Kamuf (New York: Routledge, 1993), pp. 13, 144.

4. Jürgen Habermas, *The Theory of Communicative Action*, Vol. 2, trans. by Thomas McCarthy (Boston: Beacon, 1987), p. 338.

5. Moishe Postone, *Time, Labor, and Social Domination* (New York: Cambridge University Press, 1993).

6. See especially Diana Coole, *Negativity and Politics* (London: Routledge, 2000); Judith Butler's Introduction to a new edition of *Subjects of Desire: Hegelian Reflections in 20th Century France* (New York: Columbia University Press, 1999); and Toula Nicolacopoulos and George Vassilacopoulos, *Hegel and the Logical Structure of Love* (London: Ashgate, 1999).

7. Interview with Fredric Jameson, in *Lukács after Communism, Interviews with Contemporary Intellectuals*, ed. Eva L. Corredor (Durham and London: Duke University Press, 1997), p. 93. We should add that in works such as *Dialectical Investigations* (New York: Routledge, 1993), Bertell Ollman has steadfastly defended the dialectical core of Marxism throughout the recent period, often in the face of sharp opposition to dialectical thought.

8. Many of these writings have been recently published in *The Marxist-Humanist Theory of State-Capitalism: Selected Writings by Raya Dunayevskaya* (Chicago: News and Letters, 1992), edited and introduced by Peter Hudis.

9. Some of her correspondence with James, Marcuse, and Fromm is included in this volume. Most of her other correspondence and writings have been gathered in *The Raya Dunayevskaya Collection: Marxist-Humanism—A Half-Century of Its World Development*, on deposit at the Walter Reuther Archives of Labor and Urban Affairs at Wayne State University, Detroit.

10. For some discussions of Dunayevskaya's standpoint on Hegel, see Patricia Altenbernd Johnson, "Women's Liberation: Following Dunayevskaya in Practicing Dialectics," *Quarterly Journal of Ideology*, Vol. 13: 4 (1989), pp. 65–74; Thomas M. Jeannot, "Raya Dunayevskaya's Conception of Ultimate Reality and Meaning," *Journal of Ultimate Reality and Meaning*, Vol. 22:4 (1999), pp. 276–93. See also the entry for Dunayevskaya in *Women Building Chicago, 1790–1990: A Biographical Dictionary*, ed. by Rima Lunin Schultz and Adele Hast (Bloomington: Indiana University Press, 2001).

11. G. W. F. Hegel, *Science of Logic*, trans. by A. V. Miller (New Jersey: Humanities Press, 1969), p. 113. Subsequent page references are directly in the text.

12. Engels, *Ludwig Feuerbach and the End of Classical German Philosophy*, Marx and Engels *Collected Works*, Vol. 26 (New York: International Publishers, 1990), pp. 360–61.

13. Raya Dunayevskaya, *Philosophy and Revolution, from Hegel to Sartre and from Marx to Mao* (New York: Columbia University Press, [1973] 1989), p. 26. Subsequent page references are directly in the text.

14. Georg Lukács, *The Young Hegel*, trans. Rodney Livingstone (Cambridge: MIT Press, 1975), p. 510. For background on Lukács' overall position, see especially Tom Rockmore, *Irrationalism: Lukács and the Marxist View of Reason* (Berkeley: University of California Press, 1992).

15. Lukács, *The Young Hegel*, p. 513.

16. Herbert Marcuse, *Reason and Revolution* (New York: Oxford, 1941), p. 27. The best overview of Marcuse's work remains Douglas Kellner, *Herbert Marcuse and the Crisis of Marxism* (Berkeley: University of California Press, 1984).

17. Marcuse, *Reason and Revolution*, p. 165.

18. Theodor Adorno, "Aspects of Hegel's Philosophy" (orig. German edition 1957), in *Hegel: Three Studies*, trans. by Shierry Weber Nicholsen, (Cambridge: MIT Press, 1994), p. 28. All of the following page references to Adorno are to this essay.

19. Theodor Adorno, *Negative Dialectics*, trans. by E. B. Ashton (New York: Seabury Press, 1973), orig. German edition 1966, p. 362.

20. For a critique of Moishe Postone's *Time, Labor, and Social Domination: A Reinterpretation of Marx's Critical Theory*, in which this position is articulated, see Peter Hudis, "Labor, High-Tech Capitalism, and the Crisis of the Subject: A Critique of Recent Developments in Critical Theory," *Humanity and Society*, Vol. 19:4 (1995), pp. 4–20 and "Conceptualizing an Emancipatory Alternative: István Mészáros' *Beyond Capital*," *Socialism and Democracy*, Vol. 11:1 (1997), pp. 37–54.

21. Jacques Derrida, "From Restricted to General Economy, a Hegelianism Without Reserve" (orig. French edition 1967), in *Writing and Difference*, trans. Alan Bass (Chicago: University of Chicago Press, 1978), p. 259.

22. Derrida, *Positions* (Chicago: University of Chicago Press, 1971), trans. Alan Bass, p. 44.

23. Derrida, *Glas* (Lincoln: University of Nebraska Press [orig. French edition 1974] 1986), trans. J. P. Leavey and R. Rand, pp. 200–01.

24. Marx, "Critique of the Hegelian Dialectic," in Marx and Engels, *Collected Works*, Vol. 3 (New York: International Publishers, 1975), p. 330.

25. We have used here Dunayevskaya's more lucid translation of Marx's "Critique of the Hegelian Dialectic," which appeared for the first time in English in her *Marxism and Freedom* (New York: Bookman, 1958), p. 308. See also the rendering in Marx and Engels, *Collected Works*, Vol. 3, p. 332–33.

26. Marx, *Capital* I, pp. 929–30.

27. See Ron Brokmeyer, Raya Dunayevskaya, Franklin Dmitryev, et al. *The Fetish of High Tech and Karl Marx's Unknown Mathematical Manuscripts* (Chicago: News and Letters, 1984).

28. Daniel Berthold-Bond, *Hegel's Grand Synthesis, a Study of Being, Thought and History* (Albany: SUNY Press, 1989), p. 136. See also John H. Hoffmeyer, *The Presence of the Future in Hegel's Logic* (Rutherford: Associated University Presses, 1996).

29. See "A New Revision of Marxian Economics," *American Economic Review*, Vol. 34:3 (1944), pp. 531–37. The essay has been reprinted in *The Marxist-Humanist Theory of State-Capitalism*, pp. 83–87.

30. "Is Russia Part of the Collectivist Epoch of Society?" *The Marxist-Humanist Theory of State-Capitalism*, p. 25.

31. This essay can now be found in *The Marxist-Humanist Theory of State-Capitalism*, pp. 17–23.

32. C.L.R. James, *Notes on Dialectics, Hegel, Marx, Lenin* (Westport, Connecticut: Lawrence Hill & Co., 1980), p. 119. For a critique of this book by Dunayevskaya, see her May 1972 letter "On C.L.R. James' Notes on Dialectics," reprinted in *News & Letters*, October 1997.

33. This is from a letter of Dunayevskaya's to James of March 12, 1949.

34. This statement is from a letter of James to Grace Lee on May 20, 1949. In the same letter James also says he has found nothing of significance in Hegel's *Philosophy of Mind*. The letter can be found in *The Raya Dunayevskaya Collection*, pp. 1612–15.

35. See Andy Phillips and Raya Dunayevskaya, *The Coal Miners' General Strike of 1949–50 and the Birth of Marxist-Humanism in the U.S.* (Chicago: News and Letters, 1984), as well as Dunayevskaya's *Marxism and Freedom*.

36. Dunayevskaya later reprinted this in her *Women's Liberation and the Dialectics of Revolution: Reaching for the Future* (Detroit: Wayne State University Press, 1996, orig. 1985).

37. See Dunayevskaya's discussion of this in her "Not by Practice Alone: The Movement from Theory," in Part 5, below.

38. This is from a letter of Dunayevskaya written on January 13, 1987, in *The Raya Dunayevskaya Collection*, p. 10726.

39. She was later to term this (in *Marxism and Freedom*) "the movement from practice to theory" (p. 276).

40. See the "Presentation on the Dialectics of Organization and Philosophy" (June 1, 1987), in chapter 1, below.

41. For a further discussion of her changing views about Lenin's philosophic ambivalence, see Kevin Anderson's *Lenin, Hegel, and Western Marxism* (Champaign-Urbana: University of Illinois Press, 1995).

42. Fromm included an essay by Dunayevskaya, "Marx's Humanism Today," in his *Socialist Humanism* (New York: Doubleday, 1965). He later wrote the Preface to the German edition of her *Philosophy and Revolution*. Herbert Marcuse, as mentioned above, wrote a preface to *Marxism and Freedom*.

43. See Mario Savio, Raya Dunayevskaya, and Eugene Walker, *The Free Speech Movement and the Negro Revolution* (Detroit: News and Letters, 1965). For Dunayevskaya's analysis of the Black freedom movements in the United States, see *American Civilization on Trial: Black Masses as Vanguard* (Detroit: News and Letters, 1983 [orig. 1963]).

44. Following Dunayevskaya's death in 1987, new material has been added to her Collection at the Walter Reuther Library. These are contained in the *Supplement to the Raya Dunayevskaya Collection*, and are also available on microfilm.

45. See especially *Rosa Luxemburg, Women's Liberation, and Marx's Philosophy of Revolution* (Urbana: University of Illinois Press, 1991, orig. 1982), chapter 12.

46. Many of Dunayevskaya's writings for her planned book on "Dialectics of Organization and Philosophy" are included in the *Supplement to the Raya Dunayevskaya Collection*, Vol. 13.

47. See Dunayevskaya's "Talking to Myself of June 26, 1986" on Hegel's *Phenomenology*, in Part 5, below. Hegel's famous Preface to the *Phenomenology* was actually written after the work was completed.

48. *Rosa Luxemburg, Women's Liberation, and Marx's Philosophy of Revolution*, p. xviii.

49. "The Year of Only Eight Months" (1987), in *Supplement to the Raya Dunayevskaya Collection*, p. 10690.

PART I

THE PHILOSOPHIC MOMENT
OF MARXIST-HUMANISM

∼

CHAPTER ONE

Presentation on the Dialectics of Organization and Philosophy (June 1, 1987)

Composed only a week before her death on June 9, 1987, this is Dunayevskaya's last major discussion of dialectics. Originally written in preparation for the 1987 Plenary gathering of News and Letters Committees, the organization she founded in 1955, the talk was never delivered. It develops themes from her unfinished book, "Dialectics of Organization and Philosophy: 'The Party' and Forms of Organization Born Out of Spontaneity." The original can be found in the Supplement to the Raya Dunayevskaya Collection, *p. 10737.*

The Philosophic Point

To understand today we must begin at the beginning, that is to say, as always, with Marx. Specifically the two periods are: the first and the last, the first being *the* philosophic moment, 1844.[1] That laid the ground for all future development. The last being the long hard *trek and process* of development—all the revolutions, as well as philosophic-political-economic concretizations, culminating in *Capital.* Yet the full organizational expression of all came only then, i.e., the last decade, especially the 1875 *Critique of the Gotha Program.* Why only then?

Take first another look at 1844—the philosophic moment for all of Marx's Marxism, including organization. Throughout Marx's life he reached to concretize it. But none of the concretizations, whether 1848 with the Communist League, or 1864 with the First International, or even 1871 with the Paris Commune, fully reached to the level of the philosophic moment of 1844.

3

Only with the *Critique of the Gotha Program* in 1875 did Marx fully return to that moment as it was concretized for organization, and even then, he did not call it philosophy, but "principle."[2]

The specific point that I'm singling out from the 1844 founding of a new continent of thought and of revolution is when Marx articulates the great merit of Hegel in discovering the "negation of the negation," and the great demerit of this same Hegel in enveloping it in such mysticism by dealing with it as various stages of consciousness, rather than as men and women thinking. Marx, on the other hand, declares himself not only against capitalism and "vulgar communism," but proclaims his philosophy to be "a new Humanism."[3]

To this day 1844 was the philosophic moment of Marx's discovery of that whole new continent of thought and of revolution that "Marxism" certainly lacked, and instead singled out *one* of the developments—economics—so that we didn't know "new humanism" until the Depression. But in fact, it is that which was the *ground for organization* throughout his life, from the moment he did "experience" the philosophic moment, even if it was only correspondence (letters) soon to become international correspondence.

Seriously, however, as organization, that organization—the Communist League—accepted the challenge to the existing capitalist world, and that not separated from all political tendencies and parties. I'm referring, of course, to the *Communist Manifesto*, whose second part is a critique of utopian socialism, etc. What we want to do here is to compare the 1847 *Communist Manifesto* to the 1864 First International [and in 1871] hailing the Paris Commune as *the* form, the working existence, the communal non-state as needing only release of all the mental, manual, and emotional potentiality.[4]

Why then is the actual concretization of a new unity so sharply critiqued as in the *Critique of the Gotha Program?* That becomes the whole rub and the urgent problematic of our day which must be worked out.

First, enter history. In 1847 critique meant the ruthless critique of all that exists that he spoke of in his philosophic break with the bourgeoisie and Hegel, concretized on the level of the existing "parties" in that period. (As we were to see in 1860 in his letter to Freiligrath, when Freiligrath, in refusing to get involved in the Vogt Affair,[5] said he didn't belong to the party any longer, Marx's reply was: Neither am I, to any existing party. I didn't mean it in the ephemeral sense, I meant it in the *historic*. Clearly, Marx meant that no one could rewrite the history, and both the revolution of 1848 and the *Manifesto* that anticipated it and followed it, are *historic*.)[6]

It is that historic period that changed when *international* workers got together to take a position on what was happening on a different continent.

That too had a "manifesto," perhaps not as bold as the *Communist Manifesto*, thought Marx, which was actually the preamble to the Constitution and By-laws to the First International.

At the same time, Marx didn't hesitate a second once the Paris Commune burst out, and some trade unionists didn't share the enthusiasm, to write them out of the First International. He not only declared the need to go lower and deeper, but insisted that they didn't represent the majority of the masses; the Paris Communards did, and it is that Idea that defines history now as both ongoing and the future.

Dialectics of Organization

So, what happened in 1875? Look at how the self-development of the Idea that we now call Marxism has concretized itself *when* its greatest theoretical work, *Capital*, in its French edition, is finished, and that has philosophy spelled out in the most concrete terms from fetishism of commodities to the new passions and new forces that go against the accumulation of capital. And he has the experience now of both political parties and forms of organization emerging spontaneously from the masses, *plus philosophy*.

Critique of the Gotha Program: There is no way now, no matter how Marx kept from trying to give any blueprints for the future, not to develop a general view of where we're headed for the day *after* the conquest of power, the day *after* we have rid ourselves of the birthmarks of capitalism *when* a new generation can finally see all its potentiality put an end once and for all to the division between mental and manual labor.[7]

Let me now state something general from Hegel on the question of "the philosophic point" which would also apply to us.[8]

In Hegelian dialectics, the philosophic moment is a determinant; even if the person who was driven to articulate the Idea of that "moment" was very nearly unconscious as to its depth and its ramifications, it remained the element that governed the concretization that follows the laborious birth that poured forth in a torrent nevertheless.

Specifically and concretely, in our case the moment I'm referring to is May 12 and 20, 1953.[9] The Idea is in demystifying the Absolute as either God or the closed ontology, as the unity I singled out, a dual movement, from theory to practice, from practice as well as from theory.

We were so overwhelmed with the movement from practice that we were hardly as enthusiastic or as concrete about the movement from theory, if not actually forgetting it. I therefore wish to go into great detail about those two letters in 1953, *not* as the small coin of concrete questions, but as the many universals inherent in it, so that we can see what is still new in it that we must develop for the book.[10]

Everyone has heard so much about 1953 as the stage of breakthrough on the Absolute Idea that you may think: what else is there to be said? The whole point, however, about the philosophic point that became a philosophic determinant—and not just the ground of [it], but became so startlingly new and clear with Marx—[is] that looking at it for this age, specifically [in relation to] ourselves, it began to appear in an altogether new way. Here is what I mean:

Heretofore what we stressed when we pointed to 1953 as source was the important point of 1955, when there was an actual organizational break-up.[11] Then what became clearer was that actually, insofar as the words "Marxist-Humanism" are concerned, we couldn't say 1955, but as it was expressed in written form in *Marxism* and *Freedom* in 1957.[12] Now what is clear is not that any of the other dates are wrong, but that each time it is a specific period that makes one realize that actually what wasn't clear was what was in *the* philosophic moment, and *only when* the objective and subjective merge is it "proven." Oh, the source, the ground, really also had a roof. But the context in between, the structure, couldn't be controlled without the objective situation. But that, on the other hand, made it very clear that we are back to focusing on the philosophic moment.

. . . THE IMPERATIVENESS OF BOTH THE OBJECTIVE AND SUBJECTIVE URGENCY NOW MANIFESTS THAT WHAT HAS BEEN AN UNTRODDEN PATH ALL THESE YEARS, BY ALL POST-MARX MARXISTS, INCLUDING LENIN—WHO DID DIG INTO PHILOSOPHY, BUT NOT THE PARTY, AND LUXEMBURG, WHO DID DIG INTO SPONTANEITY, BUT NOT PHILOSOPHY—IS *ORGANIZATION*, the Dialectics of Philosophy and Organization.

Why did we think once we took the big step of separating, indeed breaking, with the elitist party, that it is sufficient to do so politically without doing so philosophically?

Wasn't it because we actually had not penetrated the dialectic of organization in its relationship to dialectics of philosophy, though we certainly never stopped using the word "dialectics"? In a word, even when we used "Absolute" in relationship to method and definitely stressed that we do not mean just a tool or application, we did think that it was not just the threshold of the Absolute Idea, but the Absolute Idea as its ultimate, *as if Absolute Mind was no more than what Absolute Idea was in the "Logic" and Hegel didn't need to tell us that we better not stop there and instead go to "Philosophy of Nature" and "Philosophy of Mind."*

No wonder that when C. L. R. James said that he looked into *Philosophy of Mind*, he concluded that he found nothing there "for us."[13] I must have felt dissatisfied, since that is where I went, and precisely, I might say, on the question of what we called "dialectics of the party," specifying however, that I wasn't interested either in the mass party, which the masses will build, or in the elitist party, which we definitely oppose, but in what happens to a small group "like us" who know that nothing can be done without the masses, and are with them, but [such small groups of] theoreticians always seem to be around too. So, what is the *objectivity* which explains their presence, as the objectivity explains the spontaneous outburst of the masses? In a word, I was looking for the objectivity of subjectivity.

The one thing I did not mention in discussing 1953 is that the letter of May 20, where I suddenly speak on the *Philosophy of Mind*, came after C. L. R. James had said in his *Notes on Dialectics*[14]—or the letter accompanying his *Notes*—that he had looked into *Philosophy of Mind*, and found nothing there "for us" (naturally that means Johnson-Forest Tendency).[15] So why did I go to the *Philosophy of Mind* after connecting the end of the last few pages of *Science of Logic* with *Philosophy of Mind*? And that was directly after I repeated what the Johnson-Forest Tendency had worked out, that just as Lenin said Marx's development in the section on commodities bore resemblance to Hegel's syllogistic Universal-Particular-Individual [U-P-I][16] (we noted that chapter 1 [of *Capital*] including [the section on] fetishism bore resemblance to U-P-I), so what is further to be noted is that the accumulation of capital, its General Absolute Law, was based on the Absolute Idea. [We held] that just as that meant the dialectic of bourgeois society, its end by the revolt of the workers, so Marx "also set the limits to the dialectic of the party, which is part of bourgeois society and will wither away with the passing of the bourgeoisie. . . . " Therefore, what we were working on was *not* just a book, but a *philosophy*, a whole new philosophy of dialectics for our age of post-World War II, and that, of course, meant cracking the Absolute. That is where we all stopped. C. L. R. James promised he would do it, but he didn't. Instead, he said he had looked into the *Philosophy of Mind* and found nothing in there for us.

So, whatever it was that was driving me in 1953 to write those letters of May 12 and May 20, it suddenly became the *whole* of Hegel's work, beginning, as always, with what Marx said was most important in *Phenomenology of Mind*, going through the *Science of Logic* with Lenin, but refusing to follow either Lenin [on its] last paragraph,[17] or C. L. R. James on the fact that he found nothing in *Philosophy of Mind*. I delved not only into that work, but into [its] last final syllogisms that nobody, including bourgeois academia, had *seriously* tackled [until] the next decade.[18] I was not debating them or what they did or did not do; in this case, my "ignorance" saved me from having to argue with them or anybody, but, again it was Marx who, though he broke off his manuscript[19] before the final section of *Philosophy of Mind*, his very sharp digging in *Capital*, especially the general law of capitalist accumulation and the new passions and new forces, led me to conclude suddenly that the dialectic of the Party as well as of the contradictions in the Absolute Idea itself, resulted in my seeing what I called "the new society," i.e., the end of the division between mental and manual [labor].

Thus, that philosophic moment was the core for those heretofore formative years of News and Letters Committees which ended with the completion of *Marxism and Freedom*, where we saw that the little phrase "the movement from practice" set the whole structure of *Marxism and Freedom*. Not only that; it served both as ground and roof for the analysis of the contemporary world, both theoretically and practically, including the altogether new voices from both the proletariat and the new revolts in the Communist world, as well as the Black Revolution right here in the United States. I'm sure I don't have to repeat that to this day that first edition had one banner-raising event of world historic importance, by including the first translation both of Marx's *Humanist Essays* and Lenin's *Philosophic Notebooks*.[20]

I returned to the final chapter 12 of *Rosa Luxemburg, Women's Liberation, and Marx's Philosophy of Revolution*. Its penultimate paragraph read:

"It isn't because we are any 'smarter' that we can see so much more than other post-Marx Marxists. Rather, it is because of the maturity of our age. It is true that other post-Marx Marxists have rested on a truncated Marxism; it is equally true that no other generation could have seen the problematic of our age, much less solve our problems. Only live human beings can re-create the revolutionary dialectic forever anew. And these live human beings must do so in theory as well as in practice. It is not a question only of meeting the challenge from practice, but of being able to meet the challenge from the self-development of the Idea, and of deepening theory to the point where it reaches Marx's concept of the philosophy of 'revolution in permanence.'"

It was at that point that I asked that the following paragraph be added:

"There is a further challenge to the form of organization which we have worked out as the committee-form rather than the 'party-to-lead.' But, though committee-form and 'party-to-lead' are opposites, they are not absolute opposites. At the point when the theoretic-form reaches philosophy, the challenge demands that we synthesize not only the new relations of theory to practice, and all the forces of revolution, but philosophy's 'suffering, patience and labor of the negative,' i.e. experiencing absolute negativity. *Then and only then* will we succeed in a revolution that will achieve a classless, non-racist, non-sexist, truly human, truly new society. That which Hegel judged to be the synthesis of the 'Self-Thinking Idea'[21] and the 'Self-Bringing-Forth of Liberty,' Marxist-Humanism holds, is what Marx had called the new society.[22] The many paths to get there are not easy to work out. . . . "

Now return to our own situation, and think of the attacks that we will be facing in 1987, when we state openly that even the one post-Marx Marxist revolutionary who *did* reach deeply into philosophy—Lenin—nevertheless did not do so on the question of organization. In truth, he never renounced his position on the vanguard party set out in 1902 in *What Is To Be Done?*, though he often critiqued it himself. He profoundly extended his new breakthrough in philosophy to a concretization of the dialectics of revolution, and yet never changed his position on the need for the "thin layer of Bolsheviks" [LCW 33, p. 257] as a vanguard party organization. In 1982 in *Rosa Luxemburg, Women's Liberation, and Marx's Philosophy of Revolution*, we critiqued Lenin politically. To fully work out the dialectics of philosophy and organization for our age, it is now clear that that critique must dig deep philosophically.

The whole truth is that even Marx's *Critique of the Gotha Program*, which remains the ground for organization today, was written 112 years ago. What is demanded is not mere "updating," after all the aborted revolutions of the post-World War II world. "Ground" will not suffice alone; we have to finish the building—the roof and its contents. This is what I am working on now in the *Dialectics of Organization and Philosophy*. I would appreciate hearing from our readers on their thoughts on this.

Now then, it seems to me that in a certain sense we could call it a shock for me to have experienced *this year*, when a great deal of research was done on the many ways that spontaneity appeared in the forms of councils, soviets, committees, communes, and so forth, only to say the generalization: Yes, the party and the forms of organization born from spontaneity are opposites, but they are not *absolute* opposites. The change in the title to *Dialectics of Organization and Philosophy*[23] really means that the absolute opposite is philosophy, and that we have not yet worked out organizationally. *Because* . . .[24]

Take [Anton] Pannekoek. The Council Communists were certainly earlier on the scene and directly opposed Lenin in a friendly way, on the question of a single form of organization, insisting that when it comes to production, the people at the point of production must maintain their power after the revolution. But, did they ever give up their party? Didn't they think, along with Rosa Luxemburg, that spontaneity is no substitute for the wholeness of internationalism and theory? On the contrary, they took that for granted. What not only was not taken for granted, but never even approached in any way whatever, unless one calls "approached" a total rejection, was philosophy. Except, except, except . . .

The except of course, refers to Lenin. But he too kept to the old and Plekhanov when it came to Russia.

One must not hem in a new duality into an old reality because of the similarities of abstract opposites colliding. It is the collision of concrete opposites that demands a new unity. Without that philosophic moment there is no way to hew out a new path. And for Lenin there was no philosophic moment insofar as organization was concerned.

In the case of organization, every Left was grabbing at some old contradictions, and with them, some old solutions. Which is why the most cogent moment for our problematic, and for showing up more than ambivalence in Lenin, was the fact that Pannekoek (and Gorter), with that creative, new concept of council communism, i.e., power in the hands of the workers at the point of production, came the old, vulgarized, abysmally narrow, materialistic philosophy of Lenin's 1908 *Materialism and Empirio-Criticism*, as against Lenin's great new philosophic breakthrough on the Larger Logic, and as if that self-movement of ideas and of people was a "betrayal" of the class struggle. And to this day, that is what Council Communists are swearing by (see *Lenin as Philosopher*).[25]

Lenin, too, never raised philosophy directly in relationship to organization. It was at most a phrase, like the famous reference in the Trade Union Debate, where he brings in, in a general way only, dialectics and eclecticism (see page 65 of Volume IX of Lenin's *Selected Works*, on "a glass cylinder").[26]

And the *epigones* have been busy trying to say that whereas it was correct for Lenin not to touch the question of the party when there was the great phenomenon of soviets, "we" must no longer avoid the question of party. Whereupon, they end up just with two more reasons for being in favor of the vanguard party.

Conclusion: Untrodden Paths in Organization

In a single word, we must go into these untrodden paths. We must not, I repeat *must not*, look for a crutch just because a new epigone is using the word "democracy" to mean more than one party, and a Mao is espousing at one and the same time, "bombard the headquarters" and "the Party remains the vanguard" (+ vs. bureaucratization . . .).

Since Marx himself laid the ground [in 1875]—and that, remember, is 112 years ago—the whole of post-Marx Marxism beginning with Engels has not built on that ground. And Engels, you must remember, did fight hard to have the *Critique of the Gotha Program* published, if in a "moderated" form, and yet assented to the establishment of the Second International. And the German Social Democracy had been forced to publish it, but only as a "contribution to the discussion," not as ground for organization.

Lenin did return to Marx's roots in Hegel, and did see that the *Critique of the Gotha Program* had never really been concretized as the smashing of the bourgeois state, without which you could not have a revolution. In a word, he certainly worked out the dialectics of revolution, and made it be in Russia. But, but, but—he too didn't touch the question of the party. On the contrary, it didn't even go as far as his own varied critiques of *What Is to Be Done?*, once the Bolsheviks gained power.

With *Rosa Luxemburg, Women's Liberation, and Marx's Philosophy of Revolution*, especially chapter 11, we alone showed that Marx had created the philosophic ground for organization. But we need not only ground but a roof. And we have all these 112 years of void on organization and philosophy. There is no time in a nuclear age to put it off for another day.

That is what has been missing—the whole new concept of "post-Marx Marxism as a pejorative"—it just lay there in *Rosa Luxemburg, Women's Liberation, and Marx's Philosophy of Revolution*. . . .

NOTES

1. A reference to Marx's *Economic and Philosophical Manuscripts* of 1844, often referred to as his "Humanist Essays."

2. See Marx's covering letter to the *Critique of the Gotha Program* (letter to Wilhelm Bracke of May 5, 1875), in which he writes that "there must be no bargaining about principles" (MECW 24, p. 78).

3. See Marx's "Private Property and Communism" and "Critique of the Hegelian Dialectic" in his *Economic and Philosophic Manuscripts of 1844*. Dunayevskaya was the first to publish an English translation of these two essays, as Appendix A of her *Marxism and Freedom, from 1776 until Today* (New York: Bookman, 1958).

4. See Marx's *The Civil War in France*, where he writes "the greatest social measure of the [Paris] Commune was its own working existence" [MECW 22, p. 339].

5. In 1860, after the Bonapartist journalist Karl Vogt had slandered Marx and his colleagues in major newspapers, Marx published *Herr Vogt*, a book-length defense of the revolutionary generation of the 1840s.

6. See Marx's letter to Ferdinand Freiligrath of February 29, 1860, where he says "by party, I meant party in the eminent historical sense" [MECW 41, p. 87, trans. slightly altered].

7. This refers to Marx's discussion in *The Critique of the Gotha Program*: "In a higher phase of communist society, after the enslaving subordination of individuals under division of labor, and therewith also the antithesis between mental and physical labor, has vanished; after labor, from a mere means of life, has become the prime necessity of life; after the

productive forces have also increased with the all-round development of the individual, and all the springs of co-operative wealth flow more abundantly—only then can the narrow horizon of bourgeois right be crossed in its entirety and society inscribe on its banners: From each according to his abilities, to each according to his needs!" [MECW, 24, p. 87].

8. This sentence was written by Dunayevskaya on the outline of her talk for inclusion at this point in her presentation.

9. See chapter 2 for the texts of these 1953 letters.

10. This refers to Dunayevskaya's planned book, "Dialectics of Organization and Philosophy: The 'Party' and Forms of Organization Born Out of Spontaneity." Dunayevskaya's book was left unwritten at her death on June 9, 1987, but several hundred pages of her notes for it have been collected and donated to Wayne State University's Walter Reuther Archives of Labor and Urban Affairs, as the *Supplement to the Raya Dunayevskaya Collection*, Vol. 13. These writings are available on microfilm.

11. This refers to the break-up of the Committees of Correspondence, the organization of which Dunayevskaya was co-leader (along with C. L. R. James and Grace Lee Boggs) from 1951 to 1955. In 1955, Dunayevskaya founded News and Letters Committees, the organization she headed until her death in 1987. For Dunayevskaya's accounts of this history, see her *25 Years of Marxist-Humanism in the U.S.* (Detroit: News and Letters, 1980) and *The Coal Miners' General Strike of 1949–50 and the Birth of Marxist-Humanism in the U.S.* (Chicago: News and Letters, 1984). For intellectual biographies by writers sympathetic to James, see Paul Buhle, *The Artist as Revolutionary* (London: Verso, 1988) and Kent Worcester, *C. L. R. James: A Political Biography* (Albany: SUNY Press, 1995).

12. Although Dunayevskaya separated from James in 1955, she did not use the term "Marxist-Humanism" until the completion of *Marxism and Freedom* in 1957.

13. See the letter of C. L. R. James to Grace Lee Boggs of May 20, 1949, in *The Raya Dunayevskaya Collection*, 1612.

14. See C. L. R. James, *Notes on Dialectics: Hegel-Marx-Lenin* (Westport: Lawrence Hill, 1980, orig. 1948).

15. The "Johnson-Forest Tendency" or "State Capitalist Tendency," sometimes also termed the "Johnsonites," refers to the tendency headed by C. L. R. James, Raya Dunayevskaya, and Grace Lee Boggs within the U.S. Trotskyist movement from 1941–51, which developed the theory of state-capitalism. James used the pen name J. R. Johnson, Dunayevskaya that of F. Forest, and Grace Lee that of Ria Stone. From 1951 to 1955, the group existed independently as Committees of Correspondence. In 1955, after breaking with James, Dunayevskaya founded News and Letters Committees. Lee and James continued to work together until 1962.

16. This refers to Hegel's syllogism "Universal-Particular-Individual" (See the chapter on the "Notion" in Hegel's *Science of Logic*, also translated as the "Concept.") [SLII, pp. 234–57; SLM, pp. 600–22]. While Universal, Particular, and Individual are the most commonly used English translations for the German terms *allgemein, besonder,* and *einzeln,* these have sometimes been rendered differently. *Allgemein* has been translated not only as "universal," but also as "general"; *besonder* not only as "particular," but also as "specific" or "special"; *einzeln* not only as "individual," but also as "singular." For the relation of these

concepts to categories in Marx, see *Capital*, Vol. 1, chapter 1, "The Commodity," and chapter 25, "The General Law of Capitalist Accumulation."

17. The "last paragraph" refers to the last paragraph of Hegel's *Science of Logic*. In his 1914 "Abstract of Hegel's *Science of Logic*," Lenin wrote that the last half-paragraph of the *Logic* was "unimportant" [LCW 38, p. 234]. For Dunayevskaya's "refusal to follow" Lenin on this, see her Letter of May 12, 1953, in the next chapter.

18. The "final syllogisms" refers to paragraphs 575, 576, and 577 of Hegel's *Philosophy of Mind*, which forms the third part of his *Encyclopedia of the Philosophical Sciences*. These three final paragraphs were added to the 1830 edition of this work, a year before Hegel's death. For Dunayevskaya's view of these three final syllogisms, see her Letter of May 20, 1953, in the next chapter.

19. A reference to Marx's 1844 "Critique of the Hegelian Dialectic."

20. Dunayevskaya's "Theory/Practice" column, from which the following six paragraphs were excerpted by her, is the last writing from her pen. Entitled "On Political Divides and Philosophic New Beginnings," the full text appears in Part V, below.

21. The "Self-Thinking Idea" [*die sich denkende Idee*] is discussed in ¶574 of Hegel's *Philosophy of Mind*, where he says "This notion of philosophy is the self-thinking Idea, the truth aware of itself." Hegel returns to the concept in the final ¶577, in speaking of "The Idea of philosophy, which has self-knowing reason [*die sich wissende Vernunft*], the absolutely universal, for its middle term."

22. The phrase "self-bringing forth of liberty" can be traced to the last lines of ¶576 of Hegel's *Philosophy of Mind*. There, Hegel writes that "science appears as a subjective cognition, whose goal is liberty and which is itself the way, itself the same to bring forth" [*die Wissenschaft erscheint als ein subjektives Erkennen, dessen Zweck die Freiheit und es selbst der Weg ist, sich diesselbe hervorzubringen*]—see Hegel, *Enzyclopädie der philosophischen Wissenschaften* (1830), edited by Friedhelm Nicolin and Otto Pöggeler (Hamburg: Felix Meiner Verlag, 1975), p. 462. In his *Hegel und das Ende der Geschichte* (Stuttgart: Kohlhammer Verlag, 1965), Reinhart Klemens Maurer—whose book Dunayevskaya read, made notes on, and later discussed in her *Philosophy and Revolution*—compresses and reworks slightly Hegel's above formulation into the phrase "a self-bringing forth of liberty" [*ein sich-Hervorbringen der Freiheit*] (p. 88). Unfortunately, in the existing English edition of the *Philosophy of Mind*, translator William Wallace renders the passage from Hegel more loosely as: "philosophy appears as a subjective cognition, of which liberty is the aim, and which is itself the way to produce it."

23. The proposed title for Dunayevskaya's new book developed from "Dialectics of the Party" to "Dialectics of Organization" to "Dialectics of Organization and Philosophy: The 'Party' and Forms of Organization Born out of Spontaneity." For Dunayevskaya's discussion of the significance of these changes, see *Supplement to the Raya Dunayevskaya Collection*, Vol. 13, 10813.

24. Ellipsis in original.

25. Anton Pannekoek, *Lenin as Philosopher* (London: Merlin Press, 1975, orig. 1938).

26. See Lenin's 1920 speech "Once Again on the Trade Unions, the Current Situation and the Mistakes of Trotsky and Bukharin" [LSW 9, pp. 62–72; LCW 32, pp. 90–100].

CHAPTER TWO

~

Letters on Hegel's Absolutes
of May 12 and 20, 1953

Dunayevskaya considered her 1953 "Letters on Hegel's Absolutes" as the "philo-sophic moment" from which the whole of her concept of the dialectic and of Marxist-Humanism flowed. The first letter, of May 12, 1953, focuses on the final chapter of Hegel's Science of Logic, *"The Absolute Idea"; the second, the letter of May 20, 1953, focuses on Hegel's* Philosophy of Mind, *the concluding volume in his* Encyclopedia of the Philosophical Sciences. *The 1953 letters first appeared in mimeographed form in 1955 as part of the News and Letters pamphlet* Philosophic Notes. *These letters were reproduced, also in mimeographed form, in 1956, and (in excerpts) in 1974. The text that follows is a reproduction of the 1953 letters as pre-pared by Dunayevskaya for publication in the 1955* Philosophic Notes. *In the foot-notes, we have noted several changes introduced by the author into the text of the 1953 letters between their first appearance in 1955 and their subsequent reissuance in mimeographed form in 1956 and 1974. The original can be found in* The Raya Dunayevskaya Collection, *p. 1797.*

Letter on Hegel's *Science of Logic*
(May 12, 1953)

Dear H:[1]

I am going to take the plunge and if it turns out that I have behaved like a bull in a china shop—well, I simply have to take my chances or I will never get to sleep nights at all. There is no concrete problem that I meet daily, no matter how minor, that doesn't send me scurrying to [Hegel's] *Logic* and by now I'm so drunk with it all that I brazenly shout that in the dialectic of the Absolute Idea is the dialectic of the party and that I have just worked it out.

15

Just like that. I have taken the plunge. But I will restrain myself from beginning with the conclusions and the differentiation of us from Lenin and even us from 1948[2] but I will have you bear with me as I go through the whole last chapter of the *Logic*. However, before I do so, let me state what I am *not* doing: 1) I am not touching upon the mass party; the workers will do what they will do and until they do we can have only the faintest intimation of the great leap. 2) This is not 1948, but 1953; I am not concerned with spontaneity versus organization, nor with Stalinism which the workers will overcome.

I am concerned only with the dialectic of the vanguard party [or][3] of that *type* of grouping like ours, be it large or small, and *its* relationship to the mass.

Let's begin with the beginning: "The Absolute Idea has now turned out to be the identity of the Theoretical and the Practical Idea. . . ." [SLII, p. 446; SLM, p. 824]. *At this moment* this means to me that the party is the identity or unity of the activity of the leadership and the activity of the ranks. "Each of these by itself is one-sided and contains the Idea itself only as a sought Beyond and an unattained goal; each consequently is a synthesis of the tendency, and both contains and does not contain the Idea. . . . " [SLII, p. 466; SLM, p. 824]. And further down on the same page we have the warning that the Absolute Idea "contains the highest opposition within itself."

While the staggering truth of this last phrase sinks in, I will make one more quotation from that page: "The Absolute Idea is the only object and content of philosophy. As it contains every determinateness, and its essence is to return to itself through its self-determination or particularization, it has various phases. It is the business of philosophy to recognize it in them. Nature and Spirit are different manners of presenting its existence. . . . " [SLII, p. 466; SLM, p. 824].

Because the party is the only object and content of *our* philosophy here, I wish to make two jumps here. One is to contrast to the manner in which Other is explained on this page where "Notion . . . as person, is impenetrable and atomic subjectivity; while at the same time it is not exclusive individuality, but is, for itself, universality and cognition, and in its Other has its own objectivity for object" [SLII, p. 466; SLM, p. 824]. Here then Other is the proletariat outside. What I wish to contrast to it is the description of Other when the Notion is further developed on p. 477 where Other turns out to be, not the proletariat outside, but the party itself. Hegel says:

"The second or negative and mediated determination is at the same time the mediating determination. At first it may be taken as simple determination, but in truth it is a reference or relation; for it is negative—the negative, however, of *the positive*, and includes the latter. It is not therefore the Other of a term to which it is indifferent, for thus it would be neither an Other, nor a reference or relation; it is the Other in itself, the Other of an Other. It thus includes its own Other, and so is contradiction, or the posited dialectic of itself" [SLII, pp. 476–77; SLM, pp. 834–35].

The other jump that I referred to that I wish to make is to leave the *Logic* for a moment and go to the last chapter in [Hegel's] *Phenomenology*. In that chapter on Absolute Knowledge Hegel writes: "The object as a whole is the mediated result [the syllogism] or the passing of universality into individuality through specification, as also the reverse process from individual to universal through canceled individuality or specific determination" [PhGB, p. 790; PhGM, p. 480].

Take a second look at the phrase, "the mediated result" and remember that our object is the party and that we are working out the triangular relationship not only politically but philosophically; that, syllogistically speaking, the party is the totality, the mediated result of the three layers[4] *and at the same time* it is what it is by its relationship to the proletariat outside, on the one hand, and to the universal of socialism, on the other hand, except that the two are now not "on the one hand" and "on the other hand" but interpenetrated.

Hegel goes on (p. 804): "Spirit is the movement of the self which empties (externalizes) itself of self and sinks itself within its own substance, and *qua* subject, both has gone out of that substance into itself, making its substance an object and a content, and also supersedes this distinction of objectivity and content" [PhGB, p. 804; PhGM, p. 490].

So Socialism too as it "externalizes" itself in parties, and in this case I mean not the vanguard grouping but the Paris Commune, the Soviets, the CIO, and so is Hegel talking of history: "The other aspect, however, in which Spirit comes into being, *History*, is the process of becoming in terms of knowledge, a conscious self-mediating process—Spirit externalized and emptied into Time" [PhGB, p. 807; PhGM, p. 492]. But he does not leave it at history (which includes historic development for us not only of the above, but the historic development of the party 1903, 1920–3, now). He *ends* Absolute Knowledge with:

"The goal, which is Absolute Knowledge or Spirit knowing itself as Spirit, finds its pathway in the recollection of spiritual forms (*Geister*) as they are in themselves and as they accomplish the organization of their spiritual kingdom. Their conservation, looked at from the side of their free existence appearing in the form of contingency, is *History*; looked at from the side of their intellectually comprehended organization, it is the *Science* of the ways in which knowledge appears. Both together, or History (intellectually) comprehended (*begriffen*), form at once the recollection and the Golgotha of Absolute Spirit, the reality, the truth, the certainty of its throne, without which it were lifeless, solitary, and alone" [PhGB, p. 808; PhGM, p. 493].

Now the way I see this connect with the *Logic* [SLII, p. 466; SLM, p. 824] where I left off before I began jumping around, is that where the "various phases" could have meant stages of development *within* the party such as 1903, 1920–23, etc., the recognition of the different manners of the existence of Absolute Idea as Nature and Spirit, or the country and something like the CIO rather than a "strict party" meant you are a fool if you cannot recognize the party in that for that is socialism just as at one time it was sufficient to define it as "electricity plus soviets."[5] The *world* concepts, the *American* roots, and us. We will come back to that, but now I wish to return to Hegel as he develops his Absolute Idea logically. On the next page (467) he writes: "Thus the logical Idea has itself as infinite form for content. . . . As opposed to form, content appears as Other and as given . . . ."

"The Absolute Idea itself has only this further content, that the form-determination[6] is its own perfected totality—the pure Notion. . . . What remains therefore to be considered here is not a content as such, but the universal element of its form—that is, the *method*." [SLII, p. 468; SLM, p. 825].

In the party both as political organization and as the realization of the theory of knowledge, the "form-determinations" or form of relations between leaders and ranks, between the various layers, and within each layer tells the *whole* story. *There is no content outside of that.* Or, once again to stick close to Hegel, "The method therefore is both soul and substance, and nothing is either conceived or known in its truth except in so far as it is completely subject to the method. . . . " [SLII, p. 468; SLM, p. 826].

Hegel brings this development of method to a climax by contrasting sharply what it is to inquiring cognition where it is "in the position of a tool, of a means which stands on the subjective side, whereby the method relates itself to the object" [SLII, p. 469; SLM, p. 827] to what it is in the dialectic: "But in true cognition the method is not merely a quantity of certain determinations: it is the fact that the Notion[7] is determined in and for itself, and is the mean[8] only because it equally has the significance of objective, so that, in the conclusion, it does not merely achieve an external determinateness through the method, but is posited in its identity with the subjective Notion" [SLII, p. 469; SLM, p. 827].

It is directly after this that Hegel discloses to me the secret of something that I have been chewing over like a dog does a bone, for many a moon—the intuition of the leader which he calls "internal intuition." First, let's watch the *process* of arriving at *internal intuition:* 1) method only has to have a *beginning* and so that is where we must begin; 2) but this beginning (and he warns later that "neither in actuality nor in thought" is there any beginning "so simple and abstract as is commonly imagined") is *not* "the immediate of sensuous intuition" which "is manifold and individual"; 3) no, this beginning is "internal intuition" [SLII, pp. 470, 471; SLM, pp. 827, 828, 829].

Secondly, note the contrast between "the immediate of sensuous intuition" and which comes from that which is, from the way, we would say, the *third* layer lives, and "the internal intuition" of the leader which comes from the way he *thinks*.

Jam these two opposites together, and you will first understand a sentence back on p. 467: "The self-determination therefore in which alone the Idea is, is to hear itself speak. . . . " [SLII, p. 467; SLM, p. 825]. In a word, the self-development of socialism, objectively and subjectively, gives off impulses which come one way to the leader, another way to the *class* as a whole, but what is important is that it is *determined to appear* "to hear itself speak." And the beautiful part about the "internal intuition" is that this "beginning must be inherently defective and must be endowed with the impulse of self-development" [SLII, p. 471; SLM, p. 829].

So that, finally, we reach Hegel's conclusion that nothing in life or in thought has a beginning so simple as is imagined but that "every beginning must be made from the Absolute, while every progress is merely the exhibition of the Absolute. . . . The progress is therefore not a kind of overflow, which it would be if in truth that which begins were already the Absolute; rather the progress consists in this, that the universal determines itself and is the universal for itself, that is, is equally also individual and subject. It is the Absolute only in its completion" [SLII, pp. 471–72; SLM, p. 829].

So although we began with the universal of socialism and although we have seen socialism in the various phases of the Commune, the Soviets, the CIO, it is not yet IT for it can be it "only in its completion." The new society will not be until it is; now we see only intimations, approximations, but it is nevertheless all around us, in the lives of the workers and in the theory of the party, so until the solution of the conflict and the abolition of the division [between mental and manual labor], we are back to *stages* of development: "*cause* is the highest stage in which the concrete Notion as beginning has an immediate existence in the sphere of necessity; but it is not yet a subject which, as such, preserves itself also in its actual realization" [SLII, p. 472; SLM, p. 830].

Here I wish you to remember that in this page and in the next is where Lenin made his own 16-point definition of the dialectic, the essence of which was three-fold [LCW 38, pp. 220–22]: 1) the transformation of anything into its opposite (collapse of Second International); 2) the absolute in every relative which is the transition to something else (Monopoly as eve of socialist revolution); and 3) thought reflects reality (objective world connections).

That we can fit Lenin in too here *historically* can now be seen from the fact that in the previous section on "The Idea of Cognition" Lenin had gone *further*, saying that "Man's cognition not only reflects the objective world but creates [it]" [LCW 38, p. 212], but when he reached the Absolute Idea it was not the creativity that he developed but the objective world connections because *to him in 1915 the Idea as "objective truth"* [LCW 38, p. 217] *of necessity predominated over any actual reconstruction of society, or the 1917 "socialism looking at us through all windows"* [LCW 25, p. 363].

We, however, can go further, and not only further than Lenin but further than we ourselves did in 1948, when the Nevada Dialectics[9] so profoundly held forth on the positive in the negative. But holding fast to the positive in the negative then meant *only the general* development of socialism through overcoming Stalinism, whereas now we can be more concrete, at least in relation to our own organization where the mediating determination is a negative "but the negative of the *positive* and includes the latter" [SLII, p. 477; SLM, p. 835]. Now you can see why some 11 pages back[10] I called attention to this further determination of Other as "its own Other . . . the posited dialectic of itself" [SLII, p. 477; SLM, p. 835]: "The first or immediate term is the Notion in itself, and therefore is the negative only *in itself*; the dialectic moment with it therefore consists in this, that the *distinction* which it implicitly contains is posited in it. The second term on the other hand is itself the determinate entity, distinction or relation, hence with it the dialectic moment consists in the positing of the unity which is contained in it" [SLII, p. 477; SLM, p. 835].

We have reached the *turning point* despite the unity or the party as a totality, since "The negativity which has just been considered is the turning point of the movement of the Notion. It is the simple point of negative self-relation, the innermost source of all activity, of living and spiritual self-movement, the dialectic soul which all truth has in it and through which it alone is truth; for the transcendence of the opposition between the Notion and Reality, and that unity which is the truth, rest upon this subjectivity alone. The second negative, the negative of the negative, which we have reached, is this transcendence of the contradiction, but is no more the activity of an external reflection than the contradiction is: it is the innermost and most objective moment of Life and Spirit, by virtue of which a subject is personal and free" [SLII, pp. 477–78; SLM, p. 835].

NOW STAND UP AND SHOUT PERSONAL AND FREE, PERSONAL AND FREE, PERSONAL AND FREE AS LENIN SHOUTED LEAP, LEAP, LEAP WHEN HE FIRST SAW DIALECTICAL DEVELOPMENT TO BE THAT AND ALSO THE OBJECTIVE WORLD.[11]

I will return to freedom, and where *our* age proves it has abolished the distinction between theory and practice and that which is the preoccupation of the theorists—freedom out of one-party totalitarianism—is the preoccupation of the great masses, but now I must still stick close to Hegel for when he reaches that point he goes not into paeans of freedom but an attack on all old radical parties from the Social-Democracy (Kant to Hegel) to the SLP[12] (formalists to Hegel) and he does not let go until the method itself extends itself into a *system* (p. 480).

And on p. 482 he says "The method effects this as a *system of totality.* . . . This progress determines itself, first, in this manner, that it begins from simple determinateness and that each subsequent one is richer and more concrete." It has not been in a straight line, but an approach both *rearward* and forward so that now we can see "In the absolute method the Notion preserves itself in its otherness, and the universal in its particularization, in the *Judgment* and in reality; it raises to each next stage of determination the whole mass of its antecedent content, and by its dialectical progress not only loses nothing and leaves nothing behind, but carries with it all that it has acquired, enriching and concentrating itself upon itself" [SLII, pp. 482–83; SLM, p. 840].

So that none of the other philosophies (parties to us) just degenerated or died, but their achievements have been incorporated in the new philosophy or party and this new has been enriched "concentrating itself upon itself" for we have that new source, the third layer.

Now watch this: "Each new stage of exteriorization (that is, of further determination) is also an interiorization, and greater extension is also higher intensity" [SLII, p. 483; SLM, pp. 840–41]. What a more perfect description of going outward with B,[13] and becoming richer inward and more intense.

"The highest and acutest point is simple personality," continues Hegel, "which, by virtue alone of the absolute dialectic which is its nature, equally holds and comprehends everything within itself because it perfectly liberates itself. . . . " [SLII, p. 483; SLM, p. 841]. So we are back at liberation and until the end of The Absolute Idea that will be the theme, liberation, freedom and *an absolutely uncompromising, Bolshevik attack on impatience.* If you are right and the Unhappy Consciousness[14] should somehow go as part of Abernism— and I agree with you there—then nevertheless I will not let go of Leland.[15] Just listen to the absolutely devastating analysis by Hegel, and remember Hegel does it as he has already approached freedom and we met that type when we approached independence:[16]

p. 484: "That impatience whose only wish is to go beyond the determinate (whether in the form of beginning, object, finite, or in any other form) and to be immediately

in the absolute, has nothing before it as object of its cognition but the empty negative, the abstract infinite,—or else a would-be absolute, which is imaginary because
it is neither posited nor comprehended" [SLII, p. 484; SLM, pp. 841–42].

I am shaking all over for we have come to where we part from Lenin.[17] I
mentioned before that, although in the *approach* to the Absolute Idea Lenin
had mentioned that man's cognition not only reflects the objective world but
creates it but that *within the chapter* he never developed it. Objective world
connections, materialism, dialectical materialism it is true, but not the object
and subject as one fully developed—that's what he saw. Then he reaches the
last paragraph: "For the Idea posits itself as the absolute unity of the pure
Notion and its Reality, and thus gathers itself into the immediacy of Being;
and in doing so, as totality in this form, it is Nature" [SLII, p. 485; SLM, p.
843].

There Lenin stops—it is the *beginning* of the last paragraph—and he says:
"This phrase on the *last* page of the Logic is exceedingly remarkable. The transition of the logical idea to *Nature*. Stretching a hand to materialism. This is
not the last phrase of the *Logic*, but further till the end of the page is unimportant" [LCW 38, p. 233].

But, my dear Vladimir Ilyitch, it is not true; the end of that page *is* important; we of 1953, we who have lived three decades after you and tried to absorb
all you have left us, we can tell you that.

Listen to the very next sentence: "But this determination is not a perfected
becoming or a *transition.* . . . " [SLII, p. 485; SLM, p. 843]. Remember how
transition was everything to you in the days of Monopoly, the eve of socialism. Well, Hegel has passed *beyond* transition, he says this last determination
"the pure Idea, in which the determinateness or reality of the Notion is itself
raised to the level of Notion, is an absolute *liberation*, having no further immediate determination which is not equally *posited* and equally Notion. Consequently there is no transition in this freedom. . . . The transition here therefore must rather be taken to mean that the Idea freely releases itself in absolute
self-security and self-repose" [SLII, pp. 485, 486; SLM, p. 843].

You see, Vladimir Ilyitch, you didn't have Stalinism to overcome, when
transitions, revolutions seemed sufficient to bring the new society. Now everyone looks at the totalitarian one-party state, *that* is the new that must be overcome by a totally new revolt in which everyone *experiences* "absolute liberation." So we build with you from 1920–23 and include the experience of three
decades.

But, H (Hauser, not Hegel), I have not finished yet, not that last paragraph
in Hegel, nor my summation, for we must retrace our steps to the paragraph

before and as we do, let's keep in mind Marx's last chapter of *Capital* (Vol. I). Hegel writes: "In so far[18] the pure Idea of Cognition is enclosed in subjectivity, and therefore is an impulse to transcend the latter; and, as last result, pure truth becomes *the beginning of another sphere and science*. This transition need here only be intimated" [SLII, p. 485; SLM, p. 843]. And then he goes into how the Idea posits itself and is liberation. That, he says, he cannot fully develop here; he can only intimate it.

Now you will recall that that is precisely what Marx does in the [section on the] accumulation of capital when he reaches the laws of concentration and centralization of capital and socialization of labor. He says he cannot develop these, but he can give an intimation, and this intimation turns out to be that: 1) the ultimate would be centralization of capital "in the hands of one single capitalist corporation" [MCIF, p. 779; MCIK, p. 688]; 2) that it would not matter if that occurs peacefully or violently; 3) but that with the centralization grows also the revolt, and it is not just any revolt but one that is "organized, united, disciplined by the very mechanism of capitalist production" [MCIF, p. 929; MCIK, pp. 836–37].

H, are you as excited as I? *Just as Marx's development of the form of the commodity and money came from Hegel's syllogistic U P I, so the Accumulation of Capital (the General Absolute Law) is based on The Absolute Idea.*[19]

Remember also that we kept on repeating Lenin's aphorism that Marx may not have left us "a" Logic, but he left us the logic of *Capital* [LCW 38, p. 317; M&F 1958, p. 353]. This is it—*the logic of Capital is the dialectic of bourgeois society:* the state capitalism at one pole and the revolt at the other.

At one stage we tried to divide socialization of labor from revolt, the former being still capitalistic, and the latter the beginning of socialism.[20] We didn't get very far because that socialization was capitalistic but revolt liberates it from its capitalistic integument. Marx, however, dealing with the dialectic of *capitalist* society did not make the negation of the negation any more concrete, but, on the contrary, in the last chapter returns to the origins of capitalism.

Now we are ready to return to the last few sentences of the *Logic* ending with "But this next resolution of the pure Idea—to determine itself as external Idea—thereby only posits for itself the mediation out of which the Notion arises as free existence that out of externality has passed into itself; arises to perfect its self-liberation in the Philosophy of Spirit, and to discover the highest Notion of itself in that logical science as the pure Notion which forms a Notion of itself" [SLII, p. 486; SLM, p. 843].

Please, Hauser, can you get a hold of a copy of *Philosophy of Spirit* or is it *Mind?* I am brazen enough to want to swim there too. I have an instinct that we couldn't get very far there when we tried it before because we equated Mind to party, but now that I believe the dialectic of the Absolute Idea is the dialectic of the party, I feel that Mind is the new society gestating in the old, and I feel sure we could get a lot of very valuable dialectical developments there, and what is so significant about that also is the building of the new within the old makes it possible to stop jumping from high point to high point but rather to follow *concretely* since this new is in the *daily* struggle.)

Somewhere in the letters about Lenin's Philosophic Notebooks[21] it is stated that Lenin was aware of the gap between his Universal ("to a man"[22]) and the concrete Russian proletariat, where we are more aware of the identity of the Universal and the concrete American proletariat. What, further, these two years of our organization showed was the high stage of social consciousness of the *new layers* attracted to us: they *practice* in the paper before they join and yet they appreciate *leadership*. Perhaps I'm stretching but I feel that in the Absolute General Law[23] when Marx was developing the dialectic of bourgeois society to its limit and came up with the revolt "united, organized, and disciplined"[24] he also set the limits to the dialectic of the party which is part of bourgeois society and will wither with its passing as will the bourgeois state. It appears to me when objective and subjective are so interpenetrated that the preoccupation of the theoreticians [and][25] of the man on the street is can we be free when what has arisen is the one-party state, the assertion of freedom, "personal and free" and full liberation takes precedence over economics, politics, philosophy, or rather refuses to be rent asunder into three and wants to be one, the knowledge that you can be free.

Do you remember the letter of May 20, 1949: "We are poles apart from Hegel but very close to him in another respect. As materialists we root man in his environment, but now that the real history of humanity is about to begin, the Hegelian concept of speculative reason, comes to life with us, as never before, though *on our basis.*"[26]

W. [Raya Dunayevskaya]

Letter on Hegel's *Philosophy of Mind* (May 20, 1953)

Dear Hauser:

Please do not interpret this as any prodding of you to commit yourself on my analysis of the Absolute Idea; it is only that *I* cannot stand still and so rushed directly to the *Philosophy of Mind.* I then reread the Preface, Introduction, and Absolute Knowledge in the *Phenomenology of Mind,* the Introduction, Three Attitudes to Objectivity,[27] and the Absolute Idea in the Smaller

Logic and the Absolute Idea in the *Science of Logic*. After that I read from cover to cover Lenin's phenomenal Vol. IX[28] which is the Absolute Idea in action, reread Marx's [section on the] accumulation of capital and the fetishism of commodities in Vol. I of *Capital*, the final part in Vol. III [of *Capital*], and *The Civil War in France*. All this I did on my own time, so to speak, that is to say, between 11 p.m. and 2 a.m. after putting in very full days and evenings in concrete organizational activity. I note these facts only in order to show how this Absolute Idea has me coming and going. Along with keeping all these in the back of my head then as I read the *Philosophy of Mind*, I made up the following outline of the development of the vanguard party and its relationship to the mass movements:

> The party as a "simple" class instrument—Communist League, the First International (reflecting 1848 class struggles and the Paris Commune)
> The party as divider of *tendencies* within Marxism—Lenin's party of 1903–17 (1905 and 1917 revolutions)
> The party as divider of politics from economics—The German Social Democracy (trade union aristocracy of labor and 1914 betrayal)
> The party as different social layers—1920—(in Russia Lenin to leaders and ranks; in Germany ranks to leaders)
> The party as suppressor of ranks and destroyer of revolutionism—Stalinism—(Spanish Revolution, CIO, National Resistance Movements) 1923–53

Now ourselves, '41–'50—clarification of ideas, elaboration of theory, eyes on *mass movements*. '51–'53—life in party and third layer as source of theory. Something *totally new* appears—

> 100 years becomes practically no more than mere background for listening and digging—B,[29] Woman, Youth—*all* come from ranks—something like the Great Beginning in Russia. What is so remarkable is that it comes *not* as direct result of any revolution, but rather as the accumulated experiences and feelings and social thinking *when* placed in the proper theoretic and climatic atmosphere of live people.

To this the paper is the climax not alone because it has never been but because it *could* never have been. Only one who *knew* it could be could go through the toil of the negative, the labor and suffering, of not a single break in the cadre of the "continuators" of Leninism. *And* (note the "and" rather than a "but") only when it did *appear* can we have perspectives that we have. This therefore is not just a general interpenetration of objective and subjective but one so concrete that it is impossible to say where theory leaves off and practice begins. *This can be so only because the elements of the new society are everywhere in evidence.*

First now you are where I was as I read the *Philosophy of Mind* which, to me, is the new society. *That's* what materialistic reading of the final chapters of Hegel means to me. (To say the end of Hegel is highly idealistic is to deny that the dialectical laws apply in their *totality.* Perhaps I am very rash but that is how *I feel* at this moment. Unfortunately, in this field I can do no more than feel for I most certainly have no knowledge or practice and I am totally dependent on you.)[30]

I limit myself to the following sections of the *Philosophy of Mind:* Introduction, Free Mind, Absolute Mind.

In the Introduction Hegel states what the three stages in the development of the Mind are: 1) in the form of *self-relation* where "the *ideal* of totality of the Idea" is, it is "self-contained and free" [PM, ¶385]; 2) Moving from the Mind Subjective he comes to the second stage or *"the form of reality"* and in this objective world "freedom presents itself under the shape of necessity"; 3) From Mind Objective we reach Mind Absolute "that unity of mind as objectivity and of mind as ideality and concept, which essentially and actually is and for ever produces itself, mind in its absolute truth" [PM, ¶385].

Hegel continues: "The two first parts of the doctrine of Mind embrace the finite mind. Mind is the infinite Idea, and finitude here means the disproportion between the concept and the reality—but with the qualification that it is a shadow cast by the mind's own light—a show or illusion which the mind implicitly imposes as a barrier to itself, in order, by its removal, actually to realize and become conscious of freedom as *its* very being, i.e., to be fully *manifested.* The several steps of this activity, on each of which, with their semblance of being, it is the function of the finite mind to linger, and through which it has to pass, are steps in its liberation. In the full truth of that liberation is given the identification of the three stages—finding a world presupposed before us, generating a world as our own creation, and gaining freedom from it and in it. To the infinite form of this truth the show purifies itself till it becomes a consciousness of it."

"A rigid application of the category of finitude by the abstract logician is chiefly seen in dealing with Mind and reason: it is held not a mere matter of strict logic, but treated also as a moral and religious concern, to adhere to the point of view of finitude, and the wish to go further is reckoned a mark of audacity, if not of insanity, of thought" [PM, ¶386].

(Remember "soviets in the sky"?)[31]

If we go from this audacious thinking directly to the Free Mind or end of Section 1 of Mind Subjective, we will meet with free will in a new social order: "Actual free will is the unity of theoretical and practical mind: a free will, which realizes its own freedom of will, now that the formalism, fortuitousness, and contractedness of the practical content up to this point have been super-seded. By superseding the adjustments of means therein contained, the will is the *immediate individuality* self-instituted—an individuality, however, also purified of all that interferes with its universalism, i.e. with freedom itself" [PM, ¶481].

In a word, not the free will of the Ego, the unhappy consciousness, but the free will of the *social* individual, "an individuality . . . purified of all that inter-feres . . . with freedom itself" [PM, ¶481].

To get to the "will to liberty (which) is no longer an *impulse* which demands its satisfaction, but the permanent character—the spiritual consciousness grown into a non-impulsive nature" [PM, ¶482], Hegel cannot avoid *history*, the concrete development:

"When individuals and nations have once got in their heads the abstract concept of full-blown liberty, there is nothing like it in its uncontrollable strength, just because it is the very essence of mind, and that as its very actu-ality. Whole continents, Africa and the East, have never had this Idea, and are without it still. The Greeks and Romans, Plato and Aristotle, even the Stoics, did not have it. On the contrary, they saw that it is only by birth (as, for example, an Athenian or Spartan citizen), or by strength of character, edu-cation, or philosophy (—the sage is free even as a slave and in chains) that the human being is actually free. It was through Christianity that this Idea came into the world" [PM, ¶482].

(I'll be d—d if *for us* I will need to stop to give the materialistic explana-tion here. I'm not fighting Hegel's idealism but trying to absorb his dialectics. Anyone who *can't think* of the Industrial and French Revolutions as the begin-nings of modern society, or *know* that when will to liberty is no longer mere impulse but "permanent character," "spiritual consciousness" it means and can mean only the proletariat that has absorbed all of science in his person, that person better not try to grapple with Hegel.)

Then a rejection of property, the "have" of possession, and directly to the *is* of the new society: "If to be aware of the idea—to be aware, i.e., that men are aware of freedom as their essence, aim, and object—is matter of *specula-tion*, still this very idea itself is the actuality of men—not something which they *have*, as men, but which they *are*" [PM, ¶482].

We are ready for the Absolute Mind. I will limit myself to the concluding four paragraphs, 574–577.

Hegel begins his conclusions about philosophy which "is the self-thinking Idea, the truth aware of itself" by referring us to the Absolute Idea in the *Smaller Logic*, and there Hegel issued a warning: "It is certainly possible to indulge in a vast amount of senseless declamation about the idea absolute. But its true content is only the whole system of which we have been hitherto examining the development" [EL, ¶237].

Back to ¶574: "the logical system, but with the signification that it is universality approved and certified in concrete content as in its actuality."[32]

I'm here reminded of that total Introduction to the *Smaller Logic* (or perhaps it is time to begin calling it by its right name, *Encyclopedia of the Philosophical Sciences*, since the *Smaller Logic* is Part I of it and the *Philosophy of Mind* that concerns me now Part III) where he says "the Idea is not so feeble as merely to have a right or an obligation to exist without actually existing" [EL, ¶6]. And most certainly Socialism "is not so feeble as merely to have a right or obligation to exist without actually existing." Quite the contrary, the new society is *evident* everywhere, *appears* within the old.

Let us return to Hegel, still ¶574: "In this way the science has gone back to its beginning: its result is the logical system but as a spiritual principle: out of the presupposing judgment, in which the notion was only implicit and the beginning an immediate—and thus out of the *appearance* which it had there— it has risen into its pure principle and thus also into its proper medium."

This appearance "gives the motive of the further development" [PM, ¶575]. So, like all rational thinkers, we are back at the form of the syllogism: "The first appearance is formed by the syllogism, which is based on the Logical system as starting-point, with Nature for the middle term which couples the Mind with it. The Logical principle turns to Nature and Nature to Mind" [PM, ¶575].

The movement is from the logical principle or theory to nature or practice *and* from practice not alone to theory but to the new society which is its essence: (Note scrupulously how this development, this practice, *sunders* itself.)

"Nature, standing between the Mind and its essence, sunders itself,[33] not indeed to extremes of finite abstraction, nor itself to something away from them and independent—which, as other than they, only serves as a link between them: for the syllogism is *in the Idea* and Nature is essentially defined as a transition-point and negative factor, and as implicitly the Idea" [PM, ¶575].

Thus the sundering of practice has been neither to mount the "extremes of finite abstraction" nor as mere link between practice and theory for the triangular development here means that practice itself is "implicitly the Idea."

"Still," continues Hegel, "the mediation of the notion has the external form of *transition*, and the science of Nature presents itself as the course of necessity, so that it is only in the one extreme that the liberty of the notion is explicit as a self-amalgamation" [PM, ¶575].

By all means let's follow Hegel and hold back from skipping a single link. But also let us not forget that this is only the first syllogism, while "In the second syllogism this appearance is so far superseded, that syllogism is the standpoint of the Mind itself, which—as the mediating agent in the process—presupposes Nature and couples it with the Logical principle. It is the syllogism where Mind reflects on itself in the Idea: philosophy appears as a subjective cognition, of which liberty is the aim, and which is itself the way to produce it" [PM, ¶576].

Here then Mind itself is "the mediating agent in the process." I cannot help but think of Marx concluding that the Commune is "the form at last discovered to work out the economic emancipation of the proletariat,"[34] and of Lenin in Vol. 9[35] saying that the workers and peasants "must understand that the whole thing now is *practice*, that the historical moment has arrived when theory is being transformed into practice, is vitalized by practice, corrected by practice, tested by practice," and on the same page: "The Paris Commune gave a great example of how to combine initiative, independence, freedom of action and vigor from below with voluntary centralism free from stereotyped forms."[36] And so I repeat Mind itself, the new society, is "the mediating agent in the process."[37]

This is where Hegel arrives at Absolute Mind, the third syllogism: "The third syllogism is the Idea of philosophy, which has self-knowing reason, the absolutely-universal, for its middle term: a middle, which divides itself into Mind and Nature, making the former its presupposition, as process of the Idea's subjective activity, and the latter its universal extreme, as process of the objectively and implicitly existing Idea" [PM, ¶577].

No wonder I was so struck, when working out the layers of the party, with the Syllogism which disclosed that either the Universal or the Particular or the Individual could be the middle term. Note carefully that the "middle which divides itself" is nothing less than the absolute universal itself and that, in dividing itself into Mind and Nature, it makes *Mind* the presupposition "as process of the Idea's subjective activity" and *Nature* "as process of the objectively and implicitly existing Idea."

Here, much as I try not once again to jolt you by sounding as if I were exhorting, I'm too excited not to rejoice at what this means *for us*. But I'll stick close to Hegel and not go off for visits with Lenin and Marx. *Hegel* says that the two appearances of the Idea (Socialism in the form of the Commune and the Soviets) characterize both [as] its manifestation and in it precisely is "A unification of the two aspects":

"The self-judging of the Idea into its two appearances [¶575, 576] characterizes both as its (the self-knowing reason's) manifestations: and in it there is a unification of the two aspects:—it is the nature of the fact, the notion, which causes the movement and development, yet this same movement is equally the action of cognition. The eternal Idea, in full fruition of its essence, eternally sets itself to work, engenders and enjoys itself as absolute Mind" [PM, ¶577].

We have entered the new society.

W. [Raya Dunayevskaya]

NOTES

1. "H" stands for "Hauser," the organizational name used by Grace Lee Boggs in this period; "W," the signature at the end, stands for "Weaver," the organizational name used by Raya Dunayevskaya in this period.

2. The phrase "even us from 1948" refers to James' *Notes on Dialectics*, written in that year.

3. We have inserted "or" here, given Dunayevskaya's opposition to the vanguard party.

4. C. L. R. James developed a concept of "three layers" after the Johnson-Forest Tendency left the Socialist Workers Party, patterned on his interpretation of Vol. IX of Lenin's *Selected Works*. The term "first layer" referred to the "intellectual leadership"; "second layer" referred to the "experienced politicos"; "third layer" referred to the rank-and-file workers, women, Blacks, and youth. As a result of her 1953 "Letters on Hegel's Absolutes," Dunayevskaya worked out a new concept of the relationship between the "movement from theory" and the "movement from practice that is itself a form of theory."

5. This refers to Lenin's 1920–21 view that "Communism is Soviet power plus the electrification of the whole country" [LCW 31, pp. 419, 516].

6. For Hegel, form-determinations [*Formbestimmungen*] are specific (determinate) forms as opposed to general, contentless forms.

7. For Hegel the Notion (or Concept) [*Begriff*] signifies not abstraction from reality, but rather comprehension of its inner content. He associates the Notion with freedom. The Doctrine of the Notion is the third and last part of Hegel's *Science of Logic*.

8. In German, this is "die Mitte," alternately translated by Miller as "the middle term."

9. C. L. R. James, *Notes on Dialectics*.

10. See page 17, above.

11. In his Hegel Notebooks, Lenin writes of "Leaps!" and "breaks in gradualness" while summarizing Hegel's critique of the idea that "there are no leaps in nature" [LCW 38, p. 123]. For Hegel's concept of leaps, see SLI, pp. 388–91; SLM, pp. 368–71.

12. Socialist Labor Party, followers of Daniel DeLeon.

13. "B" refers to Charles Denby, author of *Indignant Heart*, first published in 1952. An expanded edition was published in 1978 as *Indignant Heart: A Black Worker's Journal* (Boston: South End Press); a new, further expanded edition was published in 1989 by Wayne State University Press.

14. A discussion of "Unhappy Consciousness," a mode of thought that in part pertains to Christianity, concludes the chapter on "Self-Consciousness" in Hegel's *Phenomenology*.

15. Martin Abern, one of the founders of Trotskyism in the U.S., died in 1947. Leland was the organizational secretary in 1951–52 of Correspondence Committees, the organization to which Dunayevskaya belonged from 1951 to 1955, after the Johnson-Forest Tendency left the Socialist Workers Party.

16. The Johnson-Forest Tendency "approached independence" in June, 1951, when it left the Socialist Workers Party.

17. In the 1974 edition the phrase, "where we part from Lenin," is underlined, and this entire paragraph has vertical double lines drawn alongside it.

18. The Miller translation substitutes "because" for "in so far," a more literal translation of the German "weil."

19. "UPI" refers to Hegel's syllogism "Universal-Particular-Individual." See also p. 16, note 12, as well as Marx's *Capital*, Vol. 1, chapter 1, "The Commodity," and chapter 25, "The General Law of Capitalist Accumulation."

20. This was developed by a letter of James to Dunayevskaya of June 24, 1949, in which he said "There is a deep problem, philosophical and all-inclusive around 'socialization of labor.' Socialization of labor is a capitalist category. I have thought of this almost continuously. The socialism is the *revolt*." See *The Raya Dunayevskaya Collection*, p. 1647.

21. This refers to James' letter to Dunayevskaya of May 20, 1949, in which he said that Lenin "was terribly aware of the gap between his Universal and the concrete. . . . His greatness is that he strove to bridge it. We . . . see that there is not so much a gap as a unity." See *The Raya Dunayevskaya Collection*, p. 1614.

22. A reference to Lenin's comment, in his "Report on Revising the Programme and Name of the Party" of March 8, 1918: "Every citizen to a man must act as a judge and participate in the government of the country. And what is important to us is to enlist all the toilers to a man in the government of the state. That is a tremendously difficult task. But socialism cannot be introduced by a minority, a party" [LSW 8, p. 320; LCW 27, p. 135].

23. A reference to Marx's statement in *Capital* that the "greater the social wealth" produced by capitalism, "the greater is the industrial reserve-army" of unemployed, a two-pronged process that Marx calls "the absolute general law of capitalist accumulation" [MCIF, p. 798; MCIK, p. 707].

24. In the closing pages of *Capital*, Vol. I, Marx refers to the growing "revolt of the working class, a class always increasing in numbers, and disciplined, united, organized by the very mechanism of the process of capitalist production itself" (MCIF, p. 929; MCIK, pp. 836–37).

25. We have inserted "and" for greater clarity.

26. Letter of C. L. R. James to Grace Lee Boggs of May 20, 1949. See *The Raya Dunayevskaya Collection*, p. 1613.

27. In his Smaller Logic, Hegel critiques three fundamental attitudes to objectivity: faith, empiricism, and Kantianism, and immediate knowing based on intuition.

28. This refers to Vol. IX of Lenin's *Selected Works* (New York: International Publishers, 1943), which includes many of his writings after 1917.

29. Charles Denby's *Indignant Heart* (see p. 30, note 13).

30. For the 1956 edition Dunayevskaya deleted the final two sentences within the parentheses.

31. The literary critic Irving Howe, then a Trotskyist, writing in a Workers Party discussion bulletin (Vol. 1, No. 9, March 28, 1946), attacked the Johnson-Forest Tendency for supposedly romanticizing American workers, charging them with creating "soviets in the skies."

32. In reissuing excerpts of the May 20, 1953 letter in mimeographed form in 1986, Dunayevskaya included a fuller version of this passage, from Hegel's ¶574. It reads: "This notion of philosophy is the self-thinking Idea, the truth aware of itself—the logical system, but with the signification that it is universality approved and certified in concrete content as in its actuality."

33. Later, Dunayevskaya noted that the original German read "sunders them." See this volume, p. 330.

34. Marx, *The Civil War in France*, MECW 22, p. 334.

35. This refers to Vol. IX of Lenin's *Selected Works*.

36. See Lenin's "How to Organize Competition," in *Selected Works*, Vol. 9, p. 420; LCW 26, p. 413.

37. In the 1974 edition this paragraph has vertical double lines drawn alongside it.

PART II

STUDIES IN HEGELIAN AND MARXIAN DIALECTICS, 1956–63

CHAPTER THREE

~

Notes on Hegel's *Phenomenology*

These notes, composed in December 1960, were circulated in mimeographed and pamphlet form for many years before being republished with a new Introduction in News & Letters *in May 1987, just weeks before Dunayevskaya's death. This is her first comprehensive treatment of Hegel's* Phenomenology of Mind, *and represents one of the few Marxist treatments of the book as a whole. In addition to taking up the well-known sections on "Consciousness," "Self-Consciousness" and "Reason," this text also devotes a great deal of space to the sections on "Spirit in Self-Estrangement" and "Religion," as well as the final chapter, "Absolute Knowledge." The original can be found in* The Raya Dunayevskaya Collection, *p. 2806.*

The whole of the *Phenomenology*, with its six stages of consciousness, can be divided into two major departments comprising: I. *Consciousness, Self-Consciousness and Reason*, being the summation of both the relationship, or rather awareness of a world outside oneself through feudalism to the beginning of capitalism, i.e., commercial capitalism; and II. *Spirit, Religion, and Absolute Knowledge*, which takes us from industrial capitalism and its ideological predecessors covering the field from Christianity through the enlightenment to the Jacobins of the French Revolution, all the way to "the new society" (Absolute Knowledge) with its "predecessor" in Greek Art and the Greek city-state.

In the case of Subdivision I, once we have gone from consciousness—whether that's only first awareness of things (sense-certainty) or perception, or actual understanding where the forces of the world of appearance with its laws which "leave out their specific character"—[to] immediately enter the true relationship between people and not just things. Thus, in self-consciousness we are thrust into a *production* relationship—lordship and bondage. So that once the bondsman gains "a mind of his own," he is compelled to see that there is more to freedom than either stubbornness or a mind of one's own. That is to say, if freedom is not "a type of freedom which does not get beyond the attitude of bondage," it must first now confront objective reality. Otherwise, a mind of his own would be little more than "a piece of cleverness which has mastery within a certain range, but not over the universal power, nor over the entire objective reality" [PhGB, p. 240; PhGM, p. 119].

In the struggle to realize freedom, we confront various attitudes of mind that *sound* heroic, but are in fact adaptations to one or another form of servitude. Thus, stoicism is nothing more, Hegel reminds us, than "a general form of the world spirit, only in a time of universal fear and bondage" [PhGB, p. 245; PhGM, p. 121].

Even skepticism, Hegel tells us, which corresponds to some form of independent consciousness, is very negative in its attitude, so much so that it leads to nothing but "the giddy whirl of a perpetually self-creating disorder" [PhGB, p. 249; PhGM, p. 125]. That is why both stoicism and skepticism lead to nothing but the unhappy consciousness, or Alienated Soul.

The interesting thing about this unhappy consciousness for the Christian philosopher, Hegel, is that it is a description not only of the disintegration of the Roman Empire, but the Roman Empire *at a time when* it had adopted Christianity to try to save all from the debacle. Of course, the Lutheran in Hegel may have consoled himself by the fact that this Christianity, as the Christianity of the Borgias in Renaissance Italy, was "Catholic," and it really was not until the Reformation, etc., etc. We are not interested in any rationalization, but in the objective pull upon the mind of a genius which describes this individually free person with his unhappy consciousness as a "personality confined within its narrow self and its petty activity, a personality brooding over itself, as unfortunate as it is pitiably destitute" [PhGB, p. 264; PhGM, p. 136]. You will recall that in *Marxism and Freedom*, I have a footnote on this which uses the specific personalities of the old radical who cannot find a place for himself in bourgeois society or in the movement as examples of this unhappy consciousness [M&F, p. 347]. Be that as it may, Hegel's point is that until this alienated soul has "stripped itself of its Ego" [PhGB, p. 266; PhGM, p. 137], it will not be able to execute the leap to Reason.

Before we proceed to Reason, however, let's retrace our steps back to the Preface and the Introduction, which, in a very great sense, also comprise his conclusions. At any rate, it is a constant paean to "ceaseless activity," "equal necessity of all moments," which constituted the "life of the whole"; which, however, cannot be seen before being seen, that is to say, it is all a question of a process of "working the matter out," on which the purpose depends. This constant emphasis on process, on experience (the experience of consciousness no less than "objective" experience) of self-development that must have, nay, must go through "the labor, the patience, the suffering, the seriousness of the negative" [PhGB, p. 81; PhGM, p. 10] that must not take "easy contentment in receiving, or stinginess in the giving" [PhGB, p. 73; PhGM, p. 5]—all of which signify "a birth-time and a period of transition" [PhGB, p. 75; PhGM, p. 6]—amounts to the very reason for being of Dialectics and Absolute Knowledge in his principle that "everything depends on grasping and expressing the ultimate truth, not as Substance, but as Subject as well" [PhGB, p. 80; PhGM, p. 10].

The work, the purposive activity, the mediation, the self-directive process, the subject in the objective movement, and the objective movement in the subject or mind which Hegel calls Science, is in fact not only a Preface to *his* Philosophy, but to the entire human spirit as it has developed through thousands of years, historically, nationally, internationally, and as it is going to develop via opposing *all* contemporary philosophies from mysticism to Kantianism—all this on the day after, so to speak, the French Revolution, which demands the reorganization of all previous thought. With Hegel, "immanent" rhythm and strenuous toil are one and the same thing. And finally, the man puts his faith in the *public* rather than the philosophers, "those 'representatives' who are like the dead burying their dead" [PhGB, p. 130; PhGM, p. 45]. This man was really saying, "To hell with all parties (representatives) who are out to lead." And instead, hewing a pathway to Science which would reach "a position where, in consequence, its exposition coincides with just this very point, this very stage of the science proper of mind. And finally, when it grasps this, its own essence, it will connote the nature of absolute knowledge itself" [PhGB, p. 145; PhGM, p. 57].

To return to the last section of this first major division—Reason—we see here the first Hegelian development of actuality, that is to say, the reality of the objective world and the reality of thought. The historic period is the one which preceded his own, or the period before the French Revolution. There is an awakening of the scientific world of thought which sees beyond the empirical, but cannot unify the objective and subjective. He hits out both against Kant's "Table of Categories," and against the "Abstract empty idealism" of Fichte.[1] Of Kant's discovery he says, "But to pick up the various categories again in any sort of way as a kind of happy find, hit upon, e.g., in the different judgments, and then to be content so to accept them, must really be regarded as an outrage on scientific thinking" [PhGB, p. 277; PhGM, p. 142].

He, therefore, proceeds to examine the process of observation, both of organic nature and of self-consciousness. The section on the so-called laws of thought is quite hilarious, and is a perfect slap at modern psychoanalysis, of which he knew nothing then. Indeed, if anyone thinks that the very long section on Phrenology merely reveals the backward state of science at that time, and not our age, he fails to understand that thought, or, for that matter, feelings, have no meaning apart from the reality with which thought is concerned, and which builds up "feelings."

Although we are in the realm of the phenomenal, reality and thought are so inseparable, practical reason as well as theoretical combine to show the inadequacies of mere observation, which does not mean that purposive activity can do away with one-sided subjective idealism. On the contrary, the criticism of Rousseau and the whole Romantic movement, which Hegel makes under the heading, "The Law of the Heart, and the Frenzy of Self-Conceit," apply to the labor bureaucrat and his "earnestness of high purpose, which seeks its pleasure in displaying the excellence of his own true nature, and in bringing about the welfare of mankind" [PhGB, p. 392; PhGM, p. 222]. When it meets up against mankind's opposition to this personal interpretation, "the heart-throb for the welfare of mankind passes therefore into the rage of frantic self-conceit, into the fury of consciousness to preserve itself from destruction" [PhGB, p. 397; PhGM, p. 226].

It is at this point that individualism tried to take refuge in the concept of "virtue." How many windbags, from Castro to some of our best friends, are not included in the following beautiful passage: "The vacuousness of this rhetorical eloquence in conflict with the world's process would be at once discovered if it were to be stated what all its eloquent phrases amount to. They are therefore assumed to be familiar and well-understood. The request to say what, then, this 'well-known' is would be either met by a new swell of phrases, or in reply there would be an appeal to the 'heart' which 'inwardly' tells what they mean—which is tantamount to an admission of inability to say what the meaning is" [PhGB, p. 410; PhGM, p. 234].

As Hegel hits out against this form of self-expression, he digs deep into the objective base. We reach here the section which could equally describe Mao's China, Castro's Cuba, and Djilas' counter-thesis to the new class,[2] which Hegel calls "Self-Conscious Individuals Associated as a Community of Animals and the Deception Thence Arising: The Real Fact." This section should be studied in detail, especially so pages 434–38 [PhGB, pp. 434–38; PhGM, pp. 248–52], on the "Honesty" or "Honorableness" of this type of consciousness, which, actually, since it concerns a reality not involving action, but merely good luck, is summed up simply as follows: "The true meaning of this 'honesty,' however, lies in not being so honest as it seems" [PhGB, p. 434; PhGM, p. 248]. By the time Hegel gets through exposing the deception of himself, as well as of others, his conclusion is an uncompromising one: "The moments of individuality which were taken as subject one after the other by this unreflected incoherent stage of consciousness. . ." [PhGB, p. 438; PhGM, p. 252].

The second major subdivision—Spirit—is the cornerstone of the entire work. Since alienation has by no means disappeared with the "realization of Reason," i.e., the rise of industrial capitalism, we get here the really revolutionary impact of the dialectical philosophy which refuses to be confined even where the sciences have been liberated, the individual has been freed, and production "progresses."

Whether it's nation and the family, "law and order" (legal status), or the moral laws and ethical action that proceeds with both guilt and destiny, we find that Personality or the master and lord of the world, the power of destruction, continues. Indeed, Hegel is here dealing with what he calls "titanic excess" [PhGB, p. 505; PhGM, p. 293], not only insofar as his points of reference are the Neros who fiddled while Rome burned, i.e., slave societies, but also insofar as free enterprise is concerned—Hobbes' Leviathan. Thus, not only stoicism, skepticism, the unhappy consciousness, but also Spirit finds itself estranged: "What in the case of the former was all harmony and union, comes now on the scene, no doubt in developed form, but self-estranged" [PhGB, p. 506; PhGM, p. 294].

It is this spirit in self-estrangement which Hegel also defines as "the discipline of culture." That is to say, it is a critique of everything from the Industrial Revolution to the French Revolution, and including what Marx called the "fetishism of commodities," as well as what Hegel calls a spiritual, but factual, "reign of terror"—the intellectual run amok. Throughout, we will be seeing the contradiction between the individual and society or between what we would call petty bourgeois individualism and the truly social individual.

Let us remember also that we will find here what Marx thought contained the critique, though in still mystical form, of the capitalist state: "Spirit in this case, therefore, constructs not merely one world, but a twofold world, divided and self-opposed" [PhGB, p. 510; PhGM, p. 295].

The self-opposition deepens not only because of its opposition to reality, but the internal opposition which first is "Pure Insight," which completes the stage of culture, which "extinguishes all objectiveness." That is to say, in fighting against faith and superstition, it is Enlightenment, but in trying to be an island of safety for spirit, it confines it from further self-development. In this critique of 18th century deism and utilitarianism, Hegel writes:

> Enlightenment upsets the household arrangements which spirit carries out in the
> house of faith, by bringing in the goods and furnishings belonging to the world of

Here and Now. . . . The sphere of spirit at this stage breaks up into two regions. The one is the actual world, that of self-estrangement, the other is that which spirit constructs for itself in the ether of pure consciousness, raising itself above the first. This second world, being constructed in opposition and contrast to that estrangement, is just on that account not free from it [PhGB, pp. 512–13; PhGM, pp. 296–97].

It is important to keep in mind that by culture Hegel does not mean only the Humanities or the Sciences. He means material wealth and the state, as well as the intelligentsia and their ivory towers. If you keep in mind what Marx meant by superstructure, you will be able to swim along with Hegel's critique of culture.

In criticizing Empiricism (especially Bacon's idea, "knowledge is power"),[3] Hegel criticizes not only his principles, but the reality on which these principles rest: "The extent of its culture is the measure of its reality and its power" [PhGB, p. 515; PhGM, p. 298].

He then moves from the "power of culture" to the power of state. Here we can see that ordinary psychological or moral terms like good and bad have a very different and altogether profound meaning in Hegel:

These bare ideas of Good and Bad are similarly alienated from one another; they are actually, and in actual consciousness appear as moments that are objective. In this sense, the first state of being is Power of the State, the second its Resources or Wealth [PhGB, p. 519; PhGM, p. 301].

Until Hegel reaches the attitude of "thorough-going discordance" [PhGB, p. 535; PhGM, p. 312], Hegel has the time of his life criticizing both the Good and the Bad, both the State and Wealth, both the Attitudes of Nobility and Authority in a way that could encompass everyone from Proudhon, whose anarchism had no use for the state, to Mao Zedong, who completely identifies himself with this state. This is what is so extraordinary about Hegel, that he catches the spirit of an epoch in *crisis*, and, therefore, its ramifications extend into both ages that are marked beyond the one he analyzes, and personality beyond those that he has known in his own period or in history. Think of Mao and read the following:

The noble type of consciousness, then, finds itself in the judgment related to state power. . . . This type of mind is the heroism of Service; the virtue which sacrifices individual being to the universal, and thereby brings this into existence; the type of personality which of itself renounces possession and enjoyment, acts for the sake of the prevailing power, and in this way becomes a concrete reality. . . . The result of this action, binding the essential reality and self indissolubly together is to produce a twofold actuality—a self that is truly actualized, and a state power whose authority is accepted as true. . . . It has a value, therefore, in their thoughts, and is honored accordingly. Such a type is the haughty vassal; he is active in the interests of the state-power, so far as the latter is not a personal will (a monarch) but merely an essential will [PhGB, pp. 526–28; PhGM, pp. 306–7].

Not only is the critique of state power total in its essential respects, but also in its language, for to Hegel speech contains "ego in its purity." The heroism of dumb service passes into the heroism of flattery: "This reflection of service in express language constitutes the spiritual self-disintegrating mediating term" [PhGB, p. 533; PhGM, p. 310]. One doesn't have to think or be too bright to remember, in this respect, expressions that must have been in Hegel's mind, such as that of Louis XIV, "I am the State." No wonder that Hegel added that this was the type of "pure personality to be absolutely without the character of personality" [PhGB, p. 537; PhGM, p. 314]. Indeed, on pages 537–48 [PhGB, pp. 537–48; PhGM, pp. 314–21], there is a beautiful description of Existentialists, fellow-travelers, people who break with the "East" to go to the "West" like Djilas, as well as vice-versa, like C. Wright Mills. In each case we find that "in place of revolt appears arrogance" [PhGB, p. 539; PhGM, p. 315]:

> This type of spiritual life is the absolute and universal inversion of reality and thought, their entire estrangement, the one from the other; it is pure culture. What is found out in this sphere is that neither the concrete realities, state-power and wealth, nor their determinate conceptions, good and bad, nor the consciousness of good and bad (the consciousness that is noble and the consciousness that is base) possess real truth; it is found that all these moments are inverted and transmuted the one into the other, and each is the opposite of itself [PhGB, p. 541; PhGM, p. 316].

The perversion is not ended when culture moves over to "belief and pure insight." It has always been a wonder to me how Hegel keeps trying to reassert religion as an absolute and yet at every concrete stage or form of religion, actual religion is criticized. For example, he does not deny that belief or religion has always been a form of alienation which man had to rid himself of in order to face reality; he has been devastating when it was the unhappy consciousness that confronted him, and again in the form of culture, and now as "merely belief"—in the nether world, as pure ego (see Kant: "Pure ego is the absolute unity of apperception") or "pure thought," and finally as Enlightenment. Naturally, Hegel does not deny the good enlightenment accomplished in its struggle with superstition and its clearing the ground for the French Revolution. But when it is made into something absolute, he feels the revolutionary impulse to overthrow this idol. Note in the following quotation how Hegel moves from a critique of idolatry to a critique of any "dead form of the spirit's previous state" which would equally be applicable to something like Trotsky's forced identification of nationalized property and "workers' state":

> On some "fine morning," whose noon is not red with blood, if the infection has penetrated to every organ of spiritual life. It is then the memory alone that still preserves the dead form of the spirit's previous state, as vanished history, vanished men know not how [PhGB, p. 565; PhGM, p. 332].

That is why Hegel concludes that "enlightenment itself, however, which reminds belief of the opposite of its various separate moments, is just as little enlightened regarding its own nature" [PhGB, p. 582; PhGM, p. 344].

Hegel leaves himself one loophole, that this is just an *empty* absolute. In proof of this, he hits out against what we would call vulgar materialism:

> . . . pure matter is merely what remains over when we abstract from seeing, feeling, tasting, etc., i.e., it is not what is seen, tasted, felt, and so on; it is not matter that is seen, felt or tasted, but color, a stone, a salt, and so on. Matter is really pure abstraction. . . . [PhGB, p. 592; PhGM, p. 351].

Read this along with Marx's description of the five senses in his "Private Property and Communism" [PPC, pp. 297–99; MECW 3, pp. 301–3]. Hegel is hitting out both against Descartes and the Utilitarians.

The last section of "Spirit in Self-Estrangement" that we have been dealing with Hegel entitles "Absolute Freedom and Terror." It is an analysis of what happened to the French Revolution as factionalism broke up the unity of the revolution so that for "pure personality" the world became "absolutely its own will," so that terror succeeded so-called absolute freedom, since, by being only negative, it was "merely the rage and fury of destruction" [PhGB, p. 604; PhGM, p. 359]. In a word, Hegel considers that if you have not faced the question of reconstruction on new beginnings, but only destruction of the old, you have, therefore, reached only "*death*—a death that achieves nothing, embraces nothing within its grasp; for what is negated is the unachieved, unfulfilled punctual entity of the absolutely free self" [PhGB, p. 605; PhGM, p. 360]. This is where he identifies that absolutely free self with a "*faction*. The victorious faction only is called the government . . . and its being government makes it, conversely, into a faction and hence guilty" [PhGB, p. 606; PhGM, p. 360].

It is not only government that Hegel criticizes here, but the philosophic transformation of enlightenment into Kant's "thing-in-itself."[4] In a word, he is criticizing all forms of abstraction, whether in thought or in fact, when fact is narrowed to mean not all reality, but only aspects of it. He, therefore, concludes that this self-alienated type of mind must be driven to opposition:

> Just as the realm of the real and actual world passes over into that of belief and insight, absolute freedom leaves its self-destructive sphere of reality. [PhGB, p. 610; PhGM, p. 363]

This very section is cited by Hegel in the *Science of Logic*, where, in the penultimate chapter on "The Idea of Cognition," in the final section on "The Idea of the Good," Hegel suddenly tells us that the two worlds of subjectivity and objectivity still remain in opposition: "The complete development of the unresolved contradiction, of that *absolute* end which the barrier of this actuality insuperably opposes, has been considered more closely in the *Phenomenology of Spirit*" [SLII, p. 462; SLM, p. 820; WL, pp. 544–45]. In a word, Hegel is saying, in that penultimate chapter of *Science of Logic*, where we are on the threshold of the Absolute, that the unresolved contradiction between the two worlds of subjectivity and objectivity "has been considered more closely" in his phenomenological study.[5]

This central part of the *Phenomenology*—Spirit—ends with the section called "Spirit Certain of Itself: Morality" which is just another form of talking about the state and consequently the certainty is by no means peace. On the contrary, it moves from dissemblance—which deals with what Kant called, according to Hegel, "a perfect nest of thoughtless contradictions"—through the so-called "beautiful soul" (Jacobi)[6] but which to Hegel is really "self-willed impotence" [PhGB, p. 666; PhGM, p. 400] that can only lead to hypocrisy. And on this note he ends the part of "Evil and Forgiveness" (you might return to the section on "Guilt and Destiny" [PhGB, pp. 483–99; PhGM, pp. 279–89] and compare the similarity between moral and the ethical action which had previously led us into "Spirit in Self-Estrangement" or the "Discipline of Culture and Civilization").

In a word, Spirit, as it was on the eve of the French Revolution and developed through the terror to Napoleonic France, has found no harmony either with its culture or its state, its literature or philosophy as enlightenment, or philosophy as absolute à la Jacobi. Therefore, the human spirit has not been able to shake off alienation and reaches Religion.

Religion, which is the second major section of the division into two of the whole *Phenomenology*, as I have been tracing it through here, is just one step before Absolute Knowledge. Religion is subdivided into three sections: (1) Natural, which takes up nature, plants, animals, concept of light and the "artificer" (Egyptian religion); (2) Religion in the form of art; (3) Revealed Religion or Christianity.

In his introduction to this section, Hegel says that religion has of course entered before this, i.e., in the four stages of consciousness we have heretofore dealt with, Consciousness, Self-Consciousness, Reason, and Spirit, but more or less on a low level. That is to say, when we were at the first stage of consciousness, religion was "devoid of selfhood"; when we reached Self-Consciousness, it was merely "the pain and sorrow of spirit wrestling to get itself out into objectivity once more, but not succeeding" [PhGB, p. 685; PhGM, p. 410]. The third stage of consciousness—Reason—more or less forgot about religion since it first discovered itself and, therefore, looked to the immediate present—empiricism, science, etc. Even when we reach Spirit, whether of the ethical order where we have to fight fate "devoid of consciousness," or we reached and perished in "the religion of enlightenment," or finally reached the religion of morality, the best, says Hegel, that we accomplished there was to face "Absolute Reality." Therefore, it is only now in religion that we really confront the spirit of Religion: "But only spirit which is object to itself in the shape of Absolute Spirit, is as much aware of being a free and independent reality as it remains therein conscious of itself" [PhGB, p. 688; PhGM, p. 412].

Outside of the little subsection on the artificer, which in fact relates not only to Egyptian religions and pyramids and obelisks, but to what in our age would be called "the confidence man,"[7] there isn't much that I can see in the section on Natural Religion, except I see that I wrote down two expressions, "fetishism of commodities," and "Dr. Zhivago"[8] near the following expression of Hegel: "The darkness of thought mated with the clearness of expression" [PhGB, p. 707; PhGM, p. 424]. And it is through this clearness of expression that we reach religion in the form of art, which is again subdivided into the Abstract, Living, and Spiritual Work of Art. (Since this section I took up a few days ago those two pages would be considered part of this summation and I will not concern myself here with it, except that I want to contrast the question of language as it is considered in this section with the manner in which it was considered in the section on culture.) Under culture, Hegel deals with language as still one other form of estrangement [PhGB, p. 529; PhGM, p. 308], as the speech of the ego, of the haughty vassal, of the arrogant monarch: "L'état c'est moi" (I am the State). Under Art, on the other hand, he traces language from the manner in which the idea presents itself—Epics—through the act, i.e., the drama, so that the language of the minstrel is transformed into that of Tragedy: "In regard to form, the language here ceases to be narrative, in virtue of the fact that it enters into the content, just as the content ceases to be merely one that is ideally imagined. The hero is himself the spokesman" . . .[PhGB, p. 736; PhGM, pp. 443–44]. He then breaks up the question of language as it appears when it is "double-tongued" in the oracles or via witches, and to that in which it is thought (Hamlet), and finally via action.[9] "The process of action proves their unity in the mutual overthrow of both powers and both self-conscious characters" [PhGB, p. 743; PhGM, p. 448], action both as in Tragedy and in Comedy.

The last section on Religion, which deals with Christianity, is even more contradictory, for here Hegel is supposed to reach, more or less, the height of his thought, the step before Absolute Knowledge, and [it] has been put by him in a section beyond Greek Art. And yet we know that to Hegel Greek Art was certainly a great deal greater than the appearance of One God among the Jews, or even the Christian God as it was with the Catholics, for to Hegel the Lutheran Reformation's [effort] to make the alleged unity of freedom and Christianity is anything but abstract. I have a feeling that the whole section, as it has been expanded in his volumes on the *Philosophy of Religion*, will, in actuality, turn out to be a devastating critique of the Church or the Party. But I have no chance to go into this. In any case, to make explicit what is only implicit in Religion, we must turn to Absolute Knowledge.

As we reach this apex of Hegelianism—the consummation of experience, of philosophy—we will confront the end of the division between object and subject.

This takes the form of making consciousness itself the object. Hegel lists three specific aspects: "This knowledge of which we are speaking is, however, not knowledge in the sense of pure conceptual comprehension of the object; here this knowledge is to be taken only in its development. . . . " [PhGB, p. 790; PhGM, p. 480].

Development is of the essence. It is the beginning out of which something arises. It is the middle through which something must be passed. It is the end, "the mediated result," which is really not an end of anything but a process of development which is the beginning of another process as much as it is the end of a former one. Therefore, it is development where the question is one of understanding the method of grasping the object, that is to say, confronting consciousness. In confrontation you meet the second aspect—Relatedness; from Relatedness you must go to Action. Therefore, Action, the deed, practical activity, mental activity, spiritual activity, in a word, doing something, is always the only proof there is of the thought, and therefore stands in the center of all Hegelian philosophy:

> It is through action that spirit is spirit so as definitely to exist; it raises its existence into the sphere of thought and hence into absolute opposition, and returns out of it through and within this very opposition, [PhGB, p. 797; PhGM, p. 485]

This is the movement towards science, that is to say, from individual experience through social experience, to a universal generalization of the experience which goes to make up the action: "As to the actual existence of this Notion, science does not appear in time and in reality till spirit has arrived at this stage of being conscious regarding itself" [PhGB, p. 798; PhGM, p. 486].

> Time is just the notion definitely existent. . . . Time, therefore, appears as spirit's destiny and necessity, [PhGB, p. 800; PhGM, p. 487]

It is peculiar how Hegel is constantly returning to the simple *feelings* even when he has reached Absolute Knowledge. He says, in fact, that "nothing is known which does not fall within experience, or (as it is also expressed) which is not *felt* to be true" [PhGB, p. 800; PhGM, p. 487].

We reach explicitness here, and have to deal with the transformation of Substance into Subject (not just things versus human beings, but Substance as God into living "gods" or the human and divine merged into an extension of human power).

In a single page [PhGB, p. 802; PhGM, pp. 488–89] Hegel sums up the entire development of philosophy and science from Descartes to himself. Thus, we move from Observation, which analyzes what is and "conversely it finds in its thought Existence" (Descartes), to Substance, that is to say, God as both thought and reality, though abstractly stated (Spinoza). The abstraction of this forced unity brings about "the principle of Individuality" (Leibniz). We have entered private enterprise, or the first stage of capitalism, only to move to Utilitarianism into which the Enlightenment had "perished." Here the Individual Will (Kant) comes to the rescue of Absolute Freedom, or to put it in more human language, men of good will will yet straighten out this topsy-turvy world of private capital versus labor, freedom versus terror, etc., etc., and since this really doesn't happen, we jump back from Kantianism to the Absolute Ego of Fichte, or Absolute as "intuited" by Jacobi, and finally land into the empty Absolute of Schelling.[10] In a word, Hegel shows the birth of our modern world as science rejected theology to strike out on its own, met up with a first statement of the dialectic in Kant, who tried to unify thought and science by sheer will, and when that philosophic exception failed to meet the challenge of the time, the contemporary philosopher—Fichte, Schelling, Jacobi—slid back. To go forward, Substance had to become Subject. This is where Hegel comes in. The last three pages of the *Phenomenology* are an outpouring of "simple mediating activity in thinking" where the whole process releases itself, History and Science, Nature and Spirit are "born anew from the womb of knowledge—the new state of existence, a new world and a new embodiment of spirit" [PhGB, p. 807; PhGM, p. 492].

This new world, which Hegel calls Absolute Knowledge, is the unity of the real world and the notions about it, the organization of thought and activity, which merge into the new, the whole truth of the past and the present, which anticipates the future.

NOTES

1. Johann Gottlieb Fichte (1762–1814) sought to free Kantian philosophy of the concept of the "thing-in-itself" by posing the ego as the absolute principle of reality, from which derives all direct and immediate certainty of self and objectivity. Though Hegel credited Fichte for his attempt to overcome the deficiencies of Kant, he took sharp issue with the "subjective" and "one-sided" character of his philosophy.

2. See Milovan Djilas, *The New Class: An Analysis of the Communist System* (New York: Praeger, 1957) and Dunayevskaya's critique, "Djilas' New Class," *News & Letters*, October 1957.

3. Francis Bacon (1561–1626) sought to assert the power of human knowledge over nature by developing a "map of knowledge" based on experiential reason. Hegel held that Bacon helped initiate "the universal tendency of the time and the English mode of reasoning, to proceed from facts, and to judge in accordance with them . . . he did not, however, possess the power of reasoning through thoughts and notions that are universal" (*History of Philosophy*, Vol. III, p. 173).

4. Kant maintained that our human perception can only grasp phenomena or appearances, but that beyond our reason lie noumena or "things-in-themselves" that we can never fully grasp.

5. Dunayevskaya added this paragraph when these notes were published in *News & Letters*, May 8, 1987.

6. Friedrich Heinrich Jacobi (1743–1819), an exponent of immediate knowledge or intuitionist philosophy, is critiqued at length in the section "The Third Attitude of Thought Toward Objectivity" in Hegel's Smaller Logic.

7. This is a reference to Herman Melville's novel, *The Confidence Man*.

8. For Dunayevskaya's critique of Boris Pasternak's novel, see her "Intellectualism and Creativity in the USSR" (April 28, 1959), in *The Raya Dunayevskaya Collection*, pp. 13036–42.

9. See Dunayevskaya's 1968 letter on Hegel's theory of tragedy, this volume, Part III, below.

10. Friedrich Wilhelm Joseph von Schelling (1775–1854), with whom Hegel was closely associated until breaking with him at the time of writing the *Phenomenology of Mind*, made immediate knowledge of universal substance—or "intelligent intuitive perception"—the principle of his philosophy. Hegel's most famous criticism of Schelling, found in the *Phenomenology*, centers on Schelling's presentation of a featureless absolute.

~

CHAPTER FOUR

Rough Notes on Hegel's
Science of Logic

Completed on January 26, 1961, these notes on Hegel's Science of Logic *comprise one of the few studies by a Marxist covering the whole of this text. Dunayevskaya makes her way through all three of the major sections of that work—being, essence, and notion. These notes also rely heavily, with reservations, on Lenin's 1914 "Abstract of Hegel's* Science of Logic." *Other occasional points of reference besides Lenin's work are the writings of C. L. R. James and Grace Lee, Dunayevskaya's colleagues during the years 1941–55, and those of Herbert Marcuse and Jean-Paul Sartre. The original can be found in* The Raya Dunayevskaya Collection, *p. 2806.*

Volume I: Objective Logic

Between the title of Volume I and Book One, we are confronted with two Prefaces, one of which was written when Volume I was first published in 1812, and the second Preface is one of the last things Hegel did before his death in 1831. Thus, the second Preface not only encompasses the first volume, but also the second volume (which contains Books Two and Three), which was published in 1816, and all of his other works; in fact it followed the *Encyclopedia of the Philosophical Sciences.*[1]

The historic period of Hegel's life will be one point of departure. The other point of departure will be 1914 when Lenin read this work. I will refer to his *Philosophic Notebooks* so that you in turn can study them simultaneously with the *Logic*. Finally, we must have also our own historic period in mind.

Philosophically speaking, Lenin's period was summarized by himself dialec-

tically as "the transformation into opposite"; our period has been characterized by ourselves as the Absolute Idea, or the unity of theory and practice,
which must be further concretized as Freedom—the realization of Freedom in
life most of all and in thought. That is to say, in Hegel's philosophy the
Absolute Idea also stands for unity of theory and practice and its point of
departure and return is likewise Freedom. But it is abstract.

A better way, perhaps, to express it is to say that while in Hegel the unity
of object and subject—the unity of the Universal and Individual—is in mind
alone, in the Marxist-Humanist outlook, the individual is the social entity, or
as Marx put it, there is no proof of freedom in society except through the individual who is free. I do not mean to burden these notes with too many random thoughts. On the contrary, I mean to follow Hegel in quite some detail,
but history and dialectic method *is* Hegelianism and hence very brief references to the current situation will be made.

One other item in regard to Lenin. Along with the *Philosophic Notebooks*,
we will consider the 4½ pages called "On Dialectics," which are on pp. 81–85
of his *Selected Works*, Vol. XI [see also LCW 38, pp. 355–63], but which are
actually part of his *Philosophic Notebooks*. I did not translate these because they
had already been translated, but were put in quite undialectically by the Stalinists as if they and Lenin's *Materialism and Empirio-Criticism* [1908] which follows it are by one and the same Lenin, whereas in fact the latter is quite
mechanical and the exact proof of what Lenin had in mind when he wrote at
the end of the *Notebooks* that none of the Marxists (in plural, that is, including himself, and the plural was the emphasis Lenin himself put in that word)
had understood Marx's *Capital* for the last half century. In fact, in this short
essay, "On Dialectics," he criticizes not only everyone from Plekhanov to himself, but even Engels, although he excuses the latter, who, he says, has treated
dialectics inadequately, by way of "*examples*, 'a seed,' 'for example, primitive
Communism.' The same is true of Engels. But with him it is 'in the interests
of popularization . . .' and not as a *law of knowledge* (and as a law of the objective world)" [LCW 38, p. 359].

Hegel's very first sentence to the first Preface is a reference—"The complete transformation which philosophical thought has undergone in Germany
during the last five and twenty years" [SLI, p. 33; SLM, p. 25]—to 1787 and
Kant's work.[2] Hegel's dissatisfaction with even this great step is due to the fact
that it has not lived up to the challenge of the time, i.e., the French Revolution, 1789, up to the Napoleonic Period: "There are no traces in Logic of the
new spirit which has arisen both in Learning and in Life. It is, however (let us
say it once and for all), quite vain to try to retain the forms of an earlier stage
of development when the inner structure of spirit has become transformed;

these earlier forms are like withered leaves which are pushed off by the new buds already being generated in the roots" [SLI, p. 35; SLM, p. 26].

The necessity for the new, the Hegelian departure, arises from the times *and* a new concept of philosophical method, not the dialectic in general, which [Kant] had reached for, but Hegelian Dialectic, the form of thought which was as one with the *movement* of mind: "This movement is the Absolute Method of knowledge and at the same time the immanent soul of the Content of knowledge. It is, I maintain, along this path of self-construction alone that Philosophy can become objective and demonstrated science" [SLI, pp. 36–37; SLM, p. 28].

Actually, this is only the fourth page of his Preface (the pagination of 36 and 37 is due to the fact that the stupid publishers did not use a separate pagination for Haldane's Introduction, Table of Contents, etc.) and already we have covered, or rather Hegel has covered, the two fundamental movements of his entire work—the logical-dialectical and the polemical. These, in turn, contain reality—historic reality of the period in which he lived and historic reality as evolution up to that time. And sure enough, Lenin at once noted the two essences of the dialectic: 1) The emphasis on movement, "the *movement* of scientific cognition—that is the essence"; 2) "'the *path* of self-construction' = path (here lies the nub, in my opinion) of true cognition, knowledge, movement" [LCW 38, pp. 87–88].

The Preface to the Second Edition is once again full of "immanent activity" and "necessary development," which leads Lenin to say in the very first paragraph: "What is necessary is not lifeless bones, but full-blooded life" and he stresses "an important beginning" [LCW 38, p. 89]. And Hegel, indeed, in the very approach to philosophic categories in the second paragraph is going to remind us that "so natural to man is Logic—indeed, Logic itself is just man's peculiar nature. But if Nature in general is opposed, as physical, to what is mental, then it must be said that Logic is rather that something Super-natural which enters into all the natural *behavior* of man—Feeling, Intuition, Desire, Need, Impulse—and thereby alone transforms it all to something human—to ideas and purposes" [SLI, p. 40; SLM, pp. 31–32].

For a man so full of profundities, he never forgets impulses, feelings, intuition, desires, needs; indeed, it is quite obvious that he refuses to make a distinction between physical and mental, and to this day, the so-called behavioral sciences, psychoanalysis included, cannot shine this great philosopher's shoes, much less his divine (yes, divine) concept of human ideas and purposes.

Historical materialism, strange as that may sound as any attribute of Hegel, is nevertheless basic to Hegelian analysis and in this Preface he traces philosophy back in a manner in which it is quite clear that the elements of that total philosophy with which Marx is mainly associated were present in Hegelian philosophy. This sense of history is present also in his polemical critique of Kant: "In the still spaces of Thought which has come to itself and is purely self-existent, those interests are hushed which move the lives of peoples and of individuals" [SLI, p. 42; SLM, p. 34]. Lenin emphasized this expression as well as the one in which Hegel said, "When the Critical Philosophy understands the relation of these three Terms so as to make *Thoughts* intermediary between *Us* and *Things* in such a sense that this intermediary rather excludes us from things than connects us with them. . ." [SLI, p. 44; SLM, p. 36]. At this point Lenin remarks: "In my view, the conclusion essentially is: 1) in Kant knowledge hedges off (separates) nature from man; in actuality, it unites them; 2) in Kant 'the empty abstraction' of the thing-in-itself is put in place of the living procession (*shestviya*), the movement of our ever deeper knowledge of things" [LCW 38, p. 91].

Hegel in this second Preface takes issue also with those who have criticized him since the *Phenomenology* and this first book were published. The severest of all criticisms is for those who assume a category, which, first of all, has to be proved, which he calls an "uninstructed and barbarous procedure" [SLI, p. 49; SLM, p. 41]. It is good to have in mind here our opponent, for the whole of Russian Communist theory follows precisely this barbarous procedure of assuming that Socialism already exists and then blithely goes on. If, however, one thinks that it is sufficient merely to know that the Russians assume what is first to be proven to be able to get to the bottom of their usurpation of Marxist language, Marcuse's *Soviet Marxism* is there to prove the opposite. Despite all of his *knowledge* of both Hegel and Marx and even Russian society, Marcuse still falls into the trap of apologetics on the basis that their professed theory discloses actual reality. The fundamental reason for the blindness is, of course, his complete isolation from the class struggle. But it is not the whole of the reason. The other part is the failure to create a category—state capitalism in this case—for the new state of the world economy in general and Russia in particular. Without a category, an intellectual is just lost, since he has none of the proletarian instincts to carry him through on untrodden paths, and therefore, falls into eclecticism.

Before Hegel begins Book One, we have, besides the two Prefaces, also an Introduction. In the Introduction, his reference to the *Phenomenology* will set us, too, in the proper spirit of continuity: "In the *Phenomenology of Mind* I have set forth the movement of consciousness, from the first crude opposition between itself and the Object, up to absolute knowledge. This process goes through all the forms of the relation of thought to its object, and reaches the

Concept of Science as its result" [SLI, p. 59; SLM, p. 48]. Having assumed absolute knowledge as the truth of all forms of consciousness, Hegel can now proceed to treat both knowledge and reality in the form of categories *because* they do include historical reality, present reality, as well as the long road of thought about it. That is precisely why he is opposed to the other form in which thought is presented in the philosophies that have not met the challenge of the times. Thus, in criticizing [the fact] that the structure of logic has undergone no change, despite all the revolutionary development, he says: "For when Spirit has worked on for two thousand years, it must have reached a better reflective consciousness of its own thought and its own unadulterated essence. A comparison of the form to which Spirit has risen in the worlds of Practice and Religion, and of Science in every department of knowledge Positive and Speculative, a comparison of these with the form which logic has attained shows a glaring discrepancy" [SLI, p. 62; SLM, 51].

Therefore, the need for the transformation of the structure of Logic and its actual transformation are present here. Hegel does give Kant credit for having "freed Dialectic from the semblance of arbitrariness . . . and set it forth as a *necessary procedure of Reason*," but the actual exposition is not, says Hegel, "deserving of any great praise; but the general idea upon which he builds and which he has vindicated, is the *Objectivity of Appearance* and the *Necessity of Contradiction*" [SLI, p. 67; SLM, p. 56]. It is Hegel's contention that only when you get to consider Universals, not as abstractions, but as concrete totalities of the whole historic movement, does Logic deserve to become the universal philosophy: "It is only through a profounder acquaintance with other sciences that Logic discovers itself to be subjective thought as not a mere abstract Universal, but as a Universal which comprises in itself the full wealth of Particulars" [SLI, p.69; SLM, p. 58].

It is at this point that Lenin refers the reader to *Capital*, repeating Hegel's description of logic as "not a mere abstract Universal, but as a Universal which comprises in itself the full wealth of Particulars" and then goes into paeans of praise, "a beautiful formula," and again repeats the phrase, adding "*Très bien!*" [LCW 38, p. 99]. From now on, it is *Capital* which Lenin will have in mind throughout his reading of the two volumes (three books) of *Logic*.

I would like to note also, although I will not elaborate upon this much later, that the whole of the *Logic*, as well as each section of the *Logic*, as well as each separate thought in the *Logic*, will go through the following development, both as history, as reality, as thought: the movement will always be from U (Universal) through P (Particular) to I (Individual). Lenin takes it in the same form as U-P-I, but reverses the order more often precisely because he is thinking of the *proletarian* individual, who is also the social individual and the universal of socialism. Thus, when he concludes his *Philosophic Notebooks* in those four pages of ["On] Dialectics" [which] I referred to, he says (the translator here used the word "singular," where the strict term is individual and "general" where the strict term is universal): "To begin with the simplest, most ordinary, commonest, etc., proposition, or any proposition one pleases; the leaves of a tree are green; John is a man; Fido is a dog, etc. Here already we have dialectics (as Hegel's genius recognized): the singular is the general. Consequently, opposites (the singular as opposed to the general) are identical; the singular exists only in the connection that leads to the general. The general exists only in the singular and through the singular" [LCW 38, p. 361].

In conclusion to his Introduction, Hegel returns once again to Kant, explaining that those who would just disregard him are the very ones who take his results and make the whole philosophy into a "pillow for intellectual sloth" [SLI, p. 73; SLM, p. 62]. (You will remember that that is the quotation I used in Chapter 9 in *Marxism and Freedom*, which deals with the Second International.)

We are finally ready to begin Book One, but we better remember the broad outline of the whole *Logic* into two volumes, Objective Logic and Subjective Logic; more definitely, it has three parts, namely:

1) The Logic of Being,
2) The Logic of Essence, and
3) The Logic of the Notion.

Book One: The Doctrine of Being

Section One: Determinateness (Quality)

Chapter I: Being There are only three short paragraphs in chapter I on Being, Nothing and Becoming, whereupon Hegel goes into no less than five Observations which stretch over twenty-five pages, which, in fact, cover very nearly the whole of preceding philosophies, from the Orient through the Greeks to his own time on this question of Being. Thus: *Observation One*—the Opposition of Being and Nothing in Imagination contrasts Parmenides' "pure enthusiasm of thought first comprehending itself in its absolute abstraction" to Buddhism where "Nothing or Void is the absolute principle," to Heraclitus, whose opposition to both one-sided abstractions of Being and Nothing led to the total concept of Becoming: "All things flow," which means everything is Becoming [SLI, pp. 95–96; SLM, p. 83].

But Hegel does not stop either with the Orient or with the Greeks, but proceeds to consider Spinoza, as well as the Kantian Critique. Not only that, it's quite obvious that both in philosophy and in science Hegel is the historical materialist: "What is first in science has had to show itself first too, historically" [SLI, p. 101; SLM, p. 88].

If Observation One dealt with the Unity of Being and Nothing as Becoming in a profound manner, Hegel hurries to criticize this, too, in *Observation Two*—The Inadequacy of the Expression "Unity" or "Identity of Being and Nothing." The point is that Unity "sounds violent and striking in proportion as the objects of which it is asserted obviously show themselves as distinct. In this respect therefore mere Unseparateness or Inseparability would be a good substitute for Unity; but these would not express the affirmative nature of the relation of the whole. The whole and true result, therefore, which has here been found, is Becoming. . . ." [SLI, p. 104; SLM, p. 91].

He, therefore, proceeds to *Observation Three*—The Isolation of these Abstractions, in order to stress that the Unity of Being and Nothing have to be considered in a relationship to a third, i.e., Becoming, and therefore, we must consider the *transition*. Otherwise, we would constantly be evading the internal contradictoriness, although Hegel admits that "It would be wasted labor to spread a net for all the twistings and objections of reflection and its reasonings, in order to cut off and render impossible all the evasions and digressions which it uses to hide from itself its own internal contradictoriness" [SLI, p. 106; SLM, p. 94]. He here hits out at his two main enemies, Fichte and Jacobi, whom he compares to the abstractions of Indian thought or the Brahma: "this torpid and vacuous consciousness, taken as consciousness, is Being" [SLI, p. 109; SLM, p. 97]. (With this should be read the section on Oriental philosophy [in] Hegel's *Philosophy of History*. It used to annoy me very much because I thought it showed German arrogance to Oriental philosophy. But it is, in fact, so objective an analysis of Hinduism that it will explain a great deal of modern India's difficulties in stamping out castes.)

Both in the observation "Incomprehensibility of the Beginning" and the next *Observation*—"The Expression to Transcend,'" Hegel has shifted both the actual and the philosophic, not alone from Being and Nothing to Becoming, but transcended Becoming, which is the first leap forward from an abstract being to a determinate, or specific being, with which chapter II will deal. All we need to remember at this point is that "what is transcended is also preserved" [SLI, p. 120; SLM, p. 107].

Chapter II: Determinate Being　The structure of *Logic* has now been set. We will at each point, though not in as overwhelming a manner, state a fact or proposition and then proceed to an Observation; in a word, the polemical movement in the *Logic* follows right alongside, and inseparably, with the affirmative statement. You may recall that that is the form of Marx's *Contribution* *to the Critique of Political Economy.* As you know, he was quite dissatisfied with the form, [and] discarded it for *Capital.* This was not only due to the fact that he decided that the polemical, as history of thought rather than *class struggle,* should all be placed together in a separate book (Book Four).[3] That much is obvious and would not have, in itself, produced such utter blindness on the part of Marxists who could quite easily see that the historical, to Marx, was not history of thought, but history of class struggle, since, as a matter of fact, Kautskian popularizations dealt with the class struggle without much concern to thought. No, it is the dialectics, the new, the creative dialectics of the class struggle, which did not separate philosophy—how long is my working day?—from the class struggle, which remain a mystery to the materialists who were so busy "opposing the mystical" in Hegel. But the fact that the Hegelian structure could not be "copied" by Marx, but had to be *re-created,* does not mean that the Hegelian structure *for Hegel* was wrong. On the contrary, he deals with thought, and the logical form of the Universal there *is* the Notion.

We have moved from the Universal, General, Abstract Being to a definite Being or Something, but this assumption of a definitive quality immediately moves Hegel to an observation—"Quality and Negation." "Determinateness is negation posited affirmatively, is the meaning of Spinoza's *omnis determinatio est negatio* [every determination is a negation], a proposition of infinite importance; only, negation as such is formless abstraction. Speculative philosophy must not be accused of making negation, or Nothing, its end: Nothing is the end of philosophy as little as Reality is the truth" [SLI, p. 125; SLM, p. 113].

But it must not be imagined that Hegel is only arguing with other philosophers, though that is his world. He is also moving to ever-more determinate stages of the concrete, for what pervades everything in Hegel—everything from Absolute Idea to the simple Something of a chair or a leaf or a seed—is his fundamental principle that the Truth is always concrete. Because, however, what was most concrete with him was Thought, and because this early in the *Logic* when he deals with Something, he is already dealing with it as "the first negation of the negation," Lenin gets furious with him at this point and returns to a warm feeling toward Engels by referring to the quotation about "abstract and abstruse Hegelianism" [LCW 38, p. 108]. And yet it is only a few short pages beyond this when dealing with finitude and against the Kantian thing-in-itself [that] Lenin remarks that this whole attack on the Thing-in-itself is "very profound" and again *"sehr gut!!"* [very good, LCW 38, pp. 110–11]. Lenin straightaway makes that conclusion of the essence of the dialectic which he is going to repeat throughout his reading *and* which will indeed become the basis of all his writings from there on from *Imperialism* to the *Will*. Thus, it is near Hegel's remark against the critical philosophy, i.e., Kant [SLI, p. 135, SLM, p. 122] that Lenin writes: "Dialectic is the doctrine of the *identity of opposites*—how they can be and how they become identical, transforming one into another—why the mind of man must not take these opposites for dead, blocked (*zastyvanie*), but for living, conditioned, mobile, transforming one into the other. *En lisant* [in reading] Hegel. . . ." [LCW 38, p. 109]. This, mind you, is said not in Book Three on Notion, nor even in Book Two on Essence, nor even in Section Three of Book Two on Measure where we are "practically" ready to jump into Essence, but in the very first section of Book one, chapter II.

At this point Hegel comments that in the question of determination the chief point is "to distinguish what is still *in itself* and what is *posited . . .* and being-for-other. This distinction is proper only to dialectical development and is unknown to the metaphysical (which includes the Critical) philosophy" [SLI, p. 135; SLM, p. 122]. It is here that Lenin has his first definition of dialectic as the doctrine of the identity of opposites, before which generalization, he writes: "This is very profound; the thing-in-itself and its transformation into the thing-for-other (cf. Engels). The thing-in-itself, *in general*, is an empty, lifeless abstraction. In life in the movement all and everything is *used* to being both 'in itself' and 'for other' in relation to Other, transforming itself from one condition (*sostoyaniye*) to another" [LCW 38, p. 109].

Hegel proceeds next to analyze Finitude and Ought. The Ought in turn is followed by an Observation where he tangles with Leibniz [SLI, p. 148; SLM, p. 135] and with Kant and Fichte [SLI, p. 149; SLM, p. 136] who, he insists, have the standpoint, precisely because they get stuck in Ought, "where they persist in Finitude, and (which is the same thing) in contradiction."

Lenin is again moved here to speak about the profound analysis Hegel makes of the Finite, saying "The Finite? that means *movement* has come to an end! Something? that means *not what Other is*. Being, in general? that means such indeterminateness that Being=Not-Being. All-sided, universal flexibility of concepts—flexibility reaching to the identity of opposites" [LCW 38, p. 110].

In the section which follows on Infinity, the critical point is *transition:* "Ideality[4] may be called the Quality of Infinity; but, as it is essentially the process of Becoming, it is a Transition, like that of Becoming in Determinate Being, and it must now be indicated" [SLI, p. 163; SLM, p. 150]. Two other observations followed this one, one on "Infinite Progress": "Bad Infinity,"[5] says Hegel, like progress to infinity, is really no different than Ought, "the expression of a contradiction, which pretends to be the solution and the ultimate" [SLI, p. 164; SLM, p. 150]. The second observation is on "Idealism," where he contrasts Subjective and Objective Idealism, and which brings us to chapter III, "Being-For-Self."

Somewhere in this chapter—in fact, in the first Observation—ideality is taken up both as it applies to Leibniz's Monads,[6] as well as Eleatic Being,[7] and also the Atomistic philosophy,[8] and again, there are many observations ending with the one on Kant's "Attraction and Repulsion." Now, on the one hand, Lenin is very specific in his interpretation here, calling attention to the fact that "the idea of the transformation of the ideal into the real is *profound;* very important for history . . . against vulgar materialism" [LCW 38, p. 114], and yet the whole chapter on Being-For-Self, when Lenin first approaches it, is considered by him to be "dark waters" [LCW 38, p. 114]. At this point here, during the correspondence with [C. L. R. James] and [Grace Lee] in 1949, Grace developed her thoughts on this chapter as one dealing with the developing subject as it first arose, 500 B. C., to the Absolute Idea, or the conditions for universality in the modern proletariat.[9] She seemed to think that Being-For-One coming from Being-For-Self was unclear to Lenin because he did not understand abstract labor as we did. I doubt that was the reason since in the Doctrine of Being, we are, comparatively, at a low stage of development in Hegelian thought. The fact, however, that he can at this "low stage" be so profound and point to so many of the conditions which we will meet in the Absolute Idea shows that you can, in fact, not make sharp divisions even in those most sharply pointed to by Hegel himself—Being, Essence, Notion—as is shown over and over again by the fact that he deals with Kant who was the greatest philosopher before him in this very section.

Indeed, Lenin here notes (evidently it struck him for the first time) that the self-development of the concept in Hegel is related to the entire history of philosophy. In any case, in the Observation on the Unity of the One and the Many, he deals also with the dialectic of Plato in the *Parmenides*. What is true is Hegel's very sharp opposition to so-called independence in the One: "Independence having reached its quintessence in the One which is for itself, is abstract and formal, destroying itself; it is the highest and most stubborn error, which takes itself for highest truth; appearing, more concretely, as abstract freedom, pure ego, and further as Evil. It is freedom which goes so far astray as to place its essence in this abstraction, flattering itself that, being thus by itself, it possesses itself in its purity" [SLI, p. 185; SLM, p. 172].

Section Two: Magnitude (Quantity)
We have first now reached the transformation of Quality or Determinateness into Quantity, Being-For-Self having concluded Section One, and having in turn been divided into three—Being-For-Self as such, the One and the Many, and Repulsion and Attraction.

In the first observation on Pure Quantity, as well as in the second observation on Kant's "Antinomy of the Indivisibility and Infinite Divisibility of Time, Space and Matter," the concept that we are approaching is that of Continuous and Discrete Magnitude.[10] But before he deals with these concepts, Hegel feels he must attack not only the concept of Quantity as simple unity of Discreteness and Continuity, but also the idea that Kant had of four antinomies, as if that number exhausts contradiction instead of the fact that every single concept is in fact an antinomy. In attacking Kant's *Critique of Pure Reason*, the attack is on Kant for being "apagogic" [SLI, p. 207; SLM, p. 193], that is to say, assuming what is to be proved and thus repeating the assumption in the conclusion. Hegel protests that Kant's proofs are "a forced and useless tortuosity," "an advocate's proof" [SLI, p. 208; SLM, p. 194], which sounds exactly as if it says he is a "Philadelphia lawyer." He considers the dialectic example of the old Eleatic school of thought as superior to Kant, despite the fact that so much of actual history had occurred since that period, which certainly should have led to a more profound conception of dialectic.

Discreteness, like Continuity, is a moment of Quantity and in fact it is only both moments, their unity that is, that produces Quantum.[11] At the same time, both in this chapter and in chapter II on "Quantum," we sense Hegel's sharp distaste for mathematical proof as being unworthy of philosophy, even though at its start, in the theorems of Pythagoras, they were of the essence, and there is no doubt also of their importance, and in fact necessity, to Newtonian science and differential and integral calculus. Although I know next to nothing of this, and I am sure that modern mathematics which has reached into economics, automation, and space science, that in essence all that Hegel says here is inescapably true as is all that he says on "Bad Infinity," and I dare say that any infinity that is not human is bad. I note that Lenin, who did know a great deal about calculus, makes very short shrift of this whole section precisely because he agrees with Hegel in his Analysis on Conclusions.

Section Three: Measure
With the very first statement, "Abstractly the statement may be made that in Measure, Quality and Quantity are united" [SLI, p. 345; SLM, p. 327], Lenin once again becomes excited and at the end of it, he makes all those observations—Leaps! LEAPS! LEAPS! [LCW 38, p. 123]. The observation on Nodal Lines Lenin copies out nearly in full. There is no doubt whatever that a transition from Quality into Quantity as a leap, in opposition to the concept of any gradual emergence, is the transition point for Lenin himself, breaking with the old Lenin, not because the old Lenin was ever a "gradualist," but because the *objectivity* of these leaps in *all* aspects of life is not anything merely

quantitative or merely qualitative, or as Hegel puts it: "The gradualness of arising is based upon the ideas that that which arises is already, sensibly or otherwise, *actually there*, and is imperceptible only on account of its smallness. . . . Understanding prefers to fancy identity and change to be of that indifferent and external kind which applies to the quantitative" [SLI, p. 390; SLM, p. 370].

To sharpen his own very different concept, Hegel goes over to this question of gradual transition of Quantity to Quality in Ethics, and says, "A more or less suffices to transgress the limit of levity, where something quite different, namely, crime, appears; and thus right passes over into wrong, and virtue into vice" [SLI, p. 390; SLM, p. 371].

The third chapter of this section is called "The Becoming of Essence" and is the transition, therefore, to the second Book.

Book Two: The Doctrine of Essence

Section One: Essence As Reflection Into Self

Chapter I: Show   The profundity of Hegel is seen in the fact that even where he thinks that something is relatively unessential and is, therefore, mere show, that even there the show is also objective. He considers [that] "show, then, is the *phenomenon* of skepticism . . . skepticism did not dare to affirm 'it is'; modern idealism did not dare to regard cognition as the knowledge of Thing-in-itself" [SLII, p. 22; SLM, p. 396]. Hegel hits out against all idealisms, of Leibniz, Kant, or Fichte. Hegel writes, "It is the immediacy of *Not-Being*, which constitutes Show; but this Not-Being is nothing else than the Negativity of Essence in itself" [SLII, p. 23; SLM, p. 397]. In fact, [in his comments] on the page before he [Hegel] said this, when he criticized both skepticism and idealism, Lenin noted: "You include all the manifold riches of the world in *Schein* [show] and you reject the objectivity of *Schein*!!" [LCW 38; p. 131]. And again: "Show is Essence in one of its determinations. . . *Essence* thus appears. Show is the phenomenon of Essence in itself" [LCW 38, p. 133]. Lenin further notes that in this section on the Reflection of Essence, Hegel again accuses Kant of subjectivism and insists on the objective validity of Show, "of the immediate given," and notes: "The term, '*given*' is common with Hegel in general. The little philosophers dispute whether one should take as basis the Essence or the immediately given (Kant, Hume, Machists[12]). Hegel substitutes *and* for 'or' and explains the concrete content of this 'and'" [LCW 38, p. 134].

Chapter II: The Essentialities or Determinations of Reflection   We will deal here with the three developments in Essence: first, simple self-relation or

Identity; secondly, Variety [Difference]; and thirdly, Contradiction. But before Hegel develops these three, he has an observation on so-called "Laws of Thought," which allegedly prove that A cannot be at one and the same time A and not be A. That is absolutely hilarious. "Category, according to its etymology and its Aristotelian definition, is that which is predicated or asserted of the existent.—But a determinateness of Being is essentially a transition into the opposite; the negative of any determinateness is as necessary as the determinateness itself; and each immediate determinateness is immediately opposed by the other" [SLII, p. 36; SLM, p. 410].

When Hegel gets to Observation Two, which [Aristotle] called the Law of the Excluded Middle, he again hits out at the idea that something either is or is not A, that there is no third, insisting that there *is* a third in the very thesis since A can be both +A and −A: "The something thus is itself the third term which was supposed to be excluded" [SLII, p. 66; SLM, p. 439]. At this point, Lenin remarked: "This is very profound. Every concrete thing, every concrete something stands in diverse and often contradictory relations to all others, ergo, it is itself and another" [LCW 38, p. 138].

As for the observation which follows on the law of Contradiction where Hegel defines Contradiction as the "root of all movement and life, and it is only insofar as it contains a Contradiction that anything moves and has impulse and activity" [SLII, p. 67; SLM, p. 439]. Lenin copies out in toto this entire section, at the end of which he makes his famous generalization that the idea of movement and change was disclosed in 1813 by Hegel, that is, by philosophy, and was applied by Marx first in 1847 and by Darwin in 1859 [LCW 38, p. 141]. Indeed, Lenin can hardly stop himself from becoming a complete Hegelian and stressing over and over again how stupid it is to think that Hegel is abstract and abstruse, and how profound is the concept of Contradiction as the force of Movement and how different Thinking, Reason, Notion is to ordinary understanding: "Thinking reason (notion) sharpens the blunted difference of variety, the mere manifold of imagination, to the essential difference, to *Opposition*. Only when the contradictions reach their peak does manifoldness become mobile (*regsam*)[13] and lively in relation to the other,—acquire that negativity which is the *inner-pulsation of self-movement and life*" [LCW 38, p.143; SL II, p. 69; SLM, p. 442].

Chapter III: Ground   The very first sentence—"Essence determines itself as Ground" [SLII, p. 71; SLM, p. 444]—lets us know that we are approaching the climax to Section One of Essence. As soon as Hegel, in the first observation on the Law of Ground, finishes his critique of Leibniz's Law of Sufficient Ground, he develops, in Absolute Ground, all the essentials of Form and Essence, Form and Matter, Form and Content where it becomes quite clear that these cannot be separated; that Form and Matter "presuppose one another" [SLII, p. 79; SLM, p. 452] and Content is the "unity" of Form and Matter [SLII, p. 82; SLM, p. 454]. And as we move from Absolute to Determined [Determinate] Ground and approach Complete Ground, it becomes quite clear that manifoldness or content-determinations could be used indiscriminately so that you could cite something as much *for* as *against* something, which is exactly what Socrates correctly argued against as Sophistry, because, of course, such conclusions do not exhaust the thing-in-itself in the sense of "grasp of the connection of things which contain them all" [SLII, p. 94; SLM, p. 466].

It is at this point that we reach the transition from Ground to Condition, which moves Lenin to say, "brilliant: all-world, all-sided *living* connection of everything with everything else, and of the reflection of this connection— *materialistisch auf den Kopf gestellter Hegel* [Hegel materialistically turned on his head]—in the concept of man, which must be so polished, so broken-in, flexible, mobile, relative, mutually-tied-in, united in opposition, as to embrace the world. The continuation of the work of Hegel and Marx must consist in the dialectical working out of the history of human thought, science and technique." And at the same spot, Lenin rethinks Marx's *Capital*, thus: "And a 'purely logical' working out? *Das fällt zusammen* [It coincides]. It must coincide as does induction and deduction in *Capital*" [LCW 38, p. 146].

We have now reached the third subsection of Ground—Condition, which could be defined as History. In 1950, G. [Grace Lee] wrote quite a good letter on that subsection, but J. [C. L. R. James] was no help whatsoever; indeed, he could never develop the strong point of G. on philosophy. But we can gain something by quoting her letter at this point: "The essence of Hegel's argument is this: It is necessary to get rid of the concept of Ground as a *substratum*, but when you get rid of this concept of something *behind* the immediate you have not by any means gotten rid of the fact that the immediate is the result of a MEDIATING process. It is the self-mediating, self-repelling, self-transcending relation of Ground which externalizes itself in the immediate existent. Hence the relentless phrasing and rephrasing of his thesis that 'The Fact Emerges Out of Ground.'"[14]

The exact statement from Hegel reads: "When all the Conditions of a fact are present, it enters into Existence. The fact *is* before it *exists*. . . . ." [SLII, p. 105; SLM, p. 477]. Now at this point, Lenin wrote: "Very good! What has the Absolute Idea and Idealism to find here? Remarkable, this 'derivation' of Existence" [LCW 38, p. 147]. We may be bold enough to answer the question, or better still, recognize that Lenin answered his own question when he reached the last part of Hegel precisely on the Absolute Idea, and therefore noted: 1)

That one must read the *whole* of the Logic to understand *Capital*; 2) that man's cognition not only reflects the world, but "creates" it; and 3) noted in his conclusions that there was more sense in Idealism than in vulgar materialism, which made him so anxious to try to get the *Encyclopedia Granat* to return his essay on Marx, so that he could expand the section on dialectics.

I want to return to the question of Condition as History, as well as to the expression that "The Fact *is* before it *Exists*." The History that Hegel had in mind was, of course, the historic period in which he lived, following the French Revolution, which brought not the millennium, but new contradictions, i.e., philosophically speaking, Ground had been transformed into Condition and we did get a totality of Movement—the Fact-in-itself. The *new* contradictions will once again show that facts, facts, facts can also hide[:] "the unity of Form is submerged" [SLII, p. 104; SLM, p. 475]. And of course we know that our historic epoch, much more than Hegel's, demands more of reality than just a sound of "immediates."[15] For example, scientifically with Einstein, we get to know that facts, too, are relative. So that once again we need self-transcendence and therefore, in the expression "the fact is before it exists," we recognize the process of emergence of something new, and in its emergence we therefore get the transition to Existence. In our terms, if we think of the actual historical development of the working class in Marx's *Capital*, we have "Ground in Unity with its Condition."[16]

Section Two: Appearance
Here again, the very first sentence is a leap forward: "Essence must appear" [SLII, p. 107; SLM, p. 479]. So we can no longer merely contrast Appearance to Essence, because, while there may be much Appearance that is only "show," it also contains Essence itself (which in turn will soon mean we are moving to a real crisis or Actuality).

The three sub-sections on Appearance are: 1) Existence, 2) Appearance, and 3) Essential Relation.

(I might state that Sartre's Existentialism is nowhere near this important section of Hegel's *Logic*, for in Hegel "whatever exists has a Ground and is conditioned" [SLII, p. 109; SLM, p. 481], whereas in Sartre, both the Ground and the Condition are quite subordinate to the Ego's disgust with it all.)[17]

The real tendency, as well as actuality, that we should have before us in studying this section on Appearance is Stalinism and its non-essential critique in Trotskyism. That is to say, if Essence—the present stage of capitalism or the present stage of the counter-revolutionary appearance of the labor bureaucracy—must appear, then Stalinism, which has appeared, is not just any old bureaucracy that has no connection with a new economic state of world development. On the contrary, the Appearance—Stalinism—and the Essence—state-capitalism—are one and the same, or the Form of a new Content. Trotskyism, on the other hand, by putting up a Chinese wall between what is mere Appearance to what is true Essence (and to him, the Essence is not capitalism, but the form of workers' state) has not been able to analyze either Stalinism or state-capitalism. I mean, either Stalinism as a mere perversion of the early Soviets, or Stalinism as the absolute opposite of that early workers' state.[18]

To get back to Hegel and Lenin's notes on Hegel, Lenin is quite impressed with Hegel's Analysis of the Law of Appearance, the World of Appearance and the World-in-Itself, and the Dissolution of Appearance, which are the subsections of Chapter II of this section.

Lenin keeps stressing at this point "the remarkably materialistic" analysis that flows from this objective analysis which will, of course, become the basis of Marx's analysis of the economic laws of capitalism. When Hegel writes "Law, then, is essential appearance" [SLII, p. 133; SLM, p. 504], Lenin concludes, "Ergo, Law and Essence of Concept are homogeneous (of one order) or, more correctly, uniform, expressing the deepening of man's knowledge of Appearance, the world, etc." [LCW 38, p. 152]. Finally, "The essence here is that both the World of Appearance and the World which is in and for itself are essentially *moments* of knowledge of nature by man, stages, changes or deepening (of knowledge). The movement of the world in itself ever further and further *from* the world of appearance—that is what is not yet visible in Hegel. NB. Do not the 'moments' of conception with Hegel have significance of 'moments' of transition?" [LCW 38, p. 153].

Chapter III: Essential Relation   "The truth of Appearance is Essential Relation" [SLII, p. 142; SLM, p. 512]

The relationship of the Whole and the Parts, you may recall from my various lectures on Hegel, has to me been a key, not merely to this section of Hegel, but to the entire philosophy of both Hegel and Marx. Thus, when I say that the whole is not only the sum total of the parts, but has a pull on the parts that are not yet there, even as the future has a pull on the present, it is obvious that we have moved from abstract philosophic conceptions to the actual world, and form the actual world back again to philosophy, but this time as enriched by the actual.

As Hegel puts it, "the Whole and the Parts therefore *condition* each other" [SLII, p. 145; SLM, p. 515], "the Whole is equal to the Parts and the Parts to the Whole. . . . But further, although the Whole is equal to the Parts, it is not equal *to them* as Parts; the Whole is reflected unity" [SLII, p. 146; SLM, pp. 515–16]. "Thus, the relation of Whole and Parts has passed over into a relation of Force[19] and its Manifestation" [SLII, p. 147; SLM, p. 517]. Indeed, we will move from that to the relation of Outer and Inner,[20] which will become the transition to Substance and Actuality.

On the relationship of Outer and Inner, Lenin stresses what he calls "the unexpected slipping in of the *criteria* of Hegel's Dialectic"—where Hegel notes that the relationship of Inner and Outer is apparent "in every natural, scientific, and, generally, intellectual development" [SLII, p. 157; SLM, p. 526]—and Lenin concludes, therefore, "that is where lies the *seed* of the deep truth in the mystical balderdash of Hegelianism!" [LCW 38, p. 155].

Section Three: Actuality
The introductory note will stress that "Actuality is *the unity of Essence and Existence*. . . . This unity of Inner and Outer is *Absolute Actuality*." He will divide Actuality into Possibility and Necessity as the "*formal moments*" of the Absolute, or its reflection. And finally, the unity of this Absolute and its reflection will become the Absolute Relation "or, rather, the Absolute as relation to itself,—*Substance*" [SLII, p. 160; SLM, p. 529]. At this point in the Preliminary Note [on the Absolute], Lenin gets quite peeved at the idealist in Hegel and he divides the expression that "there is no becoming in the Absolute" [SLII, p. 162; SLM, p. 531] into two sentences by stating "and other nonsense about the Absolute" [LCW 38, p. 156]. But, as usual, it will not be long before Lenin is full of praise of Hegel and his section on Actuality.

To me, the most important part of chapter I of section three, the Absolute, is the Observation [SLII, p. 167–72; SLM, pp. 536–40] on the philosophy of Spinoza: "*Determinateness is negation*—this is the absolute principle of Spinoza's philosophy, and this true and simple insight is the foundation of the absolute unity of Substance. But Spinoza does not pass on beyond negation as determinateness or quality to a recognition of it as absolute, that is, self-negative, negation" [SLII, p. 168; SLM, p. 536]. Hegel's conclusion is that though the dialectic is in it until Spinoza gets to Substance, it there stops: "Substance lacks the principle of Personality" [SLII, p. 168; SLM, p. 537]. And again later Hegel writes: "In a similar manner in the Oriental idea of *emanation* the Absolute is self-illuminating light" [SLII, p. 170; SLM, p. 538].

From now on, the polemical movement in the *Logic* will take a very subordinate place; the observations will do the same. Indeed, for the rest of the entire work, Hegel will have only two observations, as contrasted to the beginning of the *Science of Logic*, where after but one single page on Being, he had no less than four observations (really five when you consider the one on Transcendence of Becoming) which took up no less than twenty-three pages. In a word, the closer he approaches the Notion, especially the Absolute Idea, that is to say, the climax of his system as it has been comprehensively and profoundly developed both historically and polemically, the more he has absorbed all that is of value in the other systems of philosophy, rejected that which is not, and presented a truly objective worldview of history and philosophy, which contains the elements of a future society inherent in the present. (We will return to this point at the end.)

Of chapter II on Actuality, the categories dealt with—Contingency, or formal Actuality, Possibility and Necessity—are all to pave the way to chapter III, the Absolute Relation, which is the apex of the Doctrine of Essence and will bring us to the Notion.

Lenin begins to free himself of any residue of taking the empiric concrete as the Real or Actual. Near [Hegel's discussion of] the question of the relationship of Substantiality and Causality, Lenin writes: "On the one hand, we must deepen the knowledge of matter to the knowledge (to the concept) of substance, in order to find the causes of appearance. On the other hand, actual knowledge of causes is the deepening of knowledge from externality of appearance to substance. Two types of examples should explain this: 1) out of the history of natural science and 2) from the history of philosophy. More precisely: not 'examples' should be here—comparison *n'est pas raison* [comparison is not proof],—but the *quintessence* of the one and the other history—plus the history of technique" [LCW 38, p. 159].

A couple of pages later, Lenin will note that Hegel "*fully* leads up to History under Causality" and again, that the ordinary understanding of Causality fails to see that it is "only a small part of the universal connection" [LCW 38, p. 160] and that the small part is not subjective, but the objectively real connection. Indeed, Lenin very nearly makes fun, along with Hegel, of course, of Cause and Effect. Where Hegel wrote, "Effect therefore is necessary just because it is manifestation of Cause, or because it is that Necessity which is Cause" [SLII, p. 192; SLM, p. 559], Lenin noted that, of course, both Cause and Effect are "only Moments of the universal interdependence, of the universal concatenation of events, only links in the chain of the development of Matter" [LCW 38, p. 159]. And by the time he has finished with this chapter and met up with Hegel's definition of the next and final part of the Logic, the Notion, "the Realm of Subjectivity or of Freedom" [SLII, p. 205; SLM, p. 571], Lenin translates this without any self-consciousness over the word "Subjective," as follows: "NB—Freedom=subjectivity ("or") goal, consciousness, striving" [LCW 38, p. 164].

It is important to note that Herbert Marcuse in his *Reason and Revolution* also chooses this, not only as the climax, which it is, to the Doctrine of Essence, but more or less as the Essence of the whole of Hegelian philosophy. Thus, on

p. 153, he states, "Without a grasp of the distinction between Reality and Actuality, Hegel's philosophy is meaningless in its decisive principles."[21]

Volume II: Subjective Logic or the Doctrine of the Notion[22]

With the Notion, we reach, at one and the same time, that which in philosophic terms is oldest, most written about, and purely intellectualistic; and, from a Marxist point of view, least written about, most "feared" as idealistic, unreal, "pure" thought—in a word, a closed ontology.

And yet it is the Doctrine of the Notion that develops the categories of Freedom and, therefore, should mean the objective and subjective means whereby a new society is born. It is true that *consciously* for Hegel this was done only in thought, while in life contradictions persisted. But what was for Hegel consciously does not explain away the objective pull of the future on the present, and the present as history (the French Revolution for Hegel), and not just as the status quo of an existing state. Be that as it might, let's follow Hegel himself.

Before we reach section one, there is the Introductory "On the Notion in General." We will meet in Lenin constant references to Marx's *Capital* from now on. Thus, in this early section, Lenin notes that Hegel is entirely right as against Kant on the question of thought *not* separating from truth, but going toward it, as it emerges from the Concrete and moves to the Abstract: "Abstraction of *matter*, of natural *law*, of *value*, etc., in a word, *all* scientific (correct, serious, not absurd) abstractions reflect nature more deeply, truer, *fuller*. From living observation to abstract thinking, and from this to practice—such is the dialectic road to knowledge of truth, the knowledge of objective reality. Kant degrades knowledge in order to make place for belief; Hegel elevates knowledge believing that knowledge is knowledge of God. The materialist elevates knowledge of matter, of nature, throwing God and the philosophic rabble defending him into the dung heap" [LCW 38, p. 171].

The section to which Lenin refers in Hegel is: "It will always remain a matter for astonishment how the Kantian philosophy knew that relation of thought to sensuous existence, where it halted, for a merely relative relation of bare appearance, and fully acknowledged and asserted a higher unity of the two in the Idea in general, and, particularly, in the idea of an intuitive understanding; but yet stopped dead at this relative relation and at the assertion that the Notion is and remains utterly separated from reality;—so that it affirmed as true what it pronounced to be finite knowledge, and declared to be superfluous and improper figments of thought that which it recognized as truth, and of which it established the definite notion" [SLII, p. 226; SLM, p. 592].

It could also be said that Khrushchev's "peaceful coexistence" and Kant's indifferent coexistence of Absolute and the Particular or Reason and Understanding coincide also in the fact that Kant does see a dialectical relationship between the two, unlike Leibniz, who saw only harmony arising from it.

Section One: Subjectivity

Chapter I: Notion   The forms of the Notion are: Universal, Particular, Individual. These three forms of Notion are the categories which express development in this entire book, even as in the Doctrine of Essence it was the categories of Identity, Difference, and Contradiction; and in Being, it was Quantity, Quality, and Measure, with this difference: that the movement in the Doctrine of the Notion from Universal to Particular to Individual could characterize the movement of all three books of the *Science of Logic*, thus, Being standing for Universal, Particular standing for Essence, and Individual standing for Notion.

It is this first meeting with U-P-I that makes Lenin say that it reminds him of Marx's first chapter in *Capital*. Not only that; he begins immediately thereafter (that is, after dealing with chapter II—Judgment—and in the Approach to chapter III on Syllogism) to make the famous aphorism: 1) Relating to the relationship between Abstract and Concrete: "Just as the simple value form, the individual act of exchange of a given commodity with another already includes in undeveloped form all major contradictions of capitalism—so the simplest generalization, the first and simplest forming of notions (judgments, syllogisms, etc.) signifies the ever-greater knowledge of the objective world connections. Here it is necessary to seek the real sense, significance and role of Hegelian logic" [LCW 38, pp. 178–79]. 2) Where he rejects Plekhanov as a vulgar materialist, or at least having criticized Kant only as a vulgar materialist. 3) Includes himself when he says that all Marxists at the beginning of the twentieth century had done so. 4) And where he concludes that it is impossible to understand *Capital* without understanding the whole of Hegel's *Logic*. (The friends should reread the whole chapter on Lenin in *Marxism and Freedom*.)

I have had to skip a great deal which at another time must be studied more carefully, both on the question of the Judgment—where Hegel lists four major forms and a total of twelve for a subsection—and the syllogism, where we have three major sections, each containing four subsections. It is not only because I am hurrying to get to the sections which have not been dealt with in any great detail by Marxists, but because for *our* age this section on Subjectivity is *not* the subjectivity which has absorbed all objectivity and which we will first read in the Absolute Idea. One phrase from the last paragraph in Hegel's section on the Syllogism will, however, be of the Essence: "The Syllogism is Mediation—the complete Notion in its Positedness" [SLII, p. 342; SLM, p. 704]. The key word is Mediation. It is of the Essence in all thought, as well as in all struggles. Indeed, it could be said that mediation *is* the conflict of forces. For example, all of Essence could be summed up in the word Mediation, or, if instead of Essence, you're thinking concretely of production in *Capital*, then of course it is production relations. So that what U-P-I does in showing the *general* movement in *Logic*, mediation is the concrete struggle and appears in all three books: in Being, it is Measure, which is, of course, the threshold of Essence; in Essence, it is Actuality, or more specifically, Causality which, as Reciprocity, brings us to the threshold of Notion; in Notion, it is Action, Practice, which supersedes Subjectivity of Purpose and *thus* achieves unity of Theory and Practice.

Section Two: Objectivity
The three chapters in this section—I, Mechanism; II, Chemism; III, Teleology—are devastating analyses of Bukharin's *Historical Materialism* over one hundred years before it was ever written.[23] [Grace Lee] had a quite excellent, though a bit on the abstract side, thirteen-page analysis of Bukharin's work, whom she called the "philosopher of the abstract universal." It was written in October, 1949, and sometime or other should be studied since, as usual, with [C. L. R. James] it got lost in the struggle.[24]

For us, what is important is Lenin's profound understanding in 1914, as against the period when *he* gave the green light to vulgar materialism with his *Materialism and Empirio-Criticism*, of the fact that the mechanical, chemical, and even teleological—that is to say, subjectively purposeful—are no substitute for the self-developing subject. Lenin notes here that Hegel laid the basis for historical materialism, quoting Hegel's statement: "In his tools man possesses power over external nature, even though, according to his Ends, he frequently is subjected to it. But the End does not only remain outside the Mechanical process: it also preserves itself within it, and is its determination. The End, as the Notion which exists as free against the object and its process and is self-determining activity, equally is the truth which is in and for itself of Mechanism." [SLII, p. 388; SLM, p. 747].

Lenin further defends Hegel for his seeming strain to "subsume" the purposeful activity of man under the category of logic because, as Lenin states it: "There is here a very deep content, purely materialistic. It is necessary to turn this around; the practical activity of man billions of times must bring the consciousness of man to the repetition of the various logical figures, in order that these should achieve the significance of an axiom" [LCW 38, p. 190].

I believe that Hegel here is criticizing what we will much later in history know as The Plan. Intellectual planning, or what Hegel would call "Self-Determination applied externally,"[25] is certainly no substitute for the self-developing subject, not even as idealistically expressed by Hegel in the Absolute Idea.

Section Three: The Idea
Lenin notes that the introductory section to this is very nearly the best description of the dialectic. It is in this section that we will go through chapter I on Life; chapter II on the Idea of Cognition, which will not only deal with Analytic and Synthetic Cognition, but will take up the question of Practice, Volition, the Idea of the True and the Idea of the Good; and finally, Chapter III on the Absolute Idea. It is the section in which Lenin will write, although he will not develop it, that "man's cognition not only reflects the world, but creates it" [LCW 38, p. 212]. He will also stress over and over and over again *totality*, Interdependence of Notions, of *all* Notions, *Relationships*, Transitions, Unity of Opposites, and various ways of defining dialectics from the single expression that it is the transformation of one into its opposite, to the more elaborate threefold definition of dialectic, as including Determination, Contradiction, and Unity; and finally, the sixteen-point definition of dialectic, which passes through Objectivity, Development, Struggle, and finally Negation of the Negation. Lenin will also do a lot of "translations" of the word Idea, the word Absolute, which in some places he uses as no differently than Objective, but in other places as the unity of Objective and Subjective. It is obvious that Lenin is very greatly moved by the fact that Practice occupies so very great a place in Hegel, but feels that, nevertheless, this practice is limited to the theory of knowledge. I do not believe so. (See my original letters on the Absolute Idea, May 12 and 20, 1953.)[26]

Let's retrace our steps back to the beginning of this whole section on the Idea. Hegel argues against the expression *"merely Ideas:* now if thoughts are merely subjective and contingent they certainly have no further value. . . . And if conversely the Idea is not to be rated as true because, with respect to phenomena, it is transcendent, and no object can be assigned to it, in the sensuous world, to which it conforms, this is a strange lack of understanding, for so the Idea is denied objective validity because it lacks that which constitutes appearance, or the untrue being of the objective world" [SLII, p. 396; SLM, p. 756]. Hegel gives Kant credit for having rejected this "vulgar appeal" to experience, and recognized the objective validity of thought—only to never have thought and reality meet. Hegel breaks down the Determinations of Idea as, first, Universal; second, a relationship of Subjectivity to Objectivity, which is an impulse to transcend the separation; and finally, the self-identity of Identity and Process so that "in the Idea the Notion reaches Freedom" [SLII, p. 399; SLM, p. 759].

On that same page, he states, in very materialistic terms indeed, that the "Idea has its reality in some kind of matter." Hegel will then take idea through Life through what he calls the Idea of the True and the Good as Cognition and Volition.

In the Idea of Cognition, Hegel will inform us that his *Phenomenology of Mind* is a science which stands between Nature and Mind, which in a way seems contradictory since it has served as the "introduction" to his *Logic*, and he will further summarize it when he comes to the *Philosophy of Mind*.

He will hit out a great deal sharper at Jacobi than at Kant, although he gives Jacobi credit for showing that the Kantian method of demonstration is "simply bound within the circle of the rigid necessity of the finite, and that freedom (that is, the Notion, and whatever is true) lies beyond its sphere and scope" [SLII, p. 458; SLM, p. 816].

But he gets less and less interested in other philosophers, the more he reaches the question of Freedom, Liberation, Unity of Theory and Practice: "In this result then Cognition is reconstructed and united with the Practical Idea; the actuality which is found as given is at the same time determined as the realized absolute end,—not however (as in inquiring Cognition) merely as objective world without the subjectivity of the Notion, but as objective world whose inner ground and actual persistence is the Notion. This is *the Absolute Idea*" [SLII, p. 465; SLM, p. 823].

This is because, in reaching this final chapter, the Absolute Idea, he is through with all which we would politically describe as "taking over"; that is to say, capitalism will develop all technology so perfectly for us that all the proletariat will have to do will be to "take over." As we reject this concept politically, Hegel rejects it philosophically. He has now so absorbed all the other systems that, far from taking over, he is first going back to a TOTALLY NEW BEGINNING.

Here is what I mean: Take a philosopher like Spinoza. Despite his profound dialectical understanding that "every determination is a negation," he went to God taking over. This concept of Absolute, Absolute Substance, Hegel rejects, even as he rejects the Absolute Ego of Fichte and Schelling, and the Absolute of the General Good Will of Kant. Note how every single time, in no matter which section of the *Logic* you take, [when] Hegel reaches an absolute for that stage, he throws it aside to start out all over again. So that when he reaches the Notion, he is dealing with it as a new beginning *after* he rejected Absolute Substance, and that even his Notion has the dialectic of further development; indeed U-P-I is the absolute Mediation, or the development of the *Logic*. If, for example, we stop in the Absolute Idea at the Expression: "the self-determination in which alone the Idea is, is to hear itself speak" [SLII, p. 467; SLM, p. 825], we can see that the whole Logic (both logic and *Logic*) is a logic of self-determination and never more so than at the *very point* when you have reached an Absolute—say, growing internationalization of capital. You then go *not* to taking over, but breaking it down to the new beginning in the self-determination of nations; or when the state had reached the high stage of centralization, you most certainly do not go to taking over, but rather to the destruction of the state.

Hegel can reach these anticipations of the future because a very truly great step in philosophic cognition is made only when a new way of reaching freedom has become possible, as it had with the French Revolution. If at that point you do not cramp your thoughts, then you will first be amazed on how very close to reality—the reality of the present which includes the elements of the future—thought really is.

To me, that is why Hegel makes so much of the method. It is not because that is all we get from Hegel—method—but because the end and the means are absolutely inseparable. Thus, on p. 468, Hegel writes: "The method therefore is both soul and substance, and nothing is either conceived or known in its truth except in so far as it is completely subject to the method; it is the peculiar method of each individual fact because its activity is the Notion." It isn't true, for example, as Lenin stated, that Hegel ended this chapter at the point [SLII, p. 485; SLM, p. 843] where Notion and reality unite as *Nature*, which Lenin translated to mean as Practice. In this final paragraph, Hegel proceeds on to show the link back from Nature to Mind, and of course we know that those two transitions were in themselves two full books.[27] Or as Hegel puts it: "The transition here therefore must rather be taken to mean that the Idea freely releases itself in absolute self-security and self-repose. By reason of this freedom the form of its determinateness also is utterly free—the externality of space and time which is absolutely for itself and without subjectivity" [SLII, p. 486; SLM, p. 843].

Marcuse thinks that it is this statement about the Idea releasing itself freely as Nature, "this statement of putting the transition forward as an actual process in reality that offers great difficulty in the understanding of Hegel's system."[28] But he himself doesn't attempt to overcome these difficulties. On the contrary, he disregards them, accepting the idea that it is a closed ontology and the best we can do is take this method and use it as a critical theory.

One thing is clear to me, that when Hegel wrote that the "transcendence of the opposition between Notion and Reality, and that unity which is the truth, rests upon this subjectivity alone" [SLII, p. 477; SLM, p. 835], the subjectivity was certainly not to be that of the philosopher, despite all of Hegel's hopes that it would be, but that of a new, lower, deeper layer of "world spirit," or, to be specific, the proletariat and those freedom-fighters in backward Africa, who just *will* freedom so much that they make it come true. For what happens after [the revolution], however, that truth must arise not only from the movement from Practice, but also that *from Theory*. The negation of the negation will not be a generality, not even the generality of a new society for the old, but the specific of self-liberation, which is the humanism of the human *being*, as well as his philosophy.

NOTES

1. This three-volume version of Hegel's philosophy, comprising the Smaller Logic (*Encyclopedia Logic*), the *Philosophy of Nature*, and the *Philosophy of Mind* (Spirit) was first published in 1817, and then reissued with changes in 1827 and 1830.

2. In 1787 Kant published the second edition of his *Critique of Pure Reason*.

3. This refers to Marx's decision, made in the mid-1860s, to place his polemics with various theoreticians at the end of *Capital* rather than at its start, as originally intended. These polemics, which Marx consigned to Book Four of *Capital*, were published after his death as *Theories of Surplus Value*. For Dunayevskaya's discussion of this, see M&F, pp. 81–92.

4. In German the paired terms idealism and ideality are used more frequently than in English, in a sense parallel to realism and reality.

5. "Bad" or "spurious" infinity refers to the condition in which a finite thing, in reaching for infinity, becomes another finite thing, *ad infinitum*, without ever reaching true universality. In this section Hegel writes, "This spurious infinity is in itself the same thing as the perennial Ought; it is the negation of the finite it is true, but it cannot in truth free itself therefrom" [SLI, p. 155; SLM, p. 142].

6. Irreducible, fundamental substances of the universe according to Leibniz, of which the prime monad is God. In his *Lectures on the History of Philosophy*, Vol. III, Hegel attacks this "artificial system" wherein there is no inner connection between the monads and "God must then mediate among the individuals and determine the harmony in the changes of individual monads" (p. 198).

7. The Eleatics were a school founded by Parmenides who upheld a doctrine of monism wherein reality is One, motionless, undifferentiated, and unchanging.

8. The chief ancient Greek atomists were Democritus and Epicurus, who held that reality is composed of indeterminate particles called atoms, which acquire determinacies such as color and shape only through their interaction with human sense organs.

9. This refers to an unpublished letter from Lee to C. L. R. James of May 30, 1949, held by the Raya Dunayevskaya Memorial Fund, in which she wrote: "The key to the whole Logic is that 1) you have to reach Being-for-Self i.e., negation of other and Barrier so as to return

upon oneself and yet 2) that this posed abstractly, like the shot out of the pistol, results in the most abstract relation of individuals to one another. From this abstractness of their relation to one another (repulsion) results the necessity of considering them together abstractly (attraction). 'Repulsion furnishes the material for Attraction.' It is as profound an attack on the whole conception of social contract and civil society as one can project. This was the theme of Marx's first significant essay—the essay on Democritus and Epicurus. It was likewise the theme in the essays on the Jewish question. Lenin didn't understand this. . . . There was nothing in Russia to pose so concretely to Lenin that bourgeois production was based upon this abstract relation of individuals to one another in economic activity, i.e. abstract labor." Lee also discussed the section on "Being-for-self" in a letter to James of August 16, 1949. It can be found in *The Raya Dunayevskaya Collection*, pp. 1692–95.

10. To Hegel, continuous magnitude is a quantity which "propagates itself without negation . . . a context which remains at one in itself" [SLI, p. 214; SLM, p. 200]. Discrete magnitude is a quantity that is noncontinuous or interrupted; it breaks up into "a multitude of ones." The unity of both constitutes the concept of quantity.

11. To Hegel, quantum is determinate or specific quantity, with determinations such as unity, continuity, and limit. "Quantum completely posited in these determinations is Number," he writes in this chapter of the *Science of Logic* [SLI, p. 218; SLM, p. 203]. Hegel's discussion of quantity and quantum as well as measure runs nearly 200 pages.

12. "Machists" refers to the followers of Ernst Mach (1838–1916), Austrian physicist and philosopher who argued that all knowledge is a conceptual organization of the data of sensory experience. Mach's rejection of such concepts as absolute time and space helped prepare the way for Einstein's theory of relativity. Lenin took sharp issue with Mach in his *Materialism and Empirio-Criticism* (1908).

13. Lenin here puts the German word for mobile, "*regsam*," in parenthesis, but it carries no independent meaning.

14. We have not been able to locate this letter of March 22, 1950, but extracts of it appear in notes later prepared by Dunayevskaya. The notes can be found in the *Supplement to the Raya Dunayevskaya Collection*, pp. 14670–72. See also Lee's letter to James of September 4, 1949, which also takes up Ground, in *The Raya Dunayevskaya Collection*, pp. 1707–1710.

15. Hegel writes in the same paragraph that "the immediacy of Being essentially is only a *moment* of Form" [SLII, p. 104; SLM, p. 476].

16. This appears not to be a direct quote from Hegel, but instead the use of quotation marks to convey the sense of "as it were." In the penultimate paragraph of the chapter on ground, Hegel does write of the "union with conditions [which] gives ground external immediacy and the moment of Being" [SLII, p. 106; SLM, p. 478].

17. An apparent reference to Jean-Paul Sartre's *Being and Nothingness*.

18. Compare the discussion of form and essence in Dunayevskaya's 1949 "Notes on Chapter 1 of Marx's *Capital*: Its Relation to Hegel's *Logic*," in Dunayevskaya, *The Marxist-Humanist Theory of State-Capitalism*, pp. 89–94.

19. For Hegel, matter and substances do not simply *possess* various forces (such as weight or magnetism), they also *are* forces. This is in keeping with his overall view that we cannot adequately apprehend the world as substance only, but must eventually view it also as

subject. Force is not yet subject, but it does convey motion and change, rather than simple inert substantiality. In this passage, Hegel also writes that the whole and the parts are each one of them "posited. . . as transcending itself and passing over into the other" [SLII, p. 147; SLM, p. 517]. In this sense, they are not only substances but also forces.

20. Hegel writes in his observation on "the immediate identity of inner and outer" that they are not so separate as common sense would believe, that in fact "each immediately is not only its other but also the totality of the whole" [SLII, p. 157; SLM, p. 526].

21. Marcuse, *Reason and Revolution*. He writes further in this same passage: "And the reality that is actual is the one wherein the discrepancy between the possible and the real has been overcome" (p. 153).

22. Although the Doctrine of the Notion or subjective logic is, Hegel writes, "the third part of the whole" [SLII, p. 209; SLM, p. 575], it was originally published as volume two of the *Science of Logic* in 1816. Parts One and Two, the Doctrine of Being and the Doctrine of Essence were first published four years earlier in volume one, entitled "The Objective Logic."

23. Nikolai Bukharin, *Historical Materialism: A System of Sociology* (New York: International Publishers, 1925). This work was attacked for its "positivistic Aristotelianism" by Antonio Gramsci. See Gramsci, *Selections from the Prison Notebooks* (New York: International Publishers, 1971), p. 437.

24. We have not been able to locate this 13-page letter of October 21, 1949, but Dunayevskaya's extensive excerpts from it can be found in the *Supplement to the Raya Dunayevskaya Collection*, pp. 14673–80. See also Lee's letter to C. L. R. James of July 5, 1949, in which she writes that "Bukharin's ideas and the contemporary one-party state are the abstract universals." Included in *The Raya Dunayevskaya Collection*, p. 1663.

25. Dunayevskaya has here apparently shortened the phrase "self-determination is applied to them only externally." This relates to "relative ends" which essentially "are only Means" [SLII, p. 391; SLM, p. 750].

26. Included in this volume, chapter 2.

27. Hegel's *Philosophy of Nature* and *Philosophy of Mind*.

28. Marcuse, *Reason and Revolution*, p. 166.

~

CHAPTER FIVE

Notes on the Smaller Logic
from the *Encyclopedia*
of the Philosophical Sciences

Written on February 15, 1961, these notes on Hegel's Smaller Logic—the first part of his Encyclopedia of the Philosophical Sciences—*comment on all sections of the work. Dunayevskaya's notes contain an especially detailed commentary on the "Three Attitudes of Thought Toward Objectivity," a section of the Smaller Logic that does not appear in the* Science of Logic *and a theme overlooked by many writers on Hegel. Here Hegel critiques not only Kantianism and Empiricism, but also romanticism and intuitionism. The text of the Smaller Logic used by Dunayevskaya is* The Logic of Hegel, *trans. by William Wallace (Oxford: Clarendon Press, 1894), which differs in some respects from later editions of Wallace's translation. Parenthetical references are to the paragraph numbers found in all editions of Hegel's text. The original can be found in* The Raya Dunayevskaya Collection, p. 2806.*

This book is known as the Smaller Logic, and since it is Hegel's own summation of the *Science of Logic* and very much easier to read than the latter, I will be very brief in summarizing its contents, concentrating almost exclusively on the sections which are not restatements of what is in the larger *Logic*, but which are new.

The first thing that is new is both the easy style and the different subject matter taken up in the Introduction. The simplicity of the style is, of course, deceptive since it embodies as profound a theory as does the more involved style, and may lead one to think that he understands something, even though he doesn't see all of its implications. For example, ¶2 defines philosophy as a "*thinking view of things. . .* a mode in which thinking becomes knowledge, rational and comprehensive knowledge." But if the reader would then think that philosophy is then no more than common sense, he would be a victim of the simple style. In actuality that very simple introduction consisting of eighteen paragraphs is the ultimate in tracing through the development of philosophy from its first contact with religion through the Kantian revolution up to the Hegelian dialectic, and further, the whole relationship of thought to the objective world. Thus, look at the priceless formulation about "the separatist tendency" to divorce idea and reality: "This divorce between idea and reality is a favorite device of the analytic understanding in particular. Yet strangely in contrast with this separatist tendency, its own dreams, half-truths though they are, appear to the understanding something true and real; it prides itself on the imperative 'ought,' which it takes especial pleasure in prescribing on the field of politics. As if the world had waited on it to learn how it ought to be, and was not!" (¶6).

That same paragraph expresses the most profound relationship of materialism to idealism. If you will recall the chapter in *Marxism and Freedom* on the break in Lenin's thought which all hinged on a new relationship of the ideal to the real and vice-versa,[1] then this simple statement will be profoundly earth-shaking when you consider that it is an idealist who is saying it: "The idea is not so feeble as merely to have a right or an obligation to exist without actually existing."

Actuality, then, is Hegel's point of departure for thought as well as for the world and its institutions. So far as Hegel is concerned, his whole attitude to thought is the same as to experience, for in experience, says Hegel, "lies the unspeakably important truth that, in order to accept and believe any fact, we must be in contact with it" (¶7). The whole point is that philosophy sprang from the empirical sciences, and in fact, the empirical sciences themselves could not have progressed further if laws, general propositions, a theory had not resulted from them, and in turn pushed empirical facts forward.

You will be surprised to find that actually I "stole" from Hegel that sentence in *Marxism and Freedom* that created so much dispute among intellectuals, that there was nothing in thought, not even the thought of a genius, which had not previously been in the action of common man.[2] The way Hegel expressed it was by saying that while it is true that "there is nothing in thought which has not been in sense and experience," the reverse is equally true (¶8).

The reason he opposes philosophy to empiricism, then, is not because we could do without the empirical, but [because], in and of themselves, those sciences lack, 1) a Universal, are indeterminate and, therefore, not expressly (¶9) related to the Particular: "Both are external and accidental to each other, and it is the same with the particular facts which are brought into union: Each is external and accidental to the other." And 2) that the beginnings are not deduced, that is to say, you just begin somewhere without a *necessity* for so doing being apparent. Of course, says Hegel, "To seek to know before we know is as absurd as the wise resolution of Scholasticus,[3] not to venture into the water until he has learned to swim" (¶10). But, for any forward movement one must then go from the empirical to the critical to the speculative philosophy.

Not only is Hegel empirical and historical ("In philosophy the latest birth of time is the result of all the systems that have preceded it, and must include their principles") (¶13). But he insists that you cannot talk of Truth (with a capital T) in generalities: "For the truth is concrete; that is, whilst it gives a bond of principle and unity, it also possesses an internal variety of development" (¶14). In fact Hegel never wearies of saying that the truths of philosophy are *valueless* "apart from their interdependence and organic union, and must then be treated as baseless hypotheses or personal convictions."

Chapter Two—Preliminary Notion

You will note that this is something that Hegel would have opposed had someone asked him to state in a preliminary way what was his idea of Notion at the time he wrote the *Science of Logic* and told you to wait to get to the end. In fact, Marx said the same thing in *Capital* when he insisted you must begin with the concrete commodity before you go off into general absolute laws.[4] In this *Encyclopedia*, however, Hegel does give you a preview of what will follow. Some of it is in the form of extemporaneous remarks that he had made while delivering the written lectures (all of the paragraphs which are in a smaller type than the regular text were *spoken* by Hegel and taken down by his "pupils"). He is showing the connection between thought and reality, not only in general, but in the specific so that you should understand how the Greek philosophers had become the antagonists of the old religion: "Philosophers were accordingly banished or put to death as revolutionists, who had subverted religion and the state, two things which were inseparable. Thought, in short, made itself a power in the real world" (¶19). The reference, of course, is to the execution of Socrates.

Interestingly enough, Hegel is not only rooted in History, but even in the simple energy that goes into thinking: "Nor is it unimportant to study thought even as a subjective energy" (¶20). He then proceeds to trace the development of thought from Aristotle to Kant, the highest place, of course, being taken by Aristotle: "When Aristotle summons the mind to rise to the dignity of that action, the dignity he seeks is won by letting slip all our individual opinions and prejudices, and submitting to the sway of the fact" (¶23).

We get a good relationship of freedom to thought and the *Logic* in general into its various parts [when Hegel says]: "For freedom it is necessary that we should feel no presence of something else which is not ourselves" (¶24). He relates the *Logic* to the *Philosophy of Nature* and the *Philosophy of Mind*, as a syllogism: "The syllogistic form is a universal form of all things. Everything that exists is a particular, a close unification of the universal and the singular."[5] "If for instance we take the syllogism (not as it was understood in the old formal logic, but at its real value), we shall find it gives expression to the law that every particular thing is a middle term which fuses together the extremes of the Universal and the singular."

While the *Logic* is what he called "the all-animating spirit of all the sciences," it is not the individual categories he is concerned with now, but the Absolute: "The Absolute is rather the ever-present, that present which, so long as we can think, we must, though without express consciousness of it, always carry with us and always use. Language is the main depository of these types of thought" (¶24). He will not allow philosophy to be overawed by religion, though he is a very religious man, but he insists over and over again "the mind is not mere instinct: on the contrary, it essentially involves the tendency to reason and meditation." He has a most remarkable explanation of the Fall of Man and the fact that ever since his expulsion from Paradise he has had to work by the sweat of his brow: "Touching work, we remark that while it is the result of the disunion, it also is the victory over it." (Note how very much like Marx the rest of the paragraph sounds.) "The beasts have nothing more to do but to pick up the materials required to satisfy their wants; man on the contrary can only satisfy his wants by transforming, and as it were originating the necessary means. Thus even in these outside things man is dealing with himself."[6]

The last paragraph of this chapter (¶25) deals with objective thought and decides that to really deal with it, a whole chapter is necessary, and, in fact the following three chapters are devoted to the three attitudes to objectivity.

Chapter Three—First Attitude of Thought Toward the Objective World

Everything in pre-Kantian thought from faith and abstract understanding through scholasticism, dogmatism, and metaphysics is dealt with in the brief chapter of twelve pages. It is remarkable how easy it sounds when you consider the range of subjects taken up. This is something, moreover, that he has not done in the larger *Logic*. All the attitudes to objectivity are something that appear only in the Smaller Logic.

Chapter Four—Second Attitude of Thought Toward the Objective World

This deals both with the empirical school and the critical philosophy.[7] He notes that we could not have come from metaphysics to real philosophy, or from the Dark Ages to the epoch of capitalism, without empirical studies and the shaking off of the bondage of mere faith. At the same time, the method of empiricists' analysis is devastatingly criticized. Somewhere later he is to say that it is equivalent to think that you can cut off an arm from a body and still think you are dealing with a living subject, when you analyze that disjointed arm.[8] Here he states: "Empiricism therefore labors under a delusion, if it supposes that, while analyzing the objects, it leaves them as they were: it really transforms the concrete into an abstract. . . . The error lies in forgetting that this is only one-half of the process, and that the main point is the reunion of what has been divided" (¶38). And finally in that same paragraph, he states: "So long then as this sensible sphere is and continues to be for Empiricism a mere datum, we have a doctrine of bondage; for we become free, when we are confronted by no absolutely alien world, but by a fact which is our second self."

With the critical school, it is obvious that we have reached a revolution in thought and yet that it stopped being critical because of its divorce of thought from experience: "This view has at least the merit of giving a correct expression to the nature of all consciousness. The tendency of all man's endeavors is to understand the world, to appropriate and subdue it to himself; and to this end the positive reality of the world must be as it were crushed and squashed, in other words, idealized" (¶42).

He further accuses Kant of having degraded Reason "to a finite and conditioned thing, to identify it with a mere stepping beyond the finite and conditioned range of understanding. The real infinite, far from being a mere transcendence of the finite, always involved the absorption of the finite in its own fuller nature. . . . Absolute idealism, however, though it is far in advance of the vulgarly-realistic mind, is by no means merely restricted to philosophy" (¶45).

He, therefore, considers Kant's system to be "dualistic" so that "the fundamental defect makes itself visible in the inconsistency of unifying at one moment what a moment before has been explained to be independent and incapable of unification" (¶60). And yet his greatest criticism of Kant['s system] is that it fails to unify, that is to say, its form of unification was completely external and not out of the inherent unity: "Now it is not because they are subjective, that the categories are finite: they are finite by their very nature." Note how in the end Hegel both separates and unites Kant and Fichte:

> After all it was only formally, that the Kantian system established the principle that thought acted spontaneously in forming its constitution. Into details of the manner and the extent of this self-determination of thought, Kant never went. It was Fichte who first noticed the omission; and who, after he had called attention to the want of a deduction for the categories, endeavored really to supply something of the kind. With Fichte, the "Ego" is the starting-point in the philosophical development. . . . Meanwhile, the nature of the impulse remains a stranger beyond our pale. . . . What Kant calls the thing-by-itself, Fichte calls the impulse from without. (¶60)

Chapter Five—Third Attitude of Thought Toward the Objective World

To me, this chapter on what Hegel calls "Immediate or Intuitive Knowledge" and which is nearly entirely devoted to Jacobi, is the most important and essentially totally new as distinguished from the manner in which Hegel deals with the other schools of thought in his larger Logic. The newness comes not from the fact that he does not criticize Jacobi (and Fichte and Schelling), as devastatingly in the Larger Logic, but in the sense that he has made a category out of it by devoting a chapter and by making that chapter occur when, to the ordinary mind, it would have appeared that from Kant he should have gone to his own dialectical philosophy. Hegel is telling us that one doesn't necessarily go *directly* to a higher stage, but may suddenly face a throwback to a former stage of philosophy, which thereby is utterly "reactionary" (that's his word, reactionary).[9]

The first critique of Jacobi's philosophy is the analysis that even faith must be *proved*; otherwise there would be no way to distinguish in anyone's say-so whether it is something as grandiose as Christianity, or as backward as the worshiping of an ox. No words can substitute for Hegel's:

> The term faith brings with it the special advantage of reminding us of the faith of the Christian religion; it seems to include Christian faith, or perhaps even to coincide with it; and thus the Philosophy of Faith has a thoroughly pious and Christian look, on the strength of which it takes the liberty of uttering its arbitrary dicta with greater pretensions to authority. But we must not let ourselves be deceived by the semblance surreptitiously secured by means of a merely verbal similarity. The two things are radically distinct. Firstly, Christian faith comprises in it a certain author-

ity of the church; but the faith of Jacobi's philosophy has no other authority than that of the philosopher who revealed it. And, secondly, Christian faith is objective, with a great deal of substance in the shape of a system of knowledge and doctrine: while the contents of the philosophic faith are so utterly indefinite, that, while its arms are open to receive the faith of the Christian, it equally includes a belief in the divinity of the Dalai-lama, the ox, or the monkey, thus, so far as it goes, narrowing Deity down to its simplest terms, to a Supreme Being. Faith itself, taken in the sense postulated by this system, is nothing but the sapless abstraction of immediate knowledge. (¶63)

You may recall (those of you who were with us when we split from Johnson)[10] that we used this attitude as the thorough embodiment of Johnsonism [as seen in] the series of letters he issued on the fact that we must "break with the old" and stick only to the "new" without ever specifying what is old and what is new, either in a class context or even in an immediate historical frame.[11] [This is] what Hegel calls "exclusion of mediation," and he rises to his highest height in his critique of Jacobi when he states: "Its distinctive doctrine is that immediate knowledge alone, to the total exclusion of mediation, can possess a content which is true" (¶65). He further expands this thought (¶71):

> The one-sidedness of the intuitional school has certain characteristics attending upon it, which we shall proceed to point out in their main features, now that we have discussed the fundamental principle. The first of those corollaries is as follows. Since the criterion of truth is found, not in the character of the content, but in the fact of consciousness, all alleged truth has no other basis than subjective knowledge, and the assertion that we discover a certain fact in our consciousness. What we discover in our own consciousness is thus exaggerated into a fact of the consciousness of all, and even passed off for the very nature of the mind.

A few paragraphs later (¶76) is where Hegel uses the term "reactionary"— "reactionary nature of the school of Jacobi. His doctrine is a return to the modern starting point of the metaphysics in the Cartesian Philosophy." You must remember that Hegel praises Descartes as the starting point of philosophy, and even shows a justification for any metaphysical points in it just because it had broken new ground.[12] But what he cannot forgive is that in his own period, after we had already reached Kantian philosophy, one should turn backward:

> The modern doctrine on the one hand makes no change in the Cartesian method of the usual scientific knowledge, and conducts on the same plan[13] the experimental and finite sciences that have sprung from it. But, on the other hand, when it comes to the science which has infinity for its scope, it throws aside the method, and

thus, as it knows no other, it rejects all methods. It abandons itself to the control of a wild, capricious and fantastic dogmatism, to a moral priggishness and pride of feeling, or to an excessive opining and reasoning which is loudest against philosophy and philosophic themes. Philosophy of course tolerates no mere assertions, or conceits, or arbitrary fluctuations of inference to and fro (¶77).

Chapter Six—The Proximate Notion of Logic with its Subdivision

This is the last chapter before we get into the three major divisions of the Logic itself. In a word, it took Hegel six chapters, or 132 pages, to introduce the Logic which will occupy, in this abbreviated form a little less than 200 pages. On the other hand, this Smaller Logic will be such easy sailing, especially for any one who has grappled with the Larger Logic that you will almost think that you are reading a novel, and indeed, I will spend very little time in the summation because I believe you are getting ready to read it for yourself now.

To get back to the Proximate Notion, Hegel at once informs you that the three stages of logical doctrine—1) Abstract or Mere Understanding; 2) Dialectical or Negative Reason; 3) Speculative or Positive Reason—apply in fact to every logical reality, every notion and truth whatever.

There are places where Hegel is quite humorous about the dialectic as it is degraded for winning debater's points: "Often too, Dialectic is nothing more than a subjective see-saw of arguments pro and con, where the absence of sterling thought is disguised by the subtlety which gives birth to such arguments" (¶81). And yet it is precisely in this paragraph where he gives the simplest and profoundest definition of what dialectic is: "Wherever there is movement, wherever there is life, wherever anything is carried into effect in the actual world, there Dialectic is at work." Over and over again, Hegel lays stress on the fact, on the necessity to prove what one claims, and the essence of proof is that something has developed of necessity in such and such a manner, that it has been through both a historic and a self-relationship which has moved it from what it was "in itself," that is to say implicitly, through a "for itself-ness," that is to say a process of mediation or development or suffering to what it finally is "in and for itself," that is to say, explicitly. Or to put it yet another way, from potentiality to actuality, or the realization of all that is inherent in it. Finally, here is the simple way: Logic is sub-divided into three parts—I. The Doctrine of Being, II. The Doctrine of Essence, III. The Doctrine of Notion and Idea. That is, into the Theory of Thought:—I. In its immediacy: the notion implicit, and as it were in germ. II. In its reflection and mediation: the being-for-self and show of the notion. III. In its return into itself, and its being all to itself: the notion in and for itself . . . "For in philosophy, to prove means to show how the subject by and from itself makes itself what it is" (¶83).

Chapter Seven—First Subdivision of Logic—The Doctrine of Being

I will not go into the separate categories of Quality, Quantity, Measure, or the question of Being, Nothing and Becoming. Instead, all I will do here is point to the examples from the history of philosophy so that you get a feeling for yourself about the specificity of his thinking and realize that his abstractions are not abstractions at all. Two things, for example, from the section on Quality will speak for themselves:

> In the history of philosophy the different stages of the logical Idea assume the shape of successive systems, each of which is based on a particular definition of the Absolute. As the logical Idea is seen to unfold itself in a process from the abstract to the concrete, so in the history of philosophy the earliest systems are the most abstract, and thus at the same time have least in them. The relation too of the earlier to the later systems of philosophy is much like the relation of the earlier to the later stages of the logical Idea; in other words, the former are preserved in the latter, but in a subordinate and functional position. This is the true meaning of a much misunderstood phenomenon in the history of philosophy—the refutation of one system by another, of an earlier by a later. (¶86) Opinion, with its usual want of thought, believes that specific things are positive throughout, and retains them fast under the form of Being. Mere Being, however, is not the end of the matter. (¶91)

Remember that the sections in the smaller type are the ones that Hegel quotes orally and then you will get a view of his response to his audience when, say, they would look with blank faces when he would speak of something like "Being-for-self."[14] And now read the following:

> The Atomic philosophy[15] forms a vital stage in the historical growth of the Idea. The principle of that system may be described as Being-for-self in the shape of the Many. At present, students of nature who are anxious to avoid metaphysics, turn a favorable ear to Atomism. But it is not possible to escape metaphysics and cease to trace nature back to terms of thought, by throwing ourselves into the arms of Atomism. The atom in fact is itself a thought; and hence the theory which holds matter to consist of atoms is a metaphysical theory. Newton gave physics an express warning to beware of metaphysics, it is true; but to his honor, be it said, he did not by any means obey his own warning. The only mere physicists are the animals: they alone do not think: while man is a thinking being and a born metaphysician.

Read the rest for yourself—it is too important to miss ¶98.

Chapter Eight—Second Subdivision of Logic—The Doctrine of Essence

Here again I will not go into categories such as Identity, Difference, Contradiction, etc., all of which I dealt with when summarizing the Larger *Logic* and which you will find comparatively easy to read here. What interests me are the so-called examples and once in a while the easy definitions like "The aim of philosophy is to banish indifference, and to learn the necessity of things" (¶119). So we go back to the historical basis which always throws an extra illumination on the generalization that follows: "The Sophists came forward at a time when the Greeks had begun to grow dissatisfied with mere authority and tradition in the matter of morals and religion, and when they felt how needful it was to see that the sum of facts was due to the intervention and act of thought. . . . Sophistry has nothing to do with what is taught:—that may always be true. Sophistry lies in the formal circumstance of teaching it by grounds which are as available for attack as for defense" (¶121).

I want to recommend the studying in full of the final part of this section called "Actuality." It is not a question only of content or its profound insistence on the relationship of actuality to thought and vice-versa ("The idea is rather absolutely active, as well as actual") (¶142). It is a movement of and to freedom within every science, philosophy, and even class struggle, though Hegel, of course, never says that; nevertheless [one] must go through the actuality of necessity and the real world contradictions that are impossible to summarize in any briefer form than the twenty-four paragraphs Hegel does here (¶142–159). You have heard me quote often the section on Necessity, which ends with: "So long as a man is otherwise conscious that he is free, his harmony of soul and peace of mind will not be disturbed by disagreeable events. It is their view of Necessity, therefore, which is at the root of the content and discontent of man, and which in that way determines their destiny itself" (¶147). Now you go to it and study those pages.

Chapter Nine—Third Subdivision of Logic—The Doctrine of the Notion

This last section of the Logic is the philosophic framework which most applies to our age. From the very start where he says, "The Notion is the power of Substance in the fruition of its own being, and therefore, what is free," you know that on the one hand, from now on you are on your own and must constantly deepen his content through a materialistic, historical "translation." And, on the other hand, that you cannot do so unless you stand on his solid foundation: "The Notion, in short, is what contains all the earlier categories of Thought merged in it. It certainly is a form, but an infinite and creative form, which includes, but at the same time releases from itself the plenitude of all that it contains" (¶160).

I would like you to read the letter I wrote to Olga [Domanski] on Universal, Particular and Individual[16] and then read Hegel on those categories, and you will see how little of his spirit I was able to transmit and how changeable are his own definitions. For example, he says, "Individual and Actual are the same thing. . . . The Universal in its true and comprehensive meaning is one of those thoughts which demanded thousands of years before it entered into the consciousness of man" (¶163). Just ponder on this single phrase "thousands of years."

These categories—Universal, Particular and Individual—are first described in the [Doctrine of the] Notion as notion, then they enter Judgment, then Syllogism, and then throughout to the end, and in each case they are not the same, and you can really break your neck if you try to subsume them into a definitional form. They just will not be fenced in. Hegel, himself, has something to say on this fencing in of the syllogism, for example, which in "common logic" is supposed to conclude so-called elemental theory, which is then followed by a so-called doctrine of method, which is supposed to show you how to apply what you learned in Part I: "It believes Thought to be a mere subjective and formal activity; and the objective fact which confronts Thought it holds to be permanent and self-subsistent, but this dualism is a half-truth. . . . It would be truer to say that it is subjectivity itself, which, as dialectics, breaks through its own barrier and develops itself to objectivity by means of the syllogism" (¶192).

(I want to call to your attention that it is the last sentence in ¶212, which [C.L.R. James] so badly misused in justifying our return to Trotskyism. Note that the quotation itself speaks of error as *a* necessary dynamic, whereas James spoke of it as if it were *the* dynamic: "Error, or other-being, *when it is uplifted and absorbed,* is itself a necessary dynamic element of truth: for truth can only be where it makes itself its own result." (The phrase underlined was underlined by me in order to stress that James had left it out.)[17]

The final section on the Absolute Idea is extremely abbreviated and by no means gives you all that went into the *Science of Logic*, but it will serve if you read it very carefully, to introduce you to its study in the Larger Logic. I will quote only three thoughts from it:

> The Absolute Idea is, in the first place, the unity of the theoretical and practical idea, and thus at the same time, the unity of life with the idea of cognition. . . . The

defect of life lies in its being only the idea in itself or naturally: whereas cognition is in an equally one-sided way, the merely conscious idea or the idea for itself. The Unity. (¶236)

It is certainly possible to indulge in a vast amount of senseless declamation about the idea absolute, but its true content is only the whole system, of which we have been hitherto examining the development. (¶237)

I love the expression that to get to philosophic thought one must be strong enough to ward off the incessant importance of one's own opinion:

The philosophical method is analytical, as well as synthetic . . . to that end, however, there is required an effort to keep off the ever-incessant impertinence of our own fancies and opinions. (¶238)

The final sentence of the whole book in the Smaller *Logic* is what pleased Lenin so highly that he wrote as if the *Science of Logic* ended [there] by stating that the "rest of the paragraph" wasn't significant. It is on that rest of the paragraph in the Larger Logic around which the whole reason for my 1953 Letters on the Absolute Idea rests.[18] The sentence Lenin liked because it held out a hand to materialism is: "We began with Being, abstract being: where we now are we also have the idea as Being: but this idea, which has Being is Nature." This is the oral remark which followed the written last sentence: "But the idea is absolutely free; and its freedom means that it does not merely pass over into life, or as finite cognition allow life to show in it, but in its own absolute truth resolves to let the element of its particularity, or of the first characterization and other-being, the immediate idea, as its reflection, go forth freely itself from itself as Nature" (¶244).

NOTES

1. See chapter 10 of *Marxism and Freedom*, "The Collapse of the Second International and the Break in Lenin's Thought."

2. The formulation appears in *Marxism and Freedom*, in the course of discussing the impact of the French Revolution on Hegel's thought: "There is nothing in thought—not even in the thought of a genius—that has not previously been in the activity of the common man" (p. 28).

3. Scholasticus was a fictional character created by the Alexandrian neo-Platonist philosopher Hierocles.

4. In the Preface to the 1872–75 French edition of *Capital*, the last one he personally prepared for the printer, Marx termed the first chapter on commodities "rather arduous," adding that he "feared" the readers would skip too quickly ahead to the final chapters, where he took up the absolute general law of capitalist accumulation [MCIF, p. 104].

5. Just prior to this, in the same paragraph, Hegel writes, "If we consider Logic to be the system of the pure types of thought, we find that the other philosophical sciences, the Philosophy of Nature and the Philosophy of Mind, take the place, as it were, of an Applied Logic, and that Logic is the soul which animates them both."

6. Hegel stresses that the Biblical narrative of Adam and Eve being cast out from the garden of Eden ends by declaring that human beings have become godlike, with knowledge of good and evil: "On his natural side man is finite and mortal, but in knowledge infinite" (¶24). In a 1970 lecture reprinted in *Women's Liberation and the Dialectics of Revolution* (1985), Dunayevskaya writes: "Hegel had moved the myth of Adam and Eve from the theology of sin to the sphere of knowledge" (p. 23).

7. Kantianism.

8. See ¶216 of the Smaller Logic.

9. See ¶76 of the Smaller Logic.

10. C. L. R. James.

11. This refers to a series of letters written by James to his associates in early 1955, which helped lead to the breakup of the Johnson-Forest Tendency.

12. See ¶77 of the Smaller Logic: "The Cartesian philosophy, from these unproved postulates, which it assumes to be unprovable, proceeds to wider and wider details of knowledge, and thus gave rise to the sciences of modern times."

13. In the newer translation of the EL by Geraets et al., "plan" is rendered as "method."

14. Hegel defines "being-for-self" thusly: "We say that something is for itself in so far as it cancels its otherness, its relatedness to and community with Other, rejecting and abstracting from them. In it, Other only exists as having been transcended, or as its moment . . . self-consciousness is Being-for-Self accomplished and posited; the aspect of relation to an Other, an external object, has been removed" [SLI, p. 171; SLM, p. 158].

15. "The Atomic philosophy" refers to the doctrine that existence can be explained in terms of aggregates of atoms, irreducible fixed particles or units. It reached its classic expression in ancient Greece in the philosophy of Democritus. Atomism has often been connected to philosophical materialism.

16. This refers to a letter to Olga Domanski, a colleague of Dunayevskaya's, of February 27, 1961. It can be found in the *Supplement to the Raya Dunayevskaya Collection*, pp. 13842–43.

17. In 1947–48 James used the notion that "error is *the* dynamic of truth" to justify the Johnson-Forest Tendency's decision to rejoin the Socialist Workers Party, despite its "erroneous" politics, which the Tendency had long combated. See his *Notes on Dialectics*, pp. 92–93.

18. See Part I, above, and Part IV, below, where Dunayevskaya critiques Lenin's interpretation of the closing sentences of the *Science of Logic*.

CHAPTER SIX

~

Dialogue on the Dialectic

In this chapter, we include several letters from the years 1958–63 that illustrate Dunayevskaya's preliminary work toward the concept of dialectic that was to under-lie her Philosophy and Revolution: From Hegel to Sartre and from Marx to Mao *(1973).*

The letter of May 18, 1956 accompanied the first draft of the chapter of Dunayevskaya's Marxism and Freedom *dealing with Hegel and the dialectic. It summarizes some of that chapter's central arguments on Hegel and the French Revolution, while also contrasting her position to those of C. L. R. James [Johnson] and Grace Lee Boggs [Kaufman]. During the writing of* Marxism and Freedom, *Dunayevskaya circulated the draft chapters to the News and Letters local committees. In the 1957 introduction to its first edition, Dunayevskaya refers to discussions with "groups of auto workers, miners, steelworkers and student youth," which she studied "carefully" before "the book in its present form was written" (p. 24). (The original can be found in the Supplement to the Raya Dunayevskaya Collection, p. 12105.)*

The three letters to the noted Critical Theorist Herbert Marcuse elaborate on and defend the importance of Hegel's Absolute Idea for Marxist dialectics, often against objections which Marcuse had made. These letters are drawn from Dunayevskaya's extensive correspondence with Marcuse during the years 1954–79 as found in The Raya Dunayevskaya Collection *(pp. 9889–9975).[1]*

The 1960 letter to Charles Denby, editor of News & Letters, *was written at the time that Denby was writing the pamphlet* Workers Battle Automation, *published that same year. Dunayevskaya's letter offers not only a reading of French philosopher Maurice Merleau-Ponty on the dialectic, but also the most important example of her continuing efforts to carry out dialogues on philosophy with workers as well as intellectuals. Some of the results of this dialogue can be seen in the philosophical discussions in the concluding chapters of Denby's* Indignant Heart: A Black Worker's Journal *(1978).*

The 1961 letter to the noted China scholar Jonathan Spence, then a graduate student, offers an overview of the Absolute Idea chapter of Hegel's Science of Logic *which is, on the one hand, an early version of some of the discussion in* Philosophy and Revolution *and, on the other, an argument for the relevance of Hegel's dialectic to the Afro-Asian revolutions. During this period, Spence also did research for Dunayevskaya's chapter on "The Challenge of Mao Zedong," first published in the 1964 edition of her* Marxism and Freedom.

The 1963 letter to the renowned Critical Theorist and psychologist Erich Fromm connects the critique of the Enlightenment in the section on "Spirit in Self-Estrangement" in Hegel's Phenomenology of Mind *to that on "Fetishism of Commodities" in Marx's* Capital. *It forms part of Dunayevskaya's extensive correspondence with Fromm during the years 1959–78, most of which is included in* The Raya Dunayevskaya Collection, *pp. 9976–10061, and the rest of which is held by the Erich-Fromm-Archiv in Tübingen, Germany.*

Letter on Marxism and Freedom, from 1776 until Today (May 18, 1956)

Dear Friends:

I was so completely exhausted yesterday when I completed the chapter on the dialectic—The French Revolution and German Philosophy—that I did not forward a covering letter with it. This is the most difficult chapter of the whole book. At the same time there is one concrete question that I will wish discussed. It is this: Now that I have the whole material before me I feel that after the convention and discussion I will wish to rewrite chapter one on the Industrial Revolution and Classical Political Economy and this chapter two on French Revolution as one chapter and call it either "The Revolutions and Economic and Political Thought" or "The Age of Revolutions: Industrial, Social, Political, and Intellectual." The point would be to open the modern world with the revolutions that indeed laid its foundations and posed the questions as well of its ultimate development, which we are now living through.

It is only when I actually started working out the philosophic problem on black and white in its strictly philosophic implications that it finally became possible to sharpen up the great divide in the state capitalist tendency between the Johnsonites[2] and us. We did a thorough job on that politically. Now it suddenly became clear that one of the three fundamental attitudes, fundamentally *false* approaches to Hegel, was precisely the Johnsonite which is now placed along with the Communist and academic as the sheerest sophistry, one more aspect of the Existentialism which manipulates the dialectic to fit any arguments it wished like a Philadelphia lawyer arguing both, absolute opposite, sides of the question with equal glibness. Thus to [Grace Lee] Hegel was both the philosopher of the counter-revolution and of the permanent revolution while "the Absolute" was both supposed to designate us and the Existentialists as incorporating all of past culture.[3] No wonder we couldn't ever get back to the work on *Capital*, that is, Marxism.

Each generation must reinterpret Marxism for itself—Marx himself did for the three decades of his development and that of the working class movement of the 1840s through the 1848 revolutions, [as well as] the 1850s and the 1860s when a new dialectic came out of the very struggles of the workers in America and in France. Each period, as each thought; each activity as each appearance, has its own dialectic, and this you cannot learn by rote, but only after you have absorbed the past, studied concretely the present, can you finally have a contribution to make on your own. Anyone who has ever been in any of the movements that call themselves Marxist has heard, and repeated by rote, that the three elements of Marxism are: Hegelian dialectics, Classical Political Economy, and the doctrines of the French Revolution. After which they proceeded to fight for 5¢ more in wages. In a word, it meant absolutely nothing to them for their day *because* it meant nothing they needed to relive of the past. The truth is that only with the present book does each period come alive in what it meant, then when it happened; what it meant to Marx; and what it means to relive it now.

Take the French Revolution. It had a dialectic of its own [in its] development from the Bastille until the *enragés*.[4] A good way to remember the *enragés* is to remember what it means: INDIGNANT HEARTS. Now the movement used to repeat only the Jacobins as the "heroes" and as late as 1936 [C. L. R. James] made [the heroes of the Haitian Revolution] "The Black Jacobins," while there are some men who would have seen the field hands rather than the coachmen as the greatest contribution.[5] In any case, Marx saw at once, when he broke with bourgeois society and turned to study the great French Revolution, that it was the *mass* movement, the deepest layers, the self-mobilization of the urban poor, where lay the foundations for the future development of proletarian struggles. That is "one element" of the doctrine of Marxism that now comes to life and is the unifying element of the other three. That is why for the first time with us "history" of the actual class struggles has appeared as if it were something altogether new instead of the lifeblood of the Marxist theory without which it means nothing.

Now the dialectic of the French Revolution insofar as the great bourgeois thinker[6] was able to see was that it was a process of development, a constant overcoming of contradictions; you didn't get to freedom or the absolute at one fell swoop but through meeting enemies and overcoming them, through contradictions with your own previous revolutionary leaders as the Jacobins, etc. The METHOD then—despite the fact that to Hegel world history was a development of the world spirit—of revolutionary human activity, dialectical development, is what Hegel discovered while all other philosophers, when they did sense contradictions, either tried to reconcile [them] by "the men of good will"[7] or mystical evasion of all reality and running to God. At least Hegel's Absolute, though only in thought, was on this earth, not in heaven.

Hegel may not have recognized materialism, but it is materialism, dialectical materialism which can explain him for there is nothing in our thought that is not already embedded in the activity of the proletariat. A genius as great as Hegel living in a period of the French Revolution and Napoleon could not but catch the impulse, though he himself could not see the masses as living subject working out their freedom by themselves, and worked out everything only for the elite philosophers. If it needed a Marx to stand Hegel on his feet, it needed a Hegel to lay down the prerequisites for Marxism.

One final word in this introduction to the chapter on the dialectic. It cannot be separated from the Absolute for it is the method of the Absolute. If at this day and age you think of the Absolute only as thought, if at this day and age you cannot materialistically interpret that last chapter of Hegel, then you get to the freedom of socialism like a bolt from the blue, as pure empty agitation in the manner of the SLP[8] or the Johnsonites. If, on the other hand, you have worked it out, then you have faced the task imposed on you by history, of reinterpreting Marxism for your own generation. When I first said that the two poles of my book would be the Absolute Idea and Automation, people thought I was a bit off; by now I hope everyone can see what hard work awaits us now that we have recognized what specifically is our age and our job in it as part of the forward movement of the masses to full freedom.

Yours,
Raya

Letter to Herbert Marcuse
(July 15, 1958)

Dear HM,

The absoluteness of my silence is not to be construed as proof of the fact that the Absolute Idea has lost its grip on me, but only that the practical everyday life of an author whose publisher is so small as almost to unite with the politicos to silence the world and thus burdening her with all the "promotional" work as well. But, outside of an appearance on TV next week for University of Detroit, I have nearly nothing to do till Fall when I appear at Cooper Union.[9] In any case I grasp what momentary lull there is in my tours and lectures to resume where I left off when *Marxism and Freedom* ended our correspondence.

I will begin with what will not be contested, I believe; the dialectical relationship of subject and object in the process of history as the center of Hegel's Absolute Method. Or, to put it differently, the conception of reality as totality, the unity of inner and outer; the relationship between the whole and the parts which constitutes the passage from existence to reality. But the real world, even when Hegel is the Prussian philosopher glorifying the state as the combination of the ideal and the real, is not Plato's republic with its "philosopher-kings"; to Hegel not even kings can substitute for philosophers and thus, just as the Christian Hegel lets "Revealed Religion" play second fiddle to philosophy, so the state philosopher Hegel leaves the state as "Objective Mind" remain[ing] on the doorsteps [but] not in the inner sanctum of "Absolute Mind."[10]

Now Marx criticized Hegel for not having really surmounted the duality of thought and being, of theory and practice, of subject and object; that his dialectic, no more than Kant's, could in its mystical shell be the actual, interior dialectic of the historic process, but was just froth, appearance, "the origin" not the *actual history* of man. He insisted that under the circumstance Absolute Spirit was mere appearance so that, even when he had "people" as content, the expression was restricted [to] that alien man, the philosopher; and that in fact, it is always after the fact that absolute spirit makes history, so that it is not only Nature which is "unconscious" and does through necessity what Logic accomplishes freely, but Absolute Spirit as well accomplishes the real movement unconsciously: "For in effect the absolute spirit does not become conscious of itself as creator of the world until after the event and its making of history only exists in the consciousness, in the opinion and representation of the philosophers, in the speculative imagination."[11] But when "corporeal Man"[12] standing on his own feet, [is] the maker of his own history *and* his own thoughts, then first will self-knowledge and knowledge coincide, the proletariat being both subject and object of knowledge and maker of history.

There is no argument with Marx's materialism, nor did the mature Marx separate his dialectics from his materialism, but the young Marx, when the need of the hour was to free oneself and the whole generation from mysticism, did underplay (because he did not know the early works?) Hegel's insights into "peoples" and not just consciousness and self-consciousness who receive the heritage of history as "natural principles" and "have the mission of applying it."[13] In any case, I am not here interested in what Marx did or did not see (to that we will come later) but what our age can and must see and to which it has a contribution to make.

To return to Hegel, first as Absolute Knowledge appears in the *Phenomenology*, where he sums up[14] the movement from Descartes "I think therefore I am" through Spinoza's abstract unity in Substance to Leibniz's recoil from this abstraction to the Individuality of—may I add?—commercial, pre-1789 capitalism which Kant anticipated and developed further after the French Revolution as abstract freedom, or Individual Will [wherein] all good men get together and work out contradictions according to a general will. Hegel continues with his rejection of the Absolutes of other philosophies when the millennium did not follow the French Revolution and we had Fichte's analysis of reality as Ego, Schelling's "intellectual intuition" (of which Hegel says, "Substance by itself would be void and empty intuition") [PhGB, p. 803; PhGM, p. 489] and Jacobi's *"reactionary"* (my emphasis) reestablishment of Absolute as faith alone [EL, ¶76]. To this Hegel adds, "Spirit, however, has shown itself to be neither the mere withdrawal of self-consciousness into pure inwardness, nor the mere absorption of self-consciousness into Substance. . . . Spirit is the movement of the self which empties (externalizes) itself of self and sinks itself within its own substance, and qua subject." [PhGB, pp. 803–04; PhGM, p. 490]. Well, what does it accomplish "qua Subject"? 1) It "wound up [the] process of [its] embodiment" [PhGB, p. 804; PhGM, p. 490]; 2) history was born anew to combine with science of the ways in which knowledge appears and ended up as absolute spirit; but 3) "the process of releasing itself from the form of its self" which is supposed to be "the highest freedom and security of its knowledge of itself" [PhGB, p. 806; PhGM, p. 491] does not make it as happy as the ending of the *Phenomenology* would have it appear for it will reappear as Absolute Idea in the *Logic* and Absolute Mind in the *Encyclopedia*. There we will see, not the work of art with its "double-tongued equivocal character of what they gave out as certainty" [PhGB, p. 740; PhGM, p. 446], but: 1) "Individuality purified of all that interferes with its universalism, i.e., freedom itself" [PM, ¶481]; 2) freedom not as a possession but as a dimension of being; in a word 3) Absolute Mind as the *actuality* of freedom. The philosopher doth protest too much when he keeps repeating knowledge is the Olympus when all the time he comes down to earth and its freedoms and *lack* of them. That is why I said, in *Marxism and Freedom*, that translated materialistically, the fact that Nature has gone through the same dialectical development as [the] Idea shows "there is a movement *from* practice to theory as well as v.v. [vice versa]" [M&F, p. 42].

With your indulgence, therefore, I wish to look at the real world of ours and spell out this movement *from* practice to theory (for it is only there where we'll get the new insights, "the new impulses" emerging from the objective movement and the maturity of our age which will *compel* us to make concrete what was only general to Marx): 1) The period of the 1930s—not of Hitler for I am consider[ing] not the development of counter-revolution but of revolution— the French Sit-Down Strikes, the American CIO, the Spanish Revolution[,] all adding up to new forms of *workers' control of production*. That is to say, the climax in the Spanish Revolution and occupation of factories by workers showed the workers were moving from Soviets or political control to actual management of production by themselves. 2) The period of the 1940s; National Resistance Movement, including Negro demonstrations, wartime and postwar general strikes, including GI movements for returning home, ending in the flocking by the millions into the Communist Parties. All this signified, not 'backwardness' of workers, but a search for *new political forms* to work out both freedom from occupation and economic slavery. The fact that that "double-tongued" enemy—Communism in Western Europe—won the allegiance [of workers] is only one more manifestation that this is an age of absolutes, and that the counter-revolution is not only in the innards of the revolution but v.v. And because the two are so tightly linked we had stalemate. 3) But with the period of 1950s and Automation new grounds were laid for overcoming this total contradiction. Where [the theory of] state-capitalism posed, but only in general, and only for theoreticians or those where Communism actually ruled over production, the question of the *new* type of workers' revolts and the return to Marx's theories of alienation, Automation made it concrete, evoking the question: what kind of labor should man perform? If that was a cry in the wilderness during the miners' strike against [the] continuous miner [in 1949–50],[15] it began to be heard three years later during recession, and, above all, that year it was united with the cry for political freedom [from] out of totalitarianism in the East German Revolt.[16]

From then on there should have been no rest for the theoreticians until they had broken through on that Absolute Idea and absolute freedom in the manner in which Marx broke through the mystical shell, and in the concrete manner Lenin, confronted with "transformation into opposite" [LCW 38, p. 109] made his own retransformation with "Turn the imperialist war into a civil war" [LCW 21, p. 39]. But, no, the Kantian ought remained exactly as abstract as Kant had it—and no Marxist would move to make the abolition of division of mental and manual as concrete for our age as Marx had made "the general absolute law" of capitalism concretely mean for the movement the mobilization of "the new passions and new forces" for the establishment of the new society. The greatest deterrent to the indispensability of the theoretician is the theoretician himself who flocks to anything from Existentialism to Zen Buddhism and from "war guilt" to psychoanalysis—anything, anything at all to avoid the *responsibility* of the Marxist theoretician to be where the workers are.

For anyone bound for "adventures of the Hegelian dialectic,"[17] the Absolute Mind lies beckoning, but, no, we go back to repeating the old about the de-humanization of ideas that Hegel is reproached with. Now, I admit that the humanism of Hegel is not the most obvious element in the Hegelian philosophy, although I maintain that today we should see it as its innermost essence. Naturally, the academic tradition that operates on Prof. Windelband's[18] assumption that the generation that could understand Hegel's *Phenomenology* has died cannot help the youth of our epoch grasp the grandeur of the vision of the most encyclopedic mind of Europe who wrote: "Within the short span of man's own life, an individual must learn the whole long journey of mankind. This is possible only because the universal mind is operative in every individual mind and is the very substance of it."[19] It is true that Hegel himself did throw a mystical veil over his philosophy by treating it as a closed ontological system, but he also warned against those who become the self-styled "representatives" of a philosophical work who, he wrote, "are like the dead burying the dead" [PhGB, p. 130; PhGM, pp. 44–45]. He put his own faith in the public instead, not alone because of its modesty, but because "it is the nature of truth to force its way to recognition when the time comes" [PhGB, p. 129; PhGM, p. 44].

You once told me that what I wrote in the first letters in 1953 on the Absolute Idea[20] and what appeared in *Marxism and Freedom* were miles apart and, in a sense, it is. No public work, popular or unpopular, can contain the intricacies of thought as they develop in their abstract form before they become filled with more concrete content. And no doubt also part of the reason of leaving it in its undeveloped state was finding none but "dumb workers" agreeing while the theoreticians were shying away. But I do mean to follow up the book with further development and I certainly would love to have your help, no matter how sharply critical, in breaking through those murky categories. At least you shouldn't merely keep silent. I will await to hear from you before I go any further.

Did you notice the paragraph in the last issue of *American Economic Review* on *Marxism and Freedom*? It surprised me that an economic journal should be the one to stress the humanism: "The book centers on the frequently neglected or misunderstood aspects of Marxian thought; its thorough-going commitment to the humanist tradition of all earlier revolutionary and socialist movements and of German classical philosophy. The crucial significance of Marx and Engels of this basic orientation is demonstrated by a close scrutiny of their works. The student of Marxism will appreciate the appendices presenting the first English translation of important but little known philosophical statements by Marx and Lenin. The volume includes a preface by Herbert Marcuse."[21]

Yours,
Raya

Letter to Herbert Marcuse
(October 16, 1960)

Dear HM:

I hope I may intrude upon you with some [thoughts] on the Absolute Idea. You may find it useful even for your present purposes since you are dealing with sociology and technology and Nikolai Bukharin is the father, though I doubt he would like that strange progeny of Mills, Rossiter, Mallet,[22] of all mechanists. These are my "enemies" as I proceed to work out the philosophic foundations (the Hegelian Absolute Idea and Marx's Humanism) for the present day struggles for freedom in the underdeveloped economies, a sort of counterpart to *Marxism and Freedom* which limited itself to the present-day descent from ontology to technology. It should help to sharpen up the edges.

At once I must make so bold with historic background as to include both the African and Hungarian Revolutions, even as, suddenly, without anyone bothering to explain why, Latin America too is included among "backward countries," although their populations are not African but of European stock, nor do they lack either an "educated class" or railroads or aeroplanes through "jungle country." The one element of truth in the designation of "backward" pertains to the economy. But since I take man, not the "economy as such," as subject, I would like at once to make clear *what* is the "thesis" I use from Hegel's final chapter [of the *Science of Logic*]. It is to be found on p. 467: "The self-determination therefore in which alone the Idea is, is to hear itself speak" [SLII, p. 467; SLM, p. 825]. The self-determinations of people are, surely, no less important than the self-determination of the Idea. It is no accident that Nagy, the Petofi intelligentsia,[23] and the Hungarian Workers Councils all fought its ideological battles by unfolding Marxist Humanism and this same discovery appears in Senegal where Leopold Senghor, for all his apologia for De Gaulle, unfolds the same banner. (I do not recall whether I sent you my review of Senghor's *African Socialism*,[24] but I'll find a copy somewhere and send it to you.)

Now, in detail, to the unfoldment of the Absolute Idea in Hegel's *Logic*, all the way glancing at which point in it, at the various historic stages in the development of the Marxist movement, the Marxists "got caught." The significance of that first paragraph on p. 466,[25] for Lenin at end of 1914, was that the unity of the theoretic and practical idea applied not so much in action as *"precisely in the theory of knowledge."* [LCW 38, p. 219]. You may recall that just five pages before he reached that chapter, where Hegel dealt with "The Idea of the Good," Lenin stressed the actuality of the Idea and "non-actuality of the world" by writing: "Alias: Man's cognition not only reflects the objective world but creates it" [LCW 38, pp. 212–13]. But Lenin did not develop precisely that aspect, as we shall see, when we reach the end of the chapter.

That same first paragraph of the Absolute Idea contains the stopping point of today's African intelligentsia. If you are versed in their constant reiteration of the "African personality," you will recognize them easily enough in Hegel: "The Notion is not only *Seele* [soul] but also is free and subjective Notion, which is for itself and therefore has [personality . . . it is] not exclusive individuality, but is, for itself, universality and cognition, and in its Other has its own objectivity for object" [SLII, p. 466; SLM, p. 824]. Without that personality too would only be "error and gloom, opinion, striving, caprice, and transitoriness."

All the Marxists of the Second International (Lenin up to 1914 included) at the *very* best stopped on p. 467 (if even we give them credit that is of having grappled with Hegel himself instead of some tertiary summary of him) when Hegel speaks of "the universal element of its form—that is the *method*" [SLII, p. 467; SLM, p. 825]. As to vulgarization of that "method" Hegel surely had not only the Cynics and Sophists in mind [as] a few pages hence (p. 473) he says the dialectic "was often quite neglected by those who were fullest of him [Plato] in their speech" [SLII, p. 473; SLM, p. 831]. The Second International not merely neglected the dialectic, but perverted it into a sort of polish for their organic Kantianism.

Because all Marxists, not excluding Marx himself, do like to stress method rather than Absolute Idea, thus pinpointing the putting of Hegel "right side up," it is necessary to linger a bit here. Although he stresses (p. 468) that "nothing is either conceived or known in its truth except in so far as it is completely subject to the method" [SLII, p. 468; SLM, p. 826] he separates himself at once from those who would degrade method to a tool, as analysts do: "In inquiring cognition the method is likewise in the position of a tool, of a means which stands on the subjective side, whereby the method relates itself to the object. In this syllogism the subject is one extreme and the object the other. . . . The extremes remain distinct because subject, method, and object are not posited as the one identical notion" [SLII, p. 469; SLM, p. 827].

In contrast, therefore, Hegel proceeds to define method for true cognition:

"It is the fact that the Notion is determined in and for itself and is the mean[26] only because it equally has the significance of objective" [SLII, p. 469; SLM, p. 827]. The transition here is to get back to the determination of the method. "First we must begin from the *beginning*" [SLII, p. 469, SLM, p. 827] and the beginning, Hegel informs us to the consternation of philosopher and engineer alike, "must be inherently defective and must be endowed with the impulse of self-development" [SLII, p. 471; SLM, p. 829].

The self-determination of the Idea, as that of peoples, far from being worlds apart, cannot be seen in their fullness, "in and for itself" apart from each other. It is in this respect that I just get fed up with Marxists who keep harping on "method" as if it meant opposition to Absolute Idea, or, better put, want "to throw out God and the Absolute Idea" so that Idea (ideas) too is buried. In *Historical Materialism*, for example, Bukharin speaks of "society" as if indeed it was matter, dead matter. Perhaps I better follow the way of Hegel in this too and refuse to have anything to do with vulgarizers. His admonition that the vulgar refutation "be left to itself" [SLII, p. 474; SLM, p. 832] reminded me of the ghost of Hamlet's father telling him all about the corruption of the court, the murder and the vengeance he should seek, [while] nevertheless admonishing him against taking action against one of the conspirators, his mother: "Leave her to heaven." If only we had some "heaven."

What is important, says Hegel, is the source of the "prejudice" against the dialectic, i.e., that it seems to have only negative results; and therefore what is of the essence is, "To hold fast the positive in its negative, and the content of the presupposition in the result, is the most important part of rational cognition" [SLII, p. 476; SLM, p. 834]. It is here, where he deals with the second negative, or the negative "*of the positive*, and includes the latter," where Hegel stresses the subjective "for the transcendence of the opposition between Notion and Reality and that unity which is the truth, rest upon [this] subjectivity alone" [SLII, p. 477; SLM, p. 835].

We are entering the whole section where even the Lenin of post-1914 found "not clear." I believe that the fact that we live in 1960, not in 1914, and the fact that we witness both the advanced proletariat's battles with automation as well as the colonial freedom struggles, can help us break it down. I am not underestimating Lenin's conception of "the positive in the negative." One who led 1917 needs no minor league defenses. Long before he read Hegel on subjectivity, Lenin saw "Masses as Reason."[27] But if he saw that truth as long back as 1905, and was preparing to repeat that on a much grander historical scale, why then did this turning point of the movement of the Notion appear obscure to Lenin?

Hegel, on his part, hit out against the whole triplicity construction of the dialectic here, saying "If number is applicable, then the whole course of this second immediate is the third term. . . . Now, since the former (the first negative) is itself the second term, the third term may now be counted as fourth, and the abstract form of it may be taken as a quadruplicity in place of triplicity" [SLII, p. 478; SLM, p. 836]. Lenin's note here: "The distinction is not clear to me; is not the absolute equivalent to the more concrete?" [LCW 38, p. 229].

Yes and no, says Hegel, as I read him. It is concrete but it is equally subject: "The beginning was the universal; the result is the individual, the concrete and the subject" [SLII, p. 479; SLM, p. 837]. It is subject he had in mind as soon as he had reached the turning point in the movement of the motion, first stressing that the "transcendence of opposition between Notion and Reality, and that unity which is truth, rest upon this subjectivity alone" [SLII, p. 477; SLM 835]. He first stressed that transcendence of contradiction which "is the innermost and most objective moment of Life and Spirit by virtue of which a subject is personal and free" [SLII, p. 478; SLM, pp. 835–36]. And as Hegel moves to the climactic, after method is extended to system, and even though you must enter other spheres—Nature and Mind—he cannot refrain from saying that we have ended with transitions, have entered "absolute *liberation*" [SLII, p. 485; SLM, p. 843]. "The transition here therefore must rather be taken to mean that the Idea freely releases itself [. . .] the form of its determinate[ness] is utterly free . . . the Notion arises as free existence that out of externality has passed into itself; arises to perfect its self-liberation" [SLII, p. 486; SLM, pp. 843–44].

Now all this "personal and free," "individual," "liberation," "release," "utterly free," "self-liberation" cannot possibly mean only the philosopher finding his absolute, as he shows in the *Philosophy of Mind* when his own mind wanders to the struggles against slavery. (Nor do I feel like fighting with Hegel over whether Christianity or actuality brought freedom of man into the world; the Old Man was great enough and even if he did reside in ivory towers, they were awfully crowded ones—so much so that today's freedom fighters in Africa find room there too.)

In all unfairness to Lenin, I must here jump to Khrushchev and his state philosophers who are supposed to have, according to Wetter and Kline and all the specialists in *Soviet Survey*, "reconstituted the law of the negation of the negation, which had been thrown out as a feature of the dialectic" by Stalin.[28] No doubt it is true that "negation of negation" was too close for comfort to a totalitarian society—for Khrushchev as much as for Stalin. However, what is of more specific note is that Soviet science, in Stalin's time, had not yet achieved that breakthrough [so] that it had need of that law to justify "acceptance of the theory of relativity and the rejection of the idealistic interpretation in Bohr." With missile thrust and automated production achieved, they have need of the law *for the natural sciences as they practice them*.

Science is not my forte, and in any case, subjectivity is not for the vulgarly materialistic. The self-developing "subject"—the proletariat—not just negation of negation "in general" is the enemy. When Karpushin[29] asked that the Early Essays of Marx be once again included in the Complete Works of Marx, it was *not* to "*reestablish* the law of the negation of negation," but to attack, pervert, destroy if he can Marxist Humanism where Man, not Absolute Idea, became the subject of all humanity's development and the *dehumanization* of Ideas be once and for all stopped when even so great a philosopher as Hegel must perforce return to positivism.

Now then to return to Lenin—the jump to Khrushchev's Russia was only to show what can happen to a non-worked-out aspect of dialectics—Hegel made him see all the leaps where there was gradualness, all the self-movement where there was external reflection of the "International" or the *established* socialist party. The value of a theory of knowledge that has within it "all the world-connections," the motive force in the ideal as well as the real, the *individual* [as] "personal and free," how could that arise *as concrete* until after 1917 did not bring a new world social order? Something has to be left for our age, no?

In any case, where Bukharin remained in Teleology, Lenin passed on [and] saw Hegel laying the premises for historical materialism—the transformation of the subjective end to external object was only first negation, while second negation takes place *through the means*. In this relation between first and second negation, indeed, resides the relation between vulgar and dialectical materialism, for the vulgar materialist never gets beyond opposition of subjective end to external object. But the materialist in Lenin so overwhelmed him at this point of historic revelation that, you will recall, he wanted to *stop* where "Hegel stretched his hand to materialism" [LCW 38, p. 234] as he "ended" with Nature. Since that was so in the Smaller *Logic*, but there was another very important paragraph to go in the *Science of Logic*,[30] the dividing point for our epoch is precisely on this free, individual, total liberation which shows, both in thought and struggles, what they are aiming [at] and thus compelling me in any case to read and reread that Absolute Knowledge, Absolute Idea, Absolute Mind as each developing struggle on the world scene deepens.

I'll stop at this point and tell you that if you are interested and wish to comment on this, I'll continue to forward various thoughts-in-process as I work on my new book—and am just "dying" to go to Africa.

Yours,
Raya

Letter to Herbert Marcuse
(January 12, 1961)

Dear HM:

I should like to divide what I have to say into two parts, the first dealing with your question as to why I "need the Absolute Idea . . . why translate if you can speak the original language?" I disagree with you when you say that "The very concept of the Absolute Idea is altogether tied to and justifies the separation of material and intellectual productivity at the pre-technological stage." It was not the pre-technological stage that impelled Hegel to the Absolute Idea. Although he certainly lived in a pre-technological era, it was the fact that the French Revolution had not brought about the millennium— Reason, Freedom, Self-Liberation—which impelled him toward the Absolute Idea. As we know from his First System,[31] he couldn't accept the fledgling proletariat as that absolute negativity which would reconstruct society, but he didn't just "give up" when he stopped short with that work. Insofar as he compromised with the Prussian State, he *seemed* to have accepted the State as the Absolute and the opportunist in him, no doubt, did. Marx, in fact, was transformed from the petty-bourgeois intellectual into the Marx we know by so profound a critique of [Hegel's] *Philosophy of Right* that the materialist conception of history was born. But, in all fairness to Hegel the philosopher, he just couldn't stop either at the State or even Religion or its Art (Forms) of the Spirit, but proceeded on to the Absolute Idea. Why? Why, when you consider that he had broken with all preceding philosophy and had no use whatsoever for the empty Absolute of Fichte, Schelling, Jacobi?

Let's approach this from another way—Marx's constant return to Hegel and constantly breaking from him. After Marx's *Critique of Hegel's Philosophy of Right* [1843] came the "Critique of the Hegelian Dialectic" [1844]. There where he breaks with the Absolute Idea—and he had to break from it or the discovery of the materialist conception of history would have been just empirical, rather than dialectical, comprehensive, total and human—it is no longer just material foundation vs. superstructure; it is against the dehumanization of the Idea, and while he is at it, he rightly rejects the philosopher as the yardstick without forgetting, however, also to break with Feuerbach's anthropological materialism and vulgar communism.[32] By that time (he has barely mentioned Absolute Mind) the whole essay breaks off. With the 1848 Revolutions, Marx certainly has no further "use" for Hegel, and yet in 1859 he is back again. If you contrast the "copying" of Hegel in the form chosen for the *Contribution to the Critique of Political Economy* and in the language of the *Grundrisse* with his *re-creation* of the Dialectic from the life of the historic period, 1861–67,[33] you see at once that [in] this break from Hegel, the final transcendent, the Absolute, reappears but is this time split into two—for capitalism the general absolute law of capitalist accumulation, and for "the negation of the negation" the new passions and new forces. And, when he returns to *Capital* after the French Revolution (P. C.) [the Paris Commune] and inserts changes of independent "scientific value" both in chapter 1 on the *Form* of value and in the part on Accumulation [concerning] its ultimate development in the concentration of capital in the hands of a single corporation,[34] he at the same time makes the "purely technical" change of eliminating part 8 as a separate part, subordinating it to a chapter following capitalist accumulation. That is to say, the historical tendency, the whole movement from primitive accumulation through capitalis[m] to the expropriators being expropriated, now is not just a negation of the negation "in general" but the specifically self-developing subject, in its logical, philosophical, historical and individual envelopment. You will remember that he makes some cracks at the "pre-technological proletarian—the artisan—[compared] to the full-developed individual" who will have absorbed the technological achievements and we will get to this Subjectivity when we return to Hegel again.[35]

Again, why the Absolute Idea, only this time tracing it through with Lenin's need. It would, of course, be nonsense to consider that without "a transformation into opposite" that he found in Hegel, Lenin wouldn't have known what to do about the betrayal of the Second International. That man never wavered for one second on what *to do* with or without Hegel. But the need to break with his own philosophic past, that vulgar materialism to which his *Materialism and Empirio-Criticism* [1908] gave the green light, the need for *self*-liberation in thought must have been overpowering for him to have felt so very much at home with that idealist Hegel. Indeed he learned that the *leap* to freedom one gets from a generalization is a release from the empirical, the factual, the deed to where one truly reaches a new human dimension. Think of his writing, and all to himself at that, "man's cognition not only reflects the world, but creates it" [LCW 38, p. 212].

I will take only one single sentence from Hegel from the Absolute Idea chapter which so preoccupies my every waking moment, and "translate" it and you will see at once that though all translations are "correct" and surely historical, they are far from exhausting what *Hegel* meant, and therefore, the constant compulsion to return to him. The sentence is, "The self-determination in which alone the idea is, is to hear itself speak" [SLII, p. 467; SLM p. 825]. If any man understood self-determination in the Marxian sense of self-determination of nations it certainly is Lenin. At least there you would have thought he would have no need for Hegel. Yet, if you contrast what the self-determination of nations meant to Lenin pre-1914, when it was merely a principle, to what it meant post-1914 when life and theory and philosophy combined, it will be clear that two different worlds, not contradictory perhaps, but different, are at issue there. For, by 1916 when the Irish Revolution had occurred, self-determination wasn't something that was being given by principled Marxists, but something that the masses were getting and giving *to* Marxists, a new beginning for their revolution which had been betrayed, the bacillus that would bring onto the stage the proletariat in action once again. And after 1917, when it is the Bolsheviks who had to be doing the giving, and when a Bukharin was willing to take liberties with it, because now we were at a "higher" stage,[36] how that revolutionary dialectician, Lenin, hit out. [I]n his *Will* he was to remind the world that Bukharin never truly understood the Dialectic.[37] Isn't that something for a reigning statesman to bother himself with on his dying bed? (Did you know that in 1922 Lenin once again [read] Hegel's *Logic* and with it that religious philosopher Ilyin, who, in his commentary on the *Logic* was so illuminating on the question of concrete,[38] that he insisted that Ilyin, the reactionary, be freed from jail?)

Now all that meant self-determination in 1914–24. If I took only the political translation, how was I to have seen the humanism in the self-determination of the African Decade, 1950–60: "The self-determination in which alone the Idea is to hear itself speak," and it speaks with a different voice now, and to be able to hear it there is a necessity not only for the practice of hearing today's masses, but the theory of Hegel's philosophy.

If I must further justify myself, I would say that, frankly during the 1940s, when I first became enamored with the Absolute Idea, it was just out of loyalty to Marx and Lenin; Hegel was still hardly more than gibberish, although by now the *music* of his language got to me even if I couldn't read the notes. But once the new technological period of Automation got to the miners and they started asking questions about what kind of labor,[39] the return to the early Marx meant also the late Hegel. As I said, I do not agree with you that the Absolute Idea relates to a pretechnological stage. So long as classes still exist, the dialectic will, and Absolute Idea will forever show new facets. What I do agree with is that once on the world scale we have reached the ultimate in technological development, then the responses of the masses in the pre-technological underdeveloped economies are the spur to seeing the something new in the Absolute Idea. Be it backward Ireland in 1916, or backward Russia in 1917, or backward Africa in 1960, somehow that absolute negativity of Hegel comes into play.

One final word on why "translation" is no substitute for Hegel. It has to do with the limits of the age one lives with, which creates the concrete, but also exhausts it, and there is need for return to the abstract, the new universal which will become the new concrete. For example, for Lenin's age "transformation into opposite" was *the* category, while cognition not only reflecting but creating, was left alone. To get to a new relationship of theory and practice, on a new foundation, *a new concrete in life to create a new stage of philosophic cognition*, a return to Hegel was necessary. Or at least *I* needed it.

Now to the second reason for this letter. I am glad you agree that a reformulation of the relation between theory and practice and the notion of a new Subject is the key. Without a new formulation, the second negation could be diverted as it is by the Stalinists, to mean a new object—a technique, a sputnik, even an ICBM—instead of the self-developing Subject. Of course, technology means the conditions for universality, but without a new Subject one would automatically relapse to the state or "Science" doing it. I do not know whether you happen to have read the latest issue of *Technology and Culture* (Winter 1961) where A. Zvorokine, the Editor-in-Chief of the Russian *Review of the History of World Civilization* is attempting to do the same thing with technology that Leontiev and Ostrovityanov did with value, that is to say, denude [it] of its class content.[40] I am writing the Journal [*Technology and Culture*] a letter, which I will enclose for you. The point I want to make here is that vulgar materialism, which rests upon a contemplative attitude toward reality, has, when it is in power, a very vindictive attitude to the self-developing subject. This it tries to hide, either by disregarding the subject or transforming the object Science into "Subject."

A new beginning must be made, needless to say not from the Object but the Subject. That, I hope, is what you mean by "the self-transcendence of materialism." Let me return once again to Hegel and that key passage on the second negation and subjectivity: "The negativity which has just been considered is the turning-point of the movement of the Notion. It is the simple point of negative self-relation, the innermost source of all activity, of living and spiritual self-movement, the dialectic soul which all truth has in it and through which it alone is truth; for the transcendence of the opposition between the Notion and Reality, and that unity which is the truth, rest upon this subjectivity alone" [SLII, p. 477; SLM, p. 835].

To overcome the empiricism of taking the given concrete to be the real one had to do more than just to contrast essence with appearance. Lenin, in his notebooks, is happy when he gets over the final section on Essence (Causality) because it permits him to break with inconsistent empiricism, which includes the limitations of the scientific method, that is to say, the category of causality to explain the relationship between mind and matter. The categories by which we will gain knowledge of the objectively real, Lenin sees, are Freedom, Subjectivity, Notion. These, then, are the transition, or better yet transcendence, of objective idealism into materialism, as well as of vulgar materialism into true subjectivity, which has absorbed the object. And yet, it is precisely from the passage of Hegel which I just quoted that Lenin writes that this play over whether there is a triplicity or quadruplicity in the dialectic, is unclear to him.

(Incidentally, quadruplicity, instead of triplicity, had also a special, though a secondary interest for me because I used to be quite at a loss to understand why Hegel, in the *Encyclopedia*, lists Three Attitudes to Objectivity, which excludes the Hegelian dialectic, since from Kant you go not to Hegel, but backward to Jacobi. It would then mean that there is a retrogression in history and the famous triplicity of the dialectic must really become a quadruplicity before we finally reach the Freedom of the Absolute. But here, in the *Science of Logic*, we are dealing not so much with attitudes to objectivity as to self-development of self-activity. In any case, the real point to us here is the "immanent determination"—the "self-mediating movement and activity") [SLII, p. 479; SLM, p. 837].

The following and last pages are all on self-relation, "personal and free," free release, self-liberation, and it is all done via the three movements of Universal, Particular, and Individual, which characterized the *Science of Logic* as a whole, as well as in each of its sections. Let me retrace my step once again to: "The beginning was the universal; the result is the individual, the concrete, and the subject" [SLII, p. 479; SLM, p. 837].

And yet, the dialectic method, "the method of truth," has here extended itself into a *system*. Unless one fully holds on to the fact that it is only because the result has been "deduced and demonstrated" [SLII, p. 480; SLM, p. 838], he is likely to give up at this point and say that's where Hegel must really be stood on his head because he is nothing more than an idealist, after all, who has yet one other system to present as the "Absolute," and his own at that. But, neither the "system" nor the foundation is any longer a mere assumption, and we have not stopped going to the objective for proof. It does not come out of the philosopher's head at all, although "each new stage of exteriorization (that is, of further determination) is also an interiorization, and greater extension is also higher intensity" [SLII, p. 483; SLM, pp. 840–41]. No doubt, Lenin here again took heart and near the very next sentence, "the richest consequently is also the most concrete," referred us back to *Capital*. Indeed, it is at this point most likely when he wrote so frantically to the *Granat Encyclopedia*, asking whether he couldn't after all still add something on the dialectic,[41] even as he had concluded to himself what no Marxist in the past half-century had understood—*Capital*, which it is impossible to understand without the *whole* of the Logic. History, however, putting barriers even before a genius like Lenin, he remained happiest when he could "pretend" that the Logic ended with Hegel's extending a "hand to materialism" [LCW 38, p. 234]. Because as a totality the unity of Notion and Reality, after all assumed the form of *Nature*, which Lenin "translated" as "Practice."

I am certainly all for the practice of the 1917 Revolution. But even as Lenin had to live also with what "happens after," 1917–24, so we who have lived with what "happens after" for nearly four decades *must* find the self-developing Subject, the new Subject, and new, not only in a country and regarding a specific layer in the proletariat (as against our "aristocrats of labor" and for Marx's deeper and lower "strata" that have continued the revolutionary impulse), but new that embraces the whole world. That is why it is impossible to look only at the advanced economy; that is why it is necessary to look also at the most backward; and that is why the world must be our country, i.e., the country of the self-developing subject. Back then to that final paragraph of the Absolute Idea, the insistence that we have not just reached a new transition, that *this* determination is "an absolute *liberation*, having no further immediate determination which is not equally *posited* and equally Notion. Consequently there is no transition in this freedom. . . . The transition here, therefore, must rather be taken to mean that the Idea freely releases itself in absolute self-security and self-repose. By reason of this freedom the form of its determinateness also is utterly free—the externality of space and time which is absolutely for itself and without subjectivity" [SLII, pp. 485–86; SLM, p. 843].

You see I am not afraid either of the "system" of Hegelian philosophy, or of the idealism of the Absolute Idea. The Absolute Idea is the method of cognition for the epoch of the struggle for freedom, and philosophic cognition is not a system of philosophy, but the cognition of any object, our "object" being labor. The unity of object and subject, theory and practice, and the transcendence of the first negation, will come to realize itself in our time.

One minor word on the question as to why Hegel continued after he "ended" with Nature, which is the way he ended the Smaller *Logic* and which is the logical transition if you transform his *Science of Logic* into a system as he did in the *Encyclopedia* and move from Logic to Nature to Spirit or Mind. Marx, too, had three volumes to his *Capital* and likewise was going to end the first volume "logically," i.e., without entering this sphere of Accumulation. When he decided, however, to extend the book to include the Notion, not as mere "summation" of all that preceded, but, to use a Hegelian phrase once again, "the pure Notion which forms a Notion of itself" [SLII, p. 486; SLM, p. 844], he also included an anticipation of what Volumes II and III would contain. Volume II, as we know, is far from being Nature; on the contrary, it is that fantastic, pure, isolated "single society" ("socialism in one country," if you please, only Marx thought it was state capitalism). It was so pure and so logical and so unreal that it completely disorganized poor Rosa [Luxemburg] when she contrasted that phantasmagoria to the rapacious imperialism living off all those underdeveloped countries it conquered.[42] And, finally, he tells us also that he will indeed come down from those heights to face the whole concrete mess of capitalism and rates of profit and speculation and cheating, but we would only lose all knowledge of what society really is if we reversed the method. And even though Volume III stopped before he had a chance to develop the chapter on "Classes," we know that it was not really the class but the full and free development of the individual that would signify a negation of a negation that was not merely destructive of the old, but constructive of the new. In this sense, and in this sense only, Hegel's last sentence about the Notion perfecting "its self-liberation in the philosophy of Spirit" [SLII, p. 486; SLM, p. 844] must be translated, stood right-side up. And Hegel will certainly help us a lot in that book as he goes on to describe freedom, not as a "have," but as an "is" [PM, ¶482].

I hope we will get a chance to discuss all these ideas and more when I see you either the last week of February or first week of March. Let me know which is more convenient for you.

Yours,
Raya

Letter to Charles Denby
(March 10, 1960)

Dear CD:

There is a certain philosopher in France, Maurice Merleau-Ponty, who has done some very good things on Marxism, especially its humanism. One article in particular, "Marxism and Philosophy," printed as far back as 1947,[43] gave me a new insight when I reread it with Automation in mind.

So I decided to write you a letter [on it] . . . . I do not wish you to discuss it with intellectuals—they would only put in more abstract words what I have already said abstractly enough. You may, however, discuss it with a worker. The point is whether the worker is new or an old hand at Marxist Humanism, they might be able to help because even when a worker says "I don't understand," he adds something concrete. In any case do not worry if you do not grasp at once or all of it. If just a little sinks down somewhere in the unconscious, you may get help when you write the concrete about Automation, even if it is only on the question of what to put in and what to leave out.

Now then to philosophy. I'll begin with the end of that article I referred to in my first paragraph. The point that [Merleau-Ponty] makes at the end [p. 175] is why Marx at one and the same time 1) attacks philosophers ("Philosophers have interpreted the world; the point is to change it.")[44] and yet 2) attacks workers who would turn their back on philosophy "and by giving it softly and with averted glance a few ill-humored phrases."[45]

It is because you cannot "negate," that is, abolish philosophy by evading it. And the philosopher surely cannot be used as the yardstick in any case. "But," says Merleau-Ponty, "if the philosopher knows this, if he sets himself the task of following the other experiences and the other existences [. . .] instead of putting himself in their place, if he abandons the illusion of contemplating the totality of fulfilled history and feels himself, like other men, caught in it, and before a future *to build*, then philosophy realizes itself and vanishes as separate philosophy" [p. 175].

I need not tell you that "other experiences and the other existences" are those of workers, and that when philosophy "vanishes as separate" it means that thought and existence have become [one]. Since it is Automation that is in the back of my mind, I would say that when workers pose questions, *not answers, but questions*, they are well on the way to hewing out a road to the vanishing of philosophy as "separate" and to unite theory and practice.

But you have to ask the serious questions that *point* to a new direction. In Hegelian philosophy "pathway" is a very important word, a "category" which, whether it is only remembrance or description of the moment, it nevertheless cuts through a dark forest and lets you see the light, the path.

I will now jump back to the middle of the article where the subject considered is why Marx was not a vulgar materialist. (Indeed he never even used the word, materialist, by itself, to describe his philosophy. It was the unity of materialism and idealism, the *human* factor. Just as Marx refused to consider seriously "property forms," but insisted instead on *production relations* of men to men, so when he did use the expression "practical materialist" he meant practice pure and simple. Or, to put it another way, *human activity*.) You have often heard me say "philosophy in the Marxist sense of human activity." But let us never forget that that human activity was all-comprehensive and meant not only practical work but *the work of thinking*, which is just as hard labor as anything else.

Merleau-Ponty says that this introduction of the "human object" into classical philosophy "was carrying to its concrete consequences the Hegelian conception of a 'spirit-phenomenon'" [pp. 174–75].

Of all the mystical words, the one that gets the greatest laugh out of what Marx calls "vulgar materialists" and what we know as "old radicals" is this word, "spirit-phenomenon." For Hegel had dehumanized the idea and instead of seeing workers, or even people in general, saw some sort of "Spirit" or God doing the work of history. Or so *he* says. The truth is, his philosophy lives today because Marx had seen through this "spirit" and saw it was in actuality living history, or *collective men* shaping history, and doing so on the basis of a very concrete type of production, capitalistic production which "negated personality," made men into parts of machines, and therefore produced WORKERS' REVOLT.

At this point this French philosopher has something very wise to say for he stresses the fact that the so-called objectivity of scientists is itself a form of "alienation" and that it entered the Marxist movement "only when revolutionary consciousness wanes," and he points to the revisionist Bernstein [p. 173].[46]

What he is trying to do here is to sum up Marx's conception of the dialectic as TOTALITY. [It] not only denies the so-called "eternal" nature of man, and takes up a specific concrete economic epoch, and relations [of] men to each other in these historic periods of slavery and capitalism, *but even though economics was the foundation of all thought and history its proof,* history "cannot be reduced to economic skeleton." The human factor is *the* decisive factor and if that is so it is the total human being, not any single portion of him.

And because this is so, and because all history is the history of the struggles for freedom, Hegel's "Absolute Idea" was in actuality TOTAL FREEDOM. That is how Hegel and Marx met, so to speak, and why Hegel's abstract ideas are in actuality the reflections of this historic movement so that, as I put it in *Marxism and Freedom,* Hegel's *Phenomenology of Mind* is in reality the philosophy of history established by the "indignant hearts" who made the French Revolution.

Finally, to get back from the history of the French Revolution when the machine age had just begun to the age of Automation, when the machine is the full master of man and they still don't have total freedom, we have to face the specific, concrete, daily experiences AND thoughts of workers on the job.

Yours,

Raya

Letter to Jonathan Spence (June 1, 1961)

Dear Jonathan:

It is time to go straight to the most "abstract" part, essence, of Hegelian philosophy, "The Absolute Idea" of his *Science of Logic,* to show how we live in the age of absolutes, and that the "subject" (Man, though he is "dehumanized" in Hegel as mere thought) has already absorbed all "objectivity" (science, world stage of technology, past history) and now the new society depends [on] all his "subjectivity" (not petty-bourgeois ego, but what Hegel calls "the individual, purified of all that interferes with his universality" [PM, ¶481], and Marx [in 1844] calls "the *social* individual" who, however, is the only proof of the freedom of all, so that never again are we to counterpose "society" to the "individual" since he "*is* the social entity") [MECW 3, p. 299].

[Let's] follow through that last chapter, the most exciting 20 pages in all the world's literature, philosophical or real:

1) Hegel begins by saying that we have reached the Absolute Idea which "has turned out to be the identity of the Theoretical and the Practical Idea" and that this can be seen in the fact that "The Notion is not only *Seele* [soul] but also is free and subjective Notion, which is for itself and therefore has personality" [SLII, p. 466; SLM, p. 824].

Now many have stopped here and therefore I must warn you against that word "personality," so popular a word now both with African leaders *and* De Gaulle. In that very same paragraph, nay, sentence, Hegel goes on to explain that this personality "is not exclusive individuality, but is, for itself, universality and cognition, and in its Other has its own objectivity for object." The key word is "Other." It will turn out to be "its own Other" for otherwise we would once again be confronted with a subject and its "other" (or opposite) as object whereas the whole of the logic depends on doing away with the opposition of subject and object. The greatness of Hegel is that, although he worked only with thought, he got that "other" worked out not as a "have," a possession, an object, but as an "is," that is, a dimension of the human being. Until we do reach that point, and we still have nineteen pages to go, the "personality" is not much higher than Fichte's Absolute Ego.[47] The key word, "Other," then will turn out to be the universality of the individual and until that moment we are barely on the threshold of the new society (that is what Absolute Idea is, you know).

Next he equates Logic to the "self-movement of the Absolute Idea. . . . The self-determination therefore in which alone the Idea is, is to hear itself speak" [SLII, p. 467; SLM, p. 825].

The identity of history with logic so that the whole of the development has merely been the unfoldment of this Absolute sounded as the pinnacle of idealism in the 19th century. Indeed, were it not for the fact that Marx turned Hegel right side up and we could see that it wasn't "God" who "posited" himself on earth and the freedom of man came as a consequence, but, vice versa, that the struggles of man for freedom changing with each method of production on a higher level finally created the material foundations for total freedom and a new society via the class struggle. . . . until Marx, in a word, Hegel couldn't tear himself out of theology, despite the fact that in his philosophy religion takes a back seat to philosophy.

By the beginning of the 20th century "self-determination" became much more famous as self-determination of people, rather than ideas. But this shouldn't mean, either that action "takes the place of" ideas, *or* that anything less than the *unity* of theory and practice can "evolve into" a new society. If all we'll hear is Castro's voice, and *not the people speaking,* we do not get either the self-determinations of the Cubans as people or the Cubans as thinkers who have finally overcome that most monstrous fact of alienated labor that Marx showed got its apogee in the division between mental and manual labor.

It is because thought is so close to life that Hegel could, in isolating thought but carrying its development through to its logical conclusion, come to the conclusion that it is all a question of method. The Second International was fast on the trigger, and tried to isolate method as a tool that could be "used" by anyone. They therefore could never *create* or, more precisely, have the proletariat create a dialectic of its own, but retreated to Kantianism and "men of good will" solving contradictions—and ended by sending worker to shoot worker across battle lines drawn up by their bourgeoisie. Hegel here stresses that *because* logic is self-movement, that *therefore* "the logical Idea has itself as infinite form for content." In a word, you cannot abolish the difference between content and form *unless* this self-activity is its *content.* Only then, does content "as such" vanish and "the universal element of its form" is "the *method*" [SLII, p. 467; SLM, p. 825].

And only then can Hegel draw the conclusion: "The method therefore is both soul and substance, and nothing is either conceived or known in its truth except insofar as it is completely subject to method; it is the peculiar method of each individual fact because its activity is the Notion" [SLII, p. 468; SLM, p. 826].

Activity, self-activity; determination, self-determination; movement, self-movement; method that is movement, source and action, thought and practice thus becomes Absolute Method, not in heaven, but among the earth people struggling for total freedom.

Now let's break this Absolute Method down to see how it is subject, method, and object, and not a mere tool "to be used." Hegel says that, while we "must begin from the *beginning,*" [SLII, p. 469; SLM, p. 827] the beginning is nothing as simple as is usually imagined for it must be both simple and universal, and not just "abstract universality" but be "concrete universal," "that is, that which is in itself the concrete totality, but not as *posited* or *for itself*" [SLII, p. 471; SLM, p. 829] for, "It is the Absolute only in its completion" [SLII, p. 472; SLM, p. 829].

To reach completion we therefore begin with an immediate that has been mediated but still is one-sided. You can call it first negation or analytic but you know that to be *objectively* universal it must also be synthetic. It is in the unity of the two moments that we will reach the "dialectic moment," and it is here too, that we will first meet "Other" as "its own Other," thus:

"This equally synthetic and analytic moment of the Judgment, by which the original universal determines itself out of itself to be its own Other may rightly be called the dialectic moment" [SLM, p. 473; SLM, p. 831].

It is at this point that Lenin, you will recall from the *Philosophic Notebooks* at the end of *Marxism and Freedom*,[48] bursts into the definition of dialectic, singling out no less than sixteen elements—objectivity, manifold relations, development, tendencies, unity of opposites, struggles (including contradictions and impulses), unity of synthesis and analysis, summation, totality, the singular and the universal, each end the whole, transitions, new sides, deepening appearance and essence, causality and universality, content and form, negation of negation—only to sum up the whole at the end as "simply" the "doctrine of the unity of opposites" [LCW 38, pp. 221–23].

When something is as rich as the dialectic, it is indeed hard to define it as any one thing, or as 16 things, because *for each age it is different*, that is to say, it is all the things and more, but *the* one element that gets singled out as having gained by contact with the present can only be proven in life. Hegel himself, for example, to stress the primacy of Thought singles out its unity with Being: "The object in its existence without thought and Notion is an image or a name; it is what it is in the determinations of thought and Notion" [SLII, p. 475; SLM, p. 833].

For Marx it was the three volumes of his *Capital* plus the Paris Commune. For Lenin it was "the transformation into opposite" of both capital (into monopoly or imperialism) and labor (into aristocracy of labor) which finally however get resolved ("negation of negation") in the Soviet, or Russian Revolution, *plus State and Revolution*. For our age it is the unity of theory and practice, or the answer to the question of "what happens after [the revolution]," *plus* the subjectivity that has objectivity in it. So let's get to that stage:

First here we will have to watch the second negation; all the difference between revolutionaries and compromisers, which means those who retrogress in the end to the old, not forward to the new, lies in the distinction between first and second negation, that is to say, it is not just the abolition of the old, or the revolution, but the *transcendence* to what Marx [in 1844] called "*positive* Humanism, beginning from itself," *not* stalling at the first negation, or transcendence, such as communism, or atheism, for "Only by the transcendence of this mediation, which is nevertheless a necessary presupposition, does there arise positive Humanism beginning from itself" [CHD, pp. 319–20; MECW 3, pp. 341–42]. And [that is] why Marx insisted that "communism, as such, is not the goal of human development, the form of human society" [PPC, p. 303; MECW 3, p. 306].

O.K., let's get to that second negation as Hegel sums it up: "The negativity which has just been considered is the turning point of the movement of the Notion. It is the simple point of negative self-relation, the innermost source of all activity, of living and spiritual self-movement, the dialectic soul which all truth has in it and through which it alone is truth; for the transcendence of the opposition between the Notion and Reality, and that unity which is the truth, rest upon this subjectivity alone" [SLII, p. 477; SLM, p. 835].

We have reached the point in the Absolute Idea which no other age could quite see it in all its concreteness as we do when we look at the African Revolutions that have truly nought of "material foundation" and yet are so far advanced as to fight for freedom without a single look backward. And while Mao's China's shortcuts may entice their leaders, it certainly doesn't [entice the masses] who know that abolition of the opposition of Notion and Reality does in truth rest upon them alone, and because it does "rest upon this subjectivity alone" little Guinea dared say "No" to empire-builder De Gaulle.[49]

Another reason that only our age can see [it] is that no one previously, not even Lenin, could think of stopping to emphasize this passage and its paean to "personal and free": "The second negative . . . is no more the activity of an external reflection than the contradiction is: it is the innermost and most objective moment of Life and Spirit by virtue of which a subject is personal and free" [SLII, pp. 477–78; SLM, pp. 835–36]. And again: "The beginning was the universal; the result is the individual, the concrete, and the subject; what the former is *in itself*, the latter now is equally *for itself*" [SLII, p. 479, SLM, p. 837].

Nor is there any longer a difference between inner and outer: "Each new stage of exteriorization (that is, of further determination) is also an interiorization, and greater extension is also higher intensity" [SLII, p. 483; SLM, pp. 840–41].

Finally, *since* "the pure Idea of Cognition is enclosed in subjectivity and therefore is an impulse to transcend the latter; and, as last result, pure truth becomes *the beginning of another sphere and science*" (read: another society) THEREFORE *transition* is no longer "a perfected becoming" but "is an absolute *liberation*. . . . Consequently there is no transition in this freedom" [SLII, p. 485; SLM, p. 843].

All the rest of that last paragraph sings of freedom as RELEASE ("the Idea freely releases itself" [SLII, p. 486; SLM, p. 843], and "By reason of this freedom the form of its determinateness is utterly free—the externality of space and time which is absolutely for itself and without subjectivity." Because having absorbed objectivity it no longer exists "as mere objectivity," but "arises to perfect its self-liberation in the Philosophy of Spirit" [SLII, p. 486; SLM, p. 844].

It is most important, for our age, to understand why, instead of going on with the paragraph on liberation, Lenin had stopped at the very first sentence in it, which read: "For the Idea posits itself as the absolute unity of the pure Notion and its Reality, and thus gathers itself into the immediacy of Being; and in doing so, as totality in this form, it is Nature" [SLII, p. 485; SLM, p. 843]. Lenin disregards the rest of the paragraph, stressing that the Smaller Logic[50] indeed ends with this sentence, and then remarks "Stretches a hand to materialism." Further: "It is remarkable: in the whole chapter on 'The Absolute Idea' there is almost not a single word on God (scarcely a 'godly notion' slips out even accidentally) and moreover—this NB—the chapter almost does not contain *idealism* specifically, but its main object is the *dialectic* method. The sum and summation, the last word and gist of the *Logic* of Hegel is the *dialectic method*—that is extremely remarkable. And another thing: in the *most* idealistic work of Hegel there is *most* materialism. 'Contradictory' but a fact" [LCW 38, p. 234].

That is true, but it is not the whole truth, or, to be precise, it is not the whole truth for *our* epoch. We needn't prove the materialism of Hegel, but rather the idealism (materialistic idealism, but idealism nevertheless) of Marx which has been so perverted by the Stalins, Maos, and Khrushchevs. When the "what happens after" revolution's success has become that monstrous opposite, state capitalism, it is "freedom," the "release," "the personal and free," the *truth* which rests upon "subjectivity alone" that comes to the forefront, and all else are but first negation which must again be transcended and "only by transcendence of this does there arise *positive* Humanism, beginning from itself." Our task is to concretize this, *just this* Marxist Humanism.

Yours,
Raya

Letter to Erich Fromm
(November 11, 1963)

Dear Dr. Fromm:

Two matters of unequal importance prompt this letter. One is purely informational. A paperback edition of my *Marxism and Freedom* will be out early next year with a new chapter ("The Challenge of Mao Zedong"*) and a new introduction which makes reference to your *Marx's Concept of Man*. In order to make room for the new chapter the publisher has made me sacrifice my

---

*In 1961 I first analyzed "Mao Zedong: From the Beginning of Power to the Sino-Soviet Conflict." It is this which I brought up to date as the new chapter in my book. I do not have a copy of this, but I do have a copy of the original article and will be glad to send it to you, should you be interested.

translation of Marx's Early Essays. I therefore refer them to your book, calling attention to the fact that the Moscow translation is marred by footnotes which "interpret" Marx to say the exact opposite of what he is saying, whereas in your work they have both an authentic translation and valuable commentary.

The second, and central, reason for this correspondence is a sort of an appeal to you for a dialogue on Hegel between us. I believe I once told you that I had for a long time carried on such a written discussion with Herbert Marcuse, especially relating to the "Absolute Idea." With his publication of *Soviet Marxism*,[51] this became impossible because, whereas we had never seen eye to eye, until his rationale for Communism the difference in viewpoints only helped the development of ideas, but the gulf widened too much afterward. There are so few—in fact, to be perfectly frank, I know none—Hegelians in this country that are also interested in Marxism that I'm presently very nearly compelled "to talk to myself." Would a Hegelian dialogue interest you?

I should confess at once that I do not have your sympathy for Existentialism, but until Sartre's declaration that he was now a Marxist, our worlds were very far apart. With his *Critique de la Raison Dialectique* (the Introduction of which has just been published here under the title, *Search For A Method*) I felt I had to take issue. I enclose my review of it, which is mimeographed for the time being, but I hope to publish it both in English and French.[52] In any case, it was in the process of my work on this that I reread the section of Hegel's *Phenomenology of Mind* which deals with "Spirit in Self-Estrangement—the Discipline of Culture." Not only did I find this a great deal more illuminating than the contemporary works on Sartre, but I suddenly also saw a parallel between this and Marx's "Fetishism of Commodities." With your indulgence, I would like to develop this here, and hope it elicits comments from you. (On p. 6 of my review you'll find Sartre's critique of Marx's theory of fetishism.)

The amazing Hegelian critique of culture relates both to the unusual sight of an intellectual criticizing culture, the culture of the Enlightenment at that; and to the historic period criticized since this form of alienation *follows* the victory of Reason over self-consciousness. Politically speaking, such a period I would call "What Happens After?" that is to say, what happens after a revolution has succeeded and we still get, not so much a new society, as a new bureaucracy? Now let's follow the dialectic of Hegel's argument:

First of all he establishes that "Spirit in this case, therefore, constructs not merely one world, but a twofold world, divided and self-opposed" [PhGB, p. 510, PhGM, p. 295].

Secondly, it is not only those who aligned with state power ("the haughty vassal" [PhGB, p. 528; PhGM, p. 307])—from Louis XIV's "*L'état c'est moi*" to the Maos of today—who, now that they identify state power and wealth with themselves, of necessity enter a new stage: "in place of revolt appears arrogance" [PhGB, p. 539; PhGM, p. 315], who feel the potency of his dialectic. It is his own chosen field: knowledge, ranging all the way from a criticism of Bacon's "knowledge is power" [PhGB, p 515; PhGM, p. 298], to Kant's "pure ego is the absolute unity of apperception" [PhGB, p. 552; PhGM, p. 323].[53] Here is why he is so critical of thought:

> This type of spiritual life is the absolute and universal inversion of reality and thought, their entire estrangement the one from the other; it is pure culture. What is found out in this sphere is that neither the concrete realities, state power and wealth, nor their determinate conceptions, good and bad, nor the consciousness of good and bad (the consciousness that is noble and the consciousness that is base) possess real truth; it is found that all these moments are inverted and transmuted the one into the other, and each is the opposite of itself. [PhGB, p. 541; PhGM, p. 316]

Now this inversion of thought to reality is exactly what Marx deals with in "The Fetishism of Commodities," and it is the reason for his confidence in the proletariat as Reason as against the bourgeois "False Consciousness," or the fall of philosophy to ideology. Marx insists that a commodity, far from being something as simple as it appears, is a "fetish" which makes the conditions of capitalist production appear as self-evident truths of social production. All look at the appearance therefore, the duality of the commodity, of the labor incorporated in it, of the whole society based on commodity "culture." It is true that the greater part of his famous section is concerned with showing that the fantastic form of appearance of the relations between men as if it were an exchange of things is the *truth* of relations in the factory itself where the worker has been transformed into an appendage to a machine. But the very crucial footnotes all relate to the fact that even the discoverers of labor as the source of value, Smith and Ricardo, could not escape becoming prisoners of this fetishism because therein they met their historic barrier.

Whether you think of it as "fetishism of commodities" or "the discipline of culture," the "absolute inversion" of thought and reality has a dialectic all its own when it comes to the rootless intellectual. Take Enlightenment. Despite its great fight against superstition, despite its great achievement—"Enlightenment upsets the household arrangements, which spirit carries out in the house of faith, by bringing in the goods and furnishings belonging to the world of the Here and Now." [PhGB, p.512; PhGM, p.296]—it remains "an alienated type of mind": "Enlightenment itself, however, which reminds belief of the opposite of its various separate moments, is just as little enlightened regarding its own nature. It takes up a purely negative attitude to belief." [PhGB, p. 582; PhGM, p. 344].

In a word, because no new universal—Marx too speaks that only true negativity can produce the "quest for universal" and hence a new society—was born to counterpose to superstition or the unhappy consciousness, we remain within the narrow confines of "the discipline of culture"—and this even when Enlightenment has found its truth in Materialism, or Agnosticism, or Utilitarianism. For unless it has found it in freedom, there is no movement forward either of humanity or "the spirit." And what is freedom in this inverted world where the individual will is still struggling with the universal will? Well, it is nothing but—terror. The forms of alienation in "Absolute Freedom and Terror" are so bound up with "pure personality" that I could hardly keep myself, when reading, from "asking" Hegel: how did you meet Sartre? "It is conscious of its pure personality and with that of all spiritual reality; and all reality is solely spirituality; the world is for it absolutely its own will" [PhGB, p. 600; PhGM, p. 356]. And further:

> What that freedom contained was the world absolutely in the form of consciousness, as a universal will. . . . The form of culture, which it attains in interaction with that essential nature, is, therefore, the grandest and the last, is that of seeing its pure and simple reality immediately disappear and pass away into empty nothingness. . . . All these determinate elements disappear with the disaster and ruin that overtake the self in the state of absolute freedom; its negation is meaningless death, sheer horror of the negative which has nothing positive in it, nothing that gives a filling. [PhGB, p. 608; PhGM, p. 362]

This was the result of getting itself ("the pure personality") in "the rage and fury of destruction"—only to find "isolated singleness": "Now that it is done with destroying the organization of the actual world, and subsists in isolated singleness, this is its sole object, an object that has no other content left, no other possession, existence and external extension, but is merely this knowledge of itself as absolutely pure and free individual self" [PhGB, p. 605; PhGM, p. 360].

I wish also that all the believers in the "vanguard party to lead" studied hard—and not as an "idealist," but as the most far seeing realist—the manner in which Hegel arrives at his conclusions through a study that the state, far from representing the "universal will," represents not even a party, but only a *"faction"* [PhGB, p. 605; PhGM, p. 360] (Hegel's emphasis). But then it really wouldn't be "the self-alienated type of mind" Hegel is tracing, through development of the various stages of alienation in consciousness, and Marx does it in production and the intellectual spheres that correspond to these relations.

It happens that I take seriously Marx's statement [in 1844] that "*all* elements of criticism lie hidden in it [The *Phenomenology*] and are often already *prepared* and *worked out* in a manner extending far beyond the Hegelian standpoint. The sections on 'Unhappy Consciousness,' the 'Honorable Consciousness,' the fight of the noble and downtrodden consciousness, etc., etc., contain the critical elements—although still in an alienated form—of whole spheres like Religion, the State, Civic Life, etc." [MECW 3, p. 332]. Furthermore, I believe that the unfinished state of Marx's Humanist Essays makes imperative that we delve into Hegel, not for any scholastic reasons, but because it is of the essence for the understanding of today. Well, I will not go on until I hear from you.

Yours,

Raya

NOTES

1. For an overview, see Kevin Anderson, "The Marcuse-Dunayevskaya Correspondence, 1954–79," *Studies in Soviet Thought* 38 (1990), pp. 89–109.

2. Followers of C. L. R. James.

3. Grace Lee developed this in some of her philosophic letters written to Dunayevskaya and James in 1949–50. Many of them can be found in *The Raya Dunayevskaya Collection*, pp. 1735–96 and pp. 9209–37.

4. The *enragés* were the most radical, intransigent wing of the French Revolution, who opposed even the Jacobins. Later, in 1968, the term was adopted by far Left French student activists at the University of Nanterre, such as Daniel Cohn-Bendit.

5. See C. L. R. James, *The Black Jacobins: Toussaint L'Ouverture and the San Domingo Revolution* (London: Secker and Warburg, 1938), in which Toussaint, a former coachman, is portrayed as the central figure in the Haitian Revolution. Text in brackets in this sentence added by editors.

6. Hegel.

7. Kant writes in his discussion of good will and the categorical imperative: "I need no far-reaching ingenuity to find out what I have to do to possess a good will . . . I ask myself only 'Can you also will that your maxim become a universal law?'" See his *Groundwork of the Metaphysic of Morals*, trans. H. J. Paton (New York: Harper & Row, 1964, orig. 1785), p.71. Hegel writes in his *History of Philosophy*, Vol. III, that with regard to the problem of duty and good will, "the defect of the Kantian principle of freedom is that it is indeterminate" (p. 246).

8. Socialist Labor Party, followers of Daniel DeLeon.

9. Dunayevskaya's lecture at Cooper Union, given on Oct. 27, 1960, was entitled "Intellectualism and Creativity in the USSR." For the text of the talk, see *The Raya Dunayevskaya Collection*, pp. 13036–42.

10. In Hegel's philosophical system, the stage of "Objective Mind" discusses ethics as

well as political institutions like the state, civil society, and the family, and always precedes that of "Absolute Mind." See especially his *Philosophy of Mind*.

11. Marx and Engels, *The Holy Family* (1845), MECW 4, p. 86.

12. Marx, "Critique of the Hegelian Dialectic" (1844), MECW 3, p. 336.

13. An apparent reference to Hegel's essay on Natural Law (1802), where Hegel writes, "The absolute moral totality is nothing else than a people." See *Natural Law*, translated by T.M. Knox with an Introduction by H.B. Acton (Philadelphia: University of Pennsylvania Press, 1975), especially pp. 128–29.

14. This and the next sentence refer to a brief discussion in the concluding pages of the *Phenomenology*, where Hegel implicitly critiques a number of previous philosophers, from Descartes through Schelling [PhGB, pp. 802–804; PhGM, pp. 488–90]. See also Dunayevskaya's discussion of this section in her 1960 notes on Hegel's *Phenomenology*, this volume, p. 46.

15. See Andy Phillips and Raya Dunayevskaya, *The Coal Miners' General Strike of 1949–50 and The Birth of Marxist-Humanism in the U.S.* (Chicago: News & Letters, 1984).

16. A reference to the June 17, 1953, East German uprising—for a discussion by Dunayevskaya, see *Marxism and Freedom*, pp. 249–52.

17. An apparent reference to Maurice Merleau-Ponty's *Adventures of the Dialectic*, published in France in 1955.

18. Wilhelm Windelband, whose *History of Philosophy* was first published in German in 1892, was a member of the neo-Kantian Marburg school and an associate of Heinrich Rickert. Dunayevskaya is alluding to Richard Kroner's introduction to Hegel's *Early Theological Writings* (Chicago: University of Chicago Press, 1948), where he writes, "In his *History of Modern Philosophy* Wilhelm Windelband says that the generation able to understand the *Phenomenology* has died out" (p. 43).

19. This is actually not a passage from Hegel, but from Richard Kroner, who was paraphrasing Hegel's comment in the Preface to the *Phenomenology*: "What in former days occupied the energies of a man of mature mental ability, sinks to the level of information . . . in this educational progress we can see the history of the world's civilization delineated in faint outline" [PhGB, pp. 89–90; PhGM, p. 16]. See Kroner's Introduction to Hegel's *Early Theological Writings*, p. 46.

20. See the "Letters on Hegel's Absolutes," this volume, chapter 2.

21. This appears as an ad from the publisher in the *American Economic Review*, Vol. XLVIII, no. 3 (June 1958).

22. The left-wing sociologist C. Wright Mills, the liberal historian Clinton Rossiter, and the French left-wing sociologist Serge Mallet.

23. Imre Nagy was the leader of Hungary's democratic revolutionary regime before the November 1956 Russian invasion, after which he was executed. The Petofi circle united a variety of intellectuals opposed to the totalitarian regime and helped pave the way for the 1956 revolution. These intellectuals discussed Marx's humanism, especially his *Economic and Philosophical Manuscripts of 1844*.

24. Published in *News & Letters*, May 1960, pp. 5, 7. Senghor, who espoused a version of socialist humanism, led Senegal to political independence from De Gaulle's France.

25. A reference to the first paragraph in the concluding Absolute Idea chapter of Hegel's *Science of Logic*, in which he writes: "The Absolute Idea has now turned out to be the unity of the Theoretical and the Practical Idea; each of these by itself is one-sided" [SLII, p. 466; SLM, p. 824].

26. See p. 30, note 8.

27. See Lenin, "The Victory of the Cadets and the Tasks of a Workers Party" (1906) [LCW 10, p. 254.].

28. See George Kline, "'Fundamentals of Marxist Philosophy,'" in *Survey*, no. 20 (October–December 1959), p. 60, as well as Gustav Wetter, "The Soviet Concept of Coexistence," ibid., pp. 19–34. Wetter, a Jesuit specialist on Marxism, was author of *Dialectical Materialism* (London: Routledge, 1958, orig. 1952). Kline, an American philosopher, was co-editor of *Russian Philosophy*, 3 vols. (Chicago: University of Chicago Press, 1964). *Soviet Survey*, sometimes referred to as *Survey*, was an American academic journal devoted to Russian studies.

29. Dunayevskaya discussed Soviet philosopher V. A. Karpushin's interpretation of Marx's *1844 Essays* in a section of *Marxism and Freedom* entitled "Communism's Perversion of Marx's Economic-Philosophic Manuscripts" [M&F, pp. 62–66].

30. Hegel concludes the chapter on "The Absolute Idea" differently in the Smaller Logic than in the *Science of Logic*. The Smaller Logic ends with the phrase, "We began with Being, abstract Being: where we now are we also have the Idea as Being: but this Idea which has Being is Nature" [EL ¶244]. The *Science of Logic*, on the other hand, ends by posing "the next resolution of the pure Idea" which follows Nature—the *Philosophy of Mind*. Whereas Lenin quotes the phrase from the Smaller Logic in his *Philosophic Notebooks*, he dismissed the conclusion of the *Science of Logic* as "unimportant."

31. Hegel's "First System" refers to his initial outline of the *Philosophy of Mind* (Spirit), written in 1803–4, but not published until the twentieth century. It is now available in English in *System of Ethical Life and First Philosophy of Spirit*, ed. and trans. H. S. Harris and T. M. Knox (Albany: SUNY Press, 1979). There, Hegel wrote: "The more machinelike labor becomes, the less it is worth, and the more one must work in that mode . . . the value of the labor falls; the labor becomes that much deader, it becomes machine work, the skill of the single laborer is infinitely limited, and the consciousness of the single factory laborer is impoverished to the last extreme of dullness" (pp. 247, 248). This passage was discussed by Marcuse in his 1941 *Reason and Revolution*, pp. 78–79 and later by Dunayevskaya in *Marxism and Freedom*, pp. 33–34.

32. Ludwig Feuerbach (1804–72) was an important Young Hegelian philosopher whose *Essence of Christianity* (1841) contained a materialist critique of Hegelian idealism and of religion. In *Philosophy and Revolution* (1973), Dunayevskaya analyzed the differences between Marx and Feuerbach in 1844, writing that "Feuerbach's influence on Marx" is, here quoting Nicholas Lobkowicz's words, "Far less than is generally believed" (p. 302). In addition to the opening paragraphs of the "Critique of the Hegelian Dialectic" (1844), see Marx's "Theses on Feuerbach" (1845), in MECW 5, pp. 3–5, for the types of critiques to which Dunayevskaya is referring here.

33. Dunayevskaya characterized the *Critique of Political Economy* as "an *application* of di-

alectics to political economy, instead of the *creation* of the dialectic that would arise out of the workers' struggles themselves" [M&F, p. 87].

34. In *Capital*, Vol. I, Marx writes: "In any given branch of industry, centralization would reach its extreme limit if all the individual capitals invested were fused into a single corporation. In a given society this limit would be reached only when the entire social capital was united in the hands of either a single capitalist or a single capitalist company" [MCIF, p. 779; MCIK, p. 688].

35. The last two sentences of this paragraph refer to interpretations of *Capital*, Vol. I, which Dunayevskaya elaborated at greater length, especially in chapter 8 of *Marxism and Freedom* (1958) and in chapter 10 of *Rosa Luxemburg, Women's Liberation, and Marx's Philosophy of Revolution*.

36. This refers to Bukharin's opposition, in 1916–21, to the right of nations to self-determination.

37. For Lenin's discussion in his Will of how Bukharin "never fully understood the dialectic," see LCW 36, pp. 594–96.

38. Ivan Ilyin, author of *The Philosophy of Hegel as a Doctrine of the Concreteness of God and of Man* (in Russian). Ilyin stressed that the word concrete included in its Latin origin the concept of growth and also described Hegel's standpoint in a rather unusual fashion as the "empiric concrete." For a discussion, see Dunayevskaya's letter of July 6, 1949 to C. L. R. James, in *The Raya Dunayevskaya Collection*, p. 1670.

39. For a discussion, see Phillips and Dunayevskaya, *The Coal Miners' General Strike of 1949–50* (1984).

40. Dunayevskaya's critiques of Russian theoreticians' distortions of Marx's theory of value originally appeared in the *American Economic Review*, Vol. 34:3, September 1944, pp. 531–37. Her critique drew responses from Oskar Lange, Leo Rogin, Paul Baran and others, to which she responded in the *AER* of September 1945. Her original critique has been reprinted in Dunayevskaya, *The Marxist-Humanist Theory of State-Capitalism* (1992).

41. While studying Hegel, Lenin asked the *Granat Encyclopedia* if he could augment the section on "dialectics" of his article "Karl Marx." He did so in a letter dated Jan. 4, 1915 [LCW 36, p. 317].

42. A reference to Luxemburg's *Accumulation of Capital* (London: Routledge, 1951, orig. 1913). For an elaboration of Dunayevskaya's critique, see her "Marx's and Luxemburg's Theories of Accumulation of Capital, its Crises and its Inevitable Downfall," chapter three of *Rosa Luxemburg, Women's Liberation, and Marx's Philosophy of Revolution*.

43. Merleau-Ponty, "Marxism and Philosophy," *Politics*, No. 4 (1947), pp. 173–76. This special issue of *Politics*, an independent leftist journal edited by Dwight MacDonald, was devoted to "French Political Writing," and also included articles by Jean-Paul Sartre, Albert Camus, Simone de Beauvoir, and Georges Bataille. Another translation of Merleau-Ponty's article was included in his *Sense and Non-Sense* (Evanston: Northwestern University Press, 1964). Bracketed page references in the text are to the 1947 translation.

44. From Marx, "Theses on Feuerbach" (1845), MECW 5, p. 5.

45. From Marx, "Contribution to the Critique of Hegel's *Philosophy of Right:* Introduction" (1843), MECW 3, p. 180.

46. Eduard Bernstein, a major figure in German Marxism and Engels' literary executor, was termed a revisionist after he called in 1898 for the socialist movement to abandon both the perspective of revolution and the dialectic method.

47. In his 1825–26 *Lectures on the History of Philosophy*, Vol. III (Berkeley: University of California Press, 1990), Hegel critiques Fichte as follows: "Fichte's form of the I [ego-eds.] involves ambiguity between 'I' as absolute I . . . and 'I' in my particularity." (p. 259).

48. Lenin's *Philosophic Notebooks* were published in English for the first time in Dunayevskaya's *Marxism and Freedom* (1958). See also chapter 10 of *Marxism and Freedom*, "The Collapse of the Second International and the Break in Lenin's Thought."

49. A reference to Guinean President Sekou Touré's (1922–84) immensely popular refusal to join the French community, resulting in severe economic and political pressure from De Gaulle's France.

50. Toward the end of his "Abstract of Hegel's *Science of Logic*" (LCW 38) Lenin begins also to use Hegel's Smaller Logic (*Encyclopedia Logic*) alongside the Larger Logic (*Science of Logic*). For Dunayevskaya's subsequent critique of Lenin's position, see part V, chapter 17, below.

51. Marcuse, *Soviet Marxism* (New York: Columbia University Press, 1958). Dunayevskaya's critique, "Intellectuals in the Age of State Capitalism," appeared in *News & Letters*, June-July, August-September 1961, and was reprinted in *The Marxist-Humanist Theory of State-Capitalism* (1992).

52. See Jean-Paul Sartre, *Critique of Dialectical Reason* (London: NLB, 1976, orig. 1960); *Search For a Method* (New York: Knopf, 1963). Dunayevskaya's critique, "Sartre's Search for a Method to Undermine Marxism," appeared as a weekly "Political Letter," dated September 26, 1963. See also "Jean-Paul Sartre: Outsider Looking In," chapter 6 of *Philosophy and Revolution*.

53. In Kant "pure ego as the absolute unity of apperception" refers to the organization of the categories of thought by the agency of self-consciousness, the "I-think." For Hegel's detailed discussion of Kant's concept, see the section "On the Notion in General" in his *Science of Logic* [SLII, pp. 217–30; SLM, pp. 583–96].

PART III

THEORY AND PRACTICE AT A TURNING POINT, 1964–71

~

CHAPTER SEVEN

Letter of October 27, 1964,
to Herbert Marcuse

*In 1964, after having broken off their correspondence three years earlier, Dunayev-
skaya resumed her philosophic letters to Herbert Marcuse. This was a period in
which her development of Marxist-Humanism reached a critical turning point. As
her work on* Philosophy and Revolution *progressed, Dunayevskaya embarked on
new studies of the Hegelian dialectic and challenged the emerging new generation of
radicals to grapple directly with a philosophy of revolution. Her increasing emphasis
on the need to fill the theoretical void in the radical movement is reflected in this letter, which presents a brief outline of what later became the first part of* Philosophy
and Revolution *(1973). The original can be found in* The Raya Dunayevskaya
Collection, *p. 13898.*

Dear HM:

Since you once asked me why I "translate" Hegel when I know "the original" (Marx) well enough, I assume you thought that since my writings and
activity were political my veritable obsession with Hegel's Absolute Idea was
. . . an obsession. I am exaggerating, of course, but it is only because I hope
you'll permit me to write in this informal way an outline of a chapter of my
new work (which I now lean to calling "Philosophy and Revolution") that
deals with "Why Hegel? Why Now?"[1]

The chapter is to have three subsections: "Marx's Debt to Hegel"; "Lenin's
Ambivalence toward Hegel and the Shock of Recognition"; "The Philosophical Problems of Our Age." The first subsection will connect with *Marxism and
Freedom* but greatly expand why Marx couldn't "shake off" Hegel as easily as
he shook off classical political economy; once he transcended it, then his "economics" became, not a new political economy, but Marxism, a philosophy of

human activity. This was true in every single respect from the theory of value and surplus value, through rent as a "derivative" rather than making the land-lord class as fundamental a one as the new capitalist class,[2] to capital accumulation and the "law of motion" bringing about its "collapse." In all these, labor was seen as the living subject bringing all contradictions to a head and making socialism "inevitable"; at no point were economic laws independent of human activity. Regarding the Hegelian dialectic, on the other hand, despite its *re-creation* in Marxism, or what you laughingly refer to as "subversion," that is to say, transformation of dialectic from "a science of logic" to "a science" of revolution, his "attachment" to Hegel remained. This was not because Marx began as a "Left Hegelian," nor even because the Hegelian dialectic speeded him on his own voyage of discovery ("thoroughgoing Naturalism or Human-ism").[3] Indeed, when his break first came from Hegel, he *used* classical politi-cal economy to counterpose reality to "idealism," especially of the Proudhon-ist variety.[4] And yet the adieu to classical political economy was complete; the adieu to Hegelianism was not.

Take the very first, and most thorough and profound attack on Hegel's *Phi-losophy of Right*—the very critique which led to nothing short of his greatest dis-covery—the materialist conception of history.[5] A lesser man, a lesser Hegelian than Marx, would at that point have finished with Hegel. Marx, on the con-trary, proceeded to the critique of the *Phenomenology* and the *Encyclopedia*. When he broke off at the last section on the *Philosophy of Mind* [in his 1844 "Cri-tique of the Hegelian Dialectic"] to stick with what he called "that dismal sci-ence"—political economy—and engage in class struggle activities, revolutions, First International, which took the rest of his life, he still hungered to return to a presentation of "the rational form of the dialectic." Indeed, at *every* turning point, he returned to "the dialectic." You recall how happy he sounded, in 1858, in his letter to Engels when he explained that he "accidentally" came upon his library of Hegel's works and there got some "new developments" which are help-ing him complete the *Contribution to the Critique of Political Economy* (and of course you can see the results all through the *Grundrisse*).[6] Again, in 1861–63 when he first reworked it as *Capital* and made the most crucial decision on the economics presentation—not merely to break with Ricardo on land rent but to take out from Volume I all that would become Volume III and thus eliminate all relations between landlords and workers, leaving them with "pure" capital-ists alone.[7] And yet again, in 1866, when he restructured *Capital* to include [the chapter on] "The Working Day" and actually broke with the very concept of theory, both the move to the profound analysis of reification at the point of pro-duction and the fetishism of commodities, again illumined by the real Paris Commune, were still in the tightest wrappings of Hegelianism.[8]

This is exactly why Lenin wrote that it was impossible to understand *Capital*, "especially its first chapter" without the *whole* of the *Science of Logic*. And in [*Capital's*] first chapter, when you need Hegel most is where Stalin, in 1943, decided to make his theoretical break by asking that that chapter be eliminated in the "teaching" of *Capital*.[9] And, again, the last writing we have from the pen of Marx ("Marginal Notes on Wagner" and the analysis of the critiques of his own economics)[10] the constant repetition is to "the dialectic." In a word, Marx never forgot his indebtedness to Hegel because it was not a debt to the past, but a vital, living present expressing as well the pull of the future.

The new I wish to bring in here will bring in a justification for the abstractness of Hegel since there are points, critical points, turning points, when the abstract suddenly can become the concretely universal. *Capital* is concrete, an empiric study, a phenomenological as well as logical-economic analysis which "exhausts itself" in the one topic it is concerned with: capitalism. But [Hegel's] *Logic* is "without concretion of sense" [SLI, p. 69; SLM, p. 58], "applies" to all sciences, factual studies, so that when a sudden new stage is reached, and the old categories won't do, there is always a new set of categories in the *Logic* as you move from Being to Essence to Notion. That is why Lenin, who *long before* he knew the whole of the *Logic*, knew the whole of *Capital*, and wrote most profoundly of *all* the three volumes, nevertheless, suddenly, when the ground gave way before him as the Second [International] collapsed, found the new "only" in the *Logic*. That is to say, that abstract category "unity, identity, transformation into opposite," and such others as "self-transcendence" meant something so new to him also in the understanding of *Capital and* its latest stage, imperialism, that he was willing to say none, including himself, had understood *Capital* at all before that specific moment of grasping the Doctrine of the Notion in general, and the breakdown of opposition between objective and subjective that he got from the Syllogism[11] in particular.

What I am trying to say is that the minute *the actual* cannot be expressed in old terms, even when these terms are Marxian ones, it is because a new stage of cognition has not kept up with the new challenge from practice which *only philosophy* seems capable of illuminating. Old, abstruse, abstract Hegelianism made [Lenin] see what the concrete terms in *Capital* did not— that monopoly capital was not only a "stage" of centralization of capital, but a "transformation into opposite" which demanded a total reorganization and undermining of old categories, including that of labor.

This section should lead to the second subsection on Lenin's ambivalence [on] Hegel, both before the shock of recognition in 1914 and, unfortunately, after that shock, at least publicly. The duality in Lenin's philosophic heritage can no longer be put into a footnote, as I did in *Marxism and Freedom*. This ambivalence has allowed the Chinese as well as Russian Communists to per-vert Marx's Humanism by quoting *both* Lenins alongside of each other as if they were one unchangeable Lenin who never experienced a sharp break with his own philosophic past. Once, however, this is cleared, it is precisely Lenin, the Lenin of 1915–24, who allows us to jump off from the 20th rather than the 19th century precisely because his most startling and most meaningful aphorisms were expressed in "Subjective" *Logic* and he is so enthusiastic as he equates (with literal equation signs) subjectivity with freedom. You'll recall also that Lenin's Notebooks stress that *philosophy* (*Logic*, 1813) expressed "the universal movement of change" [LCW 38, p. 141] first, and only afterwards (1847) did Marx express it in politics (*The Communist Manifesto*) whereas natural science ([Darwin's] *Origin of Species*, 1859) came still later. And while it remains for our age to concretize Lenin's restatement of Hegel's apprecia-tion of the Practical Idea "precisely in the theory of knowledge" for "Cogni-tion not only reflects the objective world, but creates it," it is Lenin who put out the marker: "The continuation of the work of Hegel and Marx consists in working out dialectically the history of human thought, science and technol-ogy" [LCW 38, p. 147].

It is obvious to you, I am sure, that I do not take your position on technol-ogy. I am so Hegelian that I still consider that subject absorbs object, and not object subject which then becomes *its* extension.[12] My preference of "ontol-ogy" to "technology" in the age of automation may be said to be due to the awe I feel when confronted with the dialectic of human thought, but this would not be the whole truth since human thought is inseparable from human activity and both result from the overpowering urge to freedom. Allow me, please, to express this within the range of the types of cognition in the dialectic itself:

In inquiring cognition we face an objective world without the subjectivity of the Notion. In synthetic cognition, the objective world and subjectivity coexist[13] (and like the fragility of "peaceful coexistence"[14] which fears move-ment, so in this laying of the objective world and subjectivity side by side, there can be no transcendence). But now watch: the idea of cognition and the practical idea no sooner unite, than we are ready for the plunge to freedom.[15] Hegel begins at the bottom of page 475 [SLII, p. 475; SLM, p. 833], to review again, not dialectic "cognition" but the Absolute Method, the form of the Absolute Idea, the new stage of identity of theory and practice that we have reached as we leave behind the previous forms of cognition. (Don't forget, either, that twelve short pages after we view "the objective world whose inner ground and actual persistence is the Notion," we reach "the turning point" [SLII, p. 477; SLM, p. 835] and learn that the "transcendence of the opposi-tion between the Notion and Reality . . . rest upon this subjectivity alone.")

It appears to me also that Hegel is right when he feels it absolutely necessary that the method begin with abstract universality, abstract self-relation, the in-itselfness of the Absolute (SLII, pp. 469–72; SLM, pp. 827–30), which leads, through "the concrete totality which . . . contains as such the beginning of the progress and of development," to differentiation *within* what I would call the achieved revolution. I might as well here continue politically for I see Hegel as he finishes with subjective idealism to be finishing with reformism for whom the goal is always in the future, and shifting all his attack on the intuitionalists—Jacobi, Schelling, Fichte, especially Jacobi whom he calls a "reactionary" (*Encyclopedia*, ¶76)—or the type of *abstract* revolutionism for whom, once an "end," a revolution has been reached, there is no more negative development or mediation. All that, to *them*, that seems to be done is an organization of what has been achieved and they go at this organization in so *total* a way that they choke the spontaneous revolution, and with it all further development, to death.

Hegel, on the other hand, moves from the overcoming of the opposition between Notion and reality, resting on subjectivity alone, to paeans about "personal and free" [in the *Science of Logic*][16] and "self-liberation" in the *Philosophy of Mind*, which, to me, is the new society and not the return to metaphysics. I'm not saying that Hegel may not have consciously striven to return to metaphysics (he certainly did so personally in his apology for the Prussian state), but neither those who have tried to make him out a complete reactionary as a statist, nor those who have welcomed his glorification of "revealed religion" (Christianity in general, Lutheranism in particular, or, as Bochenski, the angry Thomist, to "deism" if not veritable atheism[17]), can explain away why his Absolute is always Idea and Mind and not *just* God. Very obviously, the ideal toward which humanity, the humanity of the French Revolution, was striving, and the ideal [of] the philosopher Hegel who wished thought to *be* so great a determinant in the transformation of reality, were not so far apart as either the ordinary or scientific mind wish to make out. For the Notion is revolutionary politics, not in the narrowly political sense as "the organizational vanguardists"* would have us believe, but in the sense of 1917: free creative power.

(When Marx is in the market he laughs at, and links, "Liberty, Equality and Bentham"[18]; when he is in proletarian politics, it is "*thinking*, bleeding Paris," so flushed with excitement at the "incubation of a new society,"[19] that it fails to see the counter-revolution, etc., etc.)

---

*The finest attack on organizational vanguardists I have read anywhere is in Hegel's *Philosophy of Religion*, in his attacks on the Church—and what a totalitarian, monolithic party medieval Catholicism was! Whoever it was who said that he who turns his back on history is doomed to relive it must have our age in mind!

The greatness of the "Absolute Method," the Hegelian dialectic, is its universals, and their distinction from the generalizations of abstract understanding, so that each universal—Being as such, Essence as such, Notion as such—is a *new* category, a leap into individuality "purified of all that interferes with its universalism" [PM, ¶481]. As Lenin put it in his Notebooks [1914–15], "The forming of abstract notions already includes consciousness of the law of the objective world connections . . . so the simplest forming of notions (judgments, syllogisms, etc.) signifies ever deeper knowledge of the *objective* world connections. Here is where we should look for the significance of Hegel's *Logic*" [LCW 38, pp. 178–79]. The important point, it seems to me, is that the new categories arise at certain turning points in history when men have such overwhelming experience that they are sure also they have found "the truth," so that, as Lenin put it, "the consciousness of the law of the objective world connections" becomes transmuted into "new categories of thoughts, or knots."[20] In a word, the Doctrine of Notion is revolutionary politics, contains the categories of Freedom, overcomes the opposition between subject and object, theory and practice, notion and reality, reaches "the second negation," not only "in general" as revolution against existing society, but in particular as the new society which has not merely the stigma of the old from which it came, but is too ready to transform the universal into a "fixed particular" (be that state property or plan or even soviet)[21] instead of *moving* forward to the abolition of the division between mental and manual work, the new *human* dimension.

That is why the polemic in the Doctrine of the Notion is so contemporary, so relevant to our day. When Hegel strikes out against transforming the universal into a fixed particular, it doesn't really matter whether he has in mind, in one case, socialism, and in the other statified property. We gain an illumination when he speaks of the universal needing to be posited as particular, but if the particular is posited as the universal, it becomes isolated or, to use Marx's expression, gains "the fixity of a popular prejudice" [MCIF, p. 152; MCIK, p. 69].

Even the bourgeois philosopher, John Findlay (whose book, despite its barbs against Marxists, I found fascinating) sees the revolutionary in Hegel as he concludes his praise of him "as the philosopher of 'absolute negativity,' the believer in nothing that does not spring from the free, uncommitted, self-committing human spirit" (*Hegel: A Reexamination* [New York: Oxford University Press, 1958], p. 354).

We certainly can no longer, as did Lenin, keep "our" philosophic notebooks private. We live in the age of absolutes, and freedom as the innermost dynamic of both life and thought demands the unity of philosophy and revolution.

Yours,
Raya

NOTES

1. In its 1973 published form, part one of *Philosophy and Revolution*, comprising chapters on Hegel, Marx and Lenin, was entitled, "Why Hegel, Why Now?"

2. This refers to Marx's critique of Ricardo, who argued that rent is based on differential rates of fertility of land. Marx argued that rent also exists independent of such differential rates of fertility (i.e., "absolute rent") in that rent is derived from the movement of capitalist production as a whole.

3. Marx, "Critique of the Hegelian Dialectic," MECW 3, p. 336.

4. Pierre-Joseph Proudhon (1809–65), French utopian socialist whose ideas Marx initially found to have some compatibility with his own. But in 1846 in his *Poverty of Philosophy* Marx began what was to become a lifelong series of criticisms of Proudhonism. For Dunayevskaya's analysis, see M&F, chapter 2.

5. See Marx's *Critique of Hegel's Philosophy of Right*, ed. with an introduction by Joseph O'Malley (Cambridge: Cambridge University Press, 1970).

6. See Marx's letter to Engels of January 14, 1858, MECW 40, p 249.

7. In the summer of 1862, in the course of working on vol. I of *Capital*, Marx broke with Ricardo's theory of ground rent, which held that rent is explained on the basis of differentials in the fertility of land. By 1863 he decided to move the discussion on ground rent from Vol. I to Vol. III of *Capital*. Dunayevskaya discussed the significance of this in a letter to C. L. R. James of January 24, 1950: "[With] 1863 . . . Capital, *Landed* Property, Wage Labor was compressed into its essentials: *Capital* and its opposite, wage labor, was to be considered in its properly subordinate place under capitalism; while landed property, as rent, was entirely discarded to be considered first as a 'particular form' of surplus value, or rather of the *transformation* of surplus value into rent, in Vol. III where forms of appearance are considered" [*The Raya Dunayevskaya Collection*, 1728].

8. For Dunayevskaya's more detailed discussion of the significance of the changes in both the 1861–63 and 1866 drafts of *Capital* in deepening Marx's concretization of the Hegelian dialectic, see chapters 5–7 of *Marxism and Freedom*, and *Rosa Luxemburg, Women's Liberation, and Marx's Philosophy of Revolution*, chapter 10.

9. See Dunayevskaya's discussion of this in *The Marxist-Humanist Theory of State Capitalism*, pp. 83–88.

10. See *Marginal Notes on Adolph Wagner's Lehrbuch der politischen Ökonomie*, MECW 24, pp. 531–62. For Dunayevskaya's early translation of this, done in the 1940s, see *The Raya Dunayevskaya Collection*, p. 1899.

11. This refers to the syllogism of "Universal-Particular-Individual." See p. 12, note 16.

12. An apparent reference to Marcuse's *One-Dimensional Man* (Boston: Beacon Press, 1964), where he wrote of the "integration" of labor with capital under automation: "The organized worker . . . is being incorporated into the technological community of the administered population" (p. 26). Dunayevskaya cites and critiques this passage in her review article, "Reason and Revolution vs. Conformism and Technology," *The Activist*, 11 (Fall 1964), pp. 32–34.

13. "Synthetic cognition" is discussed in the second section of the penultimate chapter of Hegel's *Science of Logic*, "The Idea of Cognition."

14. A reference to Nikita Khrushchev's adoption of the policy of "peaceful coexistence" between the superpowers during the Cold War.

15. The "Idea of Cognition" and the "Practical Idea" are dealt with by Hegel, in successive order, in the concluding chapters of "The Doctrine of the Notion" in his *Science of Logic*. The unity of the two is reached in the work's final chapter, "The Absolute Idea."

16. See SLI, p. 477; SLM, p. 835.

17. I.M. Bochenski, a Thomist philosopher, was a Sovietologist and author of numerous works on Marxism and European intellectual history, such as *Contemporary European Philosophy* (Berkeley: University of California Press, 1951), as well as a founder of the journal *Studies in Soviet Thought*.

18. See Marx's *Capital*, Vol. I [MCIK, p. 195; MCIF, p. 280].

19. See Marx's *Civil War in France* [MECW 22, p. 341].

20. This apparently refers to Lenin's comment, near the start of his 1914–15 *Philosophical Notebooks*, that "Logic is the science not of external forms of thought, but of the laws of development 'of all material, natural, and spiritual things,' i.e., of the development of the entire concrete content of the world and of its cognition, i.e., the sum-total, the conclusion of the *History* of knowledge of the world." Lenin then quoted Hegel's comment, "In this web, strong knots are formed now and then, which are foci of the arrest and direction of its life and consciousness" [LCW 38, pp. 92–93].

21. A reference to Leon Trotsky's insistence that the abolition of private property meant that Stalinist Russia, though "deformed," represented a "higher" form of social development than capitalism. For Dunayevskaya's critique of what she considered to be the flawed methodology which led Trotsky into such a "fixed particular," see *The Marxist-Humanist Theory of State-Capitalism*, chapter 4 of *Philosophy and Revolution*, and "Leon Trotsky as Man and as Theoretician," with a Comment by Ernest Mandel, *Studies in Comparative Communism*, Vol. X: nos. 1 and 2 (Spring/Summer 1977), pp. 166–83.

CHAPTER EIGHT

~

Hegel's Dialectic and the Freedom Struggles of the 1960s

Lecture in Japan on Hegel

In the winter of 1965–66 Dunayevskaya traveled to Japan and held discussions and meetings with student youth, auto-workers, antiwar activists, and Marxists grouped around the anti-Stalinist Zengakuren movement. At the culmination of her tour, she delivered the following lecture on Hegel on January 2, 1966 in Tokyo to a group of activists and writers from Zenshin, one of the more important anti-Stalinist organizations of the Japanese New Left. The transcript of the lecture has been slightly edited for clarity. The original can be found in The Raya Dunayevskaya Collection, *p. 9697.*

The first thing I want to make very, *very* clear is that Hegel has a validity all his own, and I want to talk about Hegel *today*. I am going to take [that] for granted instead of reiterating all the time about what Marx did or did not take from Hegel. I am taking for granted that we are Marxists. I am taking for granted we are proletarian revolutionaries. I am not going to waste one minute's time on that. If I mention Marx at all, and even Lenin, it is only in passing in order to show what each of them took from Hegel and what we have to take from Hegel. But on the whole, the subject is Hegel and no one else.

The second thing I want to make clear is that insofar as I am concerned, Hegel is his major works—that is to say, *Phenomenology of Mind, Science of Logic, Philosophy of Mind.* I am not the least bit interested in Hegel's reactionary ideas about the state, and I will not consider them. Marx said all that needs to be said on that question in his criticism of Hegel's *Philosophy of Right.* His analysis that what is a legal essence [in Hegel] is actually a legal superstructure, which reveals the actual state of production and the economy, led

137

to his discovery of the materialist foundation of history. After that, everything he criticized or took over from Hegel was as a revolutionary materialist. I am disregarding also Hegel's politics, which has absolutely nothing to do with us and is not what we take from Hegel. I am even disregarding his lectures on *The Philosophy of History* and *The History of Philosophy*, because they were his way of giving examples that his great ideas are not as abstract as they sound. But I am not interested in how he applied his ideas. I am interested only in the actual logic and movement of those ideas, which he set forth not only as a summation of all that went before, but as both the prerequisite for Marxism and as something we have not yet exhausted. We first have to work out many of the ideas before we can transcend them.

Hegel's *Phenomenology* was a summons to grasp the spirit of the times. It was a demand that the philosophers give ear to the urgency of the times. It was a challenge to all philosophers who came before him, and the greatest in modern times was Kant. [Hegel was saying] that 15 years have passed since the French Revolution and yet philosophy was still using their old categories. He was saying we have to stop using the conclusions of other philosophers, rightly or wrongly, as a pillow for our own intellectual sloth, our own laziness to meet the challenge of the times. A new thing has happened in the world in a 15-year period which compels a new stage of cognition. And a new stage of cognition means both a summation of what has happened up to your time and a recognition of the pull that the future has on you. We want to see how Hegel answered that summons and what it means for our day.

The greatest and first total statement was the *Phenomenology of Mind*. It was to have been an introduction to [his philosophic] system, but it actually [contains] his whole work. I want to make sure we realize that Hegel, despite the abstract language, is actually dealing with 2,500 years of the development of thought, mainly but not completely of Western civilization. Since we cannot go into great detail, I want to make an abstraction in one sense and follow what Marx does in Vol. II of *Capital*. Marx there says that the only way we will see the law of motion of capitalism is if we disregard anything that interferes with just two departments of production—means of production and means of consumption (constant capital and variable capital, etc.).[1] All of the time it is just two, like two classes. [Likewise,] I want to take the six stages of Hegel's development of Consciousness, Self-Consciousness, Reason, Spirit, Religion, and Absolute Knowledge [in the *Phenomenology* and divide it] into *two* major stages. One will be Consciousness, Self-Consciousness, and Reason, which I consider the development from 500 BC (slave society and Aristotle as the ancient world's greatest philosopher) to Reason, which is capitalism, the French Revolution, Lutheranism, and Kant-Hegel. The second department is all the rest: Spirit, the various forms of Alienated Spirit, and why there is still alienation even though you have reached Religion and Absolute Knowledge. So there are two departments: 1) Consciousness, Self-Consciousness, Reason; 2) Spirit, Religion, and Absolute Knowledge.

In this first department, what we have all previously emphasized from Marx is the section on "Lordship and Bondage," because we recognized that Hegel is showing the lord could demand anything and the slave was completely negative and yet the slave is the one who gets a mind of his own. The slave getting "a mind of his own" was one of the bases of Marx's great development of proletarian consciousness. (Marx didn't know Hegel's First System and all his works on labor itself.[2]) It was our proof that Hegel really did have in mind reality, which includes class structure, and he really did have in mind history, which includes labor's condition. However, today that is not the point I want to emphasize. The reason I do not want to emphasize this is because I am tracing the dialectic of thought itself. The importance of that section on "Lordship and Bondage" is that although the slave has obtained a mind of his own, there are a lot of questions about whether he will get to freedom. In becoming conscious, not only of the world and yourself as opposites, but of yourself gaining Self-Consciousness and going further to try and break down this division between opposites and yourself, you are so thrilled that you have this idea that it could become, in his words, "just a piece of cleverness, and not yet the mastery over reality" [PhGB, p. 240; PhGM, p. 119]. And because it could be just a piece of cleverness and not yet the mastery over reality, you can become just an alienated soul.

I want to take up one more thing in [the section on] Self-Consciousness, which is Stoicism. Hegel shows he is opposed not only to the alienated soul who has obtained this piece of cleverness (what we could call a Beatnik today); he is opposed to what other philosophers consider a great stage, Stoicism. Everybody thinks you are great if you are a Stoic, [since] you can withstand all sorts of things, unpleasant as well as great. [But Hegel] says, don't forget that Stoicism arises when there is universal slavery. Instead of being for the Stoics he is against them. He wants to emphasize two things. Stoicism arose because you as an individual recognized that this is a horrible society—there was universal slavery and bondage—and you *couldn't overcome* it. You weren't, so to speak, what we would call a mass movement to overcome it. So you as an individual becoming a Stoic was actually a rationalization, as in developing such stupidities as, "a philosopher is free even though he is in chains." Hegel shows that everything that appears great is only a further stage of alienation. Even when he comes to Reason (which I will get to in a moment) that will be so. The important thing about not stopping at "Lordship and Bondage" (on which we always previously have stopped) is that getting a mind of one's own is only a beginning. Hegel is showing that if you are going to master reality you are going to have to get a lot further than that. Attempts to master it by such thought as Stoicism, even when they are correct either as individual integrity or in the criticism of the rest of society, are absolutely insufficient.

Therefore I am stressing that what came out after the slave obtained a mind of his own was a new stage of, so to speak, retrogression, where the intellectuals all began saying: "Oh great, the Roman Empire is dead, but just by behaving ourselves either as stoics or in some other form, we will overcome it." And even when overcoming it sparked a real revolution, whether one considers that to be Christianity or the actual French Revolution, that is still not the answer. That is why I do not want to stop at gaining a mind of your own. I want to stress that what Hegel saw in the Alienated Soul, Stoicism, and Skepticism, were good little paths on the way to Reason that were not the answer.

As against using the conclusions of other philosophers as a pillow for intellectual sloth, Hegel is showing a new movement of history. There was an actual revolution. It broke down everything, smashed it to smithereens and started something new. And the people who did this great thing (Robespierre and the others) recognized Reason as their deity. And yet what happened? Why did the Terror follow? Why did Napoleon follow? Why didn't we yet get to the Millennium? Hegel sees Reason as a very new high stage, but [neither it nor] Spirit, which is our next department, answers or kills off all the alienations of society. It just brings them to a higher stage. So Reason ends this first great department of the *Phenomenology* on this movement from 500 BC to the French Revolution.

Now we come to department II, the central core. Everybody says, "Well if you have come to Spirit, why are there still Alienated Souls?" The alienated souls, Hegel says, have moved to a higher development, in Alienated Spirit. The higher development is that man has achieved this revolution, but he begins to identify himself either as faction or as person with the state. [Hegel has] a tremendous attack on the state—never mind that he was a Prussian philosopher. He attacked it thoroughly, totally and completely—even any future state that would come between the person and his development. There isn't a single person on our stage today, whether you take Mao, Fidel Castro, or any other person, that you cannot find described in the [section on] Alienated Spirit.[3] It is about what happens when there is a new revolution and yet somehow there is a transformation in the relationship between reality and thought in such a way that you begin to identify yourself with the state or with a single faction. You begin to have as big a Reign of Terror[4] in thought as the revolution had in action. The Reign of Terror in thought [is] against the other, the new opponents, etc. And the new opponents even include religions, although Hegel himself was a Christian (I will come to that next).

His criticism of what he called "the discipline of culture" [PhGB, pp. 507–610; PhGM, pp. 296–363] is the foundation for Marx's criticism of the superstructure. This man was no proletarian revolutionary, but he criticized all culture as having been very good for fighting against superstition and that sort of thing, but it now has imprisoned us by what Marx called the fetishism of commodities.[5] I would go so far as to say that the whole of Hegel's three volumes on the *Philosophy of Religion* are the greatest attack on the so-called vanguard party that we have ever seen. Hegel does with the church, though he is a Christian, what we want to do against the Stalinist party. He is saying, "Look at that, Christianity came in because finally we saw that, as against only a few being free who were great enough to be philosophers, Jesus insisted that man as man is free. But this one little Church, the Catholic Church, said they were the only interpreters and would not let us have a direct contact with God." Here he is supposed to be a Christian, a Lutheran that corrected such excesses both in the Catholic Church and the Terror of the French Revolution, and yet Hegel comes down and says this is not it—I have to go to philosophy. That is the basis for all the attacks on Hegel as being a hidden atheist. But the point we are trying to stress by now being in department II is that Spirit is still alienated and in the discipline of culture. Religion has been perverted and [so] man, not the Church, must decide as to what will finally evolve. It brings us to the final stage of Absolute Knowledge.

He comes to Absolute Knowledge and says: Look, this is history. This has moved in such and such stages as the phenomena of the spirit of man. Now there is also the science of this spirit, whether in religion or in actual science, and these will unite to form Absolute Knowledge. The Absolute Knowledge of science and history uniting as one becomes the transition point for the *Science of Logic* and the *Philosophy of Mind*, because everything always ends in some Absolute. One is Absolute Knowledge in the *Phenomenology*, then we have Absolute Idea in the *Science of Logic*, and then Absolute Mind in the *Philosophy of Mind*. But it is always moving in this direction.

Now Hegel comes to the *Science of Logic* and begins to talk not in stages of consciousness, as in the *Phenomenology*, but in actual philosophic categories. Each category takes up a whole stage of civilization in the same manner as each stage of consciousness. Because we are hurried in time I am not going to deal with either Being or Essence. I will go directly to "The Doctrine of the Notion" or of Freedom, and especially its last section, "The Absolute Idea." "The Doctrine of Notion" is in actuality the objective and subjective way to get to the new society. And it is this which Lenin grasped in 1915. When he saw that Hegel himself used the expression "or of Freedom" he was so thrilled he kept saying, "so what has the Absolute Idea to do with it?"[6] But when he came to the Absolute Idea itself, he didn't have so much against it either. He grasped it because we had reached an entirely new stage of development in economics, politics, etc. Lenin was compelled to return to the *Logic*, not only [because of] the betrayal of the Social Democracy or the near betrayal of his own comrades, but because he began to stand in awe of thought. He said, "Oh, my God, look at what thought does—it actually not only reflects the world but creates it. Look at what this man could have foreseen. Why didn't we see all this?" And Lenin began to try to break down the stages of Cognition, Analysis, Understanding, Reason. What are the stages of Judgment? What are the stages of Syllogism? How does the Universal of Socialism and the Particular of its appearance in any one state, a worker's state, a transitional society, all merge in this big revolution I want? What hit him was the sudden realization that Hegel is so great that it sums up a whole stage. For Hegel was the most materialist of all idealistic philosophers and Marx the most idealistic of all materialistic ones. (I will soon go over the people who are trying in an academic way to do something [with Hegel] and not getting there, precisely because they do not have the proletariat in mind [and] also do not stand in awe of thought, even though they are philosophers.)

Both Marx and Lenin, even though Lenin went further in the Absolute Idea, happened to have stopped in the Absolute. Marx said on the one hand it doesn't mean anything because Hegel returned to a closed system of thought, but on the other hand it does mean something because Marx was always returning back to it. But as it happens [Marx's 1844 "Critique of the Hegelian Dialectic"] breaks off at a certain paragraph at the very beginning of the *Philosophy of Mind*, the section which begins the Absolute.[7] When Marx finishes [his analysis of] the *Phenomenology of Mind* and deals with Absolute Knowledge, he tries to take Hegel from a different angle. He goes through Hegel's whole system, quotes two paragraphs from the *Philosophy of Nature* [and then goes] into the *Philosophy of Mind*, where the manuscript breaks off. And that is the problem of our age.

One of the central points in the Absolute Idea, just before Hegel reaches what we call the "second subjectivity," is a sentence which reads "The self-determination in which alone the Idea is, is to hear itself speak" [SLII, p. 467; SLM, p. 825]. Everybody knows what self-determination is to nations, but they don't know what self-determination means to ideas. Lenin grasped it because he was so deeply immersed in the self-determination of nations as an impulse to bring the proletarian revolution. He saw that the self-determination of ideas also has various stages of development and breaks into two. There is a movement *from* practice, [whose self-determination] is to hear itself speak. It comes, so to speak, elementally in the proletariat, as instinctive. And there is a movement from theory which doesn't come so elementally and may have many pitfalls. At this point, where the theoreticians have to listen to the masses, the question is how will the two unite?

Now at this point Hegel suddenly makes a lot of jokes. He begins to laugh at syllogisms, because you know everybody says that Hegel is supposed to stand for a Thesis, Antithesis, and Synthesis—and that is a lot of nonsense. He doesn't stand for any such formal triad. He makes a lot of jokes about people who construct mechanically. He says it could be three, four, or five. Since every beginning is a result of some other mediation, he says in essence that the unity occurs in subjectivity alone. It therefore isn't really your first negation of the thing, but the second negation [which is decisive].[8] I cannot go into all of the details of this now. But I want to stress that in the last two pages of the chapter "The Challenge of Mao Zedong" in *Marxism and Freedom*, instead of a conclusion, I give an idea of what I am going to develop in *Philosophy and Revolution* concerning "two kinds of subjectivity."[9] The first is the petty-bourgeois kind like Mao's; the second, real kind comes from the proletariat. But actually in *Marxism and Freedom* I just note it; it becomes my problem now with *Philosophy and Revolution*. The new, the greatness, the problem for our age is this second [kind of] subjectivity. In other words, how does this unity [of the theoretical and practical Idea] resolve itself in this second subjectivity?

Marcuse and the other academic Marxists approach this stage [of Hegel's dialectic] and just give up.[10] They think they are great materialists when they do so, but they are not. They say [Hegel's concept of] the Absolute Idea is the result of the fact that he lived in a pre-technological age where mental and manual labor were so far separated. They say [that with the Absolute Idea] Hegel ran back, so to speak, to what was before the beginning of industrialization. I completely and totally disagree with that because what Hegel ran back to was the state, not the Absolute Idea. The one theoretician I consider the most serious [on this] is Karl Löwith, who is a Christian.[11] He said: that is all that Hegel deserves, because he wasn't, so to speak, a true Christian. He laid the foundation for Marx, for atheism, for all that we have suffered since. So Marx is the true inheritor and God be with you if that is what you want.[12] Marcuse, because he considers himself a Marxist (and academically he is one) is trying to say: 1) The Absolute Idea is pretechnology. 2) We have to forget that part and take reality. And to him reality is that the proletariat is impotent and hasn't done the revolution for him, has not proved itself, has not made the revolution Marx had predicted. 3) He does recognize the second [kind of] subjectivity, but he interprets it as the intellectual who will do it and bring you to the new stage. It is against these three serious arguments that I want to show what I feel is the problem of the Absolute Idea.

I want to discuss it all within what we call "the historic barrier." In other words, you come to the end of all you have to say because history has now presented you with new problems. On the other hand, why is it that certain people who are not as great as Marx or Lenin, but by living in a different historic age, are compelled to deal with these problems? For example, whether or not Marcuse considers me a romantic, his Introduction to *Marxism and Freedom* (which was not reproduced in the Japanese edition) said in essence that I am great in the analysis of Marx as Marx and there has been nothing as original since the Lukács period.[13] But when it comes to all this great mass of material I have accumulated in Part I to deal with the reality of today,[14] he disagrees with it, and mainly it revolves around the role of the proletariat. So I am a romantic. Regardless of his position that I chose to believe in the proletarian revolution, the truth is that the intellectual, including the Marxist intellectual, has not been able to break down either the humanism of Marx or the fact that [Marx's 1844 Manuscripts] broke off at the Absolute Idea. The new stage for the few of us who were trying to do it came from the masses. It was the miners' strike [of 1949–50], all this upheaval in [and after] World War II.[15] Hegel has a word for it, when he says the compulsion of thought to proceed to these concrete truths demands a new stage in philosophic cognition. The new stage comes only when your philosophic categories just don't answer what has come from below. Hegel, the idealist, recognizes that fact, while these so-called materialist Marxists, including the highest of them, Marcuse, do not.

So I want to end on what I began—the need to give ear to the urgency of the times and the summons to recognize the spirit of the age by recognizing that this second [kind of] subjectivity must again be broken into two: 1) What the proletariat is going to do. They are going to do it anyway, so we better begin listening. 2) The other is what theoreticians must do. Their task isn't ended because the impulse comes from below. They have to first begin to work it out, and not just to satisfy themselves with quick political answers. And the working out of that subjectivity of the theory of our age of the Absolute Idea, in the concrete form of philosophy, theory and politics, means that we are just beginning. There is no point in saying anything about realizing philosophy if we haven't done that. That is why that is going to be the central point of *Philosophy and Revolution*.

Presentation to the Black/Red Conference

At the end of 1968, as she was drafting Philosophy and Revolution, *Dunayevskaya issued a call for a conference on the Black revolt then sweeping American soci-*

ety. Held on January 12, 1969, in Detroit, Michigan, the Black-Red Conference featured the following lecture by her. As Charles Denby, author of Indignant Heart: A Black Worker's Journal, *put it in his opening remarks to the conference: "This is the first time that such a conference of Black youth, Black workers, Black women, and Black intellectuals will have a chance to discuss with each other as well as with Marxist-Humanists, who lend the red coloration not only for the sake of color, but for the sake of philosophy, a philosophy of liberation. We hope that this will not be a one-shot conference, but a continuing dialogue of Black and white, workers and intellectuals, adults and youth, men and women, that will lead to a true unity of action and thoughts"* (The Raya Dunayevskaya Collection, p. 4338).

Let's talk—not about the moon and the stars and the planets, and little homilies from outer space, as if we don't have enough trouble on this earth—but about what is a great deal more important: the people, especially the working people, especially the Black working people.

If the Administration thinks that because we have some astronaut heroes we will thereby forget about war, racism, poverty, and the world that needs some reshaping, we will have to tell it to him like it is. Because first and foremost is MAN and LABOR. It is not the moon that came down to look at us. It is we who went up to look at the moon. And the hardware that went into that is not only a problem of science. In fact, the reason you can go to the moon, but can't solve the housing problem right here in a little slum, is because you have always had, in class society, this division between science and life. And Marx saw long, long ago—some 130 years ago—that if you're going to have a different principle for life and for science, you will be living a lie.[16] That is just what we have been living all these years. And there are reasons why there is this great division.

All of the history of mankind can be developed just on the history of labor. Even if we exclude science (which we can't), it would still be a fact that it is not only the hardware to go to the moon that labor has built. Labor has built the primary things on earth, which really make the world go around: food, shelter, clothing. Labor has built everything. But don't think that just because the working man has produced all of this, the only thing he can do is manual labor. That is what the capitalist wants you to think.

There is another kind of labor besides manual—mental activity. And this mental activity is not restricted to scientists or to other intellectuals. In fact, what they think generally comes from this movement from below. What is most important of all is that workers think their own thoughts. And the thoughts that workers think are the thoughts that *move* the world.

It is all summarized in one word: freedom. There is no such thing as thought that has any significance unless it is the thought of how to get freedom. All of man's history is various stages of the struggle for freedom. And though capitalism may be better than slavery, we still have a long way to go. So—first, we have labor as a manual activity; second, labor as a mental activity. What gets everything changed is thinking how and by what means you can move to freedom, and masses actively moving toward freedom.

Besides labor and thought, we have some colors that are not accidental which we should talk about today: Black and red. Black and red stand for the actual movement of society.

Let's start in 1831, Nat Turner's Revolt. That was the same year some whites in New England started a paper called the *Liberator,* stimulated by the movement of the slaves in the South. The coalescence of these two forces led finally to the Civil War. But that's not why I'm choosing 1831 for today's discussion. I'm choosing it for Nat Turner's Revolt—he tried to be free and he was hanged for it—and I'm choosing it because that was the year that a man named Georg Wilhelm Friedrich Hegel died. He was a German philosopher who dealt only with thought in ivory towers, yet what Nat Turner did and thought is related to Hegel, though they were of course quite unknown to each other.

Last year a prize was given to a white Southerner for a book about Nat Turner—a horrible book.[17] A lot of black intellectuals got very angry and answered the author, Styron. Theirs is not a bad answer—but what is really great is Nat Turner's own Confessions. They were made to a white racist, and Turner stressed the fact that he had the right to fight for freedom. He had heard voices and they told him to do it. Now there was another revolt that took place at the same time, and the white rulers were sure that there had been a conspiracy. Turner denied it: "I see sir, you doubt my word. But cannot you think the same idea which prompted me might prompt others as well as myself to this undertaking?"[18] Here is a supposedly unintelligent man, and he recognizes that as great as is his own struggle for freedom, it is impossible that he, though he heard the voices from heaven, thought of it alone. He is absolutely sure that the Spirit, meaning the objective movement for freedom, and the people fighting for freedom are the same thing.

How these two movements—objective and subjective, idea of freedom and people fighting for freedom—function together, is what we are going to be learning today. It is called *dialectics.* We will see how they come to jam up against each other, and coalesce or not coalesce, depending on whether you win or lose. And if we can find out what it was when the Greeks established it, and what it was when Hegel established it, and what it is with Marx—we will know all there is to know about philosophy.

Dialectics originally meant "dialect" or talking—and the Greeks had a very high opinion of it if it was the philosophers who were doing the talking. They had the first democracy for the citizens, but not for the slave laborers. The idea was that if you, the philosopher, talked to someone, and he had an idea that opposed yours, and you then contemplated, you would finally come up with an idea that was totally different than either one originally was. And it is true that you get some movement that way, but because the talk that went on was the talk of only intellectuals, it was contemplation alone or the viewing of things, not the doing of anything.

What was different about it when Hegel got to reestablish it for our age? We had moved from 500 B.C., when there was a slave society, to 1789 when there was a French Revolution, the greatest revolution that had ever happened. And the people—the *sans-culottes*, the *enragés*, the indignant hearts— had something to say about things. They were saying they were glad they got rid of Louis XVI, but what did they get with the overthrow of the monarchy? Why was there still a distinction between "passive citizens" and "active citizens"—especially when the so-called "passive citizens" were the ones who were doing all the work? They wanted to know why they all shouldn't be able to discuss things.

This French Revolution was such a challenge to the people in the ivory towers, like Hegel, that he couldn't help reflecting it. So that when he began to talk about dialectic, it didn't mean only thoughts bumping up against each other, it meant action. It meant development through contradiction, the development of ideas, and of actual history, and of the class struggle. It was this *development*—not a process of adding up how many are here in this room and contrasting that with how many voted for [George] Wallace,[19] but of seeing what the people represent and how much motion they can get going when the idea of freedom inspires them—that is of the essence.

Nevertheless, since Hegel did restrict himself to ideas, even though his philosophy reflected actual history, something more was needed. When Nat Turner led his rebellion and Hegel died in 1831, Marx was 13 years old. He didn't know anything about either one of them. But 13 years later, in 1844, he created the greatest philosophy of freedom, humanism. And he built it on the dialectic. But he said ideas don't float in air. There are people who have ideas. Marx included man himself, men who think, who struggle for freedom, who try to unite the idea of freedom with the actual struggle for freedom. He refused to bow either to capitalism or to communism. He said that in place of either the profit motive of capitalism, or the collective form of property of communism, the important thing was the *self-development of man*.

In creating this philosophy he heard about and collaborated with the

Abolitionists, Black and white, in this country who were struggling against slavery. Some so-called Marxists said well, of course, they were against slavery—but the slaves just wanted the freedom to be exploited by the capitalist.[20] The [so-called Marxists] thought they were much wiser because they wanted freedom from the capitalists, too. Marx showed them that they were crazy because freedom and thinking are always *concrete*. And in the actual dialectic of liberation—that is, in the actual relation of thought to act, in the actual development—you have to arouse and elicit from the population many, many forces. The greatest force is labor, but there are others, such as the youth, and in America the greatest of these other forces is the Black masses. Marx told the whites who thought they were superior because they were free: Look at you, you don't even have a national labor union—and you can't organize one because labor in the white skin cannot be free while labor in the black skin is branded. This wasn't only "dialectics" or "philosophy." This was the way it was. We finally had the Civil War in the United States and the first national labor union came after that.[21]

It was by establishing labor as the center, and the unity of thought and practice as necessary, and by jamming up all these new ideas into a new philosophy of liberation that Marx was able to establish the First Workingmen's International.

Okay. Now let's get down to writing our new book, *Philosophy and Revolution*. To do that, there are two more dates, this time in the 20th century, that we have to consider, before we get to the 1960s and the "Economic Reality and Dialectics of Liberation" we came to discuss. One of those dates is 1920; the other is 1936.

First, 1920. Remember, please, that past history is also present history. All history is contemporary, because we always see past history with the eyes of today. It is important to remember that, because today it is so hard to get communication started between Black and red. The Blacks who don't want to talk to the white imperialists wind up not talking to any whites. And the tragedy is that it inhibits their struggle, not the other way around—because you have to have the majority of the people to win.

Harold Cruse has just published a book called the *Crisis of the Negro Intellectual*.[22] He thinks the trouble is that the Blacks don't remember their history, the real history of the 1920s when we had the beginnings of the nationalist movement with Marcus Garvey and what was then called the "new Negro." He feels if they remembered their history, they would have their real rights. He is right and wrong at the same time. It is true you have to know your past—but the intellectuals who write today and try to tell you that W. E. B. Du Bois and Garvey were great, but Marx is not, were as far removed from Garvey and the Black masses in 1920 as anyone could possibly be.

The Garvey movement was the greatest movement America had ever seen in mass numbers. Garvey organized some six million people. The Blacks who thought the South was horrible and came North, found that the North was the same thing in a different form. The Negro was supposed to be impossible to organize. Garvey showed that was a lie. (I know people don't like the word now, but it was Garvey who fought very hard to make everyone spell Negro with a capital N. They would never have won that fight without his movement.) But because they didn't have a total philosophy, and because they were so frustrated, where did it all end? "Back to Africa." It was fantastic. They were all Americans. This is where they had labored all their lives.

What is important to remember is that the Black intellectuals didn't want to have anything to do with Garvey and his followers. The intellectuals considered them all ignorant. Du Bois even went so far as to go to the State Department to demand Garvey's deportation. Who made people look at Garvey as a revolutionary? As important? As doing more to shake up capitalism in America than all the white and black intellectuals together? Lenin.

Lenin said it was a start. It was shaking up the regime. Not only that. He said to look around the world.[23] He saw China and began to wonder if we could overthrow imperialism through the "National Question." So the actual movement, which was spontaneous as all great movements are, and which showed the true revolutionary role of the Black people in this country, revealed that the only people who were trying to get a discussion started between the Black masses and the Black intellectuals were a few white radicals who kept saying: For heaven's sake, talk to each other—this is the real revolution.

Du Bois was a very great researcher, but he never understood the Black masses—or the white masses either, because labor didn't mean anything to him. When you remember Garvey, remember that the gulf was the gulf that separated the Black masses from the Black intellectuals; remember that the few beginnings that were started then, were started by the Marxists. Cruse is trying to say that the "division" was all the Communists' fault. But the Communists of the 1920s were not the Communists we saw later.[24] The Communists had strength in 1920 because they understood the revolutionary forces. The Blacks left the Communists later—and the Black intellectuals didn't. The Black masses left the Communist Party during World War II. The minute Russia was in the war, [the Black masses were] supposed to wait until after the war was over to fight for their rights so as not to hurt the war effort. The Black masses said: I've heard that story all my life; it's never today, it's always tomorrow. And they tore up their party cards.

The other year we have to consider is 1936 when the CIO was built. Today everybody knows the CIO as a great bureaucracy, but in 1936 and 1937 it was a great movement. The first industrial union couldn't have been built without the Black workers, and everyone knew it. That was when you had the unity of white and Black. You can't rewrite history. Being against white imperialism doesn't mean that all of white labor and the radicals are the same. What the Black nationalist leaders are forgetting is plain history. Once you have that many Blacks in the same union, you can't go around pretending you're not all in the same shop. If you're going to have a revolution, you'd better have it together, or you won't have it at all.

It's one thing to say you have to operate with a Black caucus demanding various things, like upgrading and so on, but it is quite another to consider that the main enemy is not Ford or Chrysler or GM, but only Reuther.[25] You have to recognize *when* Reuther became the enemy.

Now I think we have enough of history and theory (in the 19th century we saw it through Hegel and Turner and Marx; and in the 20th century through Garvey and Lenin and labor and the Marxist-Humanists of that time) to get down to the dialectics of liberation today, in the 1960s.

Philosophy and Revolution has three parts. Part I is called "Why Hegel, Why Now?" and takes up the dialectic as the algebra of revolution, the methodology of what man has done in fighting for freedom. Once you get three things, you have the essence of it: 1) the dialectic—the actual development, through actual class struggle, through actual contradictions; 2) the right Subject—who is resolving these contradictions? Marx said it was the class force, but helped by other forces such as minorities, the Black people, and the youth; 3) how does this movement from below for freedom, from practice, unite with the movement that comes from theory? In other words, the relationship of theory to practice.

In the chapters on Marx and Lenin I take up concretely how Marx did it for his era, and how Lenin did it for his. Up to a certain stage it seemed easy, because it was only capitalism they thought they had to fight. But Lenin found, with the outbreak of World War I, that it was his co-comrades who betrayed. The fact that every unit in life has its opposite within itself, and that the counter-revolution came from within the revolution—that was the shock and the recognition that made Lenin prepare himself correctly for what was to come later. Lenin saw the aristocracy of labor as a transformation into opposite that meant a break-up within labor. But he also saw that the way to transform that into *its* opposite was by going lower and deeper, and uniting with the minority groups. That became the "National Question."

Part II of the book is called "Alternatives." Those that are the most dangerous are again those from within the Marxist movement. Lenin had to deal with the betrayal of the Second International. We have to deal with the betrayal of the Third. The three alternatives are Mao Zedong (and Castro); Leon Trotsky; and Sartre. The first two are from the Marxist movement. The last is from the intellectuals not connected with a party.

The important point to keep in mind insofar as Mao and Trotsky are concerned is that they are revolutionaries. Why did they have the wrong answers nonetheless? When you meet a new problem you can either stand still and say: this is what Trotsky did, what we call getting stuck in the fixed particular; or, as with Mao, you can say: we can't wait a thousand years, we're going to have to find some shortcuts, power comes from the barrel of a gun. But the shortcut has proved in life to be the longest way around. As far as Sartre is concerned, we find that what he wound up saying was that it was fine for all the workers to go into the Communist Party, but he wanted his own freedom as an intellectual—and you get the concept of the vanguard party coming from the man who didn't belong to any party.

What you have to ask yourself is how it happens that Blacks should follow Mao or Castro? Is it sufficient to hate and want to get rid of just your own specific capitalist? American imperialism is the enemy of Mao and Castro—and it is your enemy. But is that sufficient reason to join with Mao and Castro? Or do you have to do what Marx did and raise up an entirely new banner that will say: No, I'm not only opposed to American imperialism, but also to Russian Communism and Chinese Communism—I want an entirely new society.

Now part III is the section that isn't yet written. It is to be called "Economic Reality and the Dialectics of Liberation" and it is on two levels. One is the world level, which takes up the relationship between the advanced countries and the technologically underdeveloped countries. You see that here it is in the 1960s and never has America been so rich and powerful—in fact, the whole world is divided into two great nuclear powers, so that we may all get blown up. And here are the African Revolutions. They didn't have arms, let alone nuclear arms; they didn't have power, not even industrial power. But they dared and they won.

De Gaulle got so furious when Sekou Touré defied him and dared to tell the mighty De Gaulle: "No, we don't want to be part of the French empire," that he even tore out the telephone wires to show the Africans they could not do without the white man. Why did Touré win anyway? First of all, he had the masses with him, the entire people. And they all said "No." They dared—and a lot of white teachers and such said, "We'll help." And a lot of other Blacks said, "If Touré can win, why can't we?" That's why the Blacks are called the vanguard. The great force of an idea gained them freedom and reshaped the continent.

Why then have so many African nations moved back to a military regime by today? Or taken a side either with American imperialism or the Russian counterpart? That's where the objective movement comes in. The strength and power of these two nuclear titans will get you sucked into the vortex, *unless you rely only on the masses that brought you to liberation*. Once they got power—the Nkrumahs[26] and Tourés—they said, we're just as smart as the whites and we can play politics, too. The minute they began to play that kind of politics, they were lost. They stopped having a continuing dialogue with their own masses.

But we don't have to go to Africa to see another great form of the dialectics of liberation. We have the Blacks right here in this country. And if they shake up the world right here, all the world can be free. It was the recognition that in the most affluent society there was the greatest poverty, that in the most military power there was a revolutionary force, that made everyone turn to see what those few little Black students in North Carolina were doing when they demanded to be served at a lunch counter and refused to move.[27]

Between 1960 and 1965 the spontaneous movement of the Black youth particularly, and some labor, was the moving force. It really all started with the Montgomery Bus Boycott—and again we were the only ones who recognized it at that time, just as we were the only ones who recognized what the Mau Mau in Africa represented in the 1950s. We printed *People of Kenya Speak for Themselves* in 1955 because we recognized that the Blacks in Africa starting to throw out the white imperialists had started a new page in history that would reshape the world entirely, which it did, and in the shortest period of time, at that.[28] In 1957, in *Marxism and Freedom*, we said the two greatest forces in the world for liberation were the Hungarian Revolution and the Montgomery Bus Boycott in Alabama.[29] There was a great deal of ridicule at that time for the plane on which we had placed the Montgomery Bus Boycott. Nobody laughs at it now.

After the spontaneous movement of the Black students between 1960 and 1965, there was not only a great deal of movement on the part of white students running South to help—but there was a movement of thought, as well. Each by itself is one-sided, theory and practice. And the thinking did not begin on the question of violence or nonviolence. All the arms are in the hands of the capitalists. It is not the movement of arms that reconstructs society; only the movement of the masses does that.

The first movement on the part of Rev. King toward Humanism was when he brought the question in, in relation to the Jewish philosopher Martin Buber, who had expressed the idea that unless you recognize that it's not things, but human relations which are the crux of everything, you will never get anywhere.[30] (Rev. King didn't mention the Abolitionists, or the movement right in this country, much less Marxism.)[31]

Yet, when he moved from the South to the North, he didn't know how to function with Northern labor. His philosophy got stopped because it had to have a relationship to labor, and to Marxist Humanism as a philosophy of liberation. What came to take its place? Black power.

Now Black power may be good, but it isn't going to get you your freedom. In fact, the capitalists are trying to use Black power against you. They want to put up a few little Black capitalists and say they've done their part. No, it has to be a new unity of theory and practice, and of white and Black. Black power can be corrupted like everything else. And you can be sure that capitalism will try to buy out whomever it can.

Instead of going back to the real roots of Marxism in this country, instead of trying to work out a new relationship, there is too much trying to grab a shortcut through Castro or Mao. The most disgusting thing I ever saw occurred in New York right after Rev. King was murdered. There was the first new appearance of Black and white unity in the demonstrations after it had pretty much stopped in 1965. And right at that point, William Epton, the Maoist, got up to say: We don't mourn Rev. King—he was an obstacle to our freedom.[32] For someone who is Black to dare to do that, shows that his theory comes from a foreign land, indeed. (All the Blacks who think they're different by following Maoism should read Mao's own thought. He is so used to using black as evil, that every other word is black guards, black counter-revolution . . . with all he wants to do in Africa, somebody should at least tell him that Black is beautiful.)

Trying to be against all whites is to fail to see your real roots, and to fail to work out a new coalescence of black and white, and theory and practice. It is the present period I want you to talk about. And in becoming theoreticians, in creating a new philosophy by speaking for yourselves, you have to recognize that you speak, not as individuals (though the individual is very great) but as the new forces that are necessary—what Marx called the new passions for reconstructing society on totally new, truly human, beginnings.

Logic as Stages of Freedom, Stages of Freedom as Logic, or the Needed American Revolution

The following text is another example of Dunayevskaya's effort to relate the categories of the Hegelian dialectic to the pressing needs facing the radical movement. It consists of the final part of a Perspectives Thesis presented to a national convention of News and Letters Committees on August 30, 1969. Entitled "The Needed Ameri-

can Revolution," its third and final part on philosophy is excerpted here. The original can be found in The Raya Dunayevskaya Collection, *pp. 4385–06.*

This is the year we are to finish *Philosophy and Revolution*, which will mark 1970, the year of the 100th anniversary of Lenin's birth, as a turning point in American Marxism. As a little anticipation of the new book, I would, therefore, like to end with showing [Hegel's] *Logic* neither as only philosophic categories, nor even as Marxian economic categories, but as stages of revolution.

Since absolute negativity, or second negation, has the positive in it, the *continuous* revolution, and since this is a movement *from abstract to concrete*— from Universal to Individual, through Particular—all stages of revolution can be seen *at nodal points where "I"* [Individual] *overcomes "P"* [Particular], or, as we know it more precisely, the fixed particular of Trotskyism or nationalized property=workers state.[33]

Now then, let's take a stage from each of the three parts of *Logic* and see whether we can catch the *mass movement* in its dialectical development. How do we get to see the movement of thought, and the movement in revolution?

The *Science of Logic*, as you know, has three books, the first of which is the Doctrine of Being. We don't get the categories—Universal, Particular, and Individual—until the last book,[34] but they dominate everything—the movement from abstract, universal, to concrete, the individual. In the Doctrine of Being, you have three sections: Quality, Quantity, Measure.[35]

U=: *Quality*—a someone, a something. The Emperor, the King. *The One.*

P=: The quality gets transformed into its opposite, *Quantity*—*many ones.* People sometimes think that quantity is below quality. No, it's above it, because before you had only one, and now you have many. You have *some* democracy. Don't forget, Hegel's theory always starts at 500 B.C.

I=: Now comes *Measure*, the highest form of being. You're on the threshold, you're going into essence. What is he talking about, the "Measure of Man"? *Greek Democracy*, the polis, they had slave labor, but it was the foreigners who were slaves. The Greeks were free. So what we have is the stages of freedom: from kingdom to limited democracy, to the democratic state. You can take any section and begin saying what is the Universal, what is the Particular, what is the Individual, and you will discover that it's a stage of freedom. Hegel wasn't joking when he said all of history is the history of the consciousness of freedom.

> Book I—Doctrine of Being
> U—Quality = Emperor = One
> P—Quantity = Many = some = Democracy
> I—Measure = Greek democracy = Polis

Please note that P is the historic period, a particular, determinant *mediation*, not a description of particulars as used in the common terminology of brown hair or blue eyes or cuddly creatures to children, but the type of Particular which contains self-movement *if* it is to move to the "I," and not retrogress into a fixed particular like nationalized property.

Remember also, the "equivalent" to Being in Marx's *Capital*—"Commodities and Money," or the market place. Marx said, as he was departing form the market place (i.e., the sphere of "Liberty, Equality, Property, and Bentham") that now, as he enters the factory, the worker looks as if he expects nothing but a hiding, and that's exactly what he gets [MCIF, p. 280; MCIK, p. 195].

Lenin's profound grasp of the universal, and the individual *in* Hegel made him realize, however, that all the contradictions of capitalism are included in the simple exchange of commodities. Which is why he insisted that none of the Marxists had understood *Capital,* because it is impossible to understand chapter I for anyone who has not plodded through *the whole* of the *Logic*.

Now take the Doctrine of Essence and see the movement there through Identity, Difference and Contradiction. Or take the higher stage of Ground as classical political economy saw it—labor as *source* of value—through Essential Relation—an actual production relationship, in a hell of a battle with capitalism. You [then] reach Actuality—the class struggle itself, the crises— Hegel's first statement of the Absolute and Marx's Absolute General Law of Capitalism.[36]

This leads us to our age of Absolutes or book III, the doctrine of the Notion, that is to say the *objective and subjective ways of how a new society is born.*

In the case of Hegel, he was talking about the French Revolution. You had overthrown the king, you had a new society, you had freedom, and then you wound up with Napoleon, and not with a new society. So Hegel moved back to Mind. Notice that the movement from practice is in theory itself. When he goes over to Nature, he returns to Mind. You have a unity of what he had seen in Mind, checked against Practice, and now he will unite the two.

It didn't make any difference whether it was Being or Essence and now is Notion, it is Universal, Particular and Individual. Hegel says if you want to be bored to death, start with the syllogism the way metaphysics presents it. They tell you "all men are mortal," "Gaius is a man," therefore, "Gaius is mortal." What's new about that? It doesn't explain anything. It's been made into a cliche, it doesn't prove anything. As against boring metaphysics, let us see live rational dialectics [SLII, p. 306; SLM, p. 669].

Let's come to our age. What was Lenin's Universal? The new for Lenin was not *Imperialism*, but *State and Revolution*, and the Universal was "To a Man"—production had to be organized and run "to a man." It was a great Universal but it was general. What was the Particular that put it into effect, so to speak? You had a Russian Revolution and it nationalized all property—so that was your Particular. It was very good to begin with, but was it the concretization of all that "to a man" meant? Trotsky got stuck in this fixed Particular. The Individual, the concretization, was Workers' Councils and Intellectuals' Councils. But to make "to a man" be all that Lenin meant it to be—*the abolition of any division between mental and manual labor*—is no easy task. Yet that is our aim, and that is our new universal—the concrete that "to a man" should have been. And it is this dialectics of liberation that *Philosophy and Revolution* tries to answer.

Boring	U—"TO A MAN"
Metaphysics	P—Nationalized Property
vs.	
Live rational dialectics	I—Not only Workers' Control of Production but an absolute end to the division between mental and manual labor
"All Men are Mortal"	
vs.	
Dialectics of Liberation	

The root of *all* totalitarianism is the reduction of the "I" to Ego as petty-bourgeois self-expression, or Kantianism, away from "I" as concrete in the Hegelian sense of total; in a word, seeing in "I" a limitation instead of a RELEASE of mass creativity.

Now, how can we make it even more concrete on the very specific paragraph in the Absolute Idea regarding second negativity? Hegel says that second negativity "is the turning point of the movement of the Notion . . . for the transcendence of the opposition between Notion and Reality, and that unity which is the truth, rests upon this subjectivity alone" [SLII, p. 477; SLM, p. 835].

In the second edition of *Marxism and Freedom*, in the Mao chapter, we speak of two kinds of subjectivity.[37] It is true, but not concrete enough. So let's turn to Hegel: "Insofar as the pure idea of Cognition is enclosed in Subjectivity, and therefore is an impulse to transcend the latter. . . . (it) becomes the *beginning of another sphere and science*" [SLII, p. 485; SLM, p. 843].

Marx, in the last part of *Capital*— the [section on the] accumulation of capital—said something similar when he comes to the "Absolute General Law of Capitalist Accumulation"—the unemployed army. He notes there that he will only indicate that which will be developed in Volumes II and III. The "indication"—the "negation of the negation," "the new passions and new forces" [MCIF, pp. 929, 928; MCIK, pp. 837, 835]—is what it not only took two volumes to expand, but he again did not get to finish the final chapter [of Volume III], "Classes."

Neither did Lenin get to develop cognition as a "creative force," except in the rather hieroglyphic manner in which he referred to Bukharin as not having fully understood "the dialectic."[38] Our heritage is thus dual. We must make it single, concrete, totally philosophic, and totally revolutionary.

This is what we have *to work out*. This is our task This is where *Philosophy and Revolution* will end, and the concrete revolution begin.

NOTES

1. For Dunayevskaya's discussion of these categories of Marx, see *Marxism and Freedom*, chapter 8.

2. See p. 123, note 31.

3. This section is translated by Baillie as "Spirit in Self-Estrangement: The Discipline of Culture and Civilization" and forms the second main subdivision of the section on Spirit. For Dunayevskaya's discussion of the illumination this chapter sheds on the thought of Mao, see P&R, chapter 5.

4. A reference to the French Revolution as well as to more recent ones.

5. See Dunayevskaya's letter to Erich Fromm, pp. 117–21 above, for a further discussion of this.

6. See LCW 38, p. 164. For Hegel's equation of the Notion and Freedom, see SLII, p. 232; SLM, p. 571.

7. Marx broke off his commentary on Hegel in his 1844 "Critique of the Hegelian Dialectic" with ¶384 of Hegel's *Philosophy of Mind*.

8. Dunayevskaya here has in mind the passage from the chapter on "The Absolute Idea," where Hegel says, "The transcendence of the opposition between the Notion and Reality, and that unity which is the truth, rest upon this subjectivity alone. The second negative, the negative of the negative, which we have reached, is this transcendence of the contradiction." [SLII, p.p. 477–78; SLM, p. 835].

9. This is developed at the end of chapter 17 of *Marxism and Freedom*, entitled "The Challenge of Mao Zedong," where Dunayevskaya writes: "Two kinds of subjectivity characterize our age of state-capitalism and workers' revolts. One is the subjectivism we have been considering—Mao's—which has no regard for objective conditions . . . as if a party of the elite that is armed can both 'harness' the energies of men and 'remold' their minds. . . . The second type of subjectivity, the one which rests on 'the transcendence of the opposition between the Notion and Reality,' is the subjectivity which has 'absorbed' objectivity, that is to say, through its struggle for freedom it gets to know and cope with the objectively real" (pp. 326–27).

10. See especially Marcuse's *Reason and Revolution*. For a compilation of Dunayevskaya's

critiques of Marcuse on this point, see Kevin Anderson, "On Hegel and the Rise of Social Theory: A Critical Appreciation of Herbert Marcuse's *Reason and Revolution*, Fifty Years Later," *Sociological Theory*, Vol. 11:3 (Nov. 1993), p. 261.

11. Although he taught in the 1940s at the Hartford Seminary and wrote on Hegel and Christian thought, Löwith was Jewish. See his *My Life in Germany Before and After 1933*, trans. by Elizabeth King (Urbana: University of Illinois Press, 1994, orig. 1939).

12. See Karl Löwith, *From Hegel to Nietzsche: The Revolution in Nineteenth-Century Thought* (New York: Holt, Rinehart and Winston, 1964).

13. Marcuse's preface to the first edition of *Marxism and Freedom* is available in the recent English-language editions of that work.

14. What Dunayevskaya intended as of this point to serve as Part I of *Philosophy and Revolution* ultimately became Part III, entitled "Economic Reality and the Dialectics of Liberation." She had sent some of this material to Marcuse for comment in 1960.

15. For a further discussion of the impact of these events on the formation of Marxist-Humanism, see Phillips and Dunayevskaya, *The Coal Miners' General Strike of 1949–50 and the Birth of Marxist-Humanism in the U.S.*

16. See Marx's "Private Property and Communism" (1844): "To have one basis for life and another for science is *a priori* a lie" [MECW 3, p. 303].

17. William Styron, *The Confessions of Nat Turner* (New York: Random House, 1967).

18. For Nat Turner's confession, see *Nat Turner*, ed. by Eric Foner (Englewood Cliffs, NJ: Prentice Hall, 1971), pp. 37–55.

19. George Wallace, Alabama's segregationist governor, whose 1968 presidential campaign drew millions of votes on a "law and order" platform.

20. This position was adopted by various followers of Marx then living in the United States.

21. In August 1866 in Baltimore, a General Congress of Labor established the National Labor Union, the first nationwide labor organization in the history of the United States.

22. See Harold Cruse, *The Crisis of the Negro Intellectual* (New York: William Morrow & Co., 1967).

23. Lenin's discussion of the world significance of the Negro struggle in the United States is contained in his speeches to the Second Congress of the Communist International in 1920. See LCW 31, pp. 184–201, pp. 213–63.

24. For Dunayevskaya's semi-autobiographical analysis of the Communists of the 1920s and Black America, see her unpublished 1953 essay "Our Organization," *The Raya Dunayevskaya Collection*, pp. 2042–2116.

25. Walter Reuther, leader of the United Auto Workers from the 1940s to 1970.

26. Kwame Nkrumah, leader of Ghana's independence struggle and a Pan-Africanist theorist, was overthrown by a military coup in 1966. For Dunayevskaya's critical assessment of Nkrumah, see chapter 7 of *Philosophy and Revolution*. See also C. L. R. James's laudatory assessments which were collected in his *Nkrumah: The Ghana Revolution* (Westport: Lawrence Hill, 1977), as well as the scathing Marxist critique by Bob Fitch and Mary Oppenheimer, *Ghana: End of an Illusion* (New York: Monthly Review Press, 1966).

27. A reference to the sit-ins by students at lunch counters in Greensboro, North Carolina in February 1960.

28. This is a reference to *The People of Kenya Speak for Themselves*, by Mbiyu Koinange (Detroit: Kenya Publication Fund, 1955), published with the assistance of Dunayevskaya.

29. In *Marxism and Freedom* (1958), Dunayevskaya analyzed the Montgomery Bus Boycott. She wrote that it "contains our future," adding, "Clearly, the greatest thing of all in this Montgomery, Alabama spontaneous organization was its own working existence" (p. 281).

30. See Martin Buber, *I and Thou*, trans. by Walter Kaufmann (New York: Scribner's, 1970).

31. This is a reference to King's April 16, 1963, "Letter from Birmingham Jail," in his *Why We Can't Wait* (New York: Harper and Row, 1963).

32. William Epton made these comments at a meeting on April 8, 1968, at the City College of New York.

33. See p. 136, note 21.

34. A reference to the chapter on "The Syllogism" in Book III of the *Science of Logic*, The Doctrine of the Notion.

35. In the Doctrine of Being, Book I of the *Science of Logic*, Hegel divides the material into three sections which he entitled 1) "Determinateness (Quality)," which includes chapters on Being, Determinate Being, and Being-for-Self, 2) "Magnitude (Quantity)," 3) "Measure."

36. The "absolute general law of capitalist production" is discussed by Marx in chapter 25 of *Capital*, Vol. I.

37. See "In Place of a Conclusion: Two Kinds of Subjectivity," in *Marxism and Freedom*, pp. 326–30.

38. Lenin made this statement in his 1922 Will [LCW 36, pp. 594–96]. Dunayevskaya discusses this point in *Philosophy and Revolution*, pp. 118–19, and in her "Hegelian Leninism," pp. 159–75 in *Towards a New Marxism*, ed. by Bert Grahl and Paul Piccone (St. Louis: Telos Press, 1973).

~

CHAPTER NINE

Toward *Philosophy and Revolution*, from Hegel to Sartre and from Marx to Mao

Letter on Hegel's Theory of Tragedy
(November 17, 1968)

The following letter on Hegel's theory of tragedy, written to Richard Koffler, then a young student activist, on November 17, 1968, supplements Dunayevskaya's numerous writings on Hegel's Phenomenology of Mind, *and reflects her interest in the relation of literature and revolution. The letter was often reproduced by her along with her summary of Hegel's* Phenomenology *from 1960, which appears in part II, above.*

Dear Richard,

Now then on Hegel's theory of tragedy, there is only one good recent work which gathers together his various statements from his *Aesthetics* as well as from the *Phenomenology*.[1] There are, of course, hundreds of works written on the general subject but not very many overly relevant. So for what it's worth, I should like to call attention to a few passages in the *Phenomenology*: they are all in the section "The Spiritual Work of Art" [PhGB, pp. 730–749; PhGM, pp. 439–52]. Begin with p. 732, which will immediately introduce the question of language in general and the specific form of the epic, in particular:

> The element in which these presented ideas exist, language, is the earliest language, the *Epic* as such, which contains the universal content, at any rate universal in the sense of completeness of the world presented, though not in the sense of universal-

161

ity of thought. The Minstrel is the individual and actual spirit from whom, as a sub-ject of this world, it is produced, and by whom it is borne. His "pathos" is not the deafening power of nature, but Mnemosyne, Recollection, a gradually evolved in-wardness, the memory of an essential mode of being once directly present. [PhGB, p. 732; PhGM, p. 440–41]

Don't forget that remembering and recollection—*sich erinnern*—have a very special meaning in Hegelian terminology, based only, in part, [on the fact] that the German expression means to go into one's self, and mainly because, if you remember by "going into yourself," obviously, you have been in the "outside," i.e. the objective world and now have to communicate with yourself to bring about a new unity of objective and subjective. In the Absolute Idea, recollection is used in the manner in which we would use his-tory and in all of the consideration of Art, Hegel views [it] as a form of the Absolute Idea. Secondly, insofar as language and the epoch is concerned, as a dialectician, Hegel does not consider that you have reached the highest stage when you have expressed yourself in narrative form alone. It has to be a drama, a tragedy, a comedy, in a word a *dialogue* between antagonists. The Greek ori-gin of dialect-ic, dialect or conversation, was always that [which] produced the new ideas, the new being, neither the ideas you came with to the discus-sion nor the idea that *others* came with but a synthesis of the two which was neither the one nor the other. Now then turn to page 736, the last paragraph:

This higher language, that of *Tragedy*, gathers and keeps more closely together the dispersed and scattered moments of the inner essential world and the world of ac-tion. . . . In regard to form, the language here ceases to be narrative, in virtue of the fact that it enters into the content, just as the content ceases to be merely one that is ideally imagined. The hero is himself the spokesman, and the representation given brings before the audience—who are also spectators—*self-conscious* human beings, who know their own rights and purposes, the power and the will belonging to their specific nature, and who know how to state them. [PhGB, p. 736; PhGM, pp. 443–44]

Although Hegel doesn't use the word revolutionary, negation definitely serves that function and it is because neither the hero, as an individual, nor the chorus, because of its "powerlessness," could possibly succeed in uniting the individual and the universal that Hegel writes:

Lacking the power to negate and oppose, it is unable to hold together and keep within bounds the riches and varied fullness of divine life; it allows each individual moment to go off its own way, and in its hymns of honor and reverence praises each individual moment as an independent god, now this god and now again another. [PhGB, pp. 737–738; PhGM, p. 444]

Finally, and all too hurriedly, turn to p. 740 , and note, especially, the correct notes by Professor J. B. Baillie, who interprets the various references Hegel had in mind when he wrote the following and which I will include in parenthesis:

> He [Oedipus] who had the power to unlock the riddle of the sphinx, and he too who trusted with childlike confidence [Orestes], are, therefore, both sent to destruction through what the god reveals to them. The priestess, through whose mouth the beautiful god speaks [in the Delphic Oracle], is nothing different from the equivocal sisters of fate [the witches in Macbeth] who drive their victim to crime by their promises, and who, by the double-tongued, equivocal character of what they gave out as a certainty, deceive the King when he relies upon the manifest and obvious meaning of what they say. There is a type of consciousness that is purer than the latter [Macbeth] which believes in witches, and more sober, more thorough, and more solid than the former which puts its trust in the priestess and the beautiful god. This type of consciousness [Hamlet], therefore, lets his revenge tarry for the revelation which the spirit of his father makes regarding the crime that did him to death, and institutes other proofs in addition. [PhGB, p. 740; PhGM, p. 446]

You will note what a sharp distinction there is between Hegel's interpretation of Hamlet and the 20th century stupidities on the fact that Hamlet was "not a doer" but constantly equivocating. To think before you do is higher than to do mindlessly, not only because Hegel considered consciousness the highest form of "being," but also because we are in a totally new stage of human development—the beginnings of capitalism as against *either* the individuality that based itself on the "double-tongued" prophesy of the witches, *or* the certainties that came with the "ordered" life of feudalism. In a word, tragedy always arises even as revolutions are always defeated *when* the new society that strives to be born is not yet there, but the individual who has the "premonition" about it strives toward that universality nonetheless.

Shakespeare was an "optimist" (that is, outside of being a genius) and, therefore, no matter how many corpses at the end of a tragedy are laid out on the stage, there is always the bugle call and the new arriving, invariably late. Despite all statements to the contrary, including by himself, so is Hegel an "optimist," that is to say, he is sure that somewhere or another, at sometime or another, the individual and the universal will be united so that finally the individual will be *free* as well as pluri-dimensional, or, as he expressed it in the *Philosophy of Mind*, "individuality purified of all that interferes with its universalism, i.e. freedom" [PM, ¶481].

Marx never stopped rereading the Greek tragedies and Shakespeare and he brought in those remarkable passages from *Timon of Athens* on gold directly into both the *Grundrisse* and *Capital,* not only because they so well described the avarice and fetishism of gold but, also, because the dehumanization of man resulted from a class society.[2]

I hope this has been of some help.

Yours,

Raya

Letter on Draft of Chapter 1 of *Philosophy and Revolution* (October 13, 1968)

As the revolts of the 1960s reached their high point in the near-revolution in Paris in May 1968, and receded without the achievement of a successful revolutionary transformation, Dunayevskaya intensified her efforts to finish Philosophy and Revolution. *The following letter accompanied the completion of the draft of what later became the book's first chapter on Hegel, "Absolute Negativity as New Beginning." Written on October 13, 1968, the letter discusses the central themes of the chapter in relation to the reception of Hegel's works by orthodox Marxists, non-Marxist Hegelians, and independent Marxists such as C. L. R. James. The original can be found in the* Supplement to the Raya Dunayevskaya Collection, *p. 14043.*

Dear Friends:

This is my first letter since the convention assigned me to devote full time to trying to complete the draft of *Philosophy and Revolution.*[3] Here is chapter I, "Hegel's Absolutes as New Beginnings." As you see by its expansion to 40 pages, it may become necessary to transform the sections (each of the three sections is devoted to an outstanding work of Hegel) into three chapters.

Beginnings are always difficult and none more so than the one that attempts for the first time to deal with *all* of Hegel's major writings from a Marxist-Humanist viewpoint. Insofar as specific works of Hegel are concerned, Marx left us his analysis only of the *Phenomenology of Mind* (plus, of course, the one on Hegel's *Philosophy of Right,* which first signaled Marx's break with the bourgeoisie. But this does not directly concern us, since here I have restricted myself to the strictly philosophic works, not the philosophy of the political sphere, like the *Philosophy of Right,* or [the lectures on the] *Philosophy of Religion).* Though Marx expressed his desire to write on the "rational" in the Hegelian philosophy,[4] he did not live long enough to complete, to his own satisfaction, all his original discoveries, much less to demonstrate the dialectic process by which he arrived at his theories. That task he left for future generations; it remains our task.

Lenin did leave us his notes on the *Science of Logic,* but, indispensable as these are, they are only notes, that is to say, they have a cryptic air since they are not fully developed except in his own mind where they remained to guide him through the thrilling but also heart-breaking six years of the Russian Revolution. Though Bukharin and Deborin went on to publish them at least in Russian, their introductions are worthless, full of meaningless abstractions, since, by then, Stalin had won the power struggle and none were brave enough to dare make them *concrete.*[5] Not a single revolutionary opponent of Stalinism, from Trotsky down, bothered with laying a philosophic foundation for the struggle against Stalinism; each was too busy leaping like a bolt out of the blue to political conclusions as if these could signify *total* opposition without philosophy as *both* foundation *and* perspective for new revolutions. As a consequence, neither Trotskyism as stillbirth nor Existentialism's pretensions to Marxian Humanism are accidental. That is to say, Communism having given up its moorings in *Marxian* Hegelianism, *outsiders*—those outside the revolutionary movement, *movement* and not merely "the Party"—tried filling the vacuum.[6]

Those too young to have lived through one phase of our development—state-capitalis[t theory][7]—must nevertheless see that it is no small matter that even a correct economic analysis of the new stage of *world* capitalism and a valiant attempt to face the philosophic challenge "stopped dead" (to use a Hegelian expression of uncompleted dialectic of Kant)[8] before Hegel's Absolutes and *therefore* was overcome by the new impulses emanating from the Afro-Asian revolutions.[9] Again, the task remains for us to complete even as the singling out of the Humanism of Marxism as *the* theoretic need of our age came from us at the very moment when the *movement from practice* fulfilled the same task via actual revolutions, both in Europe and Africa as well as the Black revolt in the United States.

As for the bourgeoisie, its theoreticians have so little use for Hegel's abstractions precisely because they see in them "the algebra of revolution,"[10] that Hegel's *Science of Logic,* written in 1816–21, wasn't even translated into English till 1929!* The French, who think themselves vastly superior cultur-

---

*I should have said published rather than translated. It was translated some quarter of a century before it was published, and it is as good a demonstration of the American roots of Hegelianism as was our proof of the American roots of Marxism, and again it remains an unknown chapter of American history. At the time of the Civil War there were, in St. Louis, a German refugee, [Henry] Brockmeyer, and a New Englander, W.T. Harris whom Brockmeyer taught to love Hegel and, in turn, translated the *Science of Logic.* He also started the first philosophic journal in this country, *The Journal of Speculative Philosophy,* which was Hegelian. Since Brockmeyer decided to run—and win!—Lieutenant Governorship of Missouri and Harris became the first U.S. Commissioner of Education, the "theoretical" work went by the board. By the 1920s his heirs offered his translation of the *Science of Logic* to many publishers, none of whom accepted [it], so England gets credit for the first translation. (See footnote 53 in *Marxism and Freedom*) [M&F, p. 350].

ally to the "Anglo-Saxons," didn't tackle Hegel seriously till the period between the two world wars, and mainly through "Lectures" and "Abstracts" rather than in the original.[11] Despite the millions of words *about* Hegel's works, there is barely a work existing which tackles the *whole* of his works. It did take a new Third World to arise, though these philosophers are absolutely unconscious of the impulses pulling at them, finally to bring about, at the end of the 1950's, one good, i.e., comprehensive analysis: *Hegel: A Reexamination* by J. N. Findlay. I still consider the very finest work of analysis to be that of Karl Löwith's *From Hegel to Nietzsche* which is far superior even to Marxist works, not to mention the fact that his analysis preceded theirs without due acknowledgement. Moreover, it also has a superb analysis of the Left Hegelians which thereby gives us a chance to see them on Hegel, while they worked in collaboration with Marx, and later as they broke up.

It is true that, from a Marxist viewpoint, Herbert Marcuse's *Reason and Revolution* is outstanding. But since it is, as an intellectual, that he debates with the other interpretations, the "examples" are all about other philosophies without any examples arising either from practice or from history. The result is that even in the section on Marx, specifically on alienated labor where he does a magnificent job proving there is no difference between the young and "mature Marx," he propounds a "thesis," a thesis of humanism he has been denying ("modifying") ever since.[12]

Yours,
Raya

The Newness of our Philosophic-Historic Contribution

The following letter is one of Dunayevskaya's most important discussions of her philosophic approach to Hegel's Absolutes and Marx's Humanism. It was written in response to a paper for a study group on the draft of Dunayevskaya's Philosophy and Revolution by Richard Greeman,[13] a colleague and activist in the 1960s New Left movements. In the letter, she contrasts her concept of "Absolute Negativity as New Beginning" both to the positions of contemporary theorists like Herbert Marcuse and to those of revolutionaries such as Lenin. The letter has been excerpted here; it can be found in full in The Raya Dunayevskaya Collection, *pp. 4407–16.*

Dear Richard:

Now that your return from Europe and my hinting to you that there were serious errors in your twelve-pager ("Some Notes on Dialectic") have both receded into the past, we can let the Hegelian principle—"Error is a dynamic of truth"—direct our confrontation with error.

Let me confess at once that I am not at all sure that I understand *what* it is you were trying to do in your talk to the *Philosophy and Revolution* study group. You stated that the sessions of the class were to be a "two-way road" between author and the class members who were to become the book's "co-authors." Since, however, your talk conveyed neither what I had conceived (and taped) as the introductory lecture, and since (outside of reproducing the contents page) you made no *textual* references to the book, the draft of *Philosophy and Revolution* became, it seems to me, no more than, as you put it, "a jumping-off point for our own theoretical self-development." But can the *new* ever be fully internalized if it is conceived as no more than "a jumping-off point?"

It seemed to me that [a] salient angle protruded to lessen the impact of the philosophic journey of discovery when you said: "Let me begin by stressing philosophy AND revolution." Along with this stress on the conjunction came emphatic articulation and rearticulations of the phrase, "preparation for revolution," without you ever calling attention to the fact that the phrase was "theoretic preparation for revolution." The omission of the word, theoretic, could not help but divert from the need of a philosophic study. The proof is in the predilection for phrases like "albeit through philosophy." Indeed, you state that "under Hegel we will actually be dealing with the problems created by the Great French Revolution." But this is precisely what the author has *not* done. *Marxism and Freedom* did that.

What distinguishes *Philosophy and Revolution* from *Marxism and Freedom* is that, instead of dealing, primarily, with revolutions, and, secondarily, with the underlying philosophies; instead of so bemoaning the intellectual sloth that has accumulated in the revolutionary movement since Lenin's death that one decides *to wait for others* to come with us on that journey of discovery of Hegelian philosophy, we here take the plunge ourselves, deep, deep into "absolute negativity." *No one since Marx, not even Lenin, went that deep.* (More on that later.)

In any case, *Philosophy and Revolution*, though dependent on Lenin's "Abstract of Hegel's *Science of Logic*"[†] is far from being a mere reproduction

---

[†]I am using Lenin's own title, "Abstract of Hegel's *Science of Logic*," in order to stress that I am dealing with this, and only this, work because it is this, and only this, which discloses the *break* in Lenin's own philosophic development. What the Stalinists call *Philosophic Notebooks* (Vol. 38 of Lenin's Collected Works) contains, besides this "Abstract," a typical hodgepodge of anything philosophical Lenin wrote, except, of course, the overly touted and whole book by itself, *Materialism and Empirio-Criticism.* Neither the latter nor Vol. 38 makes it possible to see how Lenin *changed. To this day there has been no work, or a good-sized article, that has grappled with Lenin's philosophic break.* Trotskyists, as well as Stalinists, are all too anxious to take undue advantage of the fact that Lenin made "only notes for himself" as he read Hegel, and "therefore" there has been no break in Lenin. Academics play the same game.

and update of Lenin's work. Nor is it a mere popularization, or a summation of Hegel's major works—*Phenomenology of Mind, Science of Logic, Philosophy of Mind*—though it needs to be noted, also, that our new work is the first Marxist work that grapples with all three fundamental works of Hegel. (Outside of his *Philosophy of Right*, which, by being an "application" of his fundamental philosophic theses, is, to me, not *strictly* philosophic—and which in any case was already analyzed by Marx, his very first grappling with Hegelian philosophy when still a Left Hegelian and which led directly to his discovery, historical materialism—all other works of Hegel were lectures or early drafts that had not been rechecked by him before publication.) Rather, *Philosophy and Revolution* is so new a reinterpretation of Hegelian dialectics, so totally belonging to *our age*, and so linked to the revolutions-to-be, that none but Marxist-Humanists, *specifically us*, could have written it.

Now then, for error to become a dynamic of truth, what is needed is a confrontation with what Hegel called, "the suffering of the negative," and Lenin a shedding of over self-confidence. The case Lenin was referring to—Trotsky—came from the type of genius which, in military terms, saved the young workers' state, but would endanger it if extended to relations in the trade union and political fields.[14] Fortunately, we face no such serious problems, or dangers. It may even sound fantastic to look at such historic and philosophic developments for illumination on such small matters as problems of a study group in *Philosophy and Revolution*. Nevertheless, dialectic methodology must become our *daily practice*, and the problem under discussion—how to have presented the *newness* of our contribution without taking a shortcut through abbreviations and "definitions" of others on dialectic, does call for *historic* confrontations rather than presenting the new at the tail end: "Dunayevskaya is suggesting that 'Absolutes as new beginnings' is the one to look at for our time." Period. End. The time has been spent on the abbreviations which led to errors, and now there is nothing to do but say "If we don't begin, who will?" (p. 12).

That is where you should have *begun*. Let's dive into the confrontation by answering, what, *specifically*, philosophically, marks off our age from that of Lenin. By the time of the collapse of the Second International, Lenin was sufficiently disgusted with "materialists" to stand in awe of "idealist" dialectics and write: "Cognition not only reflects the world, but creates it" [LCW 38, p. 212]. Yet this isn't what he developed. That task is ours. His was, as you well know, transformation into opposite. To us, who have lived through Stalinism, to speak of transformation into opposite, could only evoke the answer: "So what else is new?" What was new was that the death of Stalin lifted an incubus from the minds of workers and intellectuals, but first of all and most seriously, from workers. And precisely because workers were girding for actual revolutionary struggles, revolutionary intellectuals no longer feared the "ontological Absolute," but began seeing it, instead, as the *concrete universal.* That is to say, the *new* in the Absolute as a unity of theory and practice was that it was being disclosed as a movement *from practice* that was on its way both to theory and a new society.

This is what I discovered in Hegel's Absolutes in May 1953, a few weeks *before* the first revolt from under totalitarianism in East Berlin on June 17th, which had put an end not only to the myth of Stalinism's invincibility but to the capitalist democracy's myth of "brainwashing." This was the *historic* breakthrough to that which separates one era—Lenin's—and another—ours. It proved also to be the point of *division* in the state-capitalist tendency which I co-founded and which had been working at the task of trying to break down that "last chapter" in Hegel, recognizing it was *task* for our age, but *collapsing as it was being concretized.*[‡]

Its first concretization was *Marxism and Freedom. Philosophy and Revolution* begins where *Marxism and Freedom* left off by having singled out Marxist-Humanism as the philosophy of our age, and the American roots, with Black as a new dimension as the parallel of the Hungarian Revolution. *Philosophy and Revolution* begins where *Marxism and Freedom* left off. What we are [now] developing as our theoretic preparation for revolution is, on the one hand, the *strictly philosophic* problems in a comprehensiveness never attempted before, and, on the other hand, "Economic Reality and the Dialectics of Liberation" appearing in so varied, contradictory forms as to fail to measure up to the challenges of the era.[15]

You told me that some European comrades agree, more or less, with that part three, but ask: why the circuitous road to get to those conclusions? What's so new about the rich getting richer and the poor poorer? Empiricism has always produced just such blindness to the concrete—concrete in the Hegelian sense of the whole, and not in the ordinary sense of the tangible. Thus, to this day, bourgeois scholars "prove" that Lenin's *Imperialism* was "not an original work," but merely an update of what the liberal economist Hobson, had done a decade before Lenin.[16] "All" Lenin was supposed to have done

---

[‡]James made it impossible to publish the original letters (May 12 and May 20, 1953) on the Absolute Idea not only by himself refusing to discuss them and stopping [Grace Lee] from continuing with her complimentary letters on them that she had written when she was away from him, but also because he had singled out for attention, not the revolutionary forces striving to be born, but the *counter*-revolutionary phenomena—the Ahabs, Hitlers, Stalins. . . . We did, however, once we were free and able to establish *News & Letters*, publish the first English translation of Lenin's *Philosophic Notebooks* (The Abstract, that is, of *Hegel's Science of Logic*) as well as the Letters on the Absolute Idea.

was to have grafted "*a priori*" political conclusions onto "objective economic statistics." With such type of "objectivity," eclectics, *including revolutionaries*, become masters at fashioning blinders to shield against all philosophic foundations other than bite size [ones], as well as against the *process of working out* revolutionary theory.

The result is that "facts" remain suspended in mid-air, the "subject," i.e. the forces of revolution, remain either unidentified or wrongly identified, and we end up with still one other defeat—or the phantasmagoria of an academic like Marcuse who now excludes the proletariat, but welcomes the lumpen as the "revolutionary force," anoints a "biological solidarity" along with the youth, indeed invents a whole "biological foundation for socialism" along with an "instinctual creative force which the young radicals see in Cuba, in the guerrillas, in the Chinese cultural revolution" (*An Essay on Liberation*).[17]

Or we are confronted with the opposite side of this eclecticism, dogmatism, which refuses to recognize anything that doesn't bow to "the vanguard Party," whether or not that did anything revolutionary. In this bowing to the "Party" there is no difference, as we saw all over again in France in Spring, 1968, between the Stalinists who played a counter-revolutionary role, and the Trotskyists who fought the Stalinists.

And the opposite of this—the glorification of spontaneity that has purged itself not just of elitism, but of philosophy à la Daniel Cohn-Bendit, who thinks he can pick up theory "en route"—only to end in "plagiarizing" (his word, not mine) the rabid, discredited, professional anti-Leninist, Chaulieu.[18] (See *Obsolete Communism*.)[19]

In place, then, of all these who indulge in what Hegel has profoundly analyzed as "the arbitrary caprice of prophetic utterance" [PhGB, p. 107; PhGM. p. 29] what we say is needed is some "labor, patience, seriousness and suffering of the negative" [PhGB, p. 81; PhGM, p. 10], which is what *Philosophy and Revolution* invites its co-authors to do. I trust, therefore, that you will allow me to conclude with a brief summation of that most difficult first chapter which, as all new beginnings, has been so troublesome not just to you, but to the whole organization.

The three forms of the Absolute in Hegel—Absolute Knowledge as the unity of history and its comprehension in the *Phenomenology of Mind;* the Absolute Idea as the unity of theory and practice in the *Science of Logic;* and Absolute Mind as the unity of the Individual and the Universal in the *Philosophy of Mind*—are approached as new beginnings because our age of absolutes sees something in them that Hegel just guessed at and yet, as genius, caught in the air of the epoch of the French Revolution. Thus, though a religious man, he ends the *Phenomenology* by a "Golgotha of Absolute Spirit," that is to say, to use a contemporary expression "God is dead." Philosophy which has been elevated above religion has reached this pinnacle, however, *when* it unites with History, *when* the remembrance of things past discloses "a new world" embedded in the present, and "therefore" "Foams forth to God his own Infinitude."[20]

Marx, who hit out sharply against any "Absolute," nevertheless stressed that Hegel, having grasped *alienation as process*, *labor as self-becoming*, actually created the dialectic not only as method but as a *critique of reality* which, however, is enveloped in "mystical form" and therefore requires historical materialism to disclose. What we did that was *new*, and could have only been seen in our era, was to grasp the *division* in the problems dealt with *before and after* the Revolution, in Hegel's case, the French Revolution, in our case, the Russian Revolution.

What we [in 1953] had singled out as new in the Absolute Idea in the *Science of Logic* was the manner in which the *second* negativity becomes "the turning point of the movement of the Notion . . . for the transcendence of the opposition between Notion and Reality, and that unity which is the truth, rest upon this subjectivity alone" [SLII, p. 477; SLM, p. 836]. With the birth of a new, Third World, the question that had to be solved was: is the new subject of revolution to be found only in the African-Asian-Latin American revolutions, or by including in "subjectivity" not only force of revolution, but also *theory in historic continuity*, [do] we retain both the proletariat in technologically advanced lands, as well as the Marxist-Humanism they brought anew onto the historic stage.

When Lenin finished reading the *Science of Logic*, he ended his analysis by stressing that Hegel, in having the Logical idea turn to Nature, was stretching "a hand to materialism" [LCW 38, p. 233], and that therefore, the remaining [part of the] paragraph was unimportant. Back in 1953, when I first broke through on the Absolute Idea, I at once took issue with that, insisting that we who had suffered through Stalinism couldn't so dismiss that last paragraph in which Hegel heaps praise on freedom, upon the Idea "that freely releases itself," "becomes utterly free" so that the "externality" of its release in Nature is but a step in its return to the "Philosophy of Spirit" where it will first "perfect its liberation" [SLII, p. 486; SLM, p. 844].[21] In a word, we are again confronted with how much more concrete for our age than for Lenin was Lenin's "idealism" on the question of cognition "creating the world."

Moreover, [whereas] Lenin didn't follow Hegel into the *Philosophy of Mind*, Marx, who did, left the analysis unfinished as he pursued his thoroughly original discovery of Historical Materialism. It did, of course, reappear as he split the Absolute into two in *Capital*.[22] But where it concerned "direct" contact with Hegel as the latter was tracing a *process*, a *philosophic* process, Marx happened to have broken off after he reached ¶384, though I didn't know this in the exhilaration over Stalin's death, when I chose to begin my analysis of the *Philosophy of Mind* with ¶385.[23]

The whole point is that each age has a task, and the drive, the self-movement, *from practice and from theory*, suddenly makes one see points, get illuminations for the tasks that confront that epoch, even from so seemingly closed an "ontological system" as Hegel's. The truth is that it was at that point that Hegel had reached the *unity* of the Individual and the Universal in a way that it seemed no problem at all to depart from Hegel who used the philosopher as yardstick for measuring the development of mankind, where the true Subject is the mass in motion. But without this *internal dialectic* it would have been impossible to work out the *concrete universal*.

Naturally, this cannot be achieved in thought alone. Naturally, men's actions alone can reconstruct society on new beginnings, can end the pre-history of mankind. Naturally, Marx's concept of *praxis*—the activity of men, mental and manual—and not Hegel's "Absolutes," contains the answer. But everyone from Marxists to anarchists never tires of speaking of *praxis* without ever, at least not since 1917, achieving a social revolution. So a new beginning, a new point of departure, a new unity of philosophy and revolution must be worked out, and it is this we invite all to help us achieve so that freedom finally becomes reality. Now that we see eye to eye, let's begin again with a view to finishing the book this year!

NOTES

1. See *Hegel on Tragedy*, edited with an Introduction by Anne and Henry Paolucci (New York: Harper & Row, 1962), in 1968 the only readily accessible source.

2. One of Marx's discussions of Greek tragedy appears in the Introduction to the *Grundrisse* (New York: Vintage, 1973), pp. 110–111. His citation from Shakespeare's *Timon of Athens* appears in *Capital*, Vol. I, chapter 3, "Money, or the Circulation of Commodities" [MCIF, p. 230; MCIK, p. 148].

3. The "convention" refers to the biennial gathering of News and Letters Committees, the Marxist-Humanist organization Dunayevskaya headed from its founding in 1955 to her death in 1987.

4. See Marx's letter to Engels of January 16, 1858, in which he expressed the desire to "write two or three sheets making accessible to the common reader the rational aspect of the method which Hegel not only discovered but also mystified" [MECW 40, p. 249].

5. Abram Deborin, a leading Soviet philosopher and editor of Lenin's works during the 1920s, was later purged by Stalin, who termed him a "Menshivizing idealist." For a discussion of Bukharin and Deborin's response to Lenin's *Philosophic Notebooks*, see David

Joravsky, *Soviet Marxism and Natural Science* (London: Routledge and Kegan Paul, 1961) and Kevin Anderson, *Lenin, Hegel, and Western Marxism*, pp. 175–77 especially.

6. See Dunayevskaya's further development of this critique in chapter 5 of *Philosophy and Revolution*, "Jean-Paul Sartre: Outsider Looking In." See also Sartre, *Existentialism and Humanism*, trans. Philip Mairet (London: Methuen, 1948, orig. 1946).

7. See *The Marxist-Humanist Theory of State-Capitalism*.

8. See SLII, p. 226; SLM, p. 592.

9. A reference to C. L. R. James.

10. This phrase was first used by the Russian Populist Alexander Herzen.

11. An apparent reference to Alexandre Kojève's lectures on Hegel's *Phenomenology* in the 1930s, translated into English as *Introduction to the Reading of Hegel*, ed. by Allan Bloom (New York: Basic Books, 1969, orig. 1947). Jean Hyppolite's two-volume French translation of Hegel's *Phenomenology* first appeared in 1939 and 1941, while a satisfactory French translation of the *Science of Logic* was published only after the Second World War.

12. For Marcuse's distancing of himself from a humanist perspective in the 1960s, see his "Socialist Humanism?" in *Socialist Humanism*, ed. by Eric Fromm (New York: Doubleday, 1965), pp. 107–117. There, Marcuse writes of the new technological "systems of domination into which the laboring classes are incorporated and incorporate themselves" (p. 99), resulting in a situation where "the objective identity of socialism and humanism is dissolved" (p. 100). Dunayevskaya's own essay, "Marx's Humanism Today," also appeared in Fromm's collection (pp. 63–76).

13. Greeman, a prominent figure in the 1968 Columbia University revolt, has been for many years the translator of and commentator on the works of the Franco-Russian revolutionary novelist and essayist Victor Serge.

14. Lenin made this critique of Trotsky during the Trade Union dispute of 1920–21. For Dunayevskaya's view of this controversy, see *Marxism and Freedom*, in which she critiques what she terms Trotsky's contention "that since Soviet Russia was a workers' state, the workers had nothing to fear from it and hence the trade unions could be incorporated into the State, and labor could be militarized" (p. 198).

15. "Economic Reality and the Dialectics of Liberation" refers to what eventually became Part III of *Philosophy and Revolution*, with chapters on revolts in the 1950s and 1960s in Africa, Eastern Europe, and the Western capitalist lands.

16. A reference to J. A. Hobson, whose work *Imperialism: A Study* appeared in 1902.

17. See *An Essay on Liberation*, by Herbert Marcuse (Boston: Beacon Press, 1969), p. 88.

18. Pierre Chaulieu was one of the pseudonyms of Cornelius Castoriadis, whom Dunayevskaya first met in Paris in 1947. For one of Dunayevskaya's critiques of Castoriadis, see her article "A Footnote on the Detractors of Lenin," in *News & Letters*, December 1969.

19. See *Obsolete Communism: The Left-Wing Alternative*, by Daniel Cohn-Bendit (New York: McGraw Hill, 1968). Cohn-Bendit was one of the prime leaders of the student revolt in Paris in May, 1968. For Dunayevskaya's analysis of France 1968, see *Philosophy and Revolution*, chapter 9, as well as her article, "Who Arrested the French Revolution?" *News & Letters*, June-July 1968.

20. See the final paragraph of Hegel's *Phenomenology of Mind*, where he writes: "The goal, which is Absolute Knowledge or Spirit knowing itself as Spirit, finds its pathway in the recollection of spiritual forms as they are in themselves and as they accomplish the organization of their spiritual kingdom. Their conservation, looked at from the side of their free existence appearing in the form of contingency, is *History*; looked at from the side of their intellectually comprehended organization, it is the *Science* of the ways in which knowledge appears. Both together, or History (intellectually) comprehended, form at once the recollection and the Golgotha of Absolute Spirit." [PhGB, p. 808; PhGM, p. 493].

21. See this volume, p. 22.

22. Dunayevskaya elaborates upon this in *Philosophy and Revolution:* " . . . where Hegel's Absolutes are always 'syntheses,' unities—of history and philosophy, theory and practice, subject and object—Marx's are always total diremptions—absolute irreconcilable contradictions." (p. 93).

23. In his 1844 "Critique of the Hegelian Dialectic," Marx broke off his commentary on Hegel's *Philosophy of Mind* with ¶384. In her l953 "Letters on Hegel's Absolutes" Dunayevskaya began her commentary on that work with ¶385. See the Letter of May 20, l953 in part I, above. At the time of writing her 1953 Letters, Dunayevskaya was not aware that Marx had stopped his commentary with ¶384.

PART IV

AFTER *PHILOSOPHY AND REVOLUTION*: HEGEL'S ABSOLUTES AND MARX'S HUMANISM, 1972–81

CHAPTER TEN

~

Hegel's Absolute as New Beginning

This text was first delivered as a paper at the biennial meeting of the Hegel Society of America, Georgetown University, October 1974. The topic of the 1974 meeting was Hegel's Aesthetics and his Logic. Dunayevskaya's paper represents a development of some of the themes from the chapter "Absolute Negativity as New Beginning: The Ceaseless Movement of Ideas and of History" of her Philosophy and Revolution: From Hegel to Sartre and from Marx to Mao, *published the preceding year. The lecture was published in* Art and Logic in Hegel's Philosophy, *ed. by Warren E. Steinkraus and Kenneth L. Schmitz (Atlantic Highlands, NJ: Humanities Press, 1980).*

In the beginning was the Word (*das ursprüngliche Wort*), not as a command, but as the philosophic utterance which vanishes into thin air.[1] The release of the self-movement of the Absolute Idea unfolds, not as if it were in repose, but so totally infected with negativity that throughout the twenty-seven paragraphs that constitute the final chapter of the *Science of Logic*, starting with the very first paragraph, we learn that the Absolute Idea contains "the highest opposition within itself" (*den höchsten Gegensatz in sich*) [SLII, p. 466; SLM, p. 824].

The dialectic would not be the dialectic and Hegel would not be Hegel if the moment of encounter with the Absolute Idea was a moment of quiescence. Thus, far from the unity of the Theoretical and Practical Idea being an ultimate, or pinnacle, of a hierarchy, the Absolute Idea is a new beginning, a new beginning that is inevitable precisely because the Absolute Idea is a "concrete totality" [SLII, p. 472; SLM, p. 830] and thus entails differentiation and impulse to transcend. To follow Hegel, step by step, without for a single moment losing sight of negativity as the driving force toward ever-new beginnings, it may be best to divide the twenty-seven paragraphs into three principal areas. The first three paragraphs, centering around that highest contradiction contained in the

Absolute Idea at the very moment of the unification of the Theoretical and Practical Idea, show its self-determination disclosing not a new content, but its universal form, *the Method*, i.e., the dialectic.

Once Hegel asserts (in the fourth paragraph) that *"Notion is everything* and its movement is the universal *absolute activity*, the self-determining and self-realizing movement" [SLII, p. 468; SLM, p. 826], Hegel divides his field of concentration in what I call the second subdivision into two: a) ¶5 to 7, stressing the new beginnings, immediacy that has resulted from mediation, and b) further opens the scope wider (¶ 8 to 15) as he sketches the development of the dialectic historically, from Plato to Kant, and differentiates his concept of second negativity as *the*

> turning point of the movement of the Notion . . . the innermost source of all activity, of all animate and spiritual self-movement, the dialectical soul that everything true possesses and through which alone it is true; for on this subjectivity alone rests the sublating of the opposition between Notion and reality, and the unity that is truth. [SLII, p. 477; SLM, p. 835]

The third subdivision I make covers the last twelve paragraphs. These disclose concreteness both in its totality and in each sphere, in each of which, as well as in the whole, inheres the impulse to transcend. And this includes the *system* itself. The intimation of totally new beginnings is not restricted to the fact that there will be other spheres and sciences Hegel plans to develop— Nature and Spirit. Inherent in these intimations are the consequences of what we have been grappling with in the whole of the *Science of Logic*.

The Absolute Idea as new beginning, rooted in practice as well as in philosophy, is the burden of this writer's contribution. While this cannot be "proven" until the end of Hegel's rigorous and yet free-flowing final chapter, it is necessary here, by way of anticipation, to call attention to the three final syllogisms in the *Encyclopedia of the Philosophical Sciences* which had not been included in the first edition of the work. To this writer, these crucial additions to the 1827 and 1830 editions constitute the summation, not alone of the *Encyclopedia*, but of the whole cycle of knowledge and reality throughout the long tortuous trek of 2,500 years of Western civilization that that encyclopedic mind of genius, Hegel, was trying to bring to a conclusion. Just as the first of those syllogisms (¶575) *shows that the very center of its structure*— Logic, Nature, Mind—is not Logic but Nature, so does the very last paragraph in the *Science of Logic*.

Whether one conceives Nature as "externality" in the Hegelian sense, or "exteriority" in the Sartrean manner, or as "Practice" in Lenin's World War I view, the point is that Hegel, not Sartre, nor Lenin, conceives Nature as mediation. When I develop this further at the end of the paper, we shall see what illumination our age casts on the movement from practice that helps us in grappling with the dialectic. But here it is best to continue with the three central divisions I suggested:

1) The same first paragraph of the Absolute Idea that riveted our attention to the highest opposition, cautioned against imposing an old duality on the new unity of opposites reached—the Theoretical and Practical Idea. "Each of these by itself is still one-sided . . . " The new, the highest opposition, rather, has to self-develop: "The Notion is not merely *soul,* but free subjective Notion that is for itself and therefore possesses *personality.*" This individuality is not "exclusive," but is "explicitly *universality* and *cognition* and in its other, has *its own* objectivity for its object" [SLII, p. 466; SLM, p. 824]. All that needs to be done, therefore, is for the Absolute Idea "to hear itself speak," to "outwardize" (*Äusserung*). Its self-determination is its self-comprehension. Or, put more precisely, "its own completed totality" is not any new content. Rather it exists wholly as *form* and "the universal aspect of its form—that is, *method.*" From that moment on Hegel will not take his mind's eye from the dialectic for, as he puts it, "nothing is known in its truth unless it is totally subject to method" (*als der Methode vollkommen unterworfen ist*) [SLII, p. 468; SLM, p. 826].

2) No less than eleven paragraphs follow the pronouncement that the Absolute form, the Method, the Notion is the whole. The pivot around which they all revolve, Hegel stresses over and over again, is the *"universal absolute activity,"* the Method which "is therefore to be recognized as . . . unrestrictedly universal" [SLII, p. 468; SLM, p. 826]. In a word, this is not just another form of cognition; it is *the unity* of the Theoretical and Practical Idea we have reached. Far from being a "merely *external* form" or the instrument it is in inquiring cognition, the method is no "mere aggregate" of determinations but "the Notion that is determined in and for itself," the middle, the mediation, *because* it is objective and it is "posited in its identity," namely "subjective Notion" [SLII, p. 469; SLM, p. 827].

To be swept up by the dialectic is to experience a plunge to freedom. Since, however, the rigor of thought cannot be allowed to dissolve into a "Bacchanalian revelry" [PhGB, p. 105; PhGM, p. 27], it is necessary to work through these paragraphs without missing any links. The first is the beginning, the *Absolute as beginning.* When Hegel refers us to the very start of the Doctrine of Being, where he first posed the question: "With What Must Science Begin?" it is not for purposes of proving that the Absolute is a mere unfolding of what was implicit from the start, the manifestations. It also becomes a totally new foundation—absolute negation. Although from the beginning, Hegel emphasized that everything, no matter how simple it sounded contained equally immediacy and mediation [SLI, p. 80; SLM, p. 68], it is now so permeated with negativity that it is no mere remembrance of things past when Hegel writes, there is nothing, whether "in *actuality* or in *thought* [that is] so simple and abstract as is commonly imagined" [SLII, p. 471; SLM, p. 829].

The long passageway through [the] "concrete totality" of diverse, contradictory forces and relations from the Doctrine of Being through Essence to Notion makes it clear that though every beginning must be made *with the Absolute*, it becomes Absolute "only in its completion" [SLII, p. 472; SLM, p. 829]. It is *in* the movement to the transcendence of the opposition between Notion and Reality that transcendence will be achieved in subjectivity and subjectivity alone. In a word, this new beginning is both in thought and in actuality, in theory and practice, that is to say, in dialectical *"mediation* which is more than a mere beginning, and is a mediation of a kind that does not belong to a comprehension by means of thinking." Rather "what is meant by it is in general the demand for the *realization of the Notion,* which realization does not lie in the *beginning* itself, but is rather the goal and the task of the entire further development of cognition" [SLII, p. 470; SLM, p. 828].

Whether or not one follows Marx's "subversion"* of the Absolute's goal, the "realization of philosophy" as a "new Humanism," the unity of the ideal and the real, of theory and practice, indeed, of philosophy and revolution,† one cannot fail to perceive Hegel's Absolute advance *(Weitergehen)* and "completion" as the conclusion *and* fulfillment, as the beginning anew from the Absolute for he never departed from conceiving all of history, of human development, not only as a history in the *consciousness* of freedom, but, as we shall see, as achievement in *actuality.* Even here, where Hegel limits himself strictly to philosophic categories, to history of thought, he maintains the need to face reality. In tracing the conceptual breakthroughs of the dialectic from Plato to Kant to his own view of second negativity, he calls attention to Plato's demand of cognition "that it should *consider things in and for themselves,* that is, should consider them partly in their universality, but also that it should not

---

*Karl Löwith writes: "Marx takes over the task of the philosophy which ended with Hegel and puts pure revolutionary Marxism, as reason becoming practical, in the place of the whole previous tradition." Then Prof. Löwith footnotes his comment by referring to Manfred Riedel's *Theorie und Praxis im Denken Hegels* (Stuttgart: 1965). It is there, continues Löwith, "where it is established for the first time that, for Hegel, theory and practice share an equal primacy, since spirit as will is a will to freedom and freedom is the origin of all historical practice" (see Löwith's "Mediation and Immediacy in Hegel, Marx and Feuerbach" in W. E. Steinkraus, ed., *New Studies in Hegel's Philosophy* (New York: Holt, Rinehart & Winston, Inc., 1971), p. 122 and note).

†See chapter 2, "A New Continent of Thought, Marx's Historical Materialism and its Inseparability from the Hegelian Dialectic," in my book, *Philosophy and Revolution* (New York: Delacorte Press, 1973).

stray away from them catching at circumstances, examples and comparisons" [SLII, p. 472; SLM, p. 830].

Considering things "in and for themselves," Hegel maintains, has made possible the working out of ever-new unities and relations between practice and theory. That is the achievement of Absolute Method. To whatever extent the method is analytic, to whatever extent synthetic as it exhibits itself as Other, the dialectic moment is not reached until (as the unity of the two), the "no less synthetic than analytic moment" determines itself as "the *other of itself*" [SLII, p. 473; SLM, p. 831]. The point is that it is the power of the negative which is the creative element. It is not the synthesis, but the absolute negativity which assures the advance movement. Since this is what separates Hegel from all other philosophers, and this philosophic ground, how a "universal first, *considered in and for itself*, shows itself to be the other of itself" [SLII, pp. 475–76; SLM, pp. 833–34], this idea will dominate the last twelve paragraphs following the encounter with

> The turning point of the movement of the Notion . . . the dialectical soul that everything true possesses and through which alone it is true; for on this subjectivity alone rests the sublating of the opposition between Notion and Reality, and the unity that is truth. [SLII, p. 477; SLM, p. 835]

Before, however, we go to those paragraphs developing second negativity to its fullest, I should like to retrace our steps to the threshold of the Absolute Idea, "The Idea of the Good," and call attention to the Russian Communist celebration of the one hundredth anniversary of Lenin's birth, which coincided with Hegel's two hundredth. This will illuminate the problematic of our day. Academician Kedrov, Director of the Institute of History of Science and Technology, embarked on still another attempt to "disengage" Lenin from Hegel with the claim that the word, "alias," before the quotation: "Cognition not only reflects the world but creates it" [LCW 38, p. 212], shows Lenin was merely restating Hegel, not bowing to Hegel's "bourgeois idealism."[‡]

The simple truth, however, is that the most revolutionary of all materialists, Vladimir Ilyitch Lenin, witnessing the simultaneity of the outbreak of World War I *and* the collapse of the Socialist International, felt compelled to return to Hegel's dialectic as that unity of opposites which might explain the counter-revolution *within* the revolutionary movement. Absolute negativity

---

[‡]See the article by Academician Kedrov printed in *Soviet Studies in Philosophy*, Summer, 1970.

became Lenin's philosophic preparation for revolution, as Lenin's *Abstract of Hegel's Science of Logic* shows.[§] By the time his notes reach the Doctrine of the Notion, Lenin states that none of the Marxists (and the emphasis on the plural makes it clear he includes himself), had fully understood Marx's greatest theoretical work, *Capital*, "*especially* its first chapter" since that is impossible "without having thoroughly studied and understood the *whole* of Hegel's *Logic*. His passion at the approach of the Doctrine of the Notion—"NB Freedom = Subjectivity, ('or') End, Consciousness, Endeavor, NB" [LCW 38, p. 164]—had made it clear that Lenin at this time, 1914, saw in freedom, in subjectivity, notion, the categories with which both to transform the world and to gain knowledge of the objectively real *because* he had already, in the Doctrine of Essence, recognized, in Hegel's critique of causality, the limitation of "science" to explain the relation between mind and matter.

Lenin then proceeded to grapple with the role of practice *in Hegel*, especially when Hegel writes of the Practical Idea as having "not only the dignity of the Universal, but also the simply actual" [SLII, p. 460; SLM, pp. 818–19]. Lenin's quotation about cognition that the Communists are presently trying to expunge is significant, *not* because he accords such "creativity" to cognition but rather because Lenin, in "granting" that creativity to cognition, had followed it up by calling attention to the fact that Hegel had used the word, Subject "here suddenly instead of Notion" [LCW 38, p. 180]. And to make matters still worse for those Russian epigoni, it was all in the sentence about "the self-certainty which the subject has in the fact of its determinateness in and for itself, a certainty of its own actuality and the *non-actuality* of the world."

Vulgar materialists are so utterly shocked at Lenin writing about the "*non-actuality* of the world" and the "self-certainty of the Subject's actuality" that, they quote, not Hegel, as Lenin did, but Lenin's "translation": "i.e., that the world does not satisfy man and man decides to change it by his activity" [LCW 38, p. 213]. But the point is that, after that "translation," Hegel is quoted in full, on the contrast between inquiring cognition where "this actuality appeared merely as an objective world, without the subjectivity of the Notion, and here it appears as an objective world whose inner ground and actual subsistence is the Notion. This is the Absolute Idea" [SLII, p. 465; SLM, p. 823; LCW 38, p. 219].

[§]This is my own translation which was published as an Appendix to my *Marxism and Freedom* (New York: 1958). However, I am cross-referencing here the "official" translation which was published out of context, in 1961, as "Conspectus of Hegel's Book, the *Science of Logic*" in Lenin's *Collected Works*, Vol. 38. See also footnote 221 on page 317 of my *Philosophy and Revolution* for evidence of the interest Lenin displayed in the study of Hegel by Prof. Ilyin who was then sitting in jail for opposing the Bolshevik revolution, and whom Lenin freed. The reference to this in the Archives of the Lenin Institute for the year 1921, was included in Russia only in the first publication of Lenin's *Philosophic Notebooks*, specifically in the Introduction by Deborin.

It is this appreciation of the Absolute Idea, not as something in heaven or in the stratosphere, but in fact in the objective world whose very ground is the Notion, that has statist Communism so worried about Lenin, ever since the East German Revolt of June 17, 1953, and the emergence of a movement from *practice* to theory *and* a new society. They have rightly sensed that Lenin's break with his own philosophic past of the photocopy theory of reality plus voluntarism[2] produced the Great Divide in the Movement that has yet to run its course.** We will take up the illumination the actual movement from practice (these past two decades) sheds on the problematic of our day at the end of this study. Here it is necessary to resume Hegel's own concentration on and development of "second negativity" in those last twelve paragraphs of Absolute Idea.

3) Beginning with ¶15, and all the way to the end of the chapter, we no sooner face the subjectivity that has overcome opposition between Notion and Reality than we learn that, since this subjective is the *"innermost"* it is also the *"most objective moment,"* [SLII, pp. 477–78; SLM, pp. 835–36] and it is this subjectivity as objectivity which is *"subject, a person, a free being."* [SLII, p. 478; SLM, p. 836]. Clearly, free creative power assures the plunge to freedom. It is the unifying force of the Absolute Idea. And since absolute negativity, the new foundation, is not "something merely picked up, but something *deduced* and *proved"* [SLII, p. 480; SLM, p. 838], this subjective could not but be objective, so much so that it extends to the *system itself*.[3]

There too we learn that the content belongs to the method, is the extension of method so that the system, too, is but another "fresh beginning" [SLII, p. 481; SLM, p. 839] which has been arrived at through an infinite remembrance of things past *and* advance signposts (*Weitergehen*). This is why the discussion in ¶20 through 25 not only never departs from absolute negativity as the transcending mediation, but shows that every advance in the system of totality becomes *"richer and more concrete"* [SLII, p. 482; SLM, p. 840].

The expression, "richer and more concrete," no more than the categories of subjectivity, reason, freedom, may not have led the reader to think of any such "materialistic" movement as the movement by which man *makes* himself free, but here is how Hegel spells out "Free Mind" in *The Philosophy of Mind* of his *Encyclopedia*:

**Elsewhere I have developed more fully the ramifications of the break in Lenin's philosophic development. See chapter 3, "The Shock of Recognition and the Philosophic Ambivalence of Lenin," in my *Philosophy and Revolution*, pp. 95–120.

> When individuals and nations have once got in their heads the abstract concept of
> full-blown liberty, there is nothing like it in its uncontrollable strength, just because
> it is the very essence of mind, and that as its very actuality . . . . The Greeks and Ro-
> mans, Plato and Aristotle, even the Stoics did not have it. . . . If to be aware of the
> Idea—to be aware, i.e., that men are aware of freedom as their essence, aim and ob-
> ject is a matter of speculation, still this very Idea itself is the actuality of men—not
> something which they have, as men, but which they are. [PM, ¶482]

The fact that, in the *Science of Logic*, the stages in dialectical advance are
not shown as so many stages in the historic development of human freedom,
but, in the end, unwind as a circle, become a circle of circles, is, however, a
constant reminder that every absolute is a new beginning, has a before and an
after; if not a "future," surely a consequence, a *"successor*—or, expressed more
accurately, *has* only the *antecedent* and *indicates* its *successor* in its conclusion"
[SLII, p. 484; SLM, p. 842]. Whatever Hegel said, and meant, about the Owl
of Minerva spreading its wings only at dusk simply does not follow from the
objectivity of the drive, the *summation* in which the advance is immanent in
the present. While he neither gave, nor was interested in, any blueprints for
the future, he was not preoccupied with death, the "end" of philosophy, much
less of the world. His philosophy is "the end" only in the sense that "up to this
moment" philosophy has reached this point with "my" philosophy of absolute
negativity. From the beginning, when his first and greatest elemental work,
The Phenomenology of Mind, ended with nothing short of the Golgotha of the
Spirit, Hegel had succeeded in describing the final act as if it were an unfolding of the everlasting. When subjected to the dialectic method from which,
according to Hegel, no truth can escape, the conclusion turns out to be a new
beginning. There is no trap in thought. Though it is finite, it breaks through
the barriers of the given, reaches out, if not to infinity, surely beyond the historic moment.

In the final two paragraphs we see that there is no rest for the Absolute
Idea, the fulfilled Being, the Notion that comprehends itself, the Notion that
has become the Idea's own content. The negativity, the urge to transcend, the
ceaseless motion will go into new spheres and sciences and first then achieve
"absolute liberation" [SLII, p. 485; SLM, p. 843]. The absolute liberation
experienced by the Absolute Idea as it "freely releases itself" does not make it
ascend to heaven. On the contrary, it first then experiences the shock of
recognition, "the *externality of space and time* existing absolutely on its own
account without the moment of subjectivity" [SLII, p. 486; SLM, p. 843].

So much for those who consider that Hegel lived far away from the concrete objective world, in some distant ivory tower in which he "deduced"
Nature from the Idea. Equally wrong, however, are those who, while recog-

nizing that Hegel presents the transition to Nature as an actual process of reality, conclude that Hegel is standing on his head. Proud as Hegel might have been of the feat, we need to turn both to the *Science of Logic*, and the *Philosophy of Mind*, especially the three final syllogisms, to see what Hegel was telling us.

What was an intimation in the Logic about Nature being the mediation is spelled out as the first syllogism at the end of the *Encyclopedia* [in the *Philosophy of Mind*]: Logic—Nature—Mind. In that paragraph Hegel further assures us that "Nature, standing between Mind and its essence, sunders them, not indeed to extremes of finite abstraction, nor stands aloof from them" [PM, ¶575].

One of the most relevant of the scholarly studies of the 1960s is Reinhart Klemens Maurer's *Hegel und das Ende der Geschichte: Interpretationen zur Phänomenologie*. He holds that it may very well be true that the first of these final syllogisms (in ¶575), which has Nature as the mediation, gives the appearance that "Hegel turns to Darwin, turns to dialectical materialism and other nature-geneses of man," and also means to turn "to Liberty," there leaving the "course of necessity," but Hegel himself brings in a "correction" in his next paragraph.[4] Here the sequence reads: Nature—Mind—Logic. Professor Maurer then proceeds to "appropriate" that syllogism as expressing the dialectic of the *Phenomenology*. Whatever one may think of that analysis as a philosophy of history or whatever, the point most Hegel scholars do agree with regarding the final syllogism [PM, ¶577], is this, in Otto Pöggeler's words of 1961: "In opposition to the usual interpretations of the Hegelian text, I should like to propose the following: that the actual science of Spirit is not the Logic, but the philosophy of Spirit."[5]

Thus the focus of the third syllogism has shifted and the stress has been correctly placed on the fact the Logic has been replaced and, in its stead, we get, not the sequential but the consequential *Self-Thinking Idea*. To Hegel this has resulted from the fact that "it is the nature of the fact, the notion, which causes the movement and development, yet this same movement is equally the action of cognition" [PM, ¶577].

Hegel's Absolutes never were a series of ascending ivory towers. Revolutionary transformation is immanent in the very form of thought. As we saw from the chapter on Absolute Idea, the unifying force was free creative power. By the time we reach the mediated final result, Absolute Mind, the absolute negativity that was the moving force in Logic, in Nature, in *Geist* where we saw them as concrete stages of human freedom, there no longer was any difference between theory and practice. This is why our age can best understand Hegel's Absolute. It has been witness to a *movement from practice* for two long decades (ever since the death of Stalin lifted the incubus from the heads of the masses in East Europe). To this writer, Hegel's genius is lodged in the fact that *his* "voyage of discovery" becomes one endless process of discovery for us. The "us" includes both Marx's new continent of thought of materialist dialectics, and Hegel scholars, as well as the movement from practice that was itself a form of theory once its spontaneity discovered the power of thought along with its physical might. This writer has followed very closely this movement of revolt ever since June 17, 1953, and saw in it a quest for universality because she had already discerned in the dialectical movement of the three final syllogisms in Absolute Mind, a new point of departure in the Idea and in the movement from practice.[6]

This movement from practice hardly had the ear of contemporary Hegelians, orthodox or Marxist, as evidenced in the erudite, Leftist director of the famous Frankfurt School, the late Theodore Adorno. His very reason for being, for thinking, for acting, was dialectics, that is to say, for negations of what is. He entitled the summation of his life's thought, his intellectual legacy, *Negative Dialectics*.[††] This book, however, has little to do with the dialectics of negativity, and least with the concept of Subject, by which Hegel distinguished his view from all other philosophers who left the search for truth at Substance only. As "concretized" by Marx for the proletarian class, Subject is supposed to have been accepted also by Adorno, but again, Adorno keeps his distance and originality locked up in what he calls *Negative Dialectics*. From the very beginning of the Preface of his work (p. xix), Adorno informs us that the positive in the negative—"the negation of the negation"—is the enemy: "This book seeks to free dialectics from such affirmative traits without reducing its determinacy." The so-called "theoretical inadequacies of Hegel and Marx" revolve around what he sees as the all-encompassing evil, the concept, that "subsuming cover," its "autarchy" [p. 12].[‡‡]

Naturally, Adorno keeps his distance from "positivists" and the vulgarisms of the knighted Karl Popper and his infamous "Hegel and Fascism" school. Nevertheless, Adorno, almost out of nothing, suddenly brings in Auschwitz and introduces some sort of kinship between it and absolute negativity. He writes: "Genocide is the absolute integration. . . . Auschwitz confirmed the

---

[††]The original German edition was published in 1966. Quotations will be made from the English translation by E. B. Ashton published in 1973 by the Seabury Press of New York.

[‡‡]Adorno's accusation of "conceptual fetishism" against Marx's famous "Fetishism of Commodities" as "truly a piece from the heritage of classic German philosophy" (p. 189f) is not relevant here. Contrast it with Karel Kosík's analysis of the very same section in a work described below.

philosopheme of pure identity as death. . . . Absolute negativity is in plain sight and has ceased to surprise anyone" (p. 362).

By "almost out of nothing," I naturally do not mean that Auschwitz was not the reality of Fascism, nor do I mean only the suddenness and shock of introducing such subject matter in the climax of a book called "Meditations on Metaphysics." Rather, I mean it is wrong. That is to say, it is totally illogical and non-dialectical, considering that Adorno devoted an adult lifetime to fighting fascist ideology as the very opposite of Hegelian dialectics and had seen the very death of dialectics in Nazi Germany. Perhaps a better word than "wrong" would be Adorno's own curse-word "naive." I mean that as late as 1957, in his *Aspects of the Hegelian Dialectic*, he almost defended a subject-object identity.

> Subject-object cannot be dismissed as mere extravagance of logical absolutism. . . .
> In seeing through the latter as mere subjectivity, we have already passed beyond the
> Speculative idealism. . . . Cognition, if it is genuine, and more than simple duplica-
> tion of the subjective, must be the subject's objectivity.[7]

And, indeed, in his *Negative Dialectics*, he reiterates the same idea when he writes that, despite the fact that Hegel "deifies" subjectivity, "he accomplishes the opposite as well, an insight into the subject as a self-manifesting objectivity" (p. 350).

Why, then, such a vulgar reduction of absolute negativity? Therein is the real tragedy of Adorno (and the Frankfurt School). It is the tragedy of a one-dimensionality of thought which results when you give up Subject, when one does not listen to the voices from below—and they were loud, clear, and demanding between the mid-fifties and mid-sixties. It is a tragedy once one returns to the ivory tower and reduces his purpose to "the purpose of discussing key concepts of philosophic disciplines and centrally intervening in those disciplines" (p. xx). The next step was irresistible, the substitution of a permanent critique not alone for absolute negativity, but also for "permanent revolution itself."

Now, whether the enduring relevance of Hegel has stood the test of time because of the devotion and analytical rigor of Hegel scholars, or because a movement of freedom surged up *from below* and was followed by new cognition studies, there is no doubt that *because* Absolute Negativity signifies transformation of reality, the dialectic of contradiction and totality of crises, the dialectic of liberation, Hegel's thought comes to life at critical points of history, called by him "birth-times of history." In addition, there were Marxist scholars, revolutionary dissidents, who built on new ground. While a scholar from the West, like Reinhart Maurer, was preoccupied with Hegel's concept of where to end, the Czechoslovakian philosopher, Karel Kosík, was preoccupied with where to begin anew. Of the Eastern European studies that accompanied the revolts, and revolved around Marx's Humanism, especially Marx's "Critique of the Hegelian Dialectic," one of the most rigorous studies was Karel Kosík's *The Dialectics of the Concrete*.§§

Nor were these serious studies limited to the "East."*** As Frantz Fanon saw it, the African struggle for freedom was "not a treatise on the universal, but the untidy affirmation of an original idea propounded as an absolute."†††
There is no doubt, of course, that once action supersedes the subjectivity of purpose, the unity of theory and practice is the form of life out of which emerge totally new dimensions. To this writer, this is only the "proof " of the ending of the *Science of Logic*, the absolute as new beginning, the self-bringing forth of liberty. Because Hegel's great work had new horizons in sight, Nature and Spirit, the Absolute Idea had to undergo "absolute liberation" (*Befreiung*). No mere transition (*Übergang*) here; Freedom is unrestricted. It will "complete" (*vollendet*) its liberation in the *Philosophy of Mind (Geist)*. But there is no doubt either in the *Science of Logic* about the Notion being Subject, being Reality, and not some sort of closed ontology. To think that Hegel referred only to the idea of Christianity in the Graeco-Roman world when he wrote about "the pivot on which the impending world revolution turned at that time"‡‡‡ is both to forget the Christians thrown to the lions, and that it was the "resigned" Hegel of the *Philosophie des Rechts* who wrote about the

§§Two of the chapters of his *Dialectics of the Concrete* have been published in English in *Telos* (Fall, 1968, and Fall, 1969). While in the second issue, Kosík contrasts the empty absolutes of Schelling with those of Hegel, who characterized the absolutes of the Romantics as having got to the Absolutes "like a shot out of the pistol" [see Karel Kosík, *Dialectics of the Concrete*, trans. Karel Kovanda and James Schmidt (Boston and Dordrecht: D. Reidel, 1976), p. 35], in the earlier, 1968 issue, Kosík wrote that Marx's beginning of *Capital* with the commodity means "it can be characterized in Hegelian terms, as the unity of being and non-being, of distinction and similarity, of identity and non-identity. All further determinations are richer definitions or characterizations of this 'absolute' of capitalist society. The dialectic of interpretation or of exegesis cannot eclipse the central problem: how does science reach the *necessary beginning of the exposition*. . . . The dialectic is not a method of reduction, *but the method of spiritual and intellectual reproduction of reality*" [*Dialectics of the Concrete*, p. 17]. The only one in the academic world in Hegel studies in the West who has dealt seriously, not with *existing, given*, established, *state* Communism, but with Marx himself and sees the transformation of the commodity as phenomenon into Notion is Karl Löwith in his *From Hegel to Nietzsche*, trans. by David Green (New York: Vintage, 1964). The original German edition appeared in 1941. [*Von Hegel bis Nietzsche* (Zurich, 1953)]

***I have limited myself to Eastern Europe, but of course I really mean the East, the Orient, and Mao's perversion of Hegelian dialectics, especially the concept of Contradiction, with which I have dealt elsewhere. (See Chapter Five, "The Thought of Mao Zedong," in my *Philosophy and Revolution*, pp. 128–150.)

†††Frantz Fanon, *The Wretched of the Earth* (New York: Grove Press, 1973), p. 33.

‡‡‡Hegel, *The Philosophy of Right*, trans. Sir T. M. Knox (Oxford: Clarendon Press, 1942), Preface, p. 10. See also the translator's note 26 on page 301.

"impending world revolution" and not the young Hegel who had earlier toasted the great French Revolution.

Is it mere accident that, after 150 years of indifference, two simultaneous translations of the *Philosophy of Nature* appeared in English? Or is it mere accident that in the new studies on Hegel, a thinker like Professor Riedel suddenly sees *in Hegel* an equal primacy of the Theoretical and the Practical Idea?[8] Or that new studies in Hegel cover East and West, North and South, and that many of the world conferences on Hegel coincide with Marx and Lenin as philosophers? Is it not rather, that the problematic of our crisis-ridden world impinges in no incidental way on the whole question of the relationship of theory to practice not just on the immediate level, but one grounded in philosophy? No doubt, as Hegel put it, to accept a category at face value is an "uninstructed and barbarous procedure" [SLI, p. 49; SLM, p. 41]. But it is also a fact that the single dialectic process surges up from thought as well as from actuality. It would be equally "uninstructed" for philosophers to act as if the relationship of theory to practice is merely a " job for politicos." Just as the objective world and the elemental quest for universality have a crucial meaning for students of the dialectic, so do the students of the dialectic have a crucial meaning for the movement from practice. Just as the movement from the abstract universal to the concrete individual through the particular, *necessitating* a double negation (and that, after all, comprises the whole movement of the *Science of Logic),* so does the "comprehension" of it. If philosophers learn to eschew elitisms, then the unity of theory and practice, of absolute as new beginning, will not remain an abstract desire, or mere will, but philosophy itself will become action.

In his *Hegel: A Reexamination*, Professor Findlay was right when he stated that Hegel's exegeses can seem "arid and false to those who see nothing mysterious and god-like in the facts of human thought."[9] But is it not equally true that philosophers who stand only in terror before revolution not only do not "comprehend" *it,* they cannot fully comprehend the revolution *in thought?* And Hegel did revolutionize philosophy. Absolute Idea as new beginning can become a new "subjectivity" for realizing Hegel's principle, that "the transcendence of the opposition between Notion and Reality, and that unity which is truth, rest upon this subjectivity alone" [SLII, p. 477; SLM, p. 835]. This is not exactly a summons to the barricades, but Hegel is asking us to have our ears as well as our categories so attuned to the "Spirit's urgency" that we rise to the challenge of working out, through "patience, seriousness, suffering and the labor of the negative" [PhGB, p. 81; PhGM, p. 10] a totally new relationship of philosophy to actuality and action as befits a "birth-time of history" [PhGB, p. 75; PhGM, p. 6]. This is what makes Hegel a contemporary.

NOTES

1. In this essay, these and other parenthetical references to the German are by the author.

2. "Photocopy theory" refers to Lenin's *Materialism and Empirio-Criticism* (1908) and "voluntarism" to his *What Is To Be Done?* (1902).

3 Hegel writes: "The method itself by means of this moment expands itself into a system" [SLII, p. 480; SLM, p. 838].

4. Reinhart Klemens Maurer, *Hegel und das Ende der Geschichte: Interpretationen zur 'Phänomenologie des Geistes'*(Stuttgart: W. Kohlhammer Verlag, 1965), p. 86.

5. Otto Pöggeler, "Zur Deutung der *Phänomenologie des Geistes*," *Hegel-Studien*, Bd. I (Bonn: Bouvier Verlag, 1961), pp. 282–83.

6. See the "Letters on Hegel's Absolutes" in part I, above.

7. Adorno, "Aspects of Hegel's Philosophy" (original German edition 1957), in *Hegel: Three Studies*, trans. Shierry Weber Nicholsen (Cambridge: MIT Press, 1993), pp. 5–6.

8. See Manfred Riedel, *Theorie und Praxis im Denken Hegels* (Stuttgart: W. Kohlhammer Verlag, 1965).

9. J. N. Findlay, *Hegel: A Reexamination* (New York: Collier, 1958), p. 346.

CHAPTER ELEVEN

~

Hegel, Marx, Lenin, Fanon, and the Dialectics of Liberation Today

Delivered on December 5, 1976, this presentation to a series of classes being held on Philosophy and Revolution in Detroit, Michigan covers the full range of Hegel's dialectic—as well as its re-creation in Marx and the attempts by Lenin and by philosophers such as Sartre, Lukács, and Adorno to concretize dialectics for the realities of their day. Coming shortly after the eruption of the Soweto revolt in South Africa in 1976, it contains one of Dunayevskaya's treatments of the thought of the African revolutionary Frantz Fanon. The original can be found in the Supplement to the Raya Dunayevskaya Collection, p. 15024.

We want to begin immediately with both *masses in motion* and the *self-determination of the Idea*, in order to stress that there is a single dialectical process in both thought and activity. And that single dialectical process is the Absolute method, that is, the dialectical method of revolution, whether in thought or in fact—and in both is what we're after.

And in order to stress that, it is important to see that even though Hegel was a bourgeois philosopher, the greatest that ever lived, he was *not* as abstract as his great philosophic works make him appear if you follow only various stages of consciousness or the philosophic categories. In fact, every philosophic category stands for a strict period in history, all of which covers the vast amount of 2,500 years. (In other words, so far as Hegel is concerned, it all began in 500 B.C. with Greek philosophy, and through the French Revolution, which is the period in which he lived.)

Because this single dialectical process is historic, and because I want you to see that it isn't something that Marx "added on" to what Hegel said, but is *in* Hegel, I want to begin with Hegel's statement that no idea is worth being called an idea unless it's an idea of freedom:

When individuals and nations have once got in their heads the concept of full-blown liberty, there is nothing like it in its uncontrollable strength, just because it is the very essence of mind, and that as its very actuality. The Greeks and Romans, Plato and Aristotle, even the Stoics did not have it. . . . If to be aware of the idea—to be aware, i.e., that men are aware of freedom as their essence, aim, and object—is a matter of speculation, still this very idea itself is the actuality of men—not something which they have, as men, but which they are. [PM, ¶482]

This appears not in an inconsequential essay, but directly in his highest book, the *Philosophy of Mind.*

Now there has to be a reason for our study a lot more urgent than what is encompassed by the word "relevance"—Hegel's "relevance for our day." [The reason is] the todayness of the Hegelian dialectic, and of Marx's new continent of thought that emerges out of two elements—both the movement from practice to theory and the movement from theory to practice. In order to get it, to grasp it, not only at its roots, but [in] its ramifications for our day, we have to grasp Marxism in its original state, in its original philosophy, which by no accident Marx called "a new Humanism." We must grasp this free from all distortions of Marxists, whether it be post-World War I, or World War II, or post-Marx (in other words, post-[Paris] Commune)—and along with that we also have to get the origin and specificity of Hegelian dialectics, because again, it is no accident that Marx considered that *the* source of all dialectics, his own included.

For us, Marx's Humanism is on the basis of our day, which began in the 1950s with the upsurge for the first time ever from under totalitarian Communism—the [1953] East German Revolution.[1] This spread all through the globe, Latin America, Africa, and so forth. The concrete specific form for our day of the Hegelian dialectic, and our original contribution, is *Absolute as New Beginning.*

Those three little words, "as new beginning," tell you that it's our day and no other day, and we will have to come through and understand this—not only because it is our original theoretic contribution, but because this is the reality of what happened in life, the momentous world historic events of the last two decades. "Absolute as new beginning" happened in life when the Hungarian revolutionaries [in 1956], and first the East Germans, brought Marx's Humanist essays from the dusty library shelves onto the historic stage of new freedom. They were also so in thought—maybe not quite the way we are saying it, though you will see that it's not too far removed, as was clear to those who recognized this passion for freedom and operated as revolutionaries. I'm referring specifically to Frantz Fanon.

There were two stages in Frantz Fanon's development that concern us, the 1950s and the 1960s (our own contribution is of course in the 1970s, even though we lived a great deal before then). Something had emerged from below with all these events occurring throughout East Europe and the beginnings of the new African revolutions. In thought what occurred was that Frantz Fanon, in *Black Skins, White Masks* had challenged Sartre (even though he himself considered himself an Existentialist) on two grounds. One is the section of *Black Skins, White Masks* where Fanon takes up "Hegel and the Negro." Hegel didn't take up the Negro question, and that is exactly what Fanon said was wrong. What Hegel took up in the *Phenomenology of Mind* was the relationship of labor to the master. Hegel's great theory of alienation was that precisely because the slave was "nothing," and had to do everything the master said, had to do all the labor, precisely *through* his labor [he] got a mind of his own, an attitude to objectivity of his own. [The slave was therefore the] person who was everything but who really had nothing. But Fanon said, nevertheless, these two opposites [of master and slave] were not as totally Absolute as they would have been had Hegel considered the Black dimension. Involved in this dialectic of the relationship of master to slave, as Hegel postulates it, was still the essence of some reciprocity. Somewhere on the way to a mind of your own, you would be able to force some recognition of yourself, as man, as woman, and not just as slave, from the master. *But,* says Fanon, Hegel didn't consider the Black, and it isn't the least bit true that the master is interested in the Black at all. The really Absolute, where there is no reciprocity, is this slave who in addition to being a slave, in addition to being the exploited labor, is Black, and is not at all recognized by the Other. Therefore, the dialectic would have to be much sharper, and see a certain transformation of reality which was deeper, than that of Hegel.[2]

For example, in my age (I'm talking as if I were Frantz Fanon) there is Sartre, and he is Left, and he is a good friend, and he is trying to establish a new philosophy for our age, which he calls Existentialism. But look what he does with those three major categories of all of philosophy, Individual, Particular, and Universal. There is a movement from the abstract Universal through the Particular, supposedly to the concrete, the Individual, who would be absolutely free, and the only proof that the Universal was a reality and not just a thought. But what does Sartre tell me in *Black Orpheus*? He tells me that Black is only a Particular, a minor term in these three terms. So then Fanon does two things in this particular section ("The Fact of Blackness"). One is that he quotes the other West Indian, Aimé Césaire, in which he tries to show the difference of the dialectic when it comes not from knowledge but from anguish [p. 123]:

Those who invented neither gunpowder nor the compass
Those who never learned to conquer steam or electricity

Those who never explored the seas or the skies
But they know the farthest corners of the land of anguish[3]

Fanon goes on to explain that *that* is what makes them the revolutionaries and what makes them strive for this philosophic expression as one of revolution. Whereupon he then quotes Sartre, on Black being only a minor, particular term, and says: "Sartre was reminding me that my Blackness was only a minor term. . . . In all truth, in all truth I tell you, my shoulders slipped out of the framework of the world, my feet could no longer feel the touch of the ground" [p. 138].

Now after this very beautiful thing, do you think Sartre changed his mind? We will see what he became. But the point is the fact that at momentous historic moments, what we call a passion for philosophy is actually the passion for freedom, which strives to acquire, to find, a philosophic expression that would not separate itself from the transformation of reality. And when we look globally at something, we realize that it's no accident that here is 1952, Frantz Fanon [is] writing this; and here is 1953, the East German Revolution; and here is 1953, Hegel's Absolute Idea being interpreted as the unity of theory and practice, the movement from practice to theory, on the part of those who were discovering Marxist-Humanism.[4] So what is the dialectic but the movement of both ideas and of masses in motion towards the transformation of reality? And this is in contrast to the lack of all method, which is reactionary, and [is] what Hegel called the Third Attitude Toward Objectivity.

We always speak—and it's easy, because it's so nice to speak of revolutions—of how, under the impact of the French Revolution, Hegel put to method the actual activity of masses in motion, the *sans culottes* in France, and so forth, and called it the dialectic.[5] But in this period there was not only revolution, but counter-revolution, and we had not the millennium, but Napoleon. So why do we only talk of the dialectical method in Hegel, and not speak about what happened on the question of counter-revolution, on the question of what Hegel himself called reactionary moves? As the philosophic expression of this tendency, this specifically concerns Jacobi.

In 1807, when he wrote the *Phenomenology of Mind*, Hegel had, so to speak, laughed at Jacobi. He didn't take him very seriously or deal with him at great length. He mentions Jacobi as part of the culture of what's called the Beautiful Soul, where the people had already gained minds of their own, and they had civilization, Enlightenment, and culture—and nobody's happy anyway.[6] Instead of trying to find out [why] there was the rift between actuality and philosophy, the people began to say, "My soul (the cultured ones) is beautiful, but these backward masses, they do not understand."[7] In passing, Hegel talks about Jacobi as part of the Beautiful Soul, as part of the Romantics [whom] he's denying if you're really going to transform reality. By 1812, when he writes the *Science of Logic*, Hegel doesn't any longer just talk of Jacobi as the Beautiful Soul (because that also included Schelling, and he was just breaking with him and all the Romantics up to his time). He does say: perhaps you have already forgotten Jacobi, he was just a minor philosopher, nevertheless it's important to recognize what he represented.[8]

There are two movements in the *Science of Logic*: the historic and dialectical movement of the self-determination of the Idea, from Being to Essence to Notion, and the polemical movement. In other words, he no sooner says something, like the first two paragraphs on Being and Nothingness, than he is off for twenty long pages on every philosopher who had ever said something on these two categories that was quite different. In the polemical movement, you already see he's denying [Jacobi] any importance.

The final year of his life, 1830–1831, was the last thing we have from him, the final three syllogisms [of the *Philosophy of Mind*]. At this late point, Jacobi gets an entire section, the Third Attitude to Objectivity. What had happened in those 14 years [since the final volume of the *Science of Logic* was published in 1816] that made Hegel change his mind? What prompted Hegel to devote an entire section to someone who was supposed to be so minor that he may have already been forgotten? Well, you not only didn't have the millennium, you also had the first capitalist crisis, 1825. This was quite a revelation for classical political economy, which was always saying that the reason for the crisis is feudalism, our little crises are just feudal blemishes; as soon as we get rid of feudalism all will be happy. But now, it isn't quite so. Hegel sees that the movement isn't always upward and onward; there is a retrogression. You come to a certain point, and instead of really transforming reality, and giving your life for it, suddenly you begin to say, "It's really faith," and [you] go back. So the idea, that this late in life, after the Enlightenment, after the French Revolution, you can still say, "Not philosophy, but Faith, God, let's go back to that"— that is the reactionary movement.

Hegel recognized this, and in 1914, in a much sharper way, Lenin recognized the same thing with the breakdown of the Second International: counter-revolution is *within* the revolution. [Lenin saw that] something is crazy, and we really have to transform all this through revolutionary movement. So we have to therefore keep in mind that in this single dialectical, revolutionary process, the *lack* of method, the lack of trying to see what you should actually do, suddenly [means] you're giving it back to faith. That is the reactionary movement.

All these beautiful syntheses are supposed to be in Hegel—the Absolute

Knowledge of the *Phenomenology of Mind* as the unity of science and history, the Absolute Idea in *Science of Logic* as the unity of theory and practice, and the Absolute Mind in *Philosophy of Mind* as the unity of the objective and the subjective. And yet what happens if there is really also retrogression? What is going to be done to stop it, to overcome it, to transcend it? Even before Marx had brought in a whole new continent of thought, and showed that it's all diremptions, and not syntheses at all, and spoke in clear language—instead of just "contradictions" he spoke of class struggles, and so forth—still there was an element of this in *thought,* in Hegel.[9] Hegel had recognized this by . . . hitting on Jacobi as the person and the attitude that is shown when the revolution has not been transformed into a new society.

So we have, therefore, in this introductory [section], the masses in motion, the self-determination of the Idea to hear itself speak, and how it develops; we have the single dialectical process of both of them. Let us see where we actually get when we come to today, and try to recapture not only Marx, but also Hegel, and within Hegel capture what was just an element, just implicit, not quite clear—because this Absolute Idea as new beginning means we have seen something in Hegel that no others have seen, because they didn't live in our age, and each age brings out something new in what the people from below have done [and in] what has happened in world historic events.

Naturally we won't be able to cover all of Hegel's works. We will be emphasizing the *Phenomenology of Mind*, the *Science of Logic*, and the *Philosophy of Mind*—and all these with Marx's original contributions, the humanist essays and *Capital*. And we will look at each one in our age who has tried a new philosophy, [such as Louis] Althusser. Althusser really goes backward. Compared to him, [Eduard] Bernstein was practically a revolutionary. Althusser wants to "drive Hegel back into the night";[10] he really wants to do more than just get rid of the "dialectical scaffolding."[11]

Let us now see what is involved in the movement of Hegel's works. You have the *Phenomenology of Mind* as different stages of consciousness: Consciousness, Self-Consciousness, Reason. Then you go into Spirit, which is supposedly the new society, but you find out that Spirit too is in Self-Estrangement, and culture really transforms into opposite the relationship of reality to thought. And when you therefore re-arise into Absolute Knowledge, there is something that is really abstract—and Hegel thought so too, but he wanted to come to a certain conclusion. Everyone, Marxists and non-Marxists, and people who don't believe in anything Hegel wrote, recognize that according to a mechanical view of things, the [*Phenomenology*] is very chaotic. Hegel originally thought he was only writing on Consciousness, Self-Consciousness, Reason; that's all he had outlined. He had planned this as a little introduction to what he would write in the *Science of Logic,* where he would write in actual scientific, i.e., philosophic categories. But what happened is that the *Phenomenology* stretched for 800 pages. The point, however, is that the *Phenomenology* reflects both the movement in life—in this case, the French Revolution—and Hegel's disgust with his colleagues, the philosophers, who were using all of the same old categories. Hegel was saying: for heaven's sake, look how the world has *changed.* We Germans just keep talking, but the French have really done everything; they've abolished the monarchy, they've established the republic—or at least part way—they've gone through things and done it. What have we done except talk? At this point—loving the French and hating the Germans—Hegel was even welcoming Napoleon, thinking: well, at least he'll get rid of feudalism in Germany (he changed his mind later on). So Hegel wasn't the least bit sad as the *Phenomenology of Mind* went to press; as editor of a daily paper, he was also witnessing Napoleon ride into Germany.

There is nothing that so excites Existentialists as the *Phenomenology of Mind.* They have built their Existentialism on it, or at least they think so. They have tried to *apply* it. *But* it is impossible—it is wrong, in addition to being impossible—to try to apply Hegel. If what Hegel described is true, you have to see that there is a dual rhythm of revolution and counter-revolution, a dual rhythm of thought and activity [which] emerges from below. You have to work out the dialectic for your age; you can't just "apply" it. But everyone has tried to apply it. Marcuse, for example, has written on "The Conquest of the Unhappy Consciousness." [In the *Phenomenology*] Hegel goes from the relationship of master and servant—in other words, self-consciousness and social relations—to Stoicism and the Unhappy Consciousness. [He shows that] you get very unhappy when feudalism falls [because] you can't find a new place for yourself in the new society. Instead of being happy and thinking the Stoics are great, Hegel says Stoicism is a philosophy in a stage of slavery. You have accepted slavery, you are not going to overthrow it—[as in the] Romans conquering Greece. Hegel was trying to see all these stages. Marcuse has a section in *One-Dimensional Man* (which actually shows his one-dimensional thought), and it's beautiful—you can laugh your head off.[12] It's about the Rand Corporation, and how they have a big map showing who would be overthrown and destroyed if there was an A-bomb and an H-bomb and so forth; everyone's supposed to be so unhappy, [since] here we are in a society that could just destroy mankind altogether. And then after they get through with the lecture, they all sit down and have coffee in this beautiful room and discuss beautiful things. But is that the conquest of the Unhappy Consciousness? That is certainly not what Hegel meant, nor can you see [in it] any dialectical development. If you're opposed to that—and certainly Marcuse was—you can only get to the Great Refusal, and that is not Hegelian.

Take Merleau-Ponty. He said that the greatest work since the *Phenomenology of Mind* was *Capital*.[13] But *Capital* is not the application, so to speak, of the *Phenomenology*. Sartre says that the fetishism of commodities, in chapter 1 of *Capital*, is the greatest thing, but it just begins our trouble.[14] Each one—even Engels—tried to apply the relationship of Hegel to Marx, instead of seeing how each arose in its time on the basis of the dialectic, and that what you have to do is *recreate* the dialectic for your age. Engels said that Being, Essence and Notion [in Hegel's *Logic*] are equivalent to the sections in *Capital* on commodity and exchange value, the market (Being); the production process, the actual exploitation (Essence); and the overthrow, the objective-subjective moment (Notion).[15] The point, however, is that Marx had to create an entirely new continent of thought to develop all of those categories in chapter 1 of *Capital*, as well as other material that is original [to] Marx and only Marx. The idea of trying to "apply" means that supposedly you are so unhappy with just abstract categories that you want to go immediately to the concrete. In fact, however, you haven't yet grasped the Hegelian dialectic.

Look at what Hegel does after he even reaches Absolute Knowledge. First of all there is the Golgotha of the Spirit—so much for synthesis. [At the end of the *Phenomenology*] Hegel makes you think you're up in heaven, but it turns out that you've just been crucified.[16] So he says: don't worry about being crucified, this is just phenomenon; wait till you get to the real science in the *Science of Logic*. Now after 800 pages of the *Phenomenology of Mind*, and Spirit in Self-Estrangement, and so forth, he begins *Science of Logic* with the question, "With what should one begin?" as if he's just brought up the question.[17] He decides to begin with the abstract, Being. Whether you think of it as God, or the human being, [it is] something quite abstract. We won't develop that here. But [for] now let's look at a person who *is* a revolutionary, who isn't trying to "apply" Hegel, but is trying to figure out what is happening in his age: Lenin.

Lenin reads the *Science of Logic* and gets very excited. He says: Oh my heavens! That Prussian philosopher, everything is self-transcendence, self-activity, self-development. What is this? This is real revolution. How come we never saw it before, or at least I didn't? But when he comes to the end of the very first section of the *Science of Logic*, [which deals with] Measure, he gets even more excited. He now writes not just of "self-development," but "Leaps! Leaps! LEAPS!" [LCW 38, p. 123]. Let's see for just a moment what is the particular section that Lenin was so crazy about. (Incidentally, people are always mistaking "Quality," [by speaking of] the transformation of Quantity into Quality. Quality is the *first* term; it is something as against just nothing. Quan-

tity is the bigger thing, because now you are a lot of people. [In] the movement to Measure, you now have so many Quantities that it becomes the Measure of man, the Measure of woman.)[18] The particular section that got Lenin
so excited is where Hegel says, "The gradualness of arising is based upon the
idea that that which arises is already, sensibly or otherwise, *actually there*, and
is imperceptible only on account of its smallness. . . . Understanding prefers
to fancy identity and change to that indifferent and external kind which
applies to the quantitative" [LCW 38, p. 124; SLI, p. 390; SLM, p. 371]. In
other words, Hegel is saying: if you think that gradual change is the same
thing, so to speak, as a revolution, you're crazy! It isn't true that if you only
waited two more days, or if you had 1,000 people instead of 100, you would
really have a new quality. The Measure will bring about such a revolution that
you will be on the threshold of an entirely new world, the world of Essence.

So when Lenin writes, "Leaps! LEAPS! *LEAPS!*" he is thinking of something very concrete. [He says to himself]: This world is crazy! It's 1914, the
world is going to pieces, the world war has happened, and what the hell do my
comrades in the Second International do about it? That original discussion
with Bernstein on "Evolution or Revolution" [in 1898–99] was poppycock
compared to what we're seeing now. So when Lenin is ready to see Measure
as the threshold of Essence and of the Revolution, he will break from within,
and not only against something else.

Now when you get to Essence, you can again be very abstract if you want
to; you can take contradiction and strip it of both its objectivity and what
Marx said it was, the class struggle, and make it contradiction in the Maoist
sense, [namely], anything that you decide is contradicted by something else.[19]
When you get to the end of th[e Doctrine of Essence], you have the first
appearance of the Absolute, but as Substance.[20] In other words, it's God.
You've seen the actuality, and you've seen what was behind the phenomenal
appearance, but Hegel says: well, if you think you've got there, you're wrong.
It's as high as Spinoza got. But so long as you don't see it developing and
emerging from itself, and how it redevelops and transforms itself, you're not
going to get there. Lenin now gained a new appreciation for the ideal as real,
for the subjective and not just objective, for a new relationship of theory and
practice, for the Doctrine of the Notion, which he decides is really the objective and subjective way of overcoming the old and establishing the new classless society.

Just as Hegel said if he had to put all his philosophy in one single sentence,
he would say that what distinguishes his from all others is that the search for
truth, the attempt to get to the ultimate, it is not just Substance, that is, a sta-
tic thing, but Subject, self-creative and developing, so Marx said that there is

only one thing that matters: labor![21] That has produced everything. It is Subject, and not only as an activity that produces [things], but as the labor*er* that
is going to be the gravedigger of this society. And therefore we have to see how
could we as revolutionaries use bourgeois terms, like "commodity" [for labor]
as if that's really it? Why don't we see that it's a fetish? And Marx had something to say on this at the end of chapter 1 of *Capital*.

But first I want to break down this idea of "application," [of] why was Engels
wrong, or at least not fully appreciative of all that Marx had done in that chapter 1 [of *Capital*]. Take that first chapter of *Capital* on the commodity. The first
three pages say every commodity is a use value—you wear it, or you sleep in
it, etc.—and an exchange value. But if you think that that's it, you're crazy.
Marx is saying: it's true I won't be able to explain to you in full the nature of
exploitation until we get to production processes, but what is it that creates
the two-fold character of labor? That is so important, that is [so much] my
original contribution, that I must immediately in section 2 of this chapter talk
about this.[22] What is this two-fold character of labor that Marx is so proud of
having discovered that he insisted it is his original contribution? Labor, too,
is a use-value: [it is] concrete and specific. You're a tailor, or a miner, or whatever; you create something that you are able to create, and whoever buys what
you create will buy it because it's useful to him. But how do you create value?
How could all these different laborers just produce congealed labor? You say
you never saw an abstract laborer? The capitalist did: it's his factory clock that
pounds you all, no matter what your specific ability is, into so much socially
necessary labor time. That's what makes this exchange of one thing for
another possible, how much labor you put into this thing and how much labor
you put into that. Now isn't [it] fantastic that you suddenly become an abstract
laborer? So if it is the factory clock that pounds you down and makes of your
congealed labor "value," could he have made of *you* a thing too? What are you
selling? Your ability to labor. Can you take your hands out of your body? They
wouldn't be any good then, they wouldn't be able to create anything. The
point is that of all the millions of commodities that are exchanged, there is
only one that is alive, the living laborer. When he or she gets into the factory,
and that factory clock tells him what to produce—yes, he becomes nothing
but an appendage to a machine. That's what capitalism has done to you. So
the capitalist has transformed you into that appendage to a machine, and
made you into abstract labor, and gotten from you much more than you have
been paid for because you definitely are producing more than he pays you.
You're going to produce as long as he tells you.

Hegel takes up 2,500 years [in his *Phenomenology of Mind*]. In chapter 1 of
Capital, [in discussing] commodities and the various forms of exchange value,

Marx takes up 6,000 years. He takes up every society that has ever existed, and what has been its measure—what did they exchange, and how much labor went into it? And he brings it up to this final machine age, where the machine makes it so easy for you to be "abstract labor." Marx contrasts Aristotle, the greatest thinker of ancient society, to an ordinary worker who, so to speak, knows "nothing." Marx says: look at Aristotle. He kept asking questions— how in the heck can a table get exchanged for a dress [or] a book? What is the common denominator? Marx says: because his was a slave society, and the free laborer didn't produce anything, Aristotle *couldn't* think of the fact that what makes them all exchangeable is labor.[23] Because you the laborer are producing, even though you don't have all of Aristotle's great knowledge, look how quickly you know the answer to these questions. Now the capitalist with the machine also "knows." At the end of chapter 1, Marx brings in the fetishism of commodities. He asks the simple question: how in the heck has everything got a commodity form? What is this fetish? That table is made of wood, it's made as a table, but it becomes a commodity to be exchanged. Suddenly it's a measure, suddenly it's something else; this has more grotesque ideas than anything! Marx even has a footnote where he contrasts the difference between the wood and the table when it becomes a commodity and gets exchanged for something else, to the Chinese Revolution, the Taiping Rebellion. He says: look at that; after the 1848 revolutions, we in Europe lost, and so now we're doing nothing—this is the quiescent 1850s. But what did the Chinese, who we think are "barbarians," do? The[y had the] Taiping Rebellion.[24] It's to encourage us not to be so dumb in the 1860s and to actually do something.[25]

So we see that he brings in, first, Being—the commodity as use-value and exchange-value; then we have Essence—production, labor; and now we come to the Doctrine of the Notion—all in this first chapter of the fetishism of commodities. In Notion he says: what is the stupid form? I know what capitalism is, I know it is exploitation, so why do *I* use the [term] *form* [in discussing the commodity]? It turns out that even when he finished chapter 1 he didn't answer that single question, what is the [secret of the] fetish[ism of commodities]? as [clearly] as he did after the Paris Commune, when he said: "clearly, it arises from this form itself" [MCIF, p. 164; MCIK, p. 82].[26] In other words, he was saying, until you are free laborers, until you have a non-state like the Paris Commune, until you make your own decisions and say, "so much I earn, and so much I do, such-and-such should be our labor, with no division between mental and manual labor and so forth," until then he couldn't answer that question, "what makes [the commodity-form] a fetish?" And after the Paris Commune he could answer [that] the commodity form itself [represents] the specificity of the capitalist system—and it will be like this until we can rip this system up. So here we have this tremendous chapter 1 of *Capital*. It is not an "application" of Hegel. Marx had found a whole new continent of thought. And in finding this new continent of thought, Marx found not only that labor is the source of all value, but that it is the Subject which will be the gravedigger of society. With labor as Subject, there will be a new classless society, where humanism is its own end and its own form. And thus what Marx had said in 1844 as a young man, "just being enthusiastic," he is now saying at the end of chapter 1 of *Capital*.

Let's look at what Sartre, Lukács, and the others did; at how they failed to recreate the dialectic for their age. Let's first take Lukács. Lukács made a great contribution in 1919, in "What Is Orthodox Marxism?" by saying that it is just fantastic to disregard Marx's origins in Hegel and to dismiss Hegel as a mystic.[27] Marx couldn't have been without Hegel; and the dialectic means development through contradiction, not only as first negation—that is, when you say *no* and overthrow what is—but on through second negativity, the establishment of something new. However, intellectuals are very funny; they get so in love with their own thought that they meanwhile forget all about the mass movement. The Second International has now been destroyed and you've shown that any kind of reformism that tries to pass as revolutionary but doesn't have the dialectic method is wrong, and you've shown the connection between economics and dialectics—beautiful! But what does Lukács do now? Well, Marx talked about the reification of labor—the fetishism of commodities, and the fact that you become an appendage to a machine. Lukács now wants to show that it's not only reification of labor, but reification of thought. He doesn't want to use Marx's idea of false ideology, that the capitalist has a false ideology because he cannot see through these things; [the capitalist] is the Spirit still in Self-Estrangement. (Incidentally, those two last paragraphs and the footnotes in chapter 1 of *Capital* is the Spirit in Self-Estrangement.)[28] Lukács develops the reification of thought to such an extent [that he acts] as if that is as important as reification of labor.[29] But how could that change the world? In that case, what will you do? Belong to the Third International instead of the Second, in other words a political answer? What is it that you're arguing *with*? How will that *change the life of the worker*? Well, Lukács doesn't bother with that. And the tragedy is, not only did he capitulate to Stalinism, but for that one moment in his life when he broke from Stalinism—in 1956 in the Hungarian Revolution—what he talked about was Democratic Socialism, and not a change in the actual conditions of labor.[30] And when he comes to his greatest work, *Social Ontology* (we don't have it yet, but some of the sections were published in *Telos*), he comes back to the fact that once you supposedly have a workers' state, you don't have to worry anymore about socially necessary labor time.[31] That is, you have to produce, and it's okay.

Now, Sartre comes to Poland and attacks the "frozen Marxism" of Lukács.[32] He's mad at Lukács (chooses the wrong day to be mad at him, incidentally), because Lukács had attacked Existentialism and tried to rate Sartre's Existentialism as if it were no different than Heidegger's (who was a fascist).[33] So here Sartre comes to Eastern Europe, which has just made *revolution* against Russian totalitarianism, and says: *I*, Sartre, have brought in the human element and showed the greatness of the Individual, the Existential and not the Essential; and now this has to be reconquered by Marxism. And how does he reconquer it? [With the concept of] the fetishism of commodities. He makes more mistakes than you could shake a stick at. (Read my chapter on Sartre in *Philosophy and Revolution*; I can't go into it all here.)[34] Everybody comes back to the [idea] that the workers are "backward," and they, the intellectuals, are so great. And Sartre comes back to a new category that is even worse than the "backwardness of the workers," the "practico-inert."[35] [It says] you're all really dumb, and you better do what the Party tells you, or what the State tells you, and so forth.

Now how does it happen that they all return to that one little thing: where is labor, and where is the laborer? And what is my role as the intellectual? I will quote from the end of the Sartre chapter in *Philosophy and Revolution*:

> One would have thought that Sartre, who returned to a work of philosophic rigor after he had become, or at least was in the process of becoming, an adherent of Marx's historical materialism, would at least in theory attempt to end the bifurcation between subject and object, would concretize his project of "going beyond" as the Subject appropriating objectivity, not vice versa. Instead, having laid a foundation for a metaphysics of Stalinism, Sartre seems totally unconscious of the fact that his methodology is at the opposite pole, not from Communism, but from the Marxism of Marx. Despite all rhetoric about praxis, Sartre's methodology does not emanate from praxis. Far from being any "algebra of revolution," Sartrean methodology is the abstraction which reduces history to illustrations and analogy. . . . The anti-Stalinist, anti-capitalist, revolutionary petty-bourgeois intellectual, himself the victim of the absolute division between mental and manual labor, the climax of centuries of division between philosophers and workers, seemed always ready to hand over the role of workers' self-emancipation to "the Party," even though its "philosophy" amounted to ordering the workers to work hard and harder. . . . The philosophy of existence fails to merge with Marxism because it has remained Subjectivity without a Subject, desire for revolution without the "new forces, new passions" for revolution. [P&R, pp. 206–07, p. 210]

It's these new forces and new passions for revolution that make us return to Hegel's Absolute Idea as new beginnings. Even though we aren't now as active as we were, say, in the 1960s, what is so great in our age is that we have reached a stage where we *are* trying to work out a new relationship of theory and practice, a new relationship of philosophy and revolution.

What are the new beginnings? They are on two levels—the actual forces of revolution, workers, Blacks, youth, and women; and then, only when you have forces of revolution, can you speak of them on the second level, not only as force but as Reason. But now, as against stressing a human force as Reason, we want to stress Reason as a *force* for revolution. You cannot subdivide, or divide in any way, the theory and the practice, and say it's only in the practice; there has to be a new unity of the two. So the "new beginning" means, "What has happened in our lifetime?" We want to take up, therefore, what happened in the last two decades, and see at which stage I was, so to speak, forced to rethink.

We have taken up the *Phenomenology of Mind* and the *Science of Logic;* now we're going to go into *Philosophy of Mind.* But I want to first say one concrete thing as to how I happened to go to those abstractions. Lenin finished his work on the *Science of Logic,* and he was very happy that in the first half of its last paragraph, Hegel had said we now go to Nature. Lenin says: Nature is practice, and hoorah! Hegel is stretching a hand to historical materialism; he was a precursor of historical materialism. Now, that is true, but we have to look at where Lenin stopped; in other words, what was in the last half paragraph? In 1953 I was rereading this for different purposes. 1953 was a lovely time for me because Stalin died! What could make me happier than that? So I'm in heaven, and thinking: well, that must be a new stage of something or other; what will the masses do now? I come to where Lenin stopped, where he says the last half paragraph after Hegel stretches his hand to Nature, is unimportant. I read the last half paragraph, and wrote a letter about it. This is what I say:

> But my dear Vladimir Ilyich, it is not true; the end of that page *is* important. We of 1953, we who have lived three decades after you and tried to absorb all you have left us, we can tell you that. Listen to the very next sentence from Hegel: "But this determination is not a perfected becoming or a transition."

(In other words, Hegel is saying Nature is not a transition.)

> Remember how transition was everything to you in the days of Monopoly, the eve of socialism. Well, Hegel has passed beyond transition; he says this last determination, "the pure Idea, in which the determinateness or reality of the Notion is itself raised to the level of Notion, is an absolute *liberation*, having no further immediate determination which is not equally posited and equally Notion. Consequently there is no transition in this freedom. . . . The transition here therefore must rather be taken to mean that the Idea freely releases itself in absolute self-security and self-repose."[36]

Where Lenin stressed the objectivity, we add the emphasis, "personal and free." (In other words, a quotation from the next sentence of Hegel.)[37] Where Lenin had next emphasized materialism, we stress the transcendence of the opposition between Notion and Reality. And where Lenin stopped a paragraph short of the end of the *Logic*, we proceed to show that Hegel's anticipation of Volumes 2 and 3 of the *Encyclopedia of the Philosophical Sciences* [the *Philosophy of Nature* and *Philosophy of Mind*] was similar to Marx's anticipation of the general law of capitalist accumulation in Volume 1 of *Capital*. (Those of you who know *Capital*, in chapter [32], on the general law of capitalist accumulation, he gives you very nearly everything in Volumes 2 and 3, right there, because he ventures to show that these new passions and new forces for the reconstruction of a new society will be human power as its own end.)[38] We concluded that what Hegel is showing in the movement from Logic to Nature to Mind was this: "The movement is from logical principle or theory, to Nature, or practice, and from practice not alone to theory, but to the new society which is its essence."[39] I then said[40] I must go to *Philosophy of Mind*. (After the *Science of Logic*, after Hegel finished the Doctrine of the Notion, he had the *Encyclopedia of the Philosophical Sciences*, where he had first the *Logic*, then the *Philosophy of Nature*, then the *Philosophy of Mind*.)

Now, in the last year of his life, Hegel decided that something wasn't kosher [in] ending [the *Philosophy of Mind*] with ¶574. He said: we have three syllogisms—Logic-Nature-Mind is the first. That sounds like he's merely repeating the titles of his books—the *Logic*, the *Philosophy of Nature*, and the *Philosophy of Mind*. But what is more important, and shows the new here, is that Nature is the mediation, the middle term; it's therefore not Logic that's the most important, it's Nature, because mediation, dialectically, is both objective and subjective. Nature turns to Mind, and it looks back at Logic, but disregards it, because it's now turning to something else. So I read this and say: Well! Hegel is not only stretching a hand to Nature, which is practice (I'm willing to accept that from Lenin and think it's great), but this syllogism shows that there is a movement from practice (that's what I was trying to point out in 1953) that is itself a form of theory.[41] What is it that the East Germans, the Hungarians—the whole of East Europe—had been showing? They not only took Marx's Humanism from the archives and put that on the historic stage, but they made something *new* with workers' councils and decentralization of the state, and so forth. So this syllogism is showing that so far as Hegel was concerned, Nature is the central thing, and there is a movement from practice which is itself a form of theory. But it simply isn't true that Hegel stops at this point, as we see immediately when we get to the second syllogism. The second syllogism is Nature-Mind-Logic. Mind becomes the central thing, the mediation. (That shows he's not just mentioning his books, because now he's turning around their order.) What is important about [doing] it that way?

Now I'll tell you something fantastic. None of the Marxists had bothered with these three categories in the *Philosophy of Mind* because we already had a new continent of thought, Marxism. There didn't seem to be any use to go back to abstractions, when Marx was so great in explaining exactly what the abstractions mean. But there is one advantage to an abstraction—if you meet a new epoch and a new crisis, a new transformation into opposite, if it's too concrete it just doesn't hold anymore. (You've now met Stalinism and not just the Second International; you're now meeting something else, and not just whatever it was before.) So therefore the abstraction makes it easier to try and see what is new in your age, what does your age think about. Now, the scholars also didn't pay any attention to these three syllogisms. I was quite shocked to find out that it was only in the mid-1960s that one of the finest, [Reinhart Klemens] Maurer, took these up. Here's what he's trying to do with that second syllogism [PM, ¶576].[42] He says: actually, it shows that this is the syllogism for the *Phenomenology of Mind* (you see, [phenomenology] becomes Nature). After all, the *Phenomenology of Mind* isn't just phenomena, but a whole philosophy of history; it takes in 2,500 years of history. Now, there's only one trouble in trying to appropriate this second syllogism for the *Phenomenology of Mind*—why did Hegel make this great work of his so inconsequential by the time he wrote the *Encyclopedia of the Philosophical Sciences*? He only gives it one single section, and under psychology, of all places! Hegel would have failed anyone who dared to say that that second syllogism was really the *Phenomenology of Mind*. But let's look at what Hegel did before this. The [chapters on the Three Attitudes of Thought Toward Objectivity] were not in the 1817 edition of the Smaller Logic.[43] The first attitude to objectivity is Faith—everything that was pre-Kantian or pre-empirical. Then the second attitude to objectivity is when you reach the Industrial Revolution in England, and the revolutionary philosophy of Kant, his introduction of dialectics. Now, if you were believing only in synthesis, your third attitude should be your dialectic, right? No. The third attitude to objectivity is the retrogression, once you have met a new crisis within that great big new beautiful civilized world of the Industrial Revolution and the French Revolution and the Kantian dialectic. So you see, Hegel is not wanting to give to Mind— as great as it is, and as the mediation—what Maurer now is saying. In other words, Hegel is now saying that as great as Mind is, and it certainly is great, by itself it's like ordering somebody suddenly to walk on his head. So what is the use of trying to tell you to walk on your head? It isn't going to help, unless it is united with something. And what is it going to be united with? If he was going to follow through by constantly turning the three categories around, then Logic would now become the mediation. And he spent all that time on the *Science of Logic*, but now he wants to throw Logic out altogether! That was just, so to speak, the excuse for you to know the categories which would help you explain reality; now you really have to *do* something. So he throws all of it out, and he says [in the final ¶577]: well, it's really the "Self-Thinking Idea," "the self-determination of the Idea, in which it alone is, is to hear itself speak."

If we listen to what the Idea is, and we know that there is no difference between Idea and freedom, then it will be equally the nature of the fact and the nature of cognition itself. That is one of the forms of getting to the transformation of reality—what Marx called the realization of freedom. That's why Marx stuck so much to the dialectic. We're not going to throw philosophy out, we have to *realize* it; that is, instead of an idea of freedom, it has to become the reality. And this reality means that when the Self-Thinking Idea and the self-movement of masses unite, then and only then will we have a new way to transform reality, a new philosophy, a new society.

We must begin, however, with Absolute Idea as new beginnings, and I want to end with that in the following way.

[Take] these three little words, "as new beginnings." Let's go through all of these Marxists that I was speaking about before, and see why they didn't get there. Lukács tried to say, "Well, since we don't believe in Absolutes, let's see what Hegel meant: he meant the unity of theory and practice, so then the key is *totality*."[44] Totality is very much superior to empiricism, it's very much superior to taking only one single question; totality means you look at the relationship between the Third World and the First World and the Second World—you look at the relationship of various ideas. But, it isn't good enough. It's just totality as the opposite of single ideas, single actions—you know, a strike instead of a revolution. That's great, but it isn't going to give you any new ideas. We're living in a world that has seen the counter-revolution within the revolution, has seen the transformation of the first workers' state into its opposite—a state capitalist society—has seen the new that was brought with Mao [which] became *its* opposite. Abstract idealism (as just the Chairman's Thought, and so forth), like abstract materialism, is vulgar, and can only help the bourgeoisie; it cannot possibly help the revolution or a new society. So it is not totality.

What did Sartre say? The "totalization"—he wants to make everything totalization. What did it bring him to, this totalization? It meant you are just a serial, just a number, like waiting for a bus at a bus station; you're one and you're ten and so forth, and you will get nowhere because there's no difference between the two. So someone has to come in from the outside, the Party, to order you about, and the Party is better than the State, or something. So it isn't totalization.[45]

What did Adorno say? Now, Adorno was the greatest of the dialecticians, so to speak "pure dialectics." And he made a *real* mess of it. You know, I was never looking forward to anything so greatly as his *Negative Dialectics*. I was dumb enough to think that that meant dialectics of negativity. Hegel says there are two negations, and the second negation is the really positive, and Marx says that that's the new society. I thought that's what Adorno would talk about. No. He is talking about negative dialectics because the fetishism is not just the commodity; he makes it now the fetishism of the *concept*. Conceptual fetishism: you've got to throw it out. What are you going to do next?

I talked to the Hegel Society of America, and there were quite a few Adorno-ites and Frankfurt School people who were trying to prove some of the better parts of Adorno.[46] So I said, I'll quote you the good parts of Adorno (from *Aspects of the Hegelian Dialectic*): "Subject-object cannot be dismissed as mere extravagance of logical absolutism . . . . In seeing through the latter as mere subjectivity, we have already passed beyond the speculative idealism . . . . Cognition, if it is genuine, and more than simple duplication of the subjective [in other words, the photocopy theory of reality—RD], must be the subject's objectivity."[47] In other words, you have to believe, because you're living in this world and you want to transform it, that your subjectivity is really a reflection of this objectivity that you want to overcome and destroy the other world. You don't think the other world is something opposite, except opposite to you in the sense of that's what you have to transform; but this represents somebody's subjectivity, the subjectivity of the capitalist. [It was] good that he said that. Why then, I ask, the vulgar reduction of absolute negativity? "Therein is the real tragedy of Adorno (and the Frankfurt School)—the inescapable one-dimensionality of thought once you 'give up' subject, once you do not listen to the voices from below—and they certainly were loud and clear and demanding in that decade of the mid-1950s to mid-1960s—once you return to the ivory tower and reduce your purpose to 'discussing key concepts of philosophic disciplines and centrally intervening in those disciplines.'" What does that mean? You're going to just see that you decategorize all of these categories, and instead of having philosophy separate, and sociology separate, and economics separate, you'll make them all into one. That's supposed to be great? Irresistibly came the next step, the substitution of a permanent critique not alone for "absolute negativity," but for what is a lot more important, absolute "permanent revolution."

Therefore, whether it's the totality as Lukács saw it, the totalization as Sartre explained it, the conceptual fetishism that Adorno developed—we really have to begin the Absolute not only as a totality, but as a new beginning on the basis of what comes from the movement from below, as well as from the Idea, and it's that unity which will finally realize the Idea of Freedom as its reality.

NOTES

1. For Dunayevskaya's discussion of the June 17, 1953, East German revolt, see *Marxism and Freedom*, pp. 249–51.

2. See Frantz Fanon, *Black Skin,White Masks* (New York: Grove Press, 1967), pp. 216–22.

3. See Aimé Césaire's *Notebook of a Return to My Native Land* (Newcastle: Bloodaxe Books, 1995, orig. 1947).

4. A reference to Dunayevskaya's 1953 letters on Hegel's Absolutes, in part I, above.

5. Dunayevskaya discusses the *sans culottes* (literally "those without breeches"), whom she terms "the deepest layers of the mass movement," in the first chapter of *Marxism and Freedom* (p. 29), in which she takes up Hegel and the French Revolution.

6. See PhGB, pp. 642–79; PhGM, pp. 383–409.

7. Not a direct quote, but Dunayevskaya's summary of his position in a dramatic form, something she did frequently with various thinkers in her lectures.

8. Hegel mentions Jacobi as "perhaps forgotten" in Observation 3 in his section on "Becoming" in the Doctrine of Being. See SLI, pp. 107–08; SLM, p. 95.

9. See page 174, note 22.

10. Louis Althusser, *For Marx* (New York: Vintage Books, 1970), p. 116. See also Dunayevskaya's "Critique of Althusser's Anti-Hegelianism," *News & Letters*, Oct. 1969.

11. This refers to Bernstein's declaration, during the Revisionism debate in German Social Democracy in 1898, that the "dialectical scaffolding" of Hegel's theories should be removed from Marxism. See his *Evolutionary Socialism* (New York: Schocken, 1961), pp. 209–11.

12. See the chapter, "The Conquest of the Unhappy Consciousness: Repressive Desublimation," in Marcuse's *One-Dimensional Man*, especially pp. 81–83.

13. See Maurice Merleau-Ponty, "Marxism and Philosophy," *Politics*, No. 4 (1947), pp. 173–76, discussed in this volume in part II, above.

14. For Sartre's discussion of the importance of Marx's concept of the fetishism of commodities, see his *Search for a Method* (New York: Vintage, 1968), pp. 77–79 especially. Dunayevskaya critiques Sartre's interpretation of Marx's concept of commodity fetishism in *Philosophy and Revolution*, pp. 200–03.

15. See Engels' letter to Conrad Schmidt of November 1, 1891, in Marx and Engels, *Selected Correspondence* (Moscow: Progress Publishers, 1975), p. 415. Engels writes: "If you compare the development from commodity to capital in Marx with the development from being to essence in Hegel you have a fairly good parallel."

16. This refers to the last paragraph of Hegel's *Phenomenology*, in which Hegel, in posing the unity of "history" and "science," writes: "Both together, or History (intellectually)

comprehended, form at once the recollection and the Golgotha of Absolute Spirit" [PhGB, p. 808; PhGM, p. 493]. In the Biblical narrative, Golgotha is the hill upon which Jesus was crucified.

17. This refers to the opening section of the Doctrine of Being in the *Science of Logic*, entitled "With What Must Science Begin?"

18. See Dunayevskaya's discussion of this in her "Rough Notes on Hegel's *Science of Logic*," in part II, above, and in her "Logic as Stages of Freedom," in part III, above.

19. Hegel discusses contradiction in the second chapter of the Doctrine of Essence. For Mao's position, see "On Contradiction," and "On the Correct Handling of Contradictions Among the People," in *Selected Works of Mao Zedong*. Five Volumes (Beijing: Foreign Languages Publishing House, 1960–65). For Dunayevskaya's critique, see the section "From Contradiction to Contradiction to Contradiction" in *Philosophy and Revolution*, pp. 160–68.

20. The first appearance of the Absolute in The Doctrine of Essence emerges in its concluding section, on "Actuality." For a further discussion of this, see Dunayevskaya's "Rough Notes on Hegel's *Science of Logic*" in part II, above.

21. See Hegel's Preface to the *Phenomenology of Mind*: "In my view . . . everything depends on grasping and expressing the ultimate truth not as Substance but as Subject as well" [PhGB, p. 80; PhGM, pp. 9–10].

22. See Marx's statement in *Capital*, Vol I: "I was the first to point out and examine critically this two-fold nature of the labor contained in commodities . . . this point is the pivot on which a clear comprehension of political economy turns" [MCIF, p. 132; MCIK, p. 48].

23. See Marx's discussion of this in MCIF, pp. 151–52; MCIK, pp. 69.

24. A massive, peasant-based anti-royalist movement during the years 1845 to 1864, and on which Marx wrote several articles.

25. The footnote in *Capital* reads: "One may recall that China and the tables began to dance when the rest of the world appeared to be standing still—to encourage the others" [MCIF, p. 164]. It was left out of previous English translations.

26. For Dunayevskaya's discussion of how the Paris Commune impacted Marx's rewriting of what became the section on commodity fetishism in the French edition of *Capital* (1872–75), see *Marxism and Freedom*, chapter 6.

27. See "What Is Orthodox Marxism?" in Georg Lukács, *History and Class Consciousness* (Cambridge: MIT Press, 1975 [orig. 1923]), pp. 1–26.

28. See MCIF, pp. 176–77; MCIK, pp. 94–96. For a further discussion of the relation between Marx's *Capital* and the section on "Spirit in Self-Estrangement" in Hegel's *Phenomenology*, see Dunayevskaya's November 11, 1963 letter to Erich Fromm, in part II, above.

29. See Lukács' essay "Reification and the Consciousness of the Proletariat," pp. 83–222 in *History and Class Consciousness*. For a more detailed critique by Dunayevskaya, see the next chapter.

30. This can especially be seen from Lukács' later (1968) work, *The Process of Democratization* (New York: SUNY press, 1991).

31. This is a reference to Lukács' *The Ontology of Social Existence*. Only two chapters of the work were translated into English as of 1976. One was published in *Telos*, Fall, 1970, as "The Dialectic of Labor: Beyond Causality and Teleology"; another appeared as "The Ontological Foundations of Human Thought and Activity" in *Contemporary East European Philosophy*, Vol. III, 1971. More of the *Social Ontology* has since been translated. See *The Ontology of Social Being. 1. Hegel*, trans. by David Fernbach (London: Merlin press, 1978), *The Ontology of Social Being. 2. Marx* (London: Merlin Press, 1978), and *The Ontology of Social Being. 3. Labour* (London: Merlin Press, 1980).

32. Sartre's attack on Lukács is contained in *Search for a Method*, p. 28 especially. Sartre chose to launch this attack in 1957, at the very moment Lukács had broken from Stalinism, had participated in the 1956 Hungarian Revolution, and had only recently been released from detention.

33. See Lukács, *Existentialisme ou Marxisme?* (Paris: Éditions Nagel, 1948), as well as his *The Destruction of Reason* (New Jersey: Humanities Press, 1981 [orig. 1954]).

34. See *Philosophy and Revolution*, pp. 202–03.

35. A central concept in Sartre's *Critique of Dialectical Reason* (London: NLB, 1976 [orig. 1960]), as well as *Search for a Method*, the latter incorporated into the former in the French edition. In *Critique of Dialectical Reason*, Sartre describes "practico-inert Being" as follows: "Thus the very praxis of individuals or groups is altered in so far as it ceases to be the free organization of the practical field and becomes the reorganization of one sector of inert materiality in accordance with the exigencies of another sector of materiality" (p. 191).

36. This is from the conclusion of the Letter of May 12, 1953. For the full text of the 1953 "Letters on Hegel's Absolutes," see part I, above.

37. An apparent reference to Hegel's phrase, "The second negative, the negation of the negation . . . [is] the innermost, most *objective* moment of life and spirit, through which a subject is *personal and free*" [SLII, p. 477; SLM, pp. 835–36].

38. Marx refers to "new passions and new forces" in Vol. I of *Capital* [MCIF, p. 928; MCIK, p. 835) and to "that development of human power, which is its own end, the true realm of Freedom" in *Capital*, Vol. III (Chicago: Charles H. Kerr, 1909), pp. 954–55—see also the newer translation by David Fernbach (New York: Vintage, 1981), p. 959.

39. This phrase is from the Letter of May 20, 1953, in Dunayevskaya's commentary on ¶575 of Hegel's *Philosophy of Mind*. For the text of the letter, see part I, above.

40. That is, in the conclusion of her letter of May 12, 1953.

41. By 1986, Dunayevskaya began to take issue with Lenin's position on "Nature" as being "Practice." See *Supplement to the Raya Dunayevskaya Collection*, p. 10883.

42. See Reinhart Klemens Maurer, *Hegel und das Ende der Geschichte* (1965).

43. The text of the transcript here reads, "The Introduction was not in the 1817 edition of the *Science of Logic*," but this appears to be a verbal slip.

44. See p. 209, note 7.

45. Totalization and seriality are key categories in Sartre's *Critique of Dialectical Reason*. Sartre distinguishes between "totality," which he regards as too often a mere "synthetic

unity" and "totalization," whose "very movement" is that of establishing "the intelligibility of dialectical reason" (pp. 45–46). However, he gives great emphasis also to "serial unities" such as people queuing for the bus in a situation where they have little real connection (pp. 256–69).

46. For the text of this lecture, see chapter 10.

47. Adorno, "Aspects of Hegel's Philosophy" (original German edition 1957), in *Hegel: Three Studies*, pp. 5–6.

CHAPTER TWELVE

On Lukács' Marxism

The following two selections, which critique the Hungarian-born Marxist philosopher Georg Lukács, were written at a moment of much rediscovery and discussion of Lukács' work by the New Left in the 1970s, especially in the journal Telos. *They represent an expansion of Dunayevskaya's critique of "alternatives" to Marx's Marxism as developed in part II of her* Philosophy and Revolution. *The first selection, a letter to colleagues written on December 14, 1972, was written shortly after Dunayevskaya's participation in a national conference hosted by* Telos. *The second, a critique of Lukács' overall philosophic position, appeared in two parts in* News & Letters, *in February and March 1973.*

Letter on Lukács (December 14, 1972)

Dear Friends,

I take for granted that insofar as our major contribution to the question of *what* is theory, and *how* it was manifested in the change in the structure of *Capital*, our friends do know: 1) the shift from history of theory to history of production relations; 2) the break with the bourgeois concept of theory by bringing the working day into the theoretical work not only as historic narrative but as historic reason; and 3) the dialectical change in the structure which separated production—about which Volume I centered alone—from the question of circulation, the market, crises—about which Volumes II and III revolve. All of this is treated in *Marxism and Freedom*, chapters 5 and 6, in which especially critical are pages 84–90 and 95–102.

At the *Telos* conference, this concept was greatly expanded because, for the first time (except, of course, in *Philosophy and Revolution*) I went into great detail on the difference between the *Grundrisse* and *Capital*, which gives me the opportunity also to take up the whole question of the concept of the primitive Oriental commune. But on the whole, the friends do have this concept, and the historic period worked out in one place or another.

What was totally new, what is not even dealt with in *Philosophy and Revolution*, was the critique of Lukács. First, I had not wished to criticize him because his 1923 work *History and Class Consciousness* remains a masterpiece insofar as the essay "What is Orthodox Marxism?" is concerned and is a ground-breaker also in the essay "Reification and the Consciousness of the Proletariat" although that is by no means totally without fault.[1] And, of course, the other essays are quite at fault. In a word, because of the attacks on Social Democracy and mechanical materialism, because of the re-creation of the Hegelian dialectic at a time when not only reformists but revolutionaries had moved away from it, and because it had been condemned by the Communist International after Lenin's death, it all deserved a new study.

What, however, had happened—and, indeed, that threatened the whole New Left as it finally tried to grapple with theory—is that intellectuals, some with great malice aforethought and some innocently but just as dangerously, had grabbed onto Lukács 1) as an escape from grappling with Lenin's *Philosophic Notebooks*, which is the only ground for a new reinterpretation of the dialectic; 2) are mixing up the 1923 Lukács with the 1967–72 Lukács during which period he worked on a work that is not yet published [in English] (and which *promises* to be great but is in truth *the* proof that intellectuals isolated from the proletariat *can't* think originally);[2] and 3) therefore, the intellectuals had to be made to confront that reality, the impossibility of *their own* self-development once they reject the proletariat as a revolutionary force.

Finally, one had also to settle scores with Merleau-Ponty who as a great philosopher, as a dialectician, as the one who broke with his cofounder of *Les Temps Modernes*, enjoyed somehow an unsullied reputation though he is the one who taught Sartre all the politics that Sartre knew. In any case, his *Adventures of the Dialectic* is presently being translated and two chapters of it on Lukács have met with great praise.[3]

Now then. First, it was necessary to show that when Merleau-Ponty calls Sartre a "super-Bolshevik," he is in fact not attacking Sartre, but Lenin. *When he speaks of the Lukácsian dialectic and acts as if Lenin did nothing other than 'Materialism and Empirio-Criticism,' it is exactly what both the Communists and the bourgeoisie are doing in a conspiracy of silence against Lenin's 'Philosophic Notebooks.'* Moreover there was absolutely no reason for him not to have grappled with Lenin's Notebooks except that they were revolutionary and would not play with the dialectic as either a literary-dramatic venture or philosophic "project" as such.

For that matter, Lukács did very nearly the same thing. It is true he mentions it in a praiseworthy manner[4] but 1) he's absolutely wrong when he says he anticipated Lenin's work. It is true that he didn't know about Lenin's work when he wrote his. It is not true that when he finally saw it there was any such affinity. 2) On the theory that Lenin was a man of practice, which he surely was, revolutionary practice, Lukács acts as if he were a philosopher only of practice, whereas in truth his greatest contribution was to theory, philosophy as a whole. 3) It is no accident that Lukács has not spoken either of the Notebooks in a serious, scrupulous, rigorous critique, or of Marx's 1844 *Manuscripts* which he did in fact anticipate, but again ONLY INSOFAR AS THE DIALECTIC IS CONCERNED, NOT INSOFAR AS THE REAL CREATIVE MARXIAN DIALECTIC, WHERE SUBJECT AND SUBJECT ALONE IS THE CREATOR OF HISTORY AND *THEREFORE* RECREATOR OF A NEW DIALECTIC.

So finally, here is the tragedy of Lukács. When in 1956 he did briefly participate in the Hungarian Revolution and that was destroyed, he retreated to his books. He no doubt corresponded with other younger intellectuals and helped many "theoretically." But never once did a single action of the Hungarian proletariat or a single thought as revolutionary humanism serve as the point of departure for this new great work he had decided to spend his last decade on. The result was that when he spoke of labor, it was never the labor*er*. Inescapably, this meant that labor became Object, not Subject. And once it became Object not Subject, then even when it was activity, it was totally abstract. The absolutely shocking descent from that to the most capitalistic of all categories—SOCIALLY NECESSARY LABOR TIME— became his preoccupation exactly as it becomes the preoccupation of any capitalist, private or state; in a word, the exploiter's bible.[5]

Thus, it was necessary to take the Telos conference on a tour of the factory to show what that damn factory clock does in pounding all concrete labor into one abstract mass, making labor a mere appendage to a machine but never once, in this reification of labor, killing what Marx called the laborer's "quest for universality"[6] and what we call "passion for philosophy and revolution."

I do not know whether I will get a chance to at least include a lengthy footnote on this in *Philosophy and Revolution* but I know that we must, in practicing the dialectic, work out ways to combat Lukácsism and establish Lenin's dialectic as the point of departure for our own very unique contributions to the dialectic. I hope this will serve as a point of departure for your own self-development.

Yours,
Raya

Lukács' Philosophic Dimension

Part I

1973 marks the 50th anniversary of the publication of *History and Class Consciousness*, and is sure to increase the deluge of articles, pamphlets and even whole books about its late famous author, Georg Lukács. These have been pouring forth the past few years from both the New Left* and the official Communist press.

In 1956, on the other hand, when Lukács briefly participated in the Hungarian Revolution despite a full quarter century of capitulation to Stalinism, the Hungarian Communists who helped the Russian counter-revolution destroy the revolution and execute its leader, Imre Nagy, expelled Lukács from the Party and unloosed still another vitriolic attack on his 1923 seminal study on Hegelian-Marxian dialectics.

The tragedy lies not in any change in the stance of the Communist Party between 1973 and 1956; it hasn't changed its counter-revolutionary nature ever since the first workers' state, Russia, was transformed into its absolute opposite, a state-capitalist society. The tragedy lies in two altogether different spheres. One is Lukács' new, monumental work, *Social Ontology*, which he considered the greatest of his life, which he was completing when he died on June 4, 1971. Whether only because this philosophic work was abstract enough to be incomprehensible, or because in reality it was not all inimical to the ruling Communist Party, the fact is that we suddenly began seeing the belated publication of Lukács' 1923 work, *History and Class Consciousness*, with a most ambient new Preface included.

The only reference the 1967 Preface makes to the 1956 Revolution is that there is no "inconsistency" between "the fact that in 1956 I had once again to take on a ministerial (!) post" (p. xxxi)[7] and the fact that he had given up political activity in the mid-1920's. As if taking on political activities—"making revolutions"—hadn't related to revolutionary dialectics, and "giving up politics" hadn't "coincided" (in Stalin's day and now!) with renunciation of, and retreat from *History and Class-Consciousness*, Lukács concludes that he is glad to be out of politics since even when he was correct "there must be grave defects in my practical political abilities" (p. xxxi). Well, it isn't his "political abilities" we are concerned with. The reason for detouring to the Preface is

---

*As one example, see *Telos*, which not only devoted two special issues (Winter 1971 and Spring 1972) plus a "memorial statement" (Spring 1971), but this was preceded by a detailed study by Paul Piccone, "Lukács' *History and Class Consciousness*, Half a Century Late," in the Fall 1969 issue. See also a book of essays, *The Unknown Dimension*, edited by Dick Howard and Karl E. Klare (New York: Basic Books, 1972).

not "politics" but the disjointedness of revolutionary philosophy from revolutionary activity.

It isn't the political double-tonguedness that manifests Lukács' philosophic retreat from working out today's revolutionary dialectics in the forthcoming *Social Ontology* (to which we'll return later). In the Preface this manifests itself in places where he is full of praise of Lenin, but in fact doesn't stand on Lenin's philosophic ground. And I don't mean Lenin's pre-1914 mechanistic *Materialism and Empirio-Criticism*, but his ground breaking 1914–15 *Philosophic Notebooks*[†] which laid the philosophic foundation both for the Great Divide in Marxism, and for the Russian Revolution as well as for new world revolutionary perspectives.

Lukács rightly shows how his work had caught the revolutionary spirit of the period, 1917–21: "A momentous world-historical change was struggling to find a theoretical expression" (p. xxv). He also points to the truth that "undoubtedly one of the great achievements of *History and Class Consciousness* [was] to have reinstated the category of totality in the central position it had always occupied throughout Marx's work." This, however, is followed up with a declaration about not knowing that Lenin was "moving in a similar direction" (p. xx). Suddenly there comes the arrogant and supercilious untitled reference to Lenin's *Philosophic Notebooks* as "philosophic fragments (that) were only published nine years after the appearance of *History and Class Consciousness*" (p. xx).[‡]

Now, to have discovered, no matter when, that the revolutionary spirit of the age was not only caught as it objectively developed, but prepared for by Lenin back in 1914 via his "return" to Hegel after the collapse of the Second International, should have been so exciting an actual and philosophic adventure that the profound philosopher Lukács, couldn't have possibly slipped into factual dating of publications relative to one "knowing" or "not knowing" about these in 1919–22, if his 1967 ear had been attuned to the living revolutionary forces. Shouldn't his recollection of the "momentous world-historical change [that] was struggling to find a theoretical expression," 1919–1922, have

---

[†]See my article, "The Shock of Recognition and the Philosophic Ambivalence of Lenin" in *Telos*, Spring, 1970.

[‡]Actually, the dating is wrong. Even before Lenin's *Philosophic Notebooks* were published in Moscow, not in 1932, but in 1929–30, sections of them began to be published soon after Lenin's death, as various factional fights developed. In view of the fact that many among the "New Left," with malice aforethought, are deliberately mixing up the Comintern's June, 1924 attack on Lukács' work with Lenin's 1920 critique of the politics of the ultra-left in *Left-Wing Communism, an Infantile Disorder*, it should be made clear that Lenin lay on his deathbed, totally paralyzed, for eight long mute tormented months in 1923. Lenin's activity was finished when the second stroke hit him on March 10, 1923; he died Jan. 21, 1924.

led him to concretize his praise of "Lenin really brought about a renewal of the Marxist method," by grappling with Lenin's Notebooks instead of skipping over those "fragments"? 1967 is, after all, a good distance from 1932, by which time not only Lenin's Notebooks, but Marx's 1844 Humanist Essays had finally been published. It is true that Lukács' 1923 work had anticipated the essays on "Alienated Labor" and "Critique of the Hegelian Dialectic." But Marx's essays also contained the sharp conclusion that "communism, as such, is not the goal of human development, the form of human society" [MECW 3, p. 306], which Lukács neither anticipated, nor knew how to relate to.

In any case, Lukács never reviewed either Lenin's or Marx's strictly philosophic works. This failure has nothing whatever to do with dates, but a great deal to do with the fact that Lukács is developing the dialectics, not of revolution, but of ontology. Whether his monumental work, *Social Ontology*, will prove to be not only his greatest work, but that dialectics of the concrete which the New Left expects all revolutionary forces to be grounded in, the indirect references to it in the new Preface to *History and Class Consciousness* do not help enhance that Preface. It isn't the Preface that will enter history, but the original work. The ambience of the Preface can no more detract from that epoch-making event than the author's renouncement of the book under Stalinism could keep it from having a most exciting underground life of its own.

One final word must be said before we can finally turn to its contents, and that is that *History and Class Consciousness* isn't a book, i.e., a whole.§ It is a collection of essays, and not all are of historic import. The two philosophic essays carried on a subterranean existence for a full half-century which has romanticized the whole, but the historic-philosophic breakthrough resides in those two central pieces—"What Is Orthodox Marxism?" and "Reification and the Consciousness of the Proletariat." It is to these we now turn.

Part II: What Is Orthodox Marxism?

> *Hegel's tremendous intellectual contribution consisted in the fact that he made theory and history dialectically relative to each other, grasped them in a dialectical reciprocal penetration.*—Lukács

It was the most unorthodox character of "What Is Orthodox Marxism?" that fired the imagination of German revolutionaries when it was first pub-

---

§Lukács himself, in the original (Christmas, 1922) Preface, made this clear with his very first sentence: "The collection and publication of these essays in book form is not intended to give them a greater importance as a whole than would be due to each individually" (p. xii).

lished in 1919 and again when it reappeared in revised form as part of the book, *History and Class Consciousness*, published in 1923.

When, by the end of the 1920s, the work was repudiated by its author as he made peace with Stalinism, the essay carried on many subterranean existences in many languages in different parts of the world: first, for those who had broken with Stalinism in the 1930s and 1940s; then for some of the "new philosophers"—French Existentialists, especially Merleau-Ponty—in the mid-1950s; and, finally, for those in the new generation of revolutionaries in the 1960s who, out of their own experiences, were turning away from sheer activism to reaching out for a "world view" of the dialectics of liberation.

The enduring relevance of the essay is proof of the fact that its explosive effect was by no means limited to the fact that it had anticipated the rediscovery of Marx's now-famous 1844 *Economic-Philosophic Manuscripts* which demonstrated how deeply rooted in Hegelian dialectics and theory of alienation were Marx's "Alienated Labor" and "Critique of the Hegelian Dialectic."

In reestablishing Marxism as a totality, never once separating the young Marx from the mature author of *Capital*, Lukács proved himself as uncompromising in his refusal to bow to scientism as to reformism.

In naming names of those who had not worked out the full implications of the revolutionary nature of the Marxian dialectic, Lukács did not stop short of criticizing Marx's closest collaborator, Engels, who "does not even mention the most vital interaction, namely the dialectical relation between subject and object in historical process" (p. 3).

The whole weight of this study in Marxian dialectics was its stress on "the transformation of reality": "It is at reality itself that Hegel and Marx part company. Hegel was unable to penetrate the real driving forces of history" (p. 17). It is true that Lukács himself so overstressed "consciousness" of the proletariat that it overshadowed its praxis which was both material force and reason so that it left room, at one and same time, for a slip back into the Hegelian idealism of "the identical subject-object," and into substituting the Party that "knows" for the proletariat.

But none noted this in the excitement generated by the essay's recapture of the revolutionary dialectical dimension of historical materialism which gave action its direction: "Marxist orthodoxy is no guardian of traditions, it is the eternally vigilant prophet proclaiming the relation between the tasks of the immediate present and the totality of the historical process" (p. 12). And that "historical process" was then concretized by the internationalism proclaimed in *The Communist Manifesto* and in the Paris Commune which Marx specified as having "no ideals to realize" but "to liberate the elements of the new society."

The essay, "Reification and Consciousness of the Proletariat" has neither the movement and verve of the first essay, nor its "orthodoxy" (and I'm using the word in the Lukácsian sense of authentic Marxism). There is no doubt, however, that it is the center of *History and Class Consciousness*.

This is not simply a matter of it being the longest piece. (As against the twenty six pages of the first essay, the essay on reification totaled no less than 139 pages.) Lukács could have called it a book, but, instead, took care to cast it in essay form. Where he shied away from claiming for it a totally new departure, a worked-out whole alternative, the intellectuals took it as such. It became the fashion to talk about "reification," "the reified world we live in." They may very well have anticipated, by three full decades, the intellectualistic rage around "One Dimensional Man," "One Dimensional Thought," "technological rationality," the move away from Reason to irrationality, or the retrogression from ontology to technology.

The "masses" (the rank and file) in the subterranean discussion of Lukács' book, on the other hand, kept their peace not merely because of lack of knowledge of "the history of philosophy," but because of a solid proletarian instinct that this was not merely a restatement of Marxism for a new epoch, but rather that it contained elements deviatory from that which was authentic Marxism.

First and most important of the distinctions between the two concepts of reification is that Marx had limited his analysis to the reification of labor, transforming it into thing, a mere appendage to a machine. Lukács, on the other hand, had transformed reification into a universal, affecting the whole of society equally: "Reification is, then, the necessary, immediate reality of every person living in capitalist society. It can be overcome only by constant and constantly renewed efforts to disrupt the reified structure of existence by relating to the concretely manifested contradictions of the total development, by becoming conscious of the immanent meanings of these contradictions for the total development" (p. 197).

Here, then, we see that reification is universalized, made a veritable "human condition"; "every person" is affected equally.

And "becoming conscious" is endowed with a "neutrality." Though Lukács is a revolutionary and quotes endlessly from Marx as to how the proletariat, and the proletariat alone, is the revolutionary force to create new human relations, it does not flow either logically or objectively, either historically or dialectically from his original theory.

Where Marx, the practitioner of the revolutionary dialectic, analyzes reification as resulting from the specifically capitalistic production process of the reification of labor, pounding labor into a thing, and thereby creating in the laborer the absolute opposite—the "quest for universality" and the revolt—

Lukács blurs totally the Marxian concept of "freely associated labor" stripping the fetishism from commodities, overcoming alienation, reshaping history.[8]

Ironically enough, it was Lukács who—in recapturing the Hegelian dimension in Marx; in delivering mighty blows to the revisionists by showing how very inseparable was their reformism, their turn away from revolution, with their abandonment of the dialectic—made his greatest contribution to authentic Marxism by interrelating and making central to his dialectic the interrelationships of the concepts of "totality" and "mediation."

In reviewing, in the 1967 Preface, what he had meant to do and what he had done, he thinks that, on the one hand, "alienation" sans objectivity was "in the air," and, on the other hand, "messianistic utopianism" led to a residue of idealism. And he adds that concerning the whole question of the relationship of "mediation to immediacy" of "economics and dialectics" that he had begun reworking in Moscow in the early thirties: "Only now, thirty years later, am I attempting to discover a real solution to this whole problem in the ontology of social existence" (p. xxxv).

Part III: The Hungarian Revolution vis-a-vis "Social Ontology"

The 1956 Revolution, with Lukács suddenly appearing as participant, revived hopes that, despite his quarter of a century of capitulation to Stalinism, Lukács would continue the revolution in thought he wrought in the early 1920s.

Every new stage of cognition is, after all, not born out of thin air. It can be born only out of praxis, the praxis of new revolutionary forces uprooting the existing social order; and the Hungarian masses were directing their revolt not against private capitalism which had already been abolished, but against the existing exploitative, ruling Communist state-power, or, more precisely put, state-capitalism calling itself Communism. With this new mass upsurge, its plunge to new freedom, there was every reason to expect the old philosopher would catch what, in the 1920s, he had called, "a momentous, world-historical change . . . struggling to find a theoretical expression."

The criticism leveled against Lukács by independent Marxists seemed to lose its validity, especially as much of it had the character of Monday morning quarterbacking raised to "wisdom" by the knowledge of some three to four decades of objective development. Considering the excitement of the new generation of Marxists over the philosophic dimension of Lukács and its impatient waiting for the comprehensive *Social Ontology* he had been writing for a decade and to which he had referred in his last years as having been the product of three decades of thought, it would indeed have been a joy to report so great a historic breakthrough—a new stage in cognition that met the challenge of the spontaneous upsurge from below, the Hungarian Revolution.

Unfortunately, nothing could be further from the truth. The truth is that, whatever deviatory—deviatory, not reinterpretative—elements were implicit in the "Reification" article, "reification of consciousness" affected Lukács, who reduced socialism to the perfection of industrial production achieving the Plan!**

Take a most crucial Hegelian category, and one central to Lukács' dialectics, mediation. As concretized by Marx, and the one Lukács tried to extend, it was, first, inseparable from the most fundamental of all Hegelian categories, their summation, subject. Secondly, and most important—since that revealed a totally new continent of thought, Historical Materialism—Marx historically, philosophically, dialectically spelled subject out as the proletariat. In a word, Marx didn't simply stand Hegel "right side up," didn't only critically transform Hegel's concept of labor as process of man's becoming, much less leave it in the realm of thought. No, as laborer, the proletariat was both opposing the capitalistic exploitation and reduction of all his concrete labors to one abstract mass by that "pendulum of the clock," and seeking "universality." Thus, he became reason as well as force, reshaped history, created new beginnings for totally new human relations.

Whatever duality there was in Lukács, and whatever abstractions—because of the emphasis on "morality" and "ethics"—the point is that the concept of concrete totality escaped him, despite the fact that totality itself, was one of his central categories. Having never grounded his concept in the concrete struggles at the point of production, in the factory he never entered; having never made the actual voices of the workers the new point of departure, labor is seen not as the laborer in revolt; labor is no more than the exercise of labor-power in the most specifically capitalistic form: socially-necessary labor time.

Where Marx used the category, socially-necessary labor time, to define that which is uniquely capitalistic, oppressive, chaotic, Lukács denudes it of its class character and makes it applicable to all societies. No wonder he begins this excursus with the statement: "Above all, we propose to examine what

---

**It no doubt is both incomplete and unfair to judge the *Social Ontology*, since the work has not yet been published. [On its subsequent publication, see p. 211, note 31.] But, no matter how the whole will reveal some partial brilliant flashes and dialectical insights, it is impossible to think that it could reverse the direction of what has been stated by Lukács in his many world interviews on the subject, in the references to it in the 1967 Preface to the 1923 work, and in the two chapters of his late writings. One was published in *Telos*, Fall, 1970, "The Dialectic of Labor: Beyond Causality and Teleology"; and the abbreviated publication of "The Ontological Foundations of Human Thought and Activity" in *Contemporary East European Philosophy*, Vol. III, 1971. (See especially pp. 223–24, pp. 228–30; the above quotations are from those pages.)

economic necessity consists of. At the outset, it would be emphasized this is not a natural, necessary process, though Marx himself, in his polemic with idealism, occasionally used such an expression."

As Lukács himself put it, he was ready "simply to skip over the most important mediating areas." By then mediation was no longer the class struggles, much less outright proletarian revolution. Mediation became subject-less; "totality" became cult.[††]

We hope we are wrong when we think that the attraction Lukács has for the New Left is due to the fact that they never were "weighted down" by any concept of the revolutionary role of the proletariat and, with Lukács at least philosophically, they are ready to scuttle Marx's theory of proletarian revolution.

NOTES

1. George Lukács, *History and Class Consciousness, Studies in Marxist Dialectics* (Merlin Press, London, 1971 [includes 1967 Preface]).

2. This is a reference to Lukács' *The Ontology of Social Being*.

3. A reference to their publication in *Telos*.

4. Lukács discussed his response to Lenin's *Philosophic Notebooks* in his 1967 Preface to *History and Class Consciousness*.

5. Marx writes in *Capital* I: "Socially necessary labor-time is the labor-time required to produce any use-value under the conditions of production normal for a given society and with the average degree of skill and intensity of labor prevalent in that society. The introduction of power-looms into England, for example, probably reduced by one half the labor required to convert a given quantity of yarn into a woven fabric" [MCIF, p. 129; MCIK, p. 46].

6. See Marx's *Poverty of Philosophy*, where he writes, "What characterizes the division of labor in the automatic workshop is that labor has there completely lost its specialized character. But the moment every special development stops, the need for universality, the tendency towards an integral development of the individual begins to be felt" [MECW 6, p. 190].

7. These and other page references in parentheses are to the 1971 English edition of Lukács' *History and Class Consciousness*.

8. In *Capital*, Vol. I, in the section on commodity fetishism, Marx writes that fetishism's "veil is not removed . . . until it becomes production by freely associated human beings" [MCIF, p. 173; MCIK, p. 92].

[††]István Mészáros, who had once been a pupil of Lukács, and remains the most profound of his sympathetic critics, calls attention to the duality in Lukács' concepts: "Even the most recent Lukács—the author of a massive *Social Ontology*—insists on a duality, on a dual causality, and on an ultimate autonomy of 'decisions between alternatives' . . . on the basis of his Ontology, the positive outcome can only be envisaged as the impact of a '*sollen*' . . . an ought to change their way of life." *George Lukács, The Man, his Work, and his Ideas*, ed. by G. H. R. Parkinson (New York: Vintage, 1970), pp. 53, 64.

⁓

CHAPTER THIRTEEN

The Hegel-Marx Relation Revisited

Letter to Harry McShane

After completing Philosophy and Revolution *in 1973, Dunayevskaya embarked on a new work focusing on the legacy of Rosa Luxemburg and today's women's liberation movement. It appeared in 1982 as* Rosa Luxemburg, Women's Liberation, and Marx's Philosophy of Revolution. *In the course of working on this, she turned to a reexamination of the totality of Marx's work, especially as illuminated by such writings from his last decade (1872–83) as his* Ethnological Notebooks. *This letter was addressed to Harry McShane, the long-time Scottish worker-militant and editor who became a Marxist-Humanist after his break with the Communist Party in 1953 and who carried on an intensive dialogue with Dunayevskaya for three decades.[1] In the letter, Dunayevskaya takes up some of her new insights on Marx which later became central to the finished book, including her critique of Engels' Origin of the Family and her analysis of Marx's* Ethnological Notebooks. *The original can be found in* The Raya Dunayevskaya Collection, *p. 6432.*

Dear Harry,

I would like to have a little theoretical discussion with you on the difference between theory and philosophy, and on the difference between a "leader" and a *founder* that may, at first sight, appear to be both abstract and, "geographically," far apart, but in fact is so crucial for our day when splits and sects are endless and yet no great divide anywhere near Lenin's great divide occurred so that the masses could sense a direction.[2] Indeed, I wish to go much deeper and further than "just" a great divide. (I do believe we Marxist-Humanists achieved that for our age by extending state-capitalist theory to Marx's Humanism, thus catching also directly where Marx had started.)[3] I wish also to go as far back as *the* founder of all of us, *Engels* and Lenin included.

Note, I include Engels of Marx's own time and place him alongside Lenin or anyone post-Marx, because it is most decisive to realize *Marxism is Marx's continent of thought and only of Marx, and not of Marx and Engels.*

Because there has been so much nonsense written by intellectuals against Engels as if he had "betrayed" Marx, and, the opposite side of the same coin, so much of Marx and Engels as if it were a hyphenated name, Marx-Engels, i.e., as if it were the same, that I have early decided to keep out and stick to fundamentals: Marx. But, in fact, though none but Engels could have brought out Marx's works; and though when Marx was alive, Engels was not just some kind of secretary, but true collaborator, and always a revolutionary, it is not true that he was anywhere near Marx in original thought. Indeed, all one has to do is read the kind of letters Engels addressed to Marx when he, *for the first time*, was reading Vol. I of *Capital* in galley proofs, to see how much Engels did *not* know.[4] But even that is not the real point, much less the need to know that it was Marx alone, and not Marx and Engels, who is responsible for that new continent of thought Marx first called "a new Humanism."

It is there, at its point of origin, which in methodology never changed though always was developing and becoming *more profound and more concrete*, at one and the same time. Let's begin at the beginning, at his very break with bourgeois society, at his 1844 *Economic-Philosophic Manuscripts*, and even that made most specific with the man/woman relationship telling all.[5] Now, generally, at least since the 1960s when both the women's liberation movement was born anew and so was a new generation of revolutionaries, male and female, so was the rediscovery of Marx's Essays. And yet what was not stressed in the same way was what Marx stressed, not just to expose the alienations and frustrations and exploitation of capitalist society, but in order to show *how total a revolution was needed.* So, the key words are *revolution,* and *totality of the uprooting,* not only of capitalism which, so to speak, was "his" task, *but all of humanity's development [that] Marx designated as "pre-history."*

Now, this brings me to how much lesser an original was Engels, and not only at the point of origin, but both in maturation and at the very climactic point of writing after Marx's death, and the very book socialist feminists surely have accepted as the best of all for that era: *Origin of the Family, Private Property, and the State.* Compare what Engels developed so fully and the mere abstracts of Marx's notations on Lewis Henry Morgan's *Ancient Society.*[6] Where[as] Engels [emphasized] the discovery of primitive communism—and it was among American Indians (the Iroquois especially) that all socialists were touting to the skies as showing how great women "were," and how, before private property, you didn't degrade women either to just an appendage of a machine if in the factory, or a breeder of children and thus the next generation of workers, but "equals"—Marx, on the other hand, while saying all this, *never* made that total, as if all we needed is to "modernize" and primitive communism becomes the communism of the future society. Quite the contrary. He showed that even in communal society, there was "slavery"—slavery of women—and it was there because we already had *division of labor*.

Now, whether one says division of labor was agricultural and men's moving to cattle breeding while women remained in agriculture—or whatever other "facts" are adduced coming to division of labor in industry—Marx's profound insight has nothing to do with anthropology or technology. No, the point was that somewhere in the "pre-history" of humanity, the division between mental and manual labor, necessary or otherwise, produced the break-up of the total being, and *its* "reunification" would first end man/woman in pre-history and start a new humanity.

So, both revolution and totality *as new beginnings* would start, not just a new continent of *thought*, but a new kind of *person*. Now, let us get down to our age and see how difficult it is to grasp that "Absolute Idea as New Beginning."

First, it appears as the unity of theory and practice. Reread *Marxism and Freedom*, where I certainly had already grasped the break-up of Absolute as the movement from practice as well as from theory, for them to unite as revolutionary practice for our age. In there, the central part which will lay the ground for our age as the age of absolute contradiction, of transformation of the first workers' state into state-capitalism, does take up all of Marx's works: philosophic, economic, historic, and political. And what do I call it? "Unity of Theory and Practice."[7] Not only that. I, in a footnote, thank Herbert Marcuse for his seminal work, *Reason and Revolution*, by saying I agree with him that Marxism went neither with Left Hegelians, nor what became of Hegelianism as that was transformed into opposite by the Right.[8] Now it is true we meant entirely different things. I meant what I was later to call a "new continent of thought," whereas Marcuse meant that since neither Left Hegelians nor Right Hegelians are true inheritors of the dialectic, "therefore" Marx went to "sociology"—Marxist, it is true, and not bourgeois, but "sociology" nevertheless.

Why, however, could I not have made myself so clear to myself as to see that, much as I learned from Marcuse, we were not only on different planets "politically" but philosophically? The answer is in fact that until *Philosophy and Revolution*, until my own return to Hegel, straight, and the new era of the 1960s incompleted in 1968, and new forces of liberation as Reason—Labor, Black Dimension, Women's Liberation, Youth—*no new stage of cognition could become concrete and profound*. And it is when I also began, with that new phrase, "new continent of thought," to see that not only was it *unity* of theory and practice, but *new beginning*—new continent, new world view, and that not only as internationalism—worker has no country; the world is his country—but Human-ism. And it is only now, in reworking for the tenth time man/woman *simultaneous with revolutionary*, that the work on Rosa Luxemburg is likewise becoming: Rosa Luxemburg, Today's Women's Liberation Movement *and* Marx's Theory of Revolution.[9]

So, if being a "philosopher"—Marx—was not just "the theoretician" Engels was in "following" *by reinterpreting Marx as he understood him*, then just think how absolutely stupid (if not idiotic) Joan Smith is in trying to correct your "very serious lack" on women, whereupon she retrogressed to the point that women just tailed "*The Party*."[10] In her case, not only is philosophy completely lacking, but theory too is reduced to "strategy," "combined strategies." Ah, well, as Hamlet's father (or his ghost) advised Hamlet not to seek revenge on his mother:

"Leave her to heaven."

On the 150th Anniversary of Hegel's Death: How Valid for our Day Are Marx's Hegelian Roots?

Dunayevskaya published the following essay in News & Letters *in December 1981, at a moment when Reaganism was beginning to make a deep mark on American politics and economics. In opposition to this emerging stage of retrogression, she here reexamines Marx's indebtedness to Hegel's dialectic, which she was studying and projecting anew as her work on* Rosa Luxemburg, Women's Liberation, and Marx's Philosophy of Revolution *was nearing completion. The original can be found in* The Raya Dunayevskaya Collection, *p. 7481.*

On the surface, any concern for the 150th anniversary of Hegel's death seems irrelevant and totally abstract in a period of Reaganomics when the deep recession at home seems on the verge of the Depression abyss; and, abroad, U.S. imperialism is, at one and the same time, propping up a genocidal war by the El Salvador neo-fascist regime against its own people, and, in West Europe, trying to introduce nuclear missiles in a competitive drive with the other nuclear titan, Russia. A careful examination, however, of the totality of the crisis—economic, political, military, ideological—that seems to spell out "Apocalypse, Now!" reveals a theoretic void on the Left that is very nearly as abysmal as that among the capitalist ideologues. This makes imperative the working out of a totally new relationship between the opposition movement from below—practice—and philosophy and revolution.

The one thing we learned from the turbulent 1960s is this: without a philosophy of revolution, near-revolutions abort. It is a fact that, because those near-revolutions had ended so disastrously, the New Left finally ended their Cohn–Bendit-like delusion that theory can be picked up "en route." A new, deeper look into Marx's philosophy of revolution was begun.

Thus, 1970, which was the 200th anniversary of Hegel's birth and 100th of Lenin's, saw a revival of both Marx and Hegel studies with conferences of each crisscrossing.* The flood of new studies, new editions, new translations that have followed that *Hegeljahr* (year of Hegel) extended into a full decade. It is still growing. Along with the Hegel studies, new studies of Marxian dialectics were published—though nowhere as comprehensive and serious as the Hegel studies.

No doubt part of the reason for the gap in seriousness between the two types of studies is due to the Russian hostility to the claim of independent Marxists about the live and so-to-speak continuing relationship of the Marxian to the Hegelian dialectic. After all, beginning in the mid-1950s and continuing to this day, the East European workers have revolted against Russian totalitarianism. Furthermore, these revolts were accompanied ideologically by a challenge to the Communist perversion of Marx's Marxism to force it to fit into the procrustean bed of Russian state-capitalist ideology. In order to separate Marx's concept of revolution from the actual revolutions against their tyranny, these state-capitalist ideologues calling themselves Communist attributed Marx's Humanism to some idealist left-over from the "mystical" Hegelian "negation of the negation." That, too, couldn't stop the revolutionaries in East Europe from translating the Hegelian phrase, as had Marx, as "revolution in permanence."[11]

Once those revolts from below placed Marx's Humanism on the historic stage of their age, there was no way to keep hidden that relationship of the Hegelian revolution in philosophy to Marx's philosophy of revolution.

Not all the blame for not developing this relationship of the Hegelian dialectics to the Marxian dialectics of liberation, however, can be [laid] on the "Russians." The truth is that the heirs of Marx, so designated by Engels who had entrusted Marx's unpublished works (and his own) to the German Social Democracy, had entombed them, christened their own mechanical material-

---

*For a fairly comprehensive summation of a decade of Hegel studies see James Schmidt in a three-article study, the first two of which have already been published in *Telos*, Winter, 1980–81, and Summer, 1981, entitled "Recent Hegel Literature, parts I and II."

ism as "Marxism"—an heirloom towards which one needs to bow, but not actualize as the transformation of reality by revolution.

It took nothing short of the outbreak of World War I and, with it, the collapse of the Second International, with the German Social Democracy at its head as the main betrayer of the proletariat, before a single revolutionary Marxist—Lenin—felt a compulsion to probe into Marx's origins in Hegel.[†] It was first then that Lenin grasped the need to study the Hegelian dialectic not alone as "source" of the Marxian dialectic, but to be probed "in and for itself." Lenin's emphasis on "the dialectic proper, as a philosophic science" [LCW 38, p. 277] separated him from all other post-Marx Marxists. It need hardly be stressed that the greatest practical revolutionary in the midst of the imperialist war was not studying Hegel for scholarly reasons.

No, as Lenin expressed it, "without having thoroughly studied and understood the whole of the *Science of Logic* . . . it is impossible completely to understand *Capital*, especially the first chapter." And Lenin concluded that "none of the Marxists understood Marx!!" [LCW 38, p. 180]. And that too was not merely a question of scholarship. Had they understood the core of the dialectic—the "transformation into opposite," "the unity and struggle of opposites"[12]—they would have understood the imperativeness of his slogan, "Turn the imperialist war into a civil war."[13]

Unfortunately, Lenin had no followers on the question of Hegelian dialectic, though the followers, Stalinist and de-Stalinized, and Trotskyist, never stopped being the most orthodox elitists in following him on the vanguard party. But then vanguardism has nothing whatever to do either with dialectics or with revolutionary spontaneism. In my new work, *Rosa Luxemburg, Women's Liberation and Marx's Philosophy of Revolution*, I go into detail on the whole question of post-Marx Marxists.[14] All that concerns us here, however, in this 150th year since Hegel's death is, how, in the last decade of Marx's life, he clung tenaciously to the Hegelian dialectic and his indebtedness to it.

Specifically, what we wish here to call attention to is the fact that Marx, even after he published his greatest theoretic work, *Capital*, Vol. I, didn't depart from his indebtedness to Hegel, though he had discovered a whole new continent of thought and of revolution that, on the surface, seems to have nothing whatever to do with "idealism." Marx was working on the seemingly

---

[†]Elsewhere I have developed this in full. See "The Collapse of the Second International and the Break in Lenin's Thought" in *Marxism and Freedom*, pp. 167–76; and "The Shock of Recognition and the Philosophic Ambivalence of Lenin" in *Philosophy and Revolution*.

"purely" materialistic Volume II of *Capital*. In a paragraph that Engels had left out of Marx's manuscripts for Volume II here is what Marx wrote:

> In a review of the first volume of *Capital*, Mr. Dühring notes that, in my zealous devotion to the schema of the Hegelian logic, I even discovered the Hegelian forms of the syllogism in the process of circulation. My relationship with Hegel is quite simple. I am a disciple of Hegel, and the presumptuous prattling of those epigones who believe they have buried this great thinker appear frankly ridiculous to me. Nevertheless, I took the liberty of adopting a critical attitude toward my master, to rid his dialectic of its mysticism and in this way to make it undergo a deep transformation, etc.[15]

Contrast this to the empty methodology of Roman Rosdolsky who, after his forced identification of the 1857–58 *Grundrisse* with the 1867–1875 *Capital*, concluded that one "no longer has to bite into the sour apple and 'thoroughly study the whole of Hegel's *Logic*' in order to understand Marx's *Capital*—one can arrive at the same end, directly, by studying the Rough Draft" (i.e., of *Capital*), which is Rosdolsky's title for the *Grundrisse*.[16]

Naturally, Marx's reference to Hegel as "master" was not meant in any schoolboy sense. Even when the young Marx had considered himself a Left Hegelian and belonged to the Doctors' Club of the Young Hegelians,[17] he was neither imitative nor arbitrary in his attitude to Hegel. Rather, as we saw from the time he worked on his doctoral thesis, he was approaching the threshold of his new continent of thought and revolution while seeing revolution lodged in the Hegelian dialectic. This is why the mature Marx kept repeating that Hegel's dialectic was the source "of all dialectic" [MCIF, p. 744; MCIK, p. 654].

Instead of using the dialectic as if it were a tool to be "applied," Marx recreated it on the objective-subjective basis as it emerged out of the production relations of labor and capital, with labor as the "grave-digger." Clearly, the unifying whole of Marx's world view was the new subject—the proletariat. The idea of history was not only as past but as that which live working men and women achieve in transforming reality, here and now—transforming themselves, as well, in the process of revolution into new, all-rounded individuals of a classless society. He would not let the Dührings treat Hegel as a "dead dog";[18] he wanted to confront them with the fact that the long, arduous, 2,500-year trek of human development that Hegel had dialectically traced was indeed, the basis of the new developments in their day.

The revolutions Marx participated in during his day and those Marxist revolutionaries who have ever since followed, are proof enough of how far distant is Marx's new continent of thought and of revolution from Hegel's bourgeois world and its idealism. The fact, however, is that the Hegelian dialectic, rooted in history and the power of negativity, remained with Marx and gained ever new creativity, whether it was in the 1844 Humanist Essays, or the outright revolutions of 1848, or even as Marx returned to the Hegelian dialectic in the 1860s and 1870s after he worked out the economic laws of capitalism, discerning the "law of motion" of capitalism to its collapse while its absolute opposite—the "new passions and new forces"—worked to reconstruct society on totally new, human beginnings, like the Paris Commune.

That is the significance of the 1870 footnote in the manuscripts for Volume II of *Capital* on which Marx worked in 1870–78 but had to leave unpublished. That volume has become the one most debated to this day. Is it too much to expect the post-Marx Marxists of our era, in this, the 150th year since Hegel's death, to recreate the Hegelian dialectic in the manner of Marx? After all, it is not the death of Hegel we are celebrating, but his philosophy. And it is a fact that the year before his death (1830), Hegel was still adding three final syllogisms to his *Philosophy of Mind*. It is these that point to the fact that, not just the "method," but the "system" itself is a process,[19] an incessant becoming which the revolutionary materialist and founder of a whole, new continent of thought and of revolution—Karl Marx—judged to be the socialist goal: "the absolute movement of becoming."[‡]

NOTES

1. For a discussion of McShane and his correspondence with Dunayevskaya, see Peter Hudis, *Harry McShane and the Scottish Roots of Marxist-Humanism* (Glasgow: The John MacLean Society, 1993). Some 190 letters between Dunayevskaya and McShane are held by The National Labour Museum, Manchester, England. See also McShane's Preface to the British edition of *Marxism and Freedom* (London: Pluto Press, 1971), pp. 9–14.

2. A reference to Lenin's philosophic break with his contemporaries in the Marxist movement with his *Philosophic Notebooks* of 1914–15.

3. A reference to the period from the May, 1953 "Letters on Hegel's Absolutes" to the publication of *Marxism and Freedom* in 1957.

4. See especially Engels' letter of June 16, 1867, in [MECW, 42, pp. 381–82], in which he discusses his problems in comprehending Marx's discussion of the value-form in chapter 1 of *Capital*.

5. In "Private Property and Communism" (1844), Marx writes: " . . . the relation of man to woman is the most natural relation of human being to human being. It therefore reveals

[‡]Elsewhere I have developed this statement of Marx from the *Grundrisse* (1857), in the context of the struggles of the 1870s. See especially chapter 1 of *Philosophy and Revolution*, and my paper, "Hegel's Absolute As New Beginning," to the Hegel Society of America [see chapter 10].

the extent to which man's natural behavior has become human." [MECW 3, p. 296). For Dunayevskaya's further discussion of this, see *Rosa Luxemburg, Women's Liberation, and Marx's Philosophy of Revolution*, and *Women's Liberation and the Dialectics of Revolution* (Detroit: Wayne State University Press, 1996 [1985]).

6. Marx's notebooks on Morgan, which Engels never published, were not published until the 1970s. See *The Ethnological Notebooks of Karl Marx*, transcribed and ed. by Lawrence Krader (Assen: Van Gorcum, 1972). For a contrast of Marx's *Notebooks* and what Engels made of them in his *Origin of the Family, Private Property, and the State*, see *RLWLKM*, chapter 12.

7. Part III of *Marxism and Freedom* is entitled "Marxism: The Unity of Theory and Practice."

8. Dunayevskaya footnoted her expression in chapter 1 of the book, " . . . Marx was *organically* a dialectician" [M&F, p. 57] by writing "In this respect Herbert Marcuse's *Reason and Revolution* is a truly pioneering and profound work, and I would like to acknowledge my debt to it" [M&F, p. 348].

9. For the development of the work which ultimately became *Rosa Luxemburg, Women's Liberation, and Marx's Philosophy of Revolution*, see part IV of Dunayevskaya's *Women's Liberation and the Dialectics of Revolution* as well as *Supplement to the Raya Dunayevskaya Collection*, pp. 14191–15377.

10. Joan Smith, a British Trotskyist, was at the time trying to arrange the publication of McShane's autobiography. For McShane's dissatisfaction with how Smith presented his autobiography in *No Mean Fighter* (London: Pluto Press, 1978), see his letter of September 5, 1974 to Dunayevskaya, contained in *The Harry McShane Collection* (National Labour Museum, Manchester, England). This is discussed in Peter Hudis, *Harry McShane and the Scottish Roots of Marxist-Humanism*.

11. See for example Marx and Engels' March 1850 "Address to the Communist League," in which they conclude that the "battle cry" of "the party of the proletariat" must be "the Revolution in Permanence" [MECW 10, p. 287]. For Dunayevskaya's discussion of this, see chapter 11, "The Philosopher of Permanent Revolution Creates New Ground for Organization," in *Rosa Luxemburg, Women's Liberation, and Marx's Philosophy of Revolution*, which also includes a critique of Trotsky's concept of permanent revolution.

12. These two phrases are used frequently by Lenin in his 1914–15 "Abstract of Hegel's *Science of Logic*" [LCW 38].

13. Lenin first used this phrase in a November 1914 article on the war [LCW 21, p. 39].

14. This is one of Dunayevskaya's first public expressions of the category "post-Marx Marxism," sometimes more sharply expressed in the formulation "post-Marx Marxism, beginning with Engels, as a pejorative." This formulation was meant to include important theoreticians and leaders such as Engels, Lenin, Luxemburg, and Trotsky, none of whom, she argued, measured up to Marx's Marxism.

15. Quoted by Maximilien Rubel in Karl Marx, *Oeuvres: Economie*, Vol. II (Paris: Éditions Gallimard, 1968) p. 528, but unavailable in other editions of *Capital*. Dunayevskaya discusses it in RLWLKM pp. 49–50.

16. Roman Rosdolsky, *The Making of Marx's 'Capital,'* (London: Pluto Press, 1977) p.

570. For Dunayevskaya's critique, see her "Rosdolosky's Methodology and Lange's Revisionism," *News & Letters* (Jan.-Feb. 1978).

17. The Doctors' Club was founded in Berlin by left-wing followers of Hegel in 1837. Marx, who was active in the club for several years, first refers to it in a letter to his father of November 10, 1837 [MECW 1, p. 19].

18. Karl Eugen Dühring (1833–1921), called Hegel a "dead horse" in his book, *Natural Dialectic*. For Marx's critique of Dühring's view, see his letter to Kugelmann of March 6, 1868 (MECW 42, p. 542).

19. In his essay "Ludwig Feuerbach and the End of Classical German Philosophy" (1886), Engels wrote: "Whoever placed the emphasis on the Hegelian *system* could be fairly conservative in both spheres [religion and politics]; whoever regarded the dialectical *method* as the main thing could belong to the most extreme opposition, in both religion and politics" [MECW 26, p. 363].

PART V

THE CHANGED WORLD AND THE NEED FOR PHILOSOPHIC NEW BEGINNINGS, 1982–87

~

CHAPTER FOURTEEN

Marxist-Humanism and the Battle of Ideas

On the Battle of Ideas:
Philosophic-Theoretic Points of Departure
as Political Tendencies Respond
to the Objective Situation

This essay, which was written as a "Political-Philosophic Letter" in October, 1982, was composed on the eve of the publication of Dunayevskaya's Rosa Luxemburg, Women's Liberation, and Marx's Philosophy of Revolution. *As part of her effort to prepare for the new battles of ideas, now that her work projected the new category "post-Marx Marxism, beginning with Engels, as pejorative," she directly discusses her own contribution to Marxism, beginning by reexamining the philosophic issues which led to the break with C.L.R. James and Grace Lee Boggs in 1955. The original can be found in* The Raya Dunayevskaya Collection, *p. 7486.*

This is being written on the centenary of Marx's discovery of still newer moments of development in life and in thought, as he 1) read Henry Lewis Morgan's *Ancient Society;* 2) visited Algeria and became aware of what we now call the Third World; and 3) projected the idea that "The Historical Tendency of Capitalist Accumulation"—so characteristic of technologically developed Western capitalism—need not be the only path for the so-called backward countries. On the contrary, concluded Marx, a backward country like Russia could achieve a revolution ahead of the West and thereby hew out still another path to "revolution in permanence."

I wish to develop this in the context of Hegel's Absolutes on the one hand, and, on the other hand, new forces of revolution and Reason for our age. Here are the three subheadings: I. The Syllogism in the Doctrine of Notion and its Impact on Lenin in 1914, and on the Johnson-Forest Tendency in 1950–53;[1] II. Dialectic Mediation and Absolute Negativity; III. Hegel's Absolute Mind (¶575, 576, 577 of the *Philosophy of Mind*); the Forces of Revolution as Reason, as they are analyzed in *Rosa Luxemburg, Women's Liberation and Marx's Philosophy of Revolution*.

I am taking advantage of the fact that we do not yet have [*Rosa Luxemburg, Women's Liberation, and Marx's Philosophy of Revolution*] in hand, which will plunge us into so many activities that we're bound to forget "abstract" philosophic points of departure. . . . [In particular, I now] find new divergences from Grace [Lee Boggs] on the politicization of the Syllogism,[2] an analysis which originally had thrilled me greatly when, in 1951, Grace had said that it signified the end of the opposition between objective and subjective. I related this expression to what Lenin had experienced as he read that section during World War I. It had led to the great divide in Marxism.

I. The Syllogism in "The Doctrine of the Notion" and its Impact on Lenin in 1914, and on the Johnson-Forest Tendency in 1950–53

Grace's 1951 philosophic letter read: "I suspect also that in the development from Judgment to Syllogism[3] is contained the development from the party of 1902 to the Soviet of 1917. The Syllogism destroys the opposition of subjectivity and objectivity."[4]

I must have disregarded the phrase "from the party of 1902 to the Soviets of 1917"—i.e., Grace's politicalization on the question of the Party as paralleling the central categories in the Doctrine of the Notion—but went the distance with the sentence "the Syllogism destroys the opposition of subjectivity and objectivity," especially as it related to the way Lenin had worked it out. The self-development of Lenin on that section of the *Logic* and its central categories, Universal, Particular, Individual [U-P-I] (which I have developed both in *Marxism and Freedom* and in *Philosophy and Revolution*) illuminates the whole question of process. Let's follow that:

1) Lenin's first comment on reaching "The Doctrine of Notion" was: "A good way to get a headache."[5]

2) In plodding through it nevertheless, he then found only one thing with which to agree with Hegel—Hegel's attack on the superficial way philosophers have of expressing U-P-I as: "All men are mortal, Gaius is a man, therefore Gaius is mortal" [LCW 38, p. 177].

But 3) Lenin no sooner reached the final section on the Syllogism than out poured tremendous aphorisms as seen in the statement: "None of the Marxists for the past half century have understood Marx!!" [LCW 38, p. 180].

Indeed, he followed up these Notebooks with an article, "On Dialectics," where he also took issue with Engels, though he forgave his not overly profound penetration of the dialectic by stating that Engels did so for "popularization" goals [LCW 38, p. 357].

Grace's politicization of the movement in "The Doctrine of the Notion," as paralleling the movement from the vanguardist party concept, 1902, to the recognition of the spontaneity of the masses in creating the Soviets, 1917, did not answer the problem that she thought she was answering; that is, whether Lenin was breaking with the vanguardist concepts. By skipping over the question of the Party, we can neither understand the tragedy as the early bureaucratization of the workers' state unfolded, nor grapple with why Lenin was still relying on the "thin stratum"—Lenin's own expression [LCW 33, p. 257]—of the Bolshevik Party, despite all the criticisms he leveled against the leadership in his Will.

I returned to the exact quotation in Hegel where Grace had made her comments, and found that it was from Section I (Subjectivity) of Doctrine of the Notion, and that Hegel then subjected the Syllogism to the experience of Section II (Objectivity), and only then arrives at the Idea.[6] That is to say, dialectical mediation becomes the key to all the "experiences" the Syllogism goes through. Indeed, when I worked out the Syllogism in [May] 1953, it was not as it was developed in the *Science of Logic* but as it appeared in the *Philosophy of Mind*.[7]

II. Dialectical Mediation and Absolute Negativity

In my [May 1953] Letters on the Absolute Idea, in which four pages are devoted to the *Philosophy of Mind*, here is what I wrote:

> Here, much as I try not once again to jolt you by sounding as if I were exhorting, I'm too excited not to rejoice at what this means *for us*. But I'll stick close to Hegel and not go off for visits with Lenin and Marx. *Hegel* says that the two appearances of the Idea (to us: Socialism in the form of either the Commune or the Soviets) characterize both its manifestation and this, *precisely*, is "A unification of the two aspects."*

---

*I should call attention to the fact that those letters, dated May 12 and May 20, 1953, use the expression Absolute Idea for all references to the Absolute. While that is acceptable in general, it is necessary here to be more precise by differentiating the Absolute: in the *Phenomenology*, Hegel used the expression Absolute *Knowledge*; in the *Science of Logic*, it is articulated as Absolute *Idea*; and in the *Philosophy of Mind*, it emerges as Absolute *Mind*. It is especially important to stress this here because the first letter on the Absolute Idea (May 12) is where I took issue with Lenin for having said that the final paragraph in the *Science of Logic* doesn't matter. Grace then took issue with my "exhortation," which concerned me enough not to continue the criticism of Lenin. Instead I followed Hegel's advice. That is, I realized that Hegel had not finished the totality of his philosophy and had advised his reader that he must now go to *Philosophy of Nature* and *Philosophy of Mind* to grasp that totality. See *The Raya Dunayevskaya Collection*, pp. 1797 and 1595.

I then quoted ¶577:

> The self-judging of the Idea into its two appearances (¶575, ¶576) characterizes both
> as its (the self-knowing reason's) manifestations: and in it there is a unification of the
> two aspects:—it is the nature of the fact, the notion, which causes the movement and
> development, yet this same movement is equally the action of cognition.

It becomes necessary to stress here, over and over again, that I had not a single word to say then about the Party or the Soviets or any form of organization. On the contrary. Here is what I then concluded: "We have entered the new society."

Philosophically, what happened was that Grace had been so enthusiastic about that May 20 letter, and had grasped how new, *historically new*, had been my singling out of the movement from practice to reach the new society, that she plunged into one of her hyperboles to say that what Lenin's *Philosophic Notebooks* had done in creating the Great Divide in Marxism in World War I, my letters on the Absolute Idea had achieved for our age.[8] It was evidently at that point that all hell broke loose as C. L. R. James not only did not answer my letters but ordered Grace, who was in California, and who had hailed those letters so enthusiastically, to return to New York at once. They both then decided that I should not demand any discussion of the letters "for the time being," and that I was to start the practical preparations for the July Convention [of Correspondence Committees]. He seemed to do likewise. But since he had to leave for England, he called the "faithful" to him there and they began preparations to split Johnson and Forest.

It is necessary now to trace what dialectic mediation achieves—precisely because it was in the middle, between the movements from practice and from theory; how it requires a *double* negation before it can reach a new society. All of it is seen first in the final syllogisms of Absolute Mind, not as any sort of God, *or* as evasion of all responsibility by dumping all responsibility on "the masses."

III. Hegel's Absolute Mind (¶575, ¶576, ¶577 of *Philosophy of Mind*); The Forces of Revolution as Reason, as analyzed in *Rosa Luxemburg, Women's Liberation, and Marx's Philosophy of Revolution*

¶575 [of Hegel's *Philosophy of Mind*] seems merely to state the obvious, the sequence of the books Hegel wrote—*Logic, Nature, Mind*. The second paragraph (576) is Nature, Mind, Logic. And since Mind is the mediation there, you first get the full impact of Hegel's concept of mediation as he lunged out against "systems" and for mediation, because *philosophic* mediation is the middle *that first creates from itself the whole.*

In a word, Hegel has now departed from both the system as well as spontaneity, *or* practice, *or* Nature as if these were the whole. He could still keep away from making his dialectic into any sort of system because, in the final paragraph (577), he *doesn't* finish that as a syllogism, that is to say, he refuses to follow the "sequence" which would have led to Logic being the mediation. What we are confronted with, as replacement for Logic, is the self-determination of the Idea and the self-bringing forth of liberty. In a word, in each case, mediation, as a transition point to something else, stops as we have reached the totality of both recollection (inwardizing) and spontaneity (Nature). Hegel replaces Logic, but will not tell us what to do. Self-knowing reason (¶577) is that self-bringing forth of liberty which is concrete, which is everywhere present, which is constantly developing.

For any to whom it may seem incongruous to have included "Forces of Revolution as Reason" in this section on Hegel's Absolute Mind, it becomes necessary to return to Marx's 1844 "Critique of the Hegelian Dialectic" to see why Marx refused to stop where Feuerbach allowed Hegel to chain the dialectic† by refusing to recognize the revolutionary nature of "negation of negation."[9] Marx unchained that most revolutionary dialectic—"negation of negation"—by demystifying it and revealing its objectively revolutionary nature. As Marx kept developing his own continent of thought and of revolution, he situated "negation of negation" by declaring that the 1848 Revolution needed further development as a "revolution in permanence." It is this which *Rosa Luxemburg, Women's Liberation, and Marx's Philosophy of Revolution* declared to be "the absolute challenge to our age." This section on Absolute Mind extends this by disclosing how the self-thinking Idea is moving toward a new unity with the self-bringing forth of liberty—that movement from practice that is itself a form of theory and thus becomes a revolutionary force that is Reason.

Where forces of revolution are Reason, Marx's demystification of double negation and its articulation as "revolution in permanence" demands that it not be left just in the field of theory but becomes ground for a new organizational form—indeed, for self-development of the Individual. It is for this reason that in all three books—*Marxism and Freedom* and *Philosophy and Revolution* as well as *Rosa Luxemburg, Women's Liberation, and Marx's Philosophy of*

---

†I felt Hegel deserved one little escape after creating so historic a revolution *in* philosophy, so I didn't include, when I quoted ¶577, that final sentence, which read: "The eternal Idea, in full fruition of its essence, eternally sets itself to work, engenders, and enjoys itself as absolute mind."

Revolution—I traced those forces of revolution through three decades, as they centered around a new generation of revolutionaries, both as Youth and as Labor from under totalitarianism calling itself Communism; or the Black dimension in the U. S. and in Africa; or a whole new Third World; or the new *world* force of revolution—Women's Liberation, having leaped from an Idea whose time has come to a movement.

Hold this in mind as you reread this year's Perspectives Thesis.[10] As preparation for our Convention, I addressed, first, a letter to the youth on August 16 which asked them:

> How will you show . . . [a] future that will be non-exploitative, non-sexist, non-racist, with truly and totally new *human* relations. . . . Take such a simple date as the early 1950s . . . which saw also the very first revolution in Latin America, Bolivia's, from Western imperialism. How do you propose to project that into the struggles against Reaganism in El Salvador in the U.S.? For that work with the Spanish-speaking dimension, we have both *Marxismo y Libertad* and *Filosofía y Revolución* as well as our bilingual pamphlet on *The Unfinished Latin American Revolutions* and much more.[11]

The following week this was followed with suggesting to the Women's Liberation-News and Letters Committees the addition of a new paragraph to Chapter 8 [of] *Rosa Luxemburg, Women's Liberation, and Marx's Philosophy of Revolution* on "The Task That Remains To Be Done: The Unique and Unfinished Contributions of Today's Women's Liberation Movement." I asked that, to the third paragraph from the end, which criticizes the old concept of woman as "helpmate," we add:

> Quite the contrary. History proves a very different truth, whether we look at February 1917, where the women were the ones who *initiated* the revolution; whether we turn further back to the Persian Revolution of 1906–11, where the women created the very first women's soviet; or whether we look to our own age in the 1970s in Portugal, where Isabel do Carmo raised the totally new concept of *apartidarismo*.[12] It is precisely because women's liberationists are both revolutionary force *and* Reason that they are crucial. If we are to achieve success in the new revolutions, we have to see that the uprooting of the old is total *from the start.*

And in the penultimate paragraph, which ends with "do not separate practice from theory," I asked that we add:

> Which is what Luxemburg meant when she defined "being human" as "joyfully throwing your life on the scales of destiny."[13]

My letter then continued:

> My point in making these two suggestions for additions is that this sort of thing must be in each one's mind very nearly every time they speak on the new book. Each one must not only concretize the book further, day in and day out, for it's only in that way that the projection of *Rosa Luxemburg, Women's Liberation and Marx's Philosophy of Revolution* will result not only in organizational growth, but, indeed, in helping to lay the ground for the American Revolution.[14]

This was followed by including, directly in the Perspectives Thesis, *What to Do*, presented on September 4, one more paragraph to add to the final page of the final chapter 12 of the new book. It would come directly after the last sentence of the penultimate paragraph and would read:

> This is the further challenge to the form of organization which we have worked out as the committee-form rather than the "party-to-lead." But, though committee-form and "party-to lead" are opposites, they are not absolute opposites. At the point when the theoretic-form reaches philosophy, the challenge demands that we synthesize not only the new relations of theory to practice, and all the forces of revolution, but philosophy's "suffering, patience and labor of the negative," i.e., experiencing absolute negativity. *Then and only then* will we succeed in a revolution that will achieve a class-less, non-racist, non-sexist, truly human, truly new society. That which Hegel judged to be the synthesis of the "self-thinking Idea" and the "self-bringing-forth of liberty," Marxist-Humanism holds, is what Marx had called the new society.[15]

Finally, with all this in mind, I just reread the Introduction to that new work and decided on still another new paragraph. Please insert it directly after the one ending with the imperial incursions into the Orient and the carving up of Africa as Marx was studying the latest empirical anthropological studies, such as Morgan's *Ancient Society*.

> That seems to have been the first point so misunderstood by post-Marx Marxists, beginning with Frederick Engels, who, without having known of the massive *Ethnological Notebooks* Marx had left behind, undertook to write his own version of Morgan's work—his *Origin of the Family*—as a "bequest" of Marx. When Ryazanov discovered these notebooks, he rushed, before he ever had a chance to decipher them, to characterize them as "inexcusable pedantry."[16] If an Engels, who was a close collaborator of Marx and without whom we could not have had Volumes II and III of *Capital,* could nevertheless suddenly have gotten so overconfident about his own prowess of interpreting Marx as to assume he was speaking for Marx; if an archivist-scholar like Ryazanov could, at a time when he was actually publishing

those magnificent early essays of Marx (the 1844 *Economic-Philosophic Manuscripts*), spend a good deal of his first report on the Archives of Marx in asking for twenty to thirty people to help him sort these manuscripts out, and yet pass judgment before he dug into them—it says a great deal about literary heirs but nothing whatsoever about so great an historic phenomenon as Marx's Marxism. Isn't it time to challenge all of the post-Marx Marxists when even those who have achieved great revolutions—and none was greater than the 1917 Russian Revolution—did not, in thought, measure up to Marx? Isn't it time to dig into what Marx, who had discovered a whole new continent of thought, had to say for himself? (Chapter 12 concentrates especially on the last writings of Marx in which this author found a trail to the 1980s.)

Just as this addition signifies that, from the very start, in the Introduction itself, I point to our challenge to all post-Marx Marxists, so it is necessary for all of us now to concretize it daily in our activities as in our meetings, as a way of building new relations.

What adds urgency to the necessity of relating both *Marxism and Freedom* and *Philosophy and Revolution* to the new book, *Rosa Luxemburg, Women's Liberation and Marx's Philosophy of Revolution*, is not only the actual movement from practice, as it developed during those three decades since 1953, but also the fact that civilization itself is under threat of nuclear annihilation. The fact that I made a category of that movement from practice—six weeks before the very first historic movement from under Communist totalitarianism on June 17, 1953, in East Germany—actually made possible the link of continuity to Marx. What opened the way for Marx to discover a whole new continent of thought and revolution was not only that he saw, and singled out as Subject, the proletariat (which was unreachable to Hegel because it was not fully developed as a class "in and for itself" during the French Revolution); it was that Marx, two years before he broke with bourgeois society, grounded in the Hegelian dialectic, was *looking for* a new beginning, and thereby experienced "the shock of recognition" in the proletariat as the new Universal. (See "Prometheus Bound, 1841–1843" in chapter 9 of *Rosa Luxemburg, Women's Liberation, and Marx's Philosophy of Revolution*.)

Once I saw that movement from practice as a philosophic category, which was not alone for our age but for Marx's as well, I could structure the whole of *Marxism and Freedom* in the context of the movement from practice, beginning with the age of revolutions—industrial, political, philosophic—and subtitling the whole work: "From 1776 until Today." Part I, "From Practice to Theory: 1776 to 1848," thus paved the way for confronting the different tendencies *within* the new proletarian revolutionary movement, as the intellectuals (specifically Marx and Lassalle) encountered the nature of the new bourgeois state. Part II, then, was entitled "Worker and Intellectual at a Turning Point in History: 1848 to 1861."‡ Because Marx's *Capital* reveals *Marx's* Marxism as a "Unity of Theory and Practice" (the title of part III), deeply rooted in history *as it was happening*, from the Civil War in the U. S. to the Paris Commune in France, it created ground for analysis of our age of state-capitalism and workers' revolts.

What followed the publication of *Marxism and Freedom* for the Marxist-Humanists of the 1960s was *News & Letters* creating a form for all the new voices to be heard, as well as for the manifestation of our unique combination of worker and intellectual. *News & Letters* published both pamphlets of the new voices—from *Workers Battle Automation* to *Freedom Riders Speak For Themselves* to *The Free Speech Movement and the Negro Revolution*[17]—and our unique combination of worker and intellectual in the form of the National Editorial Board Statement, *American Civilization on Trial*,[18] as well as my pamphlet on the Afro-Asian Revolutions.[19] By 1968, however, when the historic activities of that tumultuous decade—which had subordinated theory to activity and more activity and more activity, holding it could catch theory "en route"—ended in an aborted revolution, it was all too clear, even to those who rejected theory, that even the new movement from practice that was itself a form of theory was insufficient once theory didn't reach philosophy. It became imperative to dig back into the development of Marx's own roots in the Hegelian dialectic in the mid-19th century as well as Lenin's compulsion to return to the Hegelian dialectic in the early 20th century as the outbreak of World War I saw the collapse not only of private capitalism but also of *established* Marxism.

The writing of *Philosophy and Revolution—from Hegel to Sartre and from Marx to Mao* had still newer foundations because a new voice from the Third World and from theory was heard in the person of Frantz Fanon. He, too, was calling for a "new Humanism."[20] That affinity of ideas for a new Humanism which was circling the globe from East Europe to Africa was reflected in the collaboration I received from East European colleagues (who had to remain unnamed) in the writing of chapter 8: "State Capitalism and the East European Revolts."

The fact that I insisted on relating part III, on "Economic Reality and the Dialectics of Liberation" (which included not only "The African Revolutions and the World Economy" and "State Capitalism and the East European Revolts" but also "New Passions and New Forces," whether that be the Black

---

‡I should add here that I was most proud that some Iranian revolutionaries chose that chapter to translate into Farsi in 1979, as the Iranian Revolution was unfolding.

Dimension, the Anti-Vietnam War Youth, Rank-and-File Labor, or Women's Liberation) to Part I of the work, "Why Hegel? Why Now?"—and especially to chapter 1, "Absolute Negativity as New Beginning," which dealt with Hegel's works, in and for themselves—is what drew the sharpest critique from academic circles. Thus, George Armstrong Kelly, in his *Hegel's Retreat from Eleusis* (pp. 238–40), accused me of proposing "to substitute an unchained dialectic, which she baptizes 'Absolute Method,' a method that 'becomes irresistible . . . because our hunger for theory arises from the totality of the present global crisis.'"[21] To this writer, the critique did not appear accidental. Just as 1970, as the 100th anniversary of the birth of Lenin and the 200th of Hegel's, brought a renewed interest in both Hegel and Lenin, so 1983, as the centenary of Marx's death, will create new interest in *Marx's* Marxism and Hegel's Absolutes. Academia is forever trying to save Hegel from Marx's subversion.

The fact that in my latest work, *Rosa Luxemburg, Women's Liberation, and Marx's Philosophy of Revolution*, I trace a trail to the 1980s from the 1880s and focus on Marx's "translation" of absolute negativity as the revolution in permanence, calling that the absolute challenge to our age, will draw still greater criticism from academia and outright attacks from post-Marx Marxists. This makes it necessary to be prepared, not only for that encounter, but for further concretizing that challenge. With this in mind, I decided to add that paragraph quoted earlier directly to the Introduction. For while it is true that the actual events of the 1970s—Women's Liberation on the one hand, and the publication of Marx's *Ethnological Notebooks* on the other—are what first led to a renewed interest in Rosa Luxemburg; and while it is true also that the Women's Liberation Movement helped disclose the feminist dimension in Luxemburg never before recognized; it is not true that that is the goal of the new book.

The need to see all post-Marx Marxists in strict relationship to *Marx's* Marxism is what revealed that even so great and independent a revolutionary as Rosa Luxemburg did not fully comprehend Marx's dialectics of liberation and thereby committed her biggest error—disregard of the revolutionary nature of Polish desire for national self-determination. Put simply, *the* determinant of the new book is Marx's philosophy of revolution. This is not for any academic reason, or any sort of orthodoxy, but the fact that his works disclosed a trail to the 1980s and revealed the problematic of this age. The totally new question that Luxemburg posed—socialist democracy *after* gaining power—pointed to a new aspect of Marxism itself.[22] The new moments in Marx that the book discloses and that center around what we now call a Third World are not limited to the manner in which Marx revealed an "Asiatic mode of production" in the *Grundrisse*. Rather, this is extended to the 1880s as Marx [in his *Ethnological Notebooks*] was commenting on Morgan's *Ancient Society* and other then-new anthropological works on India, on the Australian aborigines, as well as in his letters both on his visit to Algeria and his correspondence with revolutionaries in Russia on the ancient commune there and its possible transformation into an altogether new type of revolution. In a word, it is to revolution in permanence that the book keeps returning, whether the subject is Luxemburg, or Lenin, or Women's Liberation, or the Hegelian dialectic. At the same time, we must keep in mind that, whereas it is Marx who transformed Hegel into a contemporary, and transformed the Hegelian dialectic into the Marxian dialectic of liberation, the revolution is also present *in Hegel*. Hard as Hegel tried to confine this to a revolution in thought alone, he made his presence felt in history, even as he spoke of *The Philosophy of Mind* and *History of Philosophy*. As Hegel put it:

> All revolutions, in the sciences no less than in general history, originate only in this, that the spirit of man, for the understanding and comprehension of himself, for the possessing of himself, has now altered his categories, uniting himself in a truer, deeper, more intrinsic relation with himself.[23]

Postscript

Perhaps it would be good here to trace through the entire sequence of events from 1948, when C. L. R. James' *Notes on Dialectics* inspired me to translate Lenin's *Abstract of Hegel's Science of Logic*, rather than beginning with the better-known (1953) date of my Letters on the Absolute Idea. Although I was then unaware that my brief comments in submitting the translation of Lenin's *Philosophic Notebooks* signaled a difference in interpretation of the historic and philosophic significance of those Notebooks, the truth is that that *is* the beginning of philosophic differences *within* the Johnson-Forest Tendency. (See *The Raya Dunayevskaya Collection*, pp. 1595–1734.)[24]

The Miners' General Strike, which had erupted in 1949 and continued into 1950, followed a period when C. L. R. James, who remained in New York, and I, who had moved to steel town (Pittsburgh), were hardly on speaking terms. As soon as the strike erupted, I went down to West Virginia and worked with the members of the Johnson-Forest Tendency who were very active in that strike. (The Socialist Workers Party [SWP] local there was all Johnson-Forest Tendency.) I had begun sending a very new type of article on the miners' strike and interviews with miners' wives to the *Militant*, whose editor, George Breitman, greeted them as "a breath of fresh air."[25] It was clear that the workers' attitude to the "continuous miner"—the word "Automation" had not yet been invented, and the workers simply referred to it as the "man-killer"—signified a new stage of production *and* a new stage of cognition. The predominant question in workers' minds was not just higher wages; they questioned the very kind of labor man should do, demanding to know: Why should there be this unbridgeable gulf between mental and manual labor? It is this type of question which led the Johnson-Forest Tendency to cast their summation document of ten years' development of the theory of state-capitalism in a very new way. C. L. R. James and Grace Lee came to Pittsburgh, where we jointly wrote *State-Capitalism and World Revolution*, which we were to submit to the SWP Convention that year. For the first time, we included a section on philosophy, written by our "official" philosopher, Grace Lee, and entitled "Philosophy in the Epoch of State-Capitalism."[26]

I was enthusiastic about the new section, but I had questioned two points in the draft: 1) How does it happen that Contradiction, which is the central category in Essence, becomes the central point for Lenin's philosophic reorganization when, in fact, his Notebooks show he had gone through the whole of the Doctrine of Notion? 2) Why are we omitting reference to the Absolute Idea, which C. L. R. James had posed in his *Notes on Dialectics*? The only answer James and Grace seemed to have given me was incorporated in the document: "There is no longer any purely *philosophical* answer to all this." This had been preceded by the explanation: "These intellectuals are the most cultivated in the modern world, in the sense of knowing the whole past of human culture. Having achieved what the idealism of Hegel posed as the Absolute, they are undergoing a theoretical disintegration without parallel in human history."[27]

When, in 1951, Grace tackled the Syllogism in the Doctrine of the Notion, I still seemed satisfied, but all that disappeared by 1953 when I, myself, worked out both the Absolute Idea and Absolute Mind in the letters of May 12 and May 20, 1953. It is true I was sufficiently taken aback with her critique of my "exhortation" of Lenin in the May 12 letter to begin the May 20 letter with: "Please do not interpret this as any prodding of *you* to commit yourself on my analysis of the Absolute Idea; it is only that I cannot stand still and so rushed directly to the *Philosophy of Mind*."[28] But there was no doubt by then that, hard as I tried to continue in the context that preoccupied James and Grace—the "dialectics of the party"—I was bound in a very different direction once I concentrated on Hegel's "dialectic *mediation*" rather than any sort of "media*tor*," whether the Party or otherwise. (See my "Letters on the Absolute Idea." See also my later reference to [Otto] Pöggeler's 1961 statement: "In opposition to the usual interpretations of the Hegelian text, I should like to propose the following: that the actual science of Spirit is not the Logic but the philosophy of

Spirit," which I quote in my lecture to the Hegel Society of America on "Absolute Idea as New Beginning.")[29]

It is worth noting here, also, that in plunging into the final three syllogisms, I had to dive on my own, since there was absolutely no one—not even Marx,[30] let alone Lenin, much less C. L. R. James and Grace Lee—who had written anything on that. Once I ventured out in 1953, and confronted the actual world movement from practice, the integrality of philosophy and revolution showed itself to be (or should we say, aspired to become) the solution to the problematic of the modern world. The one thing we know *as fact* in this centenary year is that—once we do know the Marx *oeuvres as totality*, and once we do have our ears to the ground of both new voices from below *and* the creative nature of Marx's mind (and Marx's alone)—then we do perceive in Marx's new moments a trail to the 1980s, be that as new Third World, or global theory reaching philosophy, a philosophy of revolution that is to become preparation for actual "revolution in permanence."

Letter on Karl Korsch (1983)

With the completion of Rosa Luxemburg, Women's Liberation, and Marx's Philosophy of Revolution, *Dunayevskaya further developed her new category — "post-Marx Marxism, beginning with Engels, as pejorative." The following letter on Karl Korsch (1886–1961),[31] one of the leading German Hegelian Marxists of the 1920s and 1930s, represents Dunayevskaya's discussion of the category in light of "Western Marxism." Written as a letter to a colleague, Michael Connolly, on February 20, 1983, it centers on a rereading of Korsch's 1923 work,* Marxism and Philosophy, *which Dunayevskaya had briefly touched upon in her* Philosophy and Revolution. *The original can be found in the* Supplement to the Raya Dunayevskaya Collection, *p. 15357.*

Although [the] "A 1980s View" section of *Rosa Luxemburg, Women's Liberation, and Marx's Philosophy of Revolution* makes it clear that the challenge to post-Marx Marxists, beginning with Engels, includes so-called Western Marxists, I nevertheless suddenly feel it necessary to make the latter reference more explicit, especially as it relates to Karl Korsch.

Ironically, one reason I consider it necessary to expand the challenge to post-Marx Marxists by focusing on "Western Marxists" is that Lukács[32] and Korsch were the very ones who did [pose] the dialectic's revolutionary nature as inseparable from actual revolutions; who did tightly relate the Second International's reformism that ended in outright betrayal once World War I erupted; and were nevertheless the very ones who, as revolutionaries, accepted Lenin's revolutionary *politics* without ever relating it to his *strictly philosophic* reorganization. Why? Why had they never seen any significance in what Lenin achieved in 1914,[33] [in what] they first worked out in 1919–1923? How could the great divide *in Marxism*, with the outbreak of World War, be left at the political level without the search for Lenin's return to the Hegelian dialectic "in and for itself"?

Heretofore I had allowed Lukács' and Korsch's disregard of Lenin's deeper penetration of the dialectic and its todayness, on the one hand, and, on the other hand, Lenin's philosophic ambivalence when it came to the question of organization,[34] i.e., his concept of "the party to lead," to rest in peace—as if so-called Western Marxists are entitled to some sort of special privileges. Now with the completion of *Rosa Luxemburg, Women's Liberation, and Marx's Philosophy of Revolution*, which could present the Marx oeuvre *as a totality* and take issue with true revolutionary giants (Lenin, Luxemburg, Trotsky) most critically, all others who claim to be Marxists must likewise be measured against *Marx's* Marxism—not Engelsianism.

The reason for focusing on Korsch is, precisely, because so-called Western Marxism was the excuse (or reason, as you wish) Jean-Paul Sartre and [Maurice] Merleau-Ponty used in the post-World War II period.[35] It is the excuse global anthropologists[36] still use when they want to escape Marxian methodology and concentrate on facts, facts, facts. It is the todayness of the past debates that have sent me back to rereading Korsch. In reading now the Korsch reference to Hegel that I quoted in *Philosophy and Revolution*[37] [from his *Marxism and Philosophy*], I became very conscious of the fact that he had allowed for altogether too many qualifications of the Hegelian dialectic as he kept repeating over and over again materialism, materialism, materialism.

In my view to skip over the dialectics of an actual new great divide in Marxism that Lenin's *Philosophic Notebooks* at the outbreak of World War I had created by saying, but Lukács and Korsch didn't know of Lenin's *Abstract of Hegel's Science of Logic* since he kept it private when they did their grappling with the Hegelian dialectic in the specific milieu of German Marxism, is a way of viewing chronology as facticity rather than dialectic sequence. The proof of that can be seen in the fact that in all the years since the publication of Lenin's 1914 *Philosophic Notebooks* they still didn't dig deep into that great divide.

It is true that they didn't know, when they were developing their view on the imperativeness of a revolutionary return to the Hegelian dialectic in 1919 to 1923, that Lenin had already achieved a much deeper and more comprehensive review of the dialectic with his *Abstract* in 1914. But they did know of the 1922 popular letter Lenin had addressed to the editors of a new journal *Under the Banner of Marxism* which called for "a systematic study of the Hegelian dialectic from a materialist standpoint."[38] Indeed, Korsch used that specific quotation as frontispiece of his *Marxism and Philosophy* without ever sensing any philosophic discontinuity between the Lenin of 1908 who had given the green light to vulgar materialism with his *Materialism and Empirio-Criticism* and the Lenin of 1914–23 who had produced the dialectical *Abstract of Hegel's "Science of Logic."* The truth is that they kept treating two very different works—*Materialism and Empirio-Criticism* and the *Abstract*[§]—as if it were one and the same continuous work, even after the latter was publicly known. Instead of digging deep into the *philosophic* great divide, they proceeded narrowly on their own way and accepted the politics of "Leninism." Thereby they did nothing to close the great philosophic void which resulted after Lenin's death even as it became *the* characteristic post-Marx Marxism with the death of Karl Marx. Nowhere is that clearer [than] in their revolutionary embrace of Lenin's great work *State and Revolution,* which however didn't work out the dialectics of the party from its 1902–03 vanguardist concept. (The fact that Party is never mentioned in that work though it is so great a recreation of Marx's *Critique of the Gotha Program* I'll deal with later.)

I was nevertheless anxious enough to give Korsch credit for reestablishing the revolutionary nature of the Hegelian dialectic to reproduce Korsch's quoting Hegel's formulation that "revolution was lodged and expressed as if in the very form of their thoughts," and stressed especially Korsch's calling attention to the fact that this use of revolution was by no means left only in the sphere of thought but was held to be "an objective component of the total social process of real revolution" (p. 41).

Clearly, it is not out of any concern for firstedness that I wish to set the record straight. The necessity for correcting the factual arises, not from facticity, but from the ambience of the dialectic. If we are not to narrow the dialectic either only to the objective or only to the subjective, the attitude to chronology cannot, must not be reduced to facticity. When all is said and done, it is the objectivity of that historic momentous event of a world war and collapse of *established* Marxism which compelled the militant materialist, Lenin, to turn to the "subjective," the "idealist" Hegel. *Marx's* Marxism

---

[§]For that matter there was no change in that false attitude when the 1914 *Philosophic Notebooks* finally were published. Nor was that failure to recognize the great divide due only to political capitulation to Stalinism. No, it was much, much deeper. Lukács, who did finally [in his *The Young Hegel* (1948)] begin making many references to the *Abstract*, made these with so false a consciousness that he paired Lenin with Stalin as an original philosopher so that both became creators of "Marxism in the age of imperialism."

was rooted therein not only as "origin" but as continuous dialectic which spells out return/recreation as the imperative need for a new relationship of theory to practice.

The relationship of theory to practice, of subject to object, so preoccupied Marx from the very first that he no sooner completed the 1844 *Economic and Philosophical Manuscripts* than he followed it with the 11 *Theses on Feuerbach*, the first of which reads: "The chief defect of all previous materialism (including Feuerbach) is that the object, actuality, sensuousness is conceived only in the form of the object of perception, but not as sensuous human activity, praxis, not subjectively. Hence, in opposition to materialism the active side was developed by idealism. . . . Feuerbach wants sensuous objects actually different from thought objects; but he does not comprehend human activity as objective. . . . Consequently, he does not comprehend the significance of 'revolutionary,' of 'practical-critical' activity" [MECW 5, p. 3].

Korsch, on the other hand, far from seeing that Marx credited, not materialism, but "idealism," i.e., the Hegelian dialectic, with the development of the "*active*" aspect of subjectivity, human activity having undergone a deeper development than from individual to social *praxis*, reduces ideas to hardly more than the mirror image of the materialist underpinning, a one to one relationship of objective to subjective. This gets further qualified by focusing on the "similarity" between Hegelian and Kantian dialectic and *other* German idealists. Thus, he no sooner quoted Hegel on the "revolution lodged in the very form of thought" but not restricted to thought, than he footnoted it with a lengthy reference to Kant's Conflict of the Faculties: "The revolution of an intellectually gifted people, such as the ones we are witnessing today, arouses all onlookers (who are not themselves directly involved) to sympathize with it in a way that approaches enthusiasm."[39]

Korsch has a peculiar way of describing the life/death of German idealism: "Instead of making an *exit*, classical German philosophy, the ideological expression of the revolutionary movement of the bourgeoisie, made a *transition* to a new science which hence forward appeared in the history of ideas as the general expression of the revolutionary movement of the proletariat: the theory of 'scientific socialism' first founded and formulated by Marx and Engels in the 1840s" (p. 41).

As we see, the qualifications Korsch introduced into the Hegelian dialectic also were extended to the Marxian. To Korsch, "The emergence of Marxist theory is, in Hegelian-Marxist terms, only the 'other side' of the emergence of the real proletarian movement; it is both sides together that comprise the concrete totality of the historical process" (p. 42).

Marx's Marxism, far from being only "the other side" of the proletarian movement, is a whole new continent of thought and of revolution in which "totality" does not stop as a mere sum of its parts. The core of the dialectic—the transformation of reality—doesn't stop at any one period.** Marx's Marxism, his Promethean vision, produced ever new moments which the "Western Marxists" failed to work out for their epoch.

Where Lenin, in his return to the Hegelian dialectic, singles out Hegel on "cognition not only reflects the world but creates it" [LCW 38, p. 212], Korsch keeps quoting over and over again from [Engels'] *Anti-Dühring* and *Ludwig Feuerbach and the End of Classical German Philosophy* as if they were Marx's works and thus falls headlong into Engelsian "positive science": "That which still survives (philosophy in Marx—RD) independently of all earlier philosophies is the science of thought and its laws—formal logic and dialectics. Everything else is subsumed in the positive science of nature and history" (p. 46).[40] This leads Korsch to become so defensive on the question of philosophy and Marxism that, despite his total break with the German Social Democracy and his magnificent connection of the Second International's reformism to its neglect of philosophy and the theory of revolution, he holds that "it is true that it appears. . . . Marxism itself is at once superseded and annihilated as a philosophical object"!

Having reduced the dialectic to "science" and history to historicism, Korsch makes it impossible to grapple with Marx's dialectics—the transformation of historic narrative into historic reason.[††] No wonder that even when he is at this most creative in revealing the relationship of the Second International's reformism to this neglect of the dialectics of revolution—the need,

---

**On that score Lukács is, at least in 1919–1923, more profoundly dialectical: "To be clear about the function of theory is also to understand its own basis, i.e., dialectical method. This point is absolutely crucial, and because it has been overlooked much confusion has been introduced into discussions of dialectics. Engels' arguments in the *Anti-Dühring* decisively influenced the later life of the theory. However we regard them, whether we grant them classical status or whether we criticize them, deem them to be incomplete or even flawed, we must still agree that this aspect is nowhere treated in them. That is to say, he contrasts the ways in which concepts are formed in dialectics as opposed to 'metaphysics'; he stresses the fact that in dialectics the definite contours of concepts (and the objects they represent) are dissolved. Dialectics, he argues, is a continuous process of transition from one definition into the other. In consequence, a one-sided and rigid causality must be replaced by interaction. But he does not even mention the most vital interaction, namely the *dialectical relation between subject and object in the historical process*, let alone give it the prominence it deserves. Yet without this factor dialectics ceases to be revolutionary, despite attempts (illusory in the last analysis) to retain 'fluid' concepts. For it implies a failure to recognize that in all metaphysics the object remains untouched and unaltered so that thought remains contemplative and fails to become practical; while for the dialectical method the central problem is *to change reality*" (*History and Class Consciousness*, p. 3).

††The one critique Korsch allowed himself of Engels' self-criticism "in an incorrect and undialectical way," Korsch never followed through with his strict Hegelianism (p. 156): "In Hegel's terms, he retreats from the height of the concept to its threshold to the categories of reacting and mutual interaction," etc.

not to "take over" the state, but for its *abolition*—Korsch sees and accepts Lenin's great divide *only politically*. He praises highly Lenin's *State and Revolution* which had recreated Marx's *Critique of the Gotha Program*, and the Paris Commune as "really no longer a state" [LCW 25, p. 424]. But since he hasn't *philosophically* worked through the great divide, he hardly can recreate it for his epoch, nor see that Lenin himself had there stopped *on the eve of* revolution, *not on what happens after* conquest of power. So blind is he to that turning point where the dialectics, far from being a question of revolution vs. reformism, would become one of confronting the most horrifying of all problems—the *counter*-revolution arising *from within* the revolution itself—that he sinks into stagifying *Marx's* Marxism.

Korsch's practice of a one to one relation of subjective to objective has him divide Marx's development into three periods, with the first being the highpoint, 1843–48. Once the 1848 revolution is defeated it is all one long retrogression which he subdivides into two: 1848–64, which he begs off from analyzing since Marx so "masterfully," in his "Inaugural Address of 1864" of the First International, described the "period of feverish industrial activity, moral degeneration and political reaction." Here is how Korsch continues with that second period: "The second period may be said to last approximately to the end of the century, leaving out all the less important divisions (the foundation and collapse of the First International; the interlude of the Commune; the struggle between Marxists and Lassalleans; the anti-socialist laws in Germany; trade unions; the founding of the Second International). The third phase extends from the start of this century to the present and into an indefinite future" (p. 51).

The logic of this illogical stagifying of Marx's development, which reduced Marx's universal of the Paris Commune into a mere interlude, stands out in all its contradictoriness when Korsch once again returns to the highpoint of his revitalization of the dialectic when the totality of his attack on the German Social Democracy is proven most dramatically by its attitude to the *Critique of the Gotha Program* in the contrast with its total opposite, Lenin's *State and Revolution*.

It takes a lot of excavating to disclose Korsch's type of Kantian dialectics at the very point when, politically, he has the deepest dialectical penetration in his rejection of the Second International's theoretical neglect of Marx's *Critique of the Gotha Program* and [he is] accepting Lenin's *State and Revolution*, especially, when at that point we need to confront Lenin's philosophic ambivalence of having stopped without tackling the dialectic of the Party and thus the 1902–03 vanguardist concept of the party was left untouched. But leave it to Korsch to come to our aid, first by focusing on Lenin's postscript [to

State and Revolution] as if that were the climax to the revolutionary analysis. That is to say, where Lenin admits he had to stop his theoretical exposé on state and revolution before he had a chance to dig into actual revolutions, either 1905 or 1917, Korsch stops also his analysis, though no revolution is knocking at his door which [made] Lenin, of course, most happy by that "interruption": "It is more pleasant and useful to go through 'the experience of revolution' than to write about it" (p. 68; [see also LCW 25, p. 497]). So, in 1923, we have yet to approach *the* problem: what happens *after* the conquest of power?

Secondly, in turning to Marx's *Critique of the Gotha Program*, Korsch still has not a word to say on the question of organization, though he is rapturous in praise of Marx's *Critique* both in the original 1923 edition of *Marxism and Philosophy* and its 1930 reprint with a new introduction as well as his special introduction that he had written to the *Critique* itself.[41] But isn't that, *that precisely*, the overriding question—the relationship of theory to organization. Wasn't that *Critique* written as "Marginal Notes" to a Party's program? Wasn't it sent to a leader (Bracke) in the parties about to be united? And wasn't that sent simultaneously with the French edition of *Capital*, Vol. I, in the very period as Marx was plunging in to a study of the Russian ancient peasant commune which disclosed such "new moments" in Marx's development as to leave a trail even for our period of the 1980s?

Let's begin at the beginning of the adventures of the *Critique*, written in 1875. The German workers party proceeded on its merry way without so much as publishing Marx's *Critique*, much less making that the foundation for the Party. Fifteen years later, when Engels finally compelled the new German Social Democracy to publish the *Critique* in 1891, it was clear that "knowing" the *Critique* had as little impact as not knowing it—just like, in Korsch's period, no new ground had been created by "knowing" instead of not knowing Lenin's 1914 breakthrough on the Hegelian dialectic.

Just as considering Marx and Engels as one led, at best, to muddying up Marx's Marxism even when no revisionism was involved, as with Engels, so not seeing Lenin's great divide philosophically resulted, at one and the same time, in the dilution of *Marx's* Marxism *and* losing the dialectical sequence for the new problems after the death of Lenin. Put simply, the challenge to post-Marx Marxists is needed, not just to clear up the debris left by Engels' interpretation of *what* were Marx's "bequests," but to be informed by Marx's inseparable new continent of thought and of revolution, *neither of which is separable from the other.*

Correctly, as Luxemburg did magnificently, to reject the very first revisionist call for the "removal of the dialectical scaffolding" from Marxism, without concretizing and deepening the dialectic for one's own age creates a gap.[42] That the historic continuity with Marx seemed to have ended with the 1848 revolution, rather than extending it to the 1850 Address on "revolution in permanence," first emerged in the 1905 Revolution. By 1907, when the International Congress [of the Second International] didn't even put that revolution on the agenda, [it] signified, as I expressed it in *Marxism and Freedom*, "The Beginning of the End of the Second International."[43] You have every right to call attention to the fact that clarification was achieved with eyes of 1957. It certainly is true that the combination of hindsight and the fact that, with the eruption of the [1956] Hungarian Revolution, came also the placing on the historic stage of Marx's 1844 humanist essays could not but reopen the relationship of philosophy to revolution. But why then, did Lenin's return to the Hegelian dialectic in 1914 lead post-Marx Marxist "Western Marxists" to skip that new ground from which to take off?

To sum up briefly, what remains of the essence is, at one and the same time, to relate historic continuity, the return to *Marx's* Marxism as a re-creation, to the *dis*continuity of the ages and, with it, to be able to meet the new challenges. As a precondition for that I hold it imperative to reconsider post-Marx Marxism, measure it against *Marx's* Marxism and, far from skipping what had been created by Lenin's great divide philosophically, to take off from that.

What a rereading of Karl Korsch's *Marxism and Philosophy* has illuminated is that the dialectic needs extension to the dialectics of the Party, which Marx had charted in *Critique of the Gotha Program,* and which even Lenin, who so freshly re-created [the *Critique*] on the question of the need to abolish the state and, with the revolution, proceeded to a new form of power that is "no longer a state" [LCW 25, p. 424], didn't have time dialectically to extend to what happens *after,* though he certainly did leave us jumping off points [which] must be worked out by this age. A first step toward that task is to make sure that not only is there no division between philosophy and revolution but also not [one] between philosophy and organization. Concretely that demands the relationship of organization to Marx's theory of "revolution in permanence." It is with that in mind that I entitled the penultimate chapter of *Rosa Luxemburg, Women's Liberation, and Marx's Philosophy of Revolution,* "The Philosopher of Permanent Revolution Creates New Ground for Organization." It is only then that the final chapter on Marx's "new moments," including his *Ethnological Notebooks* and our age's Third World, disclosed the trail to the 1980s. That doesn't mean we have the answer all signed and sealed. It does mean [that] working this out demands a challenge to post-Marx Marxists.

Marxist-Humanism: The Summation That Is a New Beginning, Subjectively and Objectively (1983)

This lecture was delivered on January 1, 1983, shortly after the publication of Rosa Luxemburg, Women's Liberation, and Marx's Philosophy of Revolution, *and shortly before Dunayevskaya embarked on an intensive national lecture tour during the period of the centenary of Marx's death (1883–1983). It focuses on how the completion of this third work of what she termed her "trilogy of revolution" shed new illumination upon both the 40-year development of Marx's Humanism and the four-decade-long development of her concept of Marxist-Humanism. The first two parts of this four-part presentation are reproduced here. The original can be found in* The Raya Dunayevskaya Collection, *p. 7639.*

Introduction: Where and How to Begin Anew?

The reason that we begin, not objectively as usual, but subjectively, is that the "here and now" demands a deeper probing into the creative mind of Marx.

The warp and woof of the Marxian dialectic, the unchained Hegelian dialectic, *the* dialectic of the revolutionary transformation is, after all, true objectively and subjectively. Yet part III of *Rosa Luxemburg, Women's Liberation, and Marx's Philosophy of Revolution* begins the probing of Marx *before* he fully broke with bourgeois society, when he worked on his doctoral thesis "On the Difference between the Democritean and Epicurean Philosophy of Nature." Thus began his very first critique of Hegel, in 1841, as it appeared in the Notes that were known only to himself. What did appear in the doctoral thesis itself was what pervaded those Notes, i.e., the question: How to begin anew?[44]

The reason that question reappears here is not to emphasize how it antedated Marx's discovery of a whole new continent of thought and revolution, but rather because it reappeared in its true profundity in Marx's own greatest work, *Capital* (I'm referring to the definitive French edition, 1875)[45] as well as in the very last decade of his life, in what we now call Marx's "new moments" of discovery.

Let me rephrase this. The crucial truth is that the question: How to begin anew? informed the whole of his dialectic methodology—even *after* his discovery of a whole new continent of thought, even *after* the publication of the first edition of *Capital* as well as the 1875 edition, *after* the Paris Commune, *when* he took issue with Mikhailovsky who had written what turned out to be what all *post*-Marx Marxists likewise accepted as the climax of the work, that is, the "Historical Tendency of Capitalist Accumulation" as a universal.[46] Marx, on the other hand, held that that summation of Western capitalist development was just that—the particular development of capitalism— which need not be the universal path of human development. Here we have the unique way Marx practiced summation as a new beginning.

The concept of totality as new beginning was true also on the organizational question: How to begin a new organization *when* it is to express a whole philosophy of revolution. Marx answered that question in his letter to Bracke, in which he enclosed what he modestly called "Marginal Notes" to the "Program of the German Workers' Party."[47] That was the letter in which he noted also that finally the French edition [of *Capital*] was out and he was sending it to Bracke. The fact that no post-Marx Marxists saw that inseparable relationship of organization to philosophy of revolution is the more remarkable when you consider that Marx's closest collaborator, Frederick Engels, was not only still alive but worked with Marx very closely in sending letters to the various so-called Marxist leaders as Marx tried to stop the unification of the Eisenachists and Lassalleans on the basis of the Gotha program.[48] Beyond the per adventure of a doubt, the *Critique of the Gotha Program* formulated a totally different basis for the establishment of a Marxist "Party."

It becomes necessary once again to emphasize that year, 1875, as not only the year in which both the French edition of *Capital* was completed and the *Critique of the Gotha Program* was written. That year also predates by two years the letter Marx wrote on Mikhailovsky (but never sent), criticizing his concept of the "historical tendency" as a universal, insisting that it was the summation of capitalist development in Western Europe and that "the Russians" could "find a path of development for their country different from that which Western Europe pursued and still pursues"—and that, in fact, if Russia didn't find that different path "she will lose the finest chance ever offered by history to a people and undergo all the fatal vicissitudes of the capitalist regime" [MECW 24, p. 199].

Think again about the question of how faithful Engels was to the Gotha Program critique, not only in the letters written when Marx was alive, but in the fact that he kept at the German Social-Democrats for a full 15 years after the Party did not publish that criticism, and only in 1891 did get it published.

The tragic truth is that it didn't make any difference when they did publish it. It didn't become ground for the new openly Social-Democratic organization. Nor was any parallel drawn by anyone, including Frederick Engels, between organization and Marx's whole philosophy, though clearly, definitively, this was what Marx's *Critique* aimed at. And just as clearly, [Marx's] covering letter warned against the unification *because* there was to be "no bargaining about principles." Quite the contrary, he "and Engels would make clear" that they had "nothing in common with it" (the Gotha Program) [MECW 24, p. 78].

In a word, it wasn't only the Eisenachists and Lassalleans who knew how to misuse the fact that Karl Marx and Frederick Engels didn't make public their break with the Gotha Program and the German Workers' Party. The truth is that the German Social-Democrats, who did consider themselves "orthodox" under its leading "Marxist" theoretician, Karl Kautsky, did the very same thing later. This time the reason rested in the claim that, since they adhered to Marx's "theories," their Party was the organization of vanguard socialism. They succeeded in so twisting the very concept of vanguardism that they made "the Party" read "the *vanguard* Party." That was *not* Marx's concept, as we shall see in a moment as we turn to the third new moment in Marx on organization. It is high time for Marxist-Humanists to concretize "Where and how to begin anew" for our age by looking at those "new moments" in Marx as the trail to the 1980s.

I. The Four New Moments in Marx That Are the 1980s Trail

The first new moment that was not grasped by the first post-Marx Marxist generation was due not merely to the fact that Engels had omitted the paragraph from the French edition of *Capital*, which had been definitively edited by Marx, when Engels transferred Marx's additions to the German.[49] Marx's point in that omitted paragraph on further industrialization (as it covered the whole nation) and, with it, the predomination of foreign over internal trade, was that although the world market annexed "vast lands in the New World, in Asia, in Australia," that wouldn't abate the general crisis of capitalism. On the contrary. The new development in capitalism meant that the ten-year cycle he had originally cited as the crisis that regularly follows capitalism's growth would occur more often.

What wasn't grasped by a less creative mind than Marx's was that, far from the climactic "Historical Tendency of Capitalist Accumulation" signifying universality for all technological development, it characterized only Western Europe while "the Russians" could choose a different path. Post-Marx Marxists failed to grasp this because they separated economic laws from the dialectics of revolution. For Marx, on the other hand, it was just this concept of revolution which changed everything, *including economic laws*. He rejected the fact of Western capitalist development as a universal for all, delved into the latest anthropological studies, and then wrote to Vera Zasulich stressing the possibility for revolution to erupt in a technologically backward country like Russia "ahead of the West." In this letter to Zasulich he had made direct reference to the "American" (he was referring to [Henry Lewis] Morgan's *Ancient Society*) whose studies of pre-capitalist societies, Marx thought, further proved that the peasant commune form of development could lead Russia, *if* the historic conditions were ripe *and* it was working with West Europe, as well, to initiate revolution.[50]

To make sure that none misunderstood his concept of revolution and the prediction of revolution in the "East" ahead of the "West," he (this time with Engels) had written a new Introduction to the Russian edition of nothing less important than his *Communist Manifesto*. There he publicly spelled out that prediction. That was 1882!

This was not the only new moment Marx discovered which post-Marx Marxists didn't grasp. The second new moment again related to theory. This time it was a new interpretation of the dialectic itself in two crucial areas in the transformation of reality. Everyone knows the 1850 Address [to the Communist League], which ended with the call for "revolution in permanence," though hardly anyone has related it to Marx's continuing concretization of the dialectic of negativity, as the dialectics of revolution.[51] None seem to have even begun to grapple with what it meant for Marx, as he was already completing economic analysis of capitalism (*and* pre-capitalist societies) in the *Grundrisse* in 1857, to have so fully integrated the dialectic and the economics as to articulate that the socialism that would follow the bourgeois form of production signified "the absolute movement of becoming" [MECW 28, pp. 411–12].* What an Hegelian expression to use to describe that full development of all the talents of the individual that would mark the new socialist society!

That the question of individual self-development and social, revolutionary, historical development would thus become one manifests itself in the *Grundrisse*. It is no accident that it was there where Marx stopped speaking of only three universal forms of human development—slave, feudal, and capitalist—and included a fourth universal form: the "Asiatic mode of production." That post-Marx Marxists failed to have that as ground for working out the reality of their age and thus anticipate what we now call a whole new Third World is exactly what this age is still suffering from.

---

*Marx was rereading Hegel's *Logic* as he worked on the *Grundrisse* and wrote to Engels on January 16, 1858, that this chance rereading was a great help to him in creating a new form for presenting his economic studies [MECW 40, p. 249]. That "new form" of integrating dialectics and economics further[more] led Marx to reworking the first draft, *Grundrisse*, into the final form, *Capital*.

The third new moment—that on organization—was not only not grasped, but actually *rejected*. Post-Marx Marxists were always "proving" that, because Marx had not worked out a "theory" of organization, while Lassalle knew how to build a mass party, he left them no model to practice. The First International, they said, had included so many contradictory tendencies that Karl Marx was forced to "consign it to die in the United States." Indeed, all of them were quick to twist the whole concept of "vanguardism" as if it meant, simply and only, "the party." Neither "Leninists" *nor opponents of Lenin* have been willing to acknowledge that the ground for [Lenin's] *What Is To be Done?* was, *precisely*, the ground of the German Social-Democracy. And that includes Rosa Luxemburg, despite all her great achievements on the actuality of spontaneity. While Lenin rejected any type of "half-way dialectic" on the National Question, he did not see that same type of "half-way dialectic" in himself on the question of the "vanguard party."

The whole truth is—and that is first and foremost—Marx never separated organization forms from his total philosophy of revolution. Indeed, as was shown when we kept stressing the year, 1875, Marx had worked out his whole theory of human development in *Capital and* in the organizational document, *The Critique of the Gotha Program*—because his principle, a philosophy of revolution, *was the ground also of organization*. In a word, it was not only the state which Marx held must be destroyed, totally uprooted. He showed that the proletarian organization likewise changed form. Thus, the First International, Marx said, "was no longer realizable in its *first historical form*" (*Critique of the Gotha Program*) [MECW 24, p. 90].

This, history shows, was not understood by the first post-Marx Marxists. It would take nothing short of the German Social-Democracy's betrayal at the outbreak of World War I before Lenin totally broke with them, and first saw Marx's *Critique of the Gotha Program* as most relevant for his day. It was then also that he spelled out most concretely how revolutionaries could not just "take over" the bourgeois state machinery. That had to be smashed to smithereens. Lenin made that revolutionary message both more concrete and more comprehensive—a true concrete Universal—when he saw, as inseparable, Marx's theory of revolution and his theory of human development, concluding, "The whole theory of Marx is an application of the theory of development."[52] Yet, as we know, Lenin still left the concept of the vanguard party in its old (though modified) form.

A new historic age was needed to work out all the ramifications. A new movement from practice as a form of theory had to emerge and be recognized before a new attitude could be worked out, and that meant, far from freeing the movement from theory of *its* responsibilities, the movement from practice was demanding that theory, too, undergo self-development so that it could concretize for a new age Marx's revolutionary dialectical philosophy, which he had called a "new Humanism." By the time, in 1956, that the Hungarian Revolution brought Marx's philosophy onto the historic stage, we had developed that new Humanism in the United States. By 1960, the Third World theorist Frantz Fanon had developed his liberation philosophy and called it "a new Humanism." By the 1970s Marx's *Ethnological Notebooks* were finally transcribed so that *Marx's* Marxism could be seen *as a totality.* It is this which *Rosa Luxemburg, Women's Liberation, and Marx's Philosophy of Revolution* is rooted in when it takes a new look at Marx's 1875 *Critique.* The new book devotes a whole chapter to the *Critique,* entitling that chapter: "The Philosopher of Permanent Revolution Creates Ground for Organization." This sums up that third new moment in Karl Marx on organization in his age and in ours.

The fourth new moment which opened with the *Ethnological Notebooks* (finally transcribed in the 1970s) reveals itself equally and even more urgently relevant to our age for Women's Liberation. It is this work which enables us to see with new eyes that Marx's 1844 concept of Man/Woman*—far from being something that only the allegedly "utopian" young Marx had articulated—was deepened throughout his life.

Thus, in 1867, as he was preparing the first edition of *Capital* for the press, and Dr. Kugelmann had given him his early essays, Marx wrote to Engels: "We have nothing to be ashamed of."[53] Marx also related these early essays to the 1867 debates around *Capital,* holding that "the feminine ferment" was inherent in revolutions *throughout history.*[54]

From his activities in the Paris Commune, we know how Marx had laid the ground in establishing the Union des Femmes, following this through by making it a principle that the First International establish autonomous women's organizations.[55] Finally, with his last work, the *Ethnological Notebooks,* he further enshrined this new attitude by showing the revolutionary presence of women throughout history, from the Iroquois women to the Irish women before British imperialism conquered Ireland.

Clearly, all four new moments, in theory and practice, in organization and spelling out "the new passions and new forces" for the reconstruction of society on new, Humanist beginnings—first naming the proletariat as Subject; then working out the revolutionary role of the peasantry, not only as in Engels' *Peasant Wars*[56] but as in the peasant communal form in the 1880s; and always

---

*One so-called independent Marxist, Hal Draper, dared to refer to these 1844 Essays as being no more than "the lucubrations of this new-fledged socialist."

singling out youth and then women as Reason as well as forces of revolution—have laid new paths of revolution, a whole trail for the 1980s.

Surely, as Marxist-Humanists, now that we do have "three books, not one,"[57] as well as all the pamphlets on the new voices from below, worldwide as well as in the United States—ranging from *Workers Battle Automation, Freedom Riders Speak for Themselves* and *Afro-Asian Revolutions* to *People of Kenya Speak for Themselves* and *Frantz Fanon, Soweto and American Black Thought*—we can now measure up to Marx's second new moment, both as a possible new path of revolution as well as the dialectics of the "absolute movement of becoming". . . . It is, indeed, the trail to the 1980s that we have been working out for three full decades.

II. The Unchained Dialectic in Marx, 1843–1883, and in Marxist-Humanism, 1953–1983

It was Marx who unchained the Hegelian dialectic by demystifying the "negation of negation," designating it as a "new Humanism" in 1844, and as "revolution in permanence" in 1850, while in 1857 recreating Hegel's "absolute movement of becoming" as integral to what would follow capitalism when revolutionary socialism came to full bloom. Nor did Marx stop in 1867 when he finished his greatest work, *Capital*, where he recreated the dialectic as "new passions and new forces" [MCIF, p. 928; MCIK, p. 835]. In the last decade of his life the creative nature of the mind of Marx, founder of a whole new continent of thought and of revolution, was still discovering "new moments."

These new revolutionary moments of human development became ground for organization. So integral were organizational forms and revolutionary principles that, as we have seen, he concluded that the form of the First International which he had headed was "no longer realizable in its *first historical form* after the fall of the Paris Commune." The point was not to "bargain about principles." Only the "all-around development of the individual" would prove that humanity reached the end of the division between mental and manual labor. Then the new society could operate on *the* new principle "from each according to his ability, to each according to his need."[58] In a word, both the destruction of the State and the end of the division between mental and manual labor must be achieved for the principle of "the absolute movement of becoming" to become reality—when *practiced* as the "all-around development of the individual." Nothing less than that could be called Communism.

When the Russian Revolution did not succeed in extending itself internationally, when world capitalism regained life and Stalin was victorious in a new form of state-capitalism, post-Marx Marxists proved incapable of following Marx's Promethean vision.

We who did fully break with Trotskyism and felt compelled to analyze the new reality of state-capitalism—and the Johnson-Forest Tendency did represent a great theoretical advance in that respect—nevertheless failed to work out what the Tendency was for instead of only what it was against. In a word, it had not reached Marxist-Humanism except in the merest embryo form— rejection of state-capitalism and looking with new eyes at labor's creativity in working out new forms of revolt. Nevertheless, were we to skip over the State-Capitalist Tendency's challenge to Trotskyism, we would leave an historic loophole on the quintessential relationship between philosophy and revolution, between theory and practice, not to mention the search for the link to the absolutely indispensable creative mind of Marx. The historic link must be reestablished if we are serious about revolution in our age. That new beginning came *before* establishment of organization—News and Letters Committees, 1955.

Before the establishment of the Committees we had, when still a part of the State-Capitalist Tendency, broken through philosophically on the Absolute Idea.[59] That happened in 1953. *It is this, just this, catching of the new in our age that laid the ground for seeing the link of continuity with Marx.* It becomes necessary to stay a little longer on those two years, 1953 to 1955, to work out, in full, our own contributions, not just as against Trotskyism but also against Johnsonism.[60]

Here, again, we need to return to what Hegel called "The Three Attitudes to Objectivity."[61] Actually it is four attitudes, but the fourth, the dialectic, being the whole, is not given a number since it occupies all the works of Hegel, and *is* Hegel *and* Marx. It is *the* "attitude" that is most relevant here. It is the relationship of subjectivity to objectivity when that subjectivity is not mere Ego, but the historic-philosophic subjectivity which, in place of stopping at first negation or mere reaction, goes on to second negation—i.e., absolute negativity which alone reveals totality by developing it as a new beginning. That new beginning relates all the four new moments in Marx to the question of philosophy of revolution as ground of organization.

Let's catch our breath right here because the "new Humanism" for our age that we represent must not be "taken for granted." It is the re-creation of Marx's new Humanism *at a time when.* But this "when" means both a "before" and "after," that is to say, it is the "when" that is our age. It signifies the stage of human development which was brought onto the historic stage of today by actual revolutions in East Europe, in the Middle East, in Africa, in the West; and in multi-colors of Black, Yellow and Brown and Red; with a whole new generation of Youth and of Women's Liberationists—as well as by a movement from theory that, though not from the same origins or as total as ours was nevertheless as philosophic as Frantz Fanon's *Wretched of the Earth*. Far from being taken for granted, our "new Humanism" must be so fully internalized as to become a second negativity type of "instinct"—that is, reappear at all historic turning points spontaneously.

This being so, we have to take a deeper look at our break from James and see that far from taking it for granted it happened "by no accident whatever." The break was not only because we were the opposite of the Johnsonism to which C. L. R. James tried to reduce the Johnson-Forest Tendency, but because the Marxist-Humanism we became is so new that the Great Divide in Marxism that Lenin represents in history became a point for further theoretic departure. Note that I say this not in the sense of a single issue as I did when I considered how wrong is Lenin's concept of the vanguard party for our age. This time the point of reference is to philosophy itself, which Lenin did finally see as "dialectic proper" but nevertheless stopped his Abstract of Hegel's *Science of Logic* half a paragraph short of the end of the Absolute Idea. It is on that point that I first took issue with his Abstract [of Hegel's *Science of Logic*] in the *Philosophic Notebooks*. It is true that I explained my "daring" as being necessitated by the objective situation which followed his death, so that whereas he saw Stalinism only in embryo, we had to suffer through a whole quarter-century of it. But that had not stopped me from refusing to remain only on the "political" scene. Instead I went on my own to the *Philosophy of Mind*, and *afterward* discovered that I had also gone past where Marx broke off in his "Critique of the Hegelian Dialectic."

Marx, unlike Lenin, had, naturally, not dismissed the rest as inconsequential. The totality of the Hegelian dialectic "in and for itself" had not only been fully inwardized, but Marx had recreated it in the fact that by then he had discovered a whole new continent of thought and of revolution which has remained the ground for Marxists, and will continue to be our ground until we have finally and totally uprooted capitalism.

Nevertheless, it is a fact that our age had to return to Hegel in order to work out that which Marx had not "translated." What had not become concrete for the other age had become imperative and urgent for ours. For our age, however, that philosophical mediation became alive as forces of revolution as Reason rather than needing any further abstract development as that middle which first creates from itself a whole. I'm referring not to the general question of absolute negativity, which Marx had fully worked out as revolution in permanence, but to the specifics of the final three syllogisms [in the *Philosophy of Mind*] that Hegel himself had worked out only the year before his death.

Even more specifically I'm limiting myself to the final paragraph (577) of Hegel's *Philosophy of Mind,* which states "it is the nature of the fact, the Notion, which causes the movement and development. Yet this same movement is equally the action of cognition." We worked this out after we rejected Lenin's stopping on the Absolute Idea before that final paragraph of the *Science of Logic,* which warned the readers that the "Absolute" has not finished its journey which must still be tested in the *Philosophy of Nature* and *Philosophy of Mind.* It was when we turned to the latter that we broke through on the Absolute Idea not only as both not being in the stratosphere and signifying a new unity of theory and practice, but also as disregarding the Party and instead facing the new society. By seeing the new unity as a new *relationship*—which demanded that the new beginning must rest in the movement from practice that is itself a form of theory, so that theory must first then work out how to reach the heights of philosophy *and depth of actual revolution*—we succeeded not only in the breakthrough on the Hegelian Absolute, but in reconnecting with Marx's "revolution in permanence."

This meeting of the spontaneous outburst of the masses and hearing the voices from below as one form of theory occurred six weeks *before* the actual revolt in East Germany on June 17, 1953—the first ever from under totalitarian Communism which found its voice once the incubus of Stalinism was removed from its head by Stalin's death.

NOTES

1. See p. 12, note 15.

2. This refers specifically to the syllogism "Universal-Particular-Individual," discussed by Hegel in the last book of his *Science of Logic,* "The Doctrine of the Notion." For one of Dunayevskaya's discussions of Hegel's syllogism, see this volume, chapter 6.

3. In Hegel's *Science of Logic* the chapter on Judgment directly precedes that on Syllogism.

4. Lee's 1951 letter has not been found. However, Dunayevskaya made excerpts from it in notes that are now included in the *Supplement to the Raya Dunayevskaya Collection,* pp. 14678–79. She there quotes Lee as writing: "I suspect that the historical content of the logical forms of Universality, Particularity, and Individuality is: U = Christianity; P = Bourgeois Democracy; I = Socialism. I suspect also that in the development from Judgment to Syllogism is combined the development of the party of 1902 to Soviets of 1917 . . . the Syllogism destroys the opposition between subjectivity and objectivity. The polemic in the realm of the Notion . . . is against elevating the U into a fixed particular (i.e., the U must be posited as P, but if the P is posited as U, the difference becomes isolated and fixed) and also against destroying the individuality of the modes by getting to the Absolute like a shot out of a pistol."

5. Lenin actually made this comment about 10 pages into his notes on the Doctrine of the Notion, as he began summarizing the first section, "Subjectivity." See LCW 38, p. 176.

6. "The Idea" is Section III of the Doctrine of the Notion.

7. See the Letter of May 20, 1953, in chapter 2, above.

8. Lee's letter of May 22, 1953 can be found in *The Raya Dunayevskaya Collection*, p. 2466.

9. In his 1844 "Critique of the Hegelian Dialectic," Marx attacks Feuerbach because the latter "regards the negation of the negation only as the contradiction of philosophy with itself." Marx points instead to "the dialectic of negativity as the moving and creating principle" in Hegel's philosophy [MECW 3, pp. 329, 332].

10. Dunayevskaya's Perspectives Thesis, a presentation given yearly to the national gathering of News and Letters Committees, was presented on September 4, 1982, under the title, "What to Do: Facing the Depth of Recession and the Myriad Global Political Crises as well as the Philosophic Void." It can be found in *The Raya Dunayevskaya Collection*, pp. 7515–38.

11. The full text of this letter can be found in the *The Raya Dunayevskaya Collection*, p. 7503.

12. For her analysis of the concept of *apartidarismo* (non-partyism) developed by do Carmo's grouping in the 1974–75 Portuguese Revolution, "Revolutionary Party of the Proletariat/Revolutionary Brigades," see Dunayevskaya's "Will the Revolution in Portugal Advance?," *News & Letters*, January-February 1976, and *Women's Liberation and the Dialectics of Revolution*.

13. These as well as other paragraphs added to *Rosa Luxemburg, Women's Liberation, and Marx's Philosophy of Revolution* after it was completed can now be found in the University of Illinois Press edition (1991) in an introductory section entitled, "New Thoughts on *Rosa Luxemburg, Women's Liberation, and Marx's Philosophy of Revolution*"(pp. xxxiii-xxxviii).

14. The full text of this letter of August 20, 1982, can be found in the *Supplement to the Raya Dunayevskaya Collection*, p. 15320.

15. The remainder of this addition can also be found in the Introduction to the 1991 edition of *Rosa Luxemburg, Women's Liberation, and Marx's Philosophy of Revolution*, pp. xxxvii–xxxviii.

16. David Ryazanov, who worked editing Marx in Soviet Russia in the 1920s, including beginning the Complete Writings of Marx and Engels (MEGA), made these remarks in a 1923 report to the Communist Academy. While the speech has not been translated into English, it is quoted and critiqued in *Rosa Luxemburg, Women's Liberation, and Marx's Philosophy of Revolution*, pp. 177–78.

17. *Workers Battle Automation*, by Charles Denby (Detroit: News and Letters, 1960); *Freedom Riders Speak for Themselves* (Detroit: News and Letters, 1961); *The Free Speech Movement and the Negro Revolution*, by Raya Dunayevskaya, Eugene Walker, and Mario Savio (Detroit: News and Letters, 1965).

18. *American Civilization on Trial*, later subtitled "Black Masses as Vanguard" (Detroit: News and Letters, 1963), reprinted with additions in 1970 and with further additions in 1983. Dunayevskaya was its principal author.

19. This refers to Dunayevskaya's *Nationalism, Communism, Marxist Humanism, and the Afro-Asian Revolutions* (1959), reprinted with a new Introduction by Dunayevskaya in 1984 (Chicago: News and Letters).

20. In his *Wretched of the Earth*, trans. Constance Farrington (New York: Grove Press, 1966 [orig. 1961]), Fanon writes that after liberation, "this new humanity . . . cannot do otherwise than define a new humanism both for itself and for others" (p. 197).

21. George Armstrong Kelly, *Hegel's Retreat from Eleusis* (Princeton: Princeton University Press, 1978), p. 239. For a further response by Dunayevskaya to Kelly's critique, see the Introduction to the 1982 edition of *Philosophy and Revolution*.

22. A reference to Rosa Luxemburg's "The Russian Revolution" (1918), where she wrote: "But socialist democracy is not something which begins only in the promised land after the foundations of socialist economy are created. . . . " See *The Russian Revolution and Leninism or Marxism* (Ann Arbor: University of Michigan Press, 1961), p. 77. Dunayevskaya discusses this in her *Rosa Luxemburg, Women's Liberation, and Marx's Philosophy of Revolution*, pp. 63–65.

23. Hegel's *Philosophy of Nature*, Vol. I, trans. by Michael John Petry (London: Unwin Brothers, 1970), p. 202, trans. by A. V. Miller (Oxford: Oxford University Press, 1970), p. 11.

24. Some of these letters to James are included in the appendix to this volume.

25. These articles can be found in *The Raya Dunayevskaya Collection*, pp. 1477–83. The article on the miners' wives was reprinted in *Women's Liberation and the Dialectics of Revolution*, pp. 29–30. See also Phillips and Dunayevskaya, *The Coal Miners' General Strike of 1949–50 and the Birth of Marxist-Humanism in the U.S.*

26. In the Johnson-Forest Tendency, James designated Lee as the specialist in philosophy, and Dunayevskaya the specialist in economics.

27. See *State-Capitalism and World Revolution*, by C. L. R. James, in collaboration with Grace Lee and Raya Dunayevskaya (Chicago: Charles Kerr, 1986, orig. 1950), p. 126.

28. See the letter of May 20, 1953, in chapter 2, above.

29. See this volume, p. 185

30. Marx broke off his "Critique of the Hegelian Dialectic" (1844) with a quotation from ¶384 of *Philosophy of Mind*. The final three syllogisms begin with ¶575, nearly 300 pages later in Hegel's text.

31. Korsch, a leading member of the German Communist Party during the years 1920–26, published the first edition of his *Marxism and Philosophy* in 1923. After Lenin's death, at the Fifth Congress of the Communist International in June/July 1924, both Korsch and Lukács were condemned as "revisionists" by Comintern leader Grigory Zinoviev, and the Cominterm program explicitly condemned "idealism." After his expulsion from the German Communist Party two years later, Korsch continued to write on Marxism, most notably in his *Karl Marx* (1938). For more background on Korsch, see Douglas Kellner's introduction to *Karl Korsch: Revolutionary Theory* (Austin: University of Texas Press, 1979) and Patrick Goode, *Karl Korsch* (London: Macmillan, 1979).

32. In his *History and Class Consciousness* (1923).

33. A reference to Lenin's 1914–15 "Abstract of Hegel's *Science of Logic*" and his other writings on Hegel in this period.

34. Dunayevskaya developed this point in chapter 3 of *Philosophy and Revolution*, "The Shock of Recognition and the Philosophic Ambivalence of Lenin."

35. Maurice Merleau-Ponty coined the phrase "Western Marxism" in his *Adventures of the Dialectic* (1955), in posing thinkers such as Lukács and Korsch as an alternative to the "orthodox Marxism" of Lenin and the Bolsheviks.

36. An apparent reference to Lawrence Krader, whose edition of *The Ethnological Notebooks of Karl Marx* (Assen: Van Gorcum, 1972) was "dedicated to the memory of Karl Korsch."

37. In *Marxism and Philosophy* Korsch commented on Hegel's statement about German idealist philosophy (from his *Lectures on the History of Philosophy*, Vol. 3, p. 409), that "revolution was lodged and expressed as if in the very form of their thought." Korsch wrote that "Hegel was not talking of what contemporary bourgeois historians of philosophy like to call a revolution in thought—a nice, quiet process that takes place in the pure realm of the study and far from the crude realm of real struggles. The greatest thinker produced by bourgeois society in its revolutionary period regarded 'revolution in the form of thought' as an objective component of the total social process of a real revolution." See *Marxism and Philosophy* (London: New Left Books, 1970), pp. 38–39. Quoted by Dunayevskaya in *Philosophy and Revolution*, p. 295.

38. This statement from Lenin serves as the opening epigraph quote in Korsch's *Marxism and Philosophy*. See also LCW 33, p. 324.

39. In citing this passage from Kant, as published in vol. I of *Politische Literatur der Deutschen im 18. Jahrhundert*, ed. Geismar, pp. 121ff., Korsch noted that "Kant also likes to use the expression 'revolution' in the realm of pure thought, but one should say that he means something much more concrete than the bourgeois Kantians of today" (p. 39).

40. This quotation is from Engels' *Anti-Dühring* [MECW 25, p. 26].

41. Korsch's 1922 Introduction to a new edition of *The Critique of the Gotha Program* is included in the English edition of *Marxism and Philosophy*.

42. Luxemburg issued this defense of the dialectic during her 1898 polemic with Eduard Bernstein, who had advocated "removing the dialectical scaffolding" from Marxism. See Luxemburg, *Reform or Revolution?* in *Rosa Luxemburg Speaks* (New York: Pathfinder Press, 1970), p. 86.

43. Dunayevskaya's analysis of the failure of the Second International to take account of the 1905 Russian Revolution is found in chapter 9 of *Marxism and Freedom*, pp. 156–60.

44. Marx's notes to his dissertation, the "Notebooks on Epicurean Philosophy," can be found in MECW 1, pp. 403–509. The dissertation, entitled "Difference Between the Democritean and Epicurean Philosophy of Nature" can be found in MECW 1, pp. 25–108.

45. During Marx's lifetime, Vol. I of *Capital* appeared in three successive editions, each of which involved substantial changes from the previous one: the 1867 first German edition, the 1872 second German edition, and the 1872–75 French edition. As Marx wrote in a letter of April 28, 1875, published as a Postface to the French edition, "Whatever the literary defects of this French edition may be, it possesses a scientific value independent of

the original and should be consulted even by readers familiar with German [MCIF, p. 105]. Dunayevskaya discussed the changes in the French edition in *Marxism and Freedom*, chapter 6, and in *Rosa Luxemburg, Women's Liberation, and Marx's Philosophy of Revolution*, pp. 139–51. See also Kevin Anderson, "The 'Unknown' Marx's *Capital*, Vol. I: The French edition of 1872–75, 100 Years Later," *Review of Radical Political Economics*, Vol. 15:4 (1983), pp. 71–80.

46. N. K. Mikhailovsky's article "Karl Marx on trial before Mr. Zhukovski," which appeared in the Russian journal *Otechestvennye Zapiski* in 1877, argued that Marx held that the "historical tendency of capitalist accumulation" traced in *Capital* was universally applicable to all societies. Marx took sharp issue with this interpretation of his work in his "Letter to the Editorial Board of *Otechestvennye Zapiski*" [MECW 24, pp. 196–201].

47. This refers to Marx's 1875 *Critique of the Gotha Program*. For the text of the covering letter to Bracke, see MECW 24, pp. 77–78.

48. Eisenachists was the popular name of the Social Democratic Party of Germany, founded in the city of Eisenach in 1869; many Eisenachists were followers of Marx. Lassalleans were the followers of Ferdinand Lassalle, whom Marx sharply opposed. The two groups united at Gotha in 1875, leading Marx to write his *Critique of the Gotha Program*.

49. This refers to the paragraph, added to chapter 25 of the French edition of *Capital*, in which Marx refers to how "the world market had successively annexed extensive areas of the New World, Asia and Australia." Left out of the supposedly definitive 1890 fourth German edition by Engels, it appears as a footnote to p. 786 of the Ben Fowkes translation of *Capital*, Vol. I [MCIF, p. 786].

50. Marx referred to Morgan in the first draft of his letter to Zasulich [MECW 24, p. 350]. For the actual letter sent to Zasulich on March 8, 1881, see MECW 24, p. 370.

51. Marx's March 1850 "Address to the Communist League" can be found in MECW 10, pp. 277–87.

52. This is a quote from Lenin's *State and Revolution* [LCW 25, pp. 462–63].

53. In a letter of April 24, 1867, Marx says, "I also found *The Holy Family* again; [Kugelmann] has presented it to me and will send you a copy. I was pleasantly surprised to find that we do not need to be ashamed of this work, although the cult of Feuerbach produces a very humorous effect upon me now" [MECW 42, p. 360].

54. In a letter to Kugelmann of December 10, 1868, Marx wrote: "Everyone who knows anything of history also knows that great social revolutions are impossible without the feminine ferment" [MECW 43, p. 185].

55. The Union des Femmes Pour la Défense de Paris et les Soins aux Blessés, the women's section of the First International, was organized by Elizabeth Dmitrieva at the suggestion of Marx. In the "Resolutions of the Conference of Delegates of the International Working Men's Association" of September 21, 1871, Marx and Engels proposed "the formation of female branches among the working class" [MECW 22, p. 424].

56. A reference to Engels' 1852 book, *The Peasant War in Germany* [MECW 10, pp. 397–482].

57. This refers to Dunayevskaya's "trilogy of revolution"—*Marxism and Freedom* (1958),

Philosophy and Revolution (1973), and *Rosa Luxemburg, Women's Liberation, and Marx's Philosophy of Revolution* (1982).

58. See Marx's 1875 *Critique of the Gotha Program* [MECW 24, pp. 87, 90].

59. A reference to Dunayevskaya's 1953 letters, included in part I, above.

60. The theories of C. L. R. James.

61. For Dunayevskaya's discussion of this, see her "Notes on the Smaller Logic" in chapter 5, above.

~

CHAPTER FIFTEEN

Forces of Revolt as Reason,
Philosophy as Force of Revolt

Not By Practice Alone: The Movement
From Theory

"Not By Practice Alone: The Movement From Theory" is the title of Part III of "Marxist-Humanist Perspectives, 1984–85," originally published by News and Letters Committees in 1984. Dunayevskaya here probes into her three major works—her "trilogy of revolution"—in terms of her contributions to the movement from theory. The full text is available in The Raya Dunayevskaya Collection, *p. 8193.*

> He who glorifies theory and genius but fails to recognize the *limits of* a theoretical work, fails likewise to recognize the *indispensability of the theoretician.* All of history is the history of the struggle for freedom. If, as a theoretician, one's ears are attuned to the new impulses from the workers, new "categories" will be created, a new way of thinking, a step forward in philosophic cognition.
>
> Marxism and Freedom, p. 89

1. The New Sense of Objectivity;
The Theory of State-Capitalism and New
Forms of Workers' Revolts

Heretofore we criticized the theory of state-capitalism by stressing that, without developing into the philosophy of Marxist-Humanism, it was incomplete. While that is true, it would have been impossible to get to the philosophy of Marxist-Humanism without the theory of state-capitalism. We would certainly have had to find the important missing link in our encounter with state-capitalist society, as is all too obvious from Herbert Marcuse and other Left intellectuals who, without the ground worked out by the state-capitalist theory, had no theory for criticizing "Soviet" regimes and, by no accident whatever, fell into the trap of apologists for these regimes. (See my critique of Marcuse's *Soviet Marxism* titled "Intellectuals in the Age of State Capitalism," *News & Letters*, June-July 1961.)[1]

The Draft Perspectives 1984–85 states correctly: "Put another way, since the new enemy comes, not alone from traditional capitalism, but from state-capitalism masquerading as Communism and continuing to use Marxist language, the struggle for total freedom becomes both more arduous and in need of a totally new relationship of practice to theory."[2]

At the same time we must not forget that those who could not break through to the Absolute Idea and thus the road to Marxist-Humanism—the Johnsonites[3]—kept using the *word*, state-capitalism, as if that alone exhausted the theory for meeting the challenge of the new reality.* It becomes imperative to look deeply into the period, 1941 to 1953, as it actually developed. There we will see the points in which the *Idea* of Marxist-Humanism was implicit—i.e., the movement from practice as well as from theory—and have hindsight help us grasp how different were the views of C. L. R. James and Raya Dunayevskaya toward these movements from below when we were on the threshold of breaking through to the Absolute Idea which had led us to Marxist-Humanism.

There is not time to go into the whole decade when we were functioning as a united Tendency on the theory of state-capitalism. Thus, we will leave aside the fact that as early as 1941, when I was completing work on the Five-Year Plans from original Russian sources, I found an article by Marx on "Alienated Labor." It is true I did not know that this was part of the famous 1844 *Economic and Philosophical Manuscripts*. But I quoted it at the top of the section titled "Labor and Society," both in order to show the transformation into opposite of that workers' state into a state capitalist society *and* to point to new forms of workers' revolts.[4] Thus, the 1943–44 period became most crucial to our whole political analysis of new types of mass revolts, with the heroic Warsaw Uprising of the Jewish ghetto in 1943, and in 1944 the whole Polish nation rising up against the Nazi occupier, only to have the "Red" Army remain outside the Warsaw gates to let the nation bleed to death. Our analy-

---

*It is not quite correct that this means all the Johnsonites, as James' (Johnson) co-leader, Grace Lee ... enthusiastically greeted my Letters on the Absolute Idea as doing "for our age" what "Lenin's Philosophic Notebooks had done for his."

sis was called "All Roads Lead to Warsaw." Thus, when the Black Dimension burst forth in 1943, at the same time as the *first-time-ever* in wartime miners' general strike, its global dimension could be seen in the Madagascar Revolt that became the De Gaulle massacre in that same fateful 1943.

Now let's examine the critical years, 1950–53, which I designate as "On The Threshold," which will be further developed in the next section. It is sufficient here just to single out the year 1950, because it is there, *precisely there*, where those two "subjectivities"—Johnson and Forest—in their attitude to the *masses in motion*, acted totally differently.

We are first now getting reacquainted with that period through the new pamphlet on the Miners' General Strike.[5] But, please note carefully that it is by no accident that we do so with eyes of this year, that is to say, not only because it is the 1980s, but because we now stress not only the spontaneous new stage of revolt which we finally saw also as a category, as a form of theory itself, but the movement *from theory*, in turn, that was on the way to philosophic second negativity. Let's tarry also on 1952 and the Bolivian Revolution, its uniqueness:

Here are its achievements: 1) It was not only the first post-war national revolution in Latin America, which would have given it sufficient historic importance. Nor 2) was it only a peasant revolution, which again would have granted it an outstanding place, historically speaking, as well as concretely speaking. No, 3) its outstanding, unique feature was that the miners on strike and peasants in revolt—*jointly* challenging the big imperialist behemoth of U.S. imperialism as well as its own rulers—made the revolution of such new *world* importance that, along with all the new passions and forces in 1950 and the final break with Trotskyism in 1951, the Latin American dimension nudged us to that new second great divide in post-Marx Marxism—Marxist-Humanism.

A new sense of objectivity cried out to be released, but none were there to embrace it as two kinds of subjectivity engaged in *internal* tensions, inevitable but nevertheless diversionary from the objectively developing new situation. We were nearing the eve of 1953, that is to say, the philosophic breakthrough in the Absolute Idea, which saw in it not only a movement from theory but *from practice* which led to recapturing the philosophy of Marx's Humanism and the departure of those who refused to go beyond the theory of state-capitalism. Johnsonites separated from Forest and the majority, especially proletarian, membership.

Because state-capitalism is not just a Russian but a *world* phenomenon, it gave capitalism a new lease on life. While the first appearance of state-capitalism was via counter-revolution, transforming the workers' state into a state-capitalist society, the objective pull from world production and the world market imposed itself on the new national revolutions in the post-World War II era, as they remained in a statist framework. That absolute contradiction remains to plague us. Thus, with the very first test which came in 1961 with the Bay of Pigs invasion of Cuba, we felt it imperative to declare that, although we had already shown that Cuba was being pulled into the state-capitalist orbit of Russia, we were under no circumstances going to let that keep us from fighting U.S. imperialism's invasion of that country and its revolution to free itself of the U.S. imperialist stranglehold.

Quite the contrary. We at once started something new, in order not to wait for the next issue of News & Letters, which was, after all, unfortunately just a monthly. Instead, the same day, we began Weekly Political Letters. Do reread them (they are in Vol. V of The Raya Dunayevskaya Collection, beginning on p. 2906); or at least reread the abbreviated version in 25 Years of Marxist-Humanism in the U.S. [Detroit: News and Letters, 1980], especially pp. 8–10, singling out from p. 9 what we stress in no uncertain terms:

"This is beyond the Cuban struggle. This is the American revolution. This is the world anti-war struggle." This was further developed not only in our 1960 Resolution on "War and Peace," but led to our Resolution on "War and Revolution" the following decade.[6] In a word, principles of revolution do not change, be it directly against the enemy at home—U.S. capitalism—or in *critical* solidarity work with Left groups.

These political principles of revolution must under no circumstances be separated from the philosophical principles. That is the whole significance of our expression of the whole body of Marxist-Humanist philosophy contained in "the trilogy of revolution"—Marxism and Freedom; Philosophy and Revolution; and Rosa Luxemburg, Women's Liberation, and Marx's Philosophy of Revolution. These must never be reduced either to a mere abstraction or to the so-immediate concrete that we hardly become distinguishable from some sort of "popular front" in the solidarity committees. We are, after all, indigenous to the Latino world and have used precisely Marx's theory of the philosophy of revolution in permanence, not as an abstraction but as the actual concrete needed in order both to be armed against being pulled into the world market of the whirlpool of capitalism, state as well as private, *and* as requiring a decentralized organization whose ground is that continuing "revolution in permanence."

Here is how I put it in my May 15, 1978 essay on "The Latin American Unfinished Revolutions" after we had worked out the movement from practice: As for the claimant, J. Posadas,[7] holding that he is the "real" Fourth

International, by further twisting Trotsky's theory of permanent revolution not only to give "primacy" to the colonial revolutions, but actually elevating that as the "World Development of Permanent Revolution," this further proves the theoretical void left by Lenin's death. It was certainly not filled by Trotskyism, be it "orthodox" or flowing from the new claimants to the title. No matter where the place was, the question reemerged—whether in Bolivia, where they had actually become part of the class-collaborationist government, *or* in Cuba, acting as if Castro were a composite of both Lenin and Trotsky—the point was that we had to know how, at one and the same time, to be part of solidarity support committees but to do so very critically. Nicaragua demands the same type of critical activity.

Here are other contradictory manifestations in the Third World, not only in Latin America but in Africa, where along with the revolutionary upsurges that were successful in gaining independence, they also bore the mark of the single party state. Since, however, these came about not, as in Russia, through the workers' state being transformed into its opposite—a state-capitalist society—but through revolution against imperialism which a unified people fought as one, we wanted to examine "in person," so to speak.

It was for this reason that the 1962 trip to Africa was, at one and the same time, the revelation of all the new passions and forces for a new social order.[†] Which didn't change my critical attitude to the new rulers who had been revolutionaries, and who still thought of themselves as such. Clearly, they thought their anti-imperialism sufficed without realizing that it's the internal production relations of ruler to ruled that are *decisive*. It is this which cannot be covered up by focusing only on the outside imperialist.

The outside imperialist will persist, as neocolonialism proves. But genuine revolutions cannot, must not, become half-way houses. It is this I warned against in the pamphlet on *Nationalism, Communism, Marxist-Humanism, and the Afro-Asian Revolutions,* as I developed the danger in any administrative mentality in revolutionaries which first became visible after power was gained, but in fact was inherent in the Second International.

2. What Was Marx's Dialectics of Revolution to the Post-Marx Marxists of the Second International?

We first developed the question of the administrative mentality as a danger to the revolution when we realized that Mao was offering himself as the

---

[†]See my writings from Africa, titled "1962: Year of the Africa Trip," in Vol. 5 of the Archives, starting on p. 3184 [of *The Raya Dunayevskaya Collection*].

"new" international (vs. the Russians) Marxist to lead the national revolutions and one who had all the answers, but in fact was only packaging his own *national* revolution as an international, fully social revolution.

When we developed the question of the administrative mentality in the second edition *of Marxism and Freedom,* we did not hurry to a conclusion on "The Challenge of Mao Zedong" (the chapter we added to that new (1964) edition). Instead, we projected the needed task as "In Place of a Conclusion: Two Kinds of Subjectivity." This was rooted philosophically both in Hegel's second negativity (which we would first develop in *Philosophy and Revolution)* and in Marxist-Humanism.

The administrative mentality that the intellectual in a state-capitalist society displayed all too clearly was actually inherent in the Second International in their failure to grapple with Marx's dialectics of revolution. What looked as only an organizational question in the *Critique of the Gotha Program* was the dialectics of revolution *in the concrete.* In our age it appeared as if it were characteristic of revolutionaries bottled up in academia. Thus, Marcuse, even after having written so seminal a work as *Reason and Revolution,* had regressed, first very nearly to approve of—surely to discuss as if it were just a matter of discussion instead of attack—what he called *Soviet Marxism,* uncritically going for Angela Davis, and still refusing to be armed with the theory of state-capitalism, and at the end fairly falling into the trap of Mao's "Cultural Revolution"—on the American scene at that.

We, on the other hand, long before we created the phrase "trilogy of revolution" with the completion of *Rosa Luxemburg, Women's Liberation, and Marx's Philosophy of Revolution,* did not fail to give our support critically only, not even if the subject was so great a hero as Che (Guevara). After the aborted 1968 French near-revolution, it became imperative not to leave loopholes for the 1960s generation of revolutionaries to think that by activity alone one can achieve a successful revolution by merely picking up theory "en route." Theory is a hard taskmaster as it develops into a full philosophy of revolution. It is for this reason we returned to the Hegelian dialectic "in and for itself," through *Philosophy of Mind,* where none had trod before, in "Why Hegel? Why Now?"

The movement from theory that is the concern for our age is not of theory "in general," but a most concrete manifestation of *Marx's Marxism,* today's Marxist-Humanism. Naturally, the revolutions of Marx's day *as Marx saw them* continue to be the primary ground for our day. The 20th century revolutions, whether of the early 20th century—1905, 1917, 1919—*or* those of post-World War II, no matter how more relevant to our day, need to be measured against the philosophy of revolution of the founder of all of us—Karl Marx.

The fact that this was not evident to any revolutionary as a great divide before World War I broke out and the Second International betrayed, proves how far all post-Marx Marxists had not fully grasped that "philosophy," *to Marx,* continued to be a determinant for judging whether there truly was a movement towards new human relations, a new "social order." That was not all due to the unavailability of all of Marx's works: there was enough available as we shall see, especially regarding the *Critique of the Gotha Program,* as Lenin reread it when the betrayal had occurred. Even then (1914), however, only one revolutionary theoretician—Lenin—felt any compulsion to dig into Marx's origins in the Hegelian dialectic. That philosophy did not loom as a "principle" that was a necessity for "practical fighters" (Luxemburg's phrase for the stagnation that Marx's enemies did see in post-Marx Marxism)[8] hindsight can see most clearly in the attitude to the 1905–07 Russian Revolution on the part of the most active revolutionaries—Luxemburg, Lenin, Trotsky.

Here was that great, unexpected Russian Revolution. Here was Luxemburg, so original as to deny it was merely the continuation of the 19th century revolution, insisting most presciently that, on the contrary, it was the first of a series of altogether new revolutions—and we better all learn how to "speak Russian." Here was Lenin, great enough to recognize its internationalism as well as the revolutionary nature of the peasantry along with that of the proletariat. And here was Trotsky, so far ahead of his period that when a Menshevik declared Trotsky's description of the 1905 *Soviet* revolution as "permanent revolution," though he had skipped over the role of the peasantry, Trotsky gladly accepted that designation. Yet when it came to the 1907 Russian [Social-Democratic Labor Party] Congress which had all the tendencies there not only refusing, along with the Mensheviks, to put the nature of the 1905–07 Revolution on the agenda, Trotsky was vulgarly—I naturally mean *theoretically* vulgarly—saying he didn't come for a gabfest; he wanted a "program of action," what to do, as if that could be spelled out when one is bereft of a theory.

To put it in a nutshell—and this became clear at the 1907 Second International Stuttgart Congress—all revolutionaries were still under the illusion that an amendment to the anti-war resolution would theoretically patch up any differences and result in a unified International. Unity they achieved, but this could not, and did not, prevent total collapse and betrayal.

What created new beginnings and a successful 1917 Revolution was that *after* that Great Divide between reformists, who became betrayers, and revolutionaries, it was not only as a political division, but the fact that Lenin then returned to Marx's origins in the Hegelian dialectic and worked out anew, in his *Philosophic Notebooks,* the philosophic-theoretic preparation for revolution. Unfortunately, Lenin kept these *Notebooks* private so that, while it had such great revolutionary consequences in 1917, they were no help once Lenin died. The consequences of the theoretic-philosophic void left by Lenin's death surfaced the very next year by the total incapacity to deal with the 1925–27 revolution in China. Chiang Kai-shek's barbarous counter-revolution went on unhampered.

The great defeat that followed, however, was not all due to Stalin's disastrous policies. Trotsky, while great in exposing how Stalin's "socialism in one country" contributed to the defeat, once again showed in what a vise he was kept by his refusal to face the revolutionary nature of the peasantry. Indeed, it was not only Stalin or Trotsky, in different ways, but the whole leadership of the Third International; as for the Chinese Revolution, Trotsky had united with the other Opposition to Stalin's China policies—the Leningrad and Moscow Oppositions, [Grigori] Zinoviev—signing a joint statement which, far from mentioning permanent revolution, quoted Lenin's Second [Communist International] Resolution on the "Colonial and National Revolutions Question," with the slogan of a revolutionary democratic worker-peasant government. Young Mao was hardly on the scene as any sort of leader yet, and in any case was no match for the "Russian theoretical leadership." He had singled out the peasantry as the revolutionary force and went his own way (see the "Hunan Report").[9]

Contrast this to the maturity of our age, and not alone with hindsight and experience, nor only on Cuba, i.e., the Western hemisphere, but with philosophy—the breakthrough on the Absolute Idea—to see the ramifications of 1905–07 for what is now known as the Third World, specifically the revolution in Iran in 1979. We had singled out from 1905–07 what had happened in what was then Persia, not alone as proletariat and peasantry and internationalism, but also Women's Liberation.

The impact of 1905 on Iran, which created the ground for analyzing the 1979 Revolution there, was indeed seeing for the first time the uniqueness of the women's *anjumen* in 1906–11. We were thus prepared for Chapter Two of the 1979 Iranian Revolution opened by *today's* Women Liberationists; practical fighters, indeed, for a second chapter which much of the other Left "practicals" aided in squashing![10]

At the same time, however, we must not skip the period when we were only on the threshold of Marxist-Humanism, 1950–53. It is necessary to reexamine the State-Capitalist Tendency when it was still a united Johnson-Forest Tendency. *State-Capitalism and World Revolution*, the summation document of 10 years of existence that we wrote in 1950, showed us trying—trying very hard—to meet philosophic demands.[11] Not, however, having broken through on the Absolute Idea, the Tendency nevertheless rushed to "conclusions." What that accomplished was to have me become aware of the differences that were emerging.

Where Marxist-Humanism now checks before and after each movement from practice also the movement from theory, and measures how we anticipated some of the events as well as created the fabric-the single dialectic in both subjectivity and objectivity—that was not so when we were a united Tendency in the critical period of 1950–53, when the theory of state-capitalism still operated as a united Johnson-Forest Tendency.

Instead, *State-Capitalism and World Revolution*, in its section on philosophy, focused on Contradiction rather than second negativity and Absolute Idea, which would have brought us to Marx's Humanism. Grace [Lee], who is the author of that philosophic section, considered Humanism merely as either Christian or Existentialist Humanism, naturally rejecting both. In so doing, the Tendency went no further than analyzing "The Philosophy of State-Capitalism." Indeed, that is what it openly called that section. In a word, it went no further philosophically than we had already worked out in economic and political terms for the decade of 1941–50.

There was a possibility of another direction: the ongoing miners' general strike and our listening to the voices from below, as we worked out philosophically the meaning of that strike. Instead, we "stopped dead," to use Hegel's phrase against Kant, who was on the threshold of the dialectic, being the first to reintroduce it into modem philosophy, but had not worked the dialectic out fully, i.e., concretely at the same time. In a political way, that is what was happening to the Johnson-Forest Tendency as differences began to surface between Johnson and Forest. (See *The Coal Miners' General Strike of 1949–50 and the Birth of Marxist-Humanism in the U.S.*)

3. The Absolute Method—The Unchained Dialectic

> . . . our epoch is a birth time, and a period of transition. . . .
> —Hegel, *Phenomenology of Mind*. [PhGB, p. 75, PhGM, p. 6]

The body of ideas comprising Marxist-Humanism is rooted in the new postwar movements both from practice and from theory. *Marxism and Freedom*, structured on the movement from practice, and *Philosophy and Revolution*, tracing the movement from theory, were not only worked out while deeply participating in all movements of the new age of revolutions, be it the 1950s or 1960s and 1970s, but were equally rooted in the past, i.e., history. In a word, the period was the whole expanse of the modern world that began with the industrial revolution—indeed, we called the very first part of *Marxism and Freedom* "The Age of Revolutions"—industrial, political, economic, intellectual.

With *Philosophy and Revolution*, we had a new situation. It is not alone all the new passions and forces of the 1960s with which the book ends, but the fact that the philosophic predominates over the historic, the theory over the practice; indeed, the very fact that the structure is the exact opposite of what *Marxism and Freedom* was—that is, not the movement from practice, but the movement from theory—gave the whole question of Hegelian dialectics "in and for itself" a totally new meaning, in the sense that it demanded detailing not only the movement from practice but that from theory. That movement from theory becomes the uniqueness of Marxist-Humanist philosophy and our original contribution to *Marx's* Marxism. That happens to be exactly where Marx left off in his critique of Hegel's *Philosophy of Mind*, once he discovered his new continent of thought and of revolution. The totality of the crises of our age compelled us to rediscover the rest of the *Philosophy of Mind*, especially the final three paragraphs, where, suddenly, as Hegel reached what was supposed to be the final syllogism, the sequence is broken. What would have been Nature-Logic-Mind, which would have meant Logic was the mediation, is Logic replaced with the Self-Thinking Idea. But even when the absolutely Universal becomes mediation, it is no beyond, no abstraction, but is concrete and everywhere, and Absolute Method which is simultaneously objective and subjective. Such a vision, precisely, is what has made Hegel a contemporary of the 1960s and 1970s. And it is such a method that Marx worked at in his final decade, as he worked out a new relationship of the precapitalist societies to his age. "Why Hegel? Why Now?" is exactly what gave *Philosophy and Revolution: From Hegel to Sartre, and from Marx to Mao* its structure.

Rosa Luxemburg, Women's Liberation, and Marx's Philosophy of Revolution did more than merely permit us to refer to our major theoretical works as the "trilogy of revolution." With the availability of Marx's *Ethnological Notebooks* and, in general, "new moments" Marx discovered in his last decade making it possible finally to view Marx's Marxism *as a totality*, it is clear also that our own contributions to *Marx's* Marxism helped articulate Marxism for our age. Surely, the trail to the 1980s that Marx left us in the new moments in his last decade is not something one "picks up" en route to somewhere else. It requires labor, hard labor, to work out, and the work is never done until, once and for all, we're done with capitalism and have achieved new human relations. The dialectics of revolution keep reemerging in ever newer appearances, as new forces and new passions are born anew. And yet the dialectic *principle* of second negativity never changes. Take the trail to the 1980s that Marx left us from the 1880s.

We have been tracing this ever since Marx first uttered the phrase, when he broke with capitalism in 1843, and worked at its special significance when he reiterated "revolution in permanence" in the 1850 *Address to the Communist League*, after the 1848–49 revolutions were defeated. He wrote it to his organization, the first time he had an organization—the Communist League.

What makes 1875 so crucial a year in Marx's life is that, at one and the same time, he completed the definitive French edition of *Capital*, Vol. 1, and the *Critique of the Gotha Program*, and that these two set the methodological foundation for absorbing all the new he began seeing in anthropological empiric studies. That illuminated for him what had been only a "vision" of the Man/Woman relationship he had developed when he first discovered his continent of thought and of revolution. Human development was, indeed, an "absolute movement of becoming."

This is what makes it imperative that, to work out the new relationship of practice to theory, and theory to practice, we do not stop with Hegel's Absolutes—Knowledge, Idea, Mind—but recreate, as Marx did, Absolute Method—the unchained dialectic. In challenging post-Marx Marxists, we are articulating Marx's Marxism for our age.

The Absolute Method works out a correct Notion (Concept) from the very start, even "just" the immediate, or "just" organization, seeing everything in that conceptual fabric. The point is that *each*—both the concrete and the universal; both the organizational and the philosophic-theoretical—*moves*. There is one dialectic for the objective and the subjective. Listen to how concretely (Antonio) Gramsci envisioned the Absolute as "Absolute humanism":

"It has been forgotten that in the case of a very common expression (historical materialism) one should put the accent on the first term—'historical'—and not on the second which is of metaphysical origin. The philosophy of praxis is absolute 'historicism,' the absolute humanism of history. It is along this line that one must trace the thread of the new conception of the world."[12]

Absolute humanism is surely the articulation needed to sum up a class*less*, *non*-racist, *non*-sexist society, where truly new human relations self-develop. Gramsci, however, like Lenin, didn't shed the concept of the vanguard party. Which is why I didn't for a second let go of Marx's *Critique of the Gotha Program*.

What has brought us to a reunion with Marx's Marxism is the trilogy of revolution to back up our activities as they *flow from* Absolute Method, whether that is expressed in our view of the 1905 Russian Revolution or 1952 Bolivian Revolution or the philosophic encounter with Silvio Frondizi[13] or 1982 "simple" activities in Latin American or African solidarity movements, or 1984–85 Perspectives. Needed for spelling this out organizationally is a summation of the movements both from practice and from theory, beginning with the period of transition, 1950–53.

4. On The Threshold 1950–53:
The Relationship of Abstract/Concrete

> Every emancipation is a restoration of the human world and of human relationships to man himself.
>
> —Marx, *On the Jewish Question*. [MECW 3, p. 168]

Now that we have briefly traced the body of ideas worked out by Marxist-Humanism from the mid-1950s to the present, a look back at the transition period, 1950–53, will help illuminate that historic movement from practice that was made into a philosophic category and became dialectically inseparable *when* theory, i.e., the theory of state-capitalism, reached philosophy, specifically that of Marx's Humanism as it merged subjectivity and objectivity with our age's breakthrough on the Absolute Idea as a movement from practice as well as from theory.

With our new pamphlet now on the 1949–50 miners' general strike, we can see *as a unity* the spontaneous activity and what philosophic problems were being worked out simultaneously. The objectivity of the movement *from practice* became international on June 17, 1953, when, for the first time ever, there was a spontaneous, mass revolt from under Russian totalitarianism—a revolt which combined economics and politics as the East German workers revolted against the "norms of work" and lack of political freedom, succinctly expressed in the slogan "Bread and Freedom!"

Let us now follow, month by month, those four decisive months, March to June, in 1953 that witnessed the birth of a totally new, historic stage, economically, politically, and philosophically:

1) March. With the death of Stalin, an incubus was removed from the heads of the masses who were preparing themselves, for the first time ever, to openly revolt from under Communist totalitarianism. That brought about a political crisis also in the Johnson-Forest Tendency, as I was writing the analysis of [Stalin's death].‡ Suddenly what was disclosed was the apoliticalization which deepened when, after our final break with Trotskyism in 1951, we failed to face the public either with our theory of state-capitalism, or the magnificent experience in the Miners' General Strike followed by the seniority strikes in 1951. As against Johnson's co-leader, Grace, who wished to continue with the so-called "underground" apolitical existence, Charles Denby saw so great an affinity of the American workers' daily battles against the labor bureaucracy that he asked me to reproduce my analysis of the 1921 Trade Union Debate between Lenin and Trotsky, in the context of the ramifications of the 1953 death of Stalin and the workers' revolts that were sure to follow.

2) *April.* In a word, the analysis of the significance of Stalin's death in March was followed with an analysis I made of "The Trade Unions, Then and Now."[14] This, in the 1953 context of both Russian and East European battles against Stalinism and U.S. labor wildcatting against the labor bureaucracy, was mimeographed and distributed at factory gates.

3) *May* (12th and 20th) came the Letters on the Absolute Idea. Johnson's refusal to discuss them only led to our publishing them in our (News and Letters Committees') very first (1955) bulletin that followed first issuing *News & Letters,* and never again will there be any separation of politics from philosophy.

4) *June 17, 1953.* The new sense of objectivity which we then began to discuss in relationship to the stage of state-capitalism began to be seen in the context of Marx's new sense of objectivity in relationship to all human activity. Of course, we've been looking at some history with hindsight. But the question is not one of rewriting history, whether it be Cuba, 1959, whether that be the 1905 Revolution, or the 1955 establishment of News and Letters Committees. First, it was 1905–07 that at once confronted us with the "Organizational Question." Secondly, the pointing at the maturity of our age plus the digging into Hegelian dialectics made it possible to retrieve Lenin's *Philosophic Notebooks because* we understood fully his compulsion both to return to Hegelian dialectics (*not* for any scholastic purposes), and to make sure never

---

‡The debate on the significance of the death of Stalin resulted from the fact that, although we broke from the Socialist Workers Party in 1951, we did not appear publicly until the fall of 1953 when it became clear that the very high tensions within the Johnson-Forest Tendency resulted from the apoliticalization we had undergone. Those tensions became especially clear when the very first issue of *Correspondence* appeared and my political analysis of the Beria purge met with opposition, supposedly from outside sources. All these differences in 1953 came to a climax at the end of 1954 and early 1955, and resulted in the Johnson group breaking from the Tendency. This finally led to the creation of the fully independent State-Capitalist Tendency inseparable from its philosophic political views. Our very first decision was to publish our own paper, *News & Letters,* and to do that on the day—June 17—in honor of the 1953 East German revolt.

again to separate it from dialectics of revolution. This is the kind of dialectical methodology that is needed, not just for "classes" but for the analysis of everyday events, especially those of our age which we have characterized as the movement from practice that is itself a form of theory.

Our present tracing also of the movement from theory is not the first time we have engaged in it. On the contrary, in the very first major theoretical work of our body of ideas—*Marxism and Freedom*—structured on the movement from practice, we devoted considerable space to the break of Lenin with his philosophic past, which we designated as the Great Divide in Marxism. We now face a new Divide, and this time the return to Marx's philosophic roots in the Hegelian dialectic was not to be kept in private notes, but to be developed openly, publicly, and collectively. It is of the essence not to turn the trilogy of revolution into an abstraction.

Today we can surely show the trilogy of revolution as a concrete Universal—whether that be in the United States, or in the work in Latin American solidarity committees; whether it be directly in reference to Marx's *Capital*, or on the peasant question and the Third World—and always, this concrete Universal must not be presented as an abstraction, but as the concrete need to be armed against being pulled into the vortex of the world market. Reread, please, the footnote in *Capital*, Vol. I, in the section on Fetishism [MCIF, p. 171; MCIK, p. 89] where Marx writes: "A more exhaustive study of the Asiatic . . . form of common property would indicate the way in which different forms of spontaneous, primitive communal property give rise to different forms of its dissolution." *Dissolution* is the key to the whole question of what is private property, what is communal form of property, what is *class* structure. That appears during the transition period.

It is the clearest demonstration of what a different world Marx's Promethean vision extended to its multilinearism vs. the narrow unilinearism of Engels, and not alone on the "Woman Question" but on primitive communism in general and, above all, on the dualities that are present in the communal form which will lead to private property, capitalism, and are already present in the differences between chiefs (leaders) and ranks. In a word, it is present in the *gens itself*, irrespective of sex or culture.

The new sense of objectivity, be it in relation to state-capitalism or to human activity, and two kinds of subjectivity—the masses in motion vs. that of the leader—point to the need to be related to the questions of abstract and concrete. Without that, we run the risk of making an abstraction of the trilogy of revolution. It is exactly what happened on the question of dialectics which was made into an abstraction, an icon everyone bowed to, but none recreated concretely. The contrast between abstract and concrete—as if one is Universal and the other concrete—does not free you of the danger of transforming the *concrete Universal* into an abstraction.

Thus, to bandy about the expression "trilogy of revolution" means to act as if, at one and the same time, "everybody" knows about it, and all that needs to be done is to assert, as "conclusion," that all will need to study it in the manner in which one gets a degree, instead of seeing it as an urgent task *to do*. That only transforms it into an abstraction.

What the new moments of Marx's last decade show is that long before the new empiric anthropological studies he was then digging into, for Marx, *Capital* (1867), too, pointed to the significance of those pre-capitalist societies—the *gens* in primitive communism—that resided in the form of their dissolution. Indeed, the proof that the new moments, far from being a "break" from the "classic" Marx, were a *development of* Marx—the young, the old, the mature, the in-between—is the *Grundrisse*, 1857. It is there that Marx first worked out the Asiatic Mode of Production. Moreover, he considered it of such fundamental historic significance in human development, that he designated it as the "fourth form." He repeated that conclusion in the most famous of all historic materialist definitions, in the Preface to the *Critique of Political Economy* (1859), and it has never stopped being used as the perfect expression of historical materialism.

Anyone who doesn't see that fully today will fall, knowingly or unknowingly, into the statist mold of property-form instead of the key *production relationship* Marx taught us along with his theory of "revolution in permanence." Which is how we were emboldened to criticize the heroic Che who nevertheless was wrong both in the concrete in Bolivia and in the whole theory of shortcuts to revolution and "Leader Maximum."

Hold tight to *Marxism and Freedom*'s structure. Note that part in the section titled "Organizational Interlude." Though it is an analysis of the whole of the Second International—the established, so-called "orthodox" Marxists—what we focus on is not its life, but its *death*. Because Marx's Marxism taught us never to separate revolution from organization, the fact that the 1905–07 Revolution did not become a point on the agenda of the 1907 Second International Congress is what brought us to consider that it signaled the death of the Second International. *Philosophically*, there were indications before the outbreak of the betrayal-to-be in World War I, not to mention that, being burdened with the concept of a "party to lead," it blinded them to the priority of philosophy rather than leadership.

It is this which emboldens us to call the great revolutionary, Rosa Luxemburg—who has so much to say to us on spontaneity, on woman, on revolution—nevertheless nearly totally deaf on philosophy. We have, after all, by now broken also with Lenin not just politically, against any elitist organization, which we had done way back as still a united Johnson-Forest Tendency. No, this time it was philosophically, and on the very text Lenin himself had to return to as ground for *State and Revolution*, that is, Marx's *Critique of the Gotha Program*, which Lenin read profoundly enough when it came to smashing the bourgeois state, but managed to escape saying anything on Party structure, for which Marx had laid a totally different ground.

Indeed, not only ground, but "Absolute." Philosophy of "revolution in permanence" cannot possibly be only ground, or even content, substance; it is Subject, and that both objectively and subjectively. The unchained dialectic—both as dialectics of liberation and dialectics of thought, dialectics of self-development—that self-development is both Individual and Universal. The achievement of that can only come with sharp awareness of the absolute contradictions in the nuclear world state-capitalist reality; to project Marx's philosophy of revolution *concretely*, its Absolutes as concrete Universals, not abstractions, becomes imperative. This lays ground for daily practical work and not just books or essay writing. That is our organizational task.

Letter to the Youth on the Needed Total Uprooting of the Old and the Creation of New Human Relations

As early as the 1950s, Dunayevskaya had singled out youth as a revolutionary category. She wrote in 1958, "Even though the youth are not directly involved in production, they are the ones whose idealism in the finest sense of the word combines with opposition to existing adult society in so unique a way that it literally brings them alongside the workers as builders of a new society." [15] *This letter, written to the youth of News and Letters Committees on August 13, 1983, represents one of her many efforts to develop the connection between dialectical philosophy and her concept of youth as a revolutionary category. The original can be found in* The Raya Dunayevskaya Collection, p. 7803.

> "Human concepts are subjective in their abstractness, separateness, but objective as a whole, in the process, in the sum-total, in the tendency, in the source."
>
> —Lenin, Abstract of Hegel's *Science of Logic*. [LCW 38, p. 208]

> "I love all men who *dive*. Any fish can swim near the surface, but it takes a great whale to go downstairs five miles or more; and if he don't attain the bottom, why all the lead in Galena[16] can't fashion the plummet that will. I'm not

talking about Mr. Emerson now—but of the whole corps of thought-divers, that have been diving and coming up again with bloodshot eyes since the world began."

—Melville, Letter of March 3, 1849[17]

Because of my deep confidence in the youth striving to be "thought-divers" (whether or not they are superb swimmers just by being young and strong), I'd like to appeal to you to dive into the battle of challenging post-Marx Marxism. That battle will reveal the much greater maturity of this historic period as against that of the generation of the 1960s. It is true that they were so massively active in that decade that 1968 had reached the threshold of a revolution. The fact, however, that it remained an unfinished act made it clear to the following generation that they had better probe deeply into how the lack of serious theory vitiated activism's goals. The idea that activity, activity, activity would absolve them from the hard labor of recreating Marx's theory of "revolution in permanence" for their age and that theory picked up "en route" would solve the totality of the economic-political-social crises, as well as end U.S. imperialism's war in Vietnam, ended in total failure.[18]

Nevertheless, one of the most famous debates in that period was that between Sartre and [Claude] Lévi-Strauss (not exactly youth themselves, but accepted as gurus by the youth movement), as the 1960s generation continued to follow new philosophies like Existentialism and Structuralism, instead of trying to find the historic link of continuity with "old" Marxism. While Lévi-Strauss critiqued Sartre's adherence to dialectics,[19] holding that Structuralism required the analytic, empiric, scientific method, Sartre—since he, himself, was enamored with Structuralism and had as ahistorical an outlook as Lévi-Strauss—could hardly win the argument for meaning as against Lévi-Strauss's emphasis on non-meaning. Here is how Lévi-Strauss put it:

. . . in my perspective, meaning is never the primary phenomenon; meaning is always reducible. In other words, behind all meaning there is a non-meaning, while the reverse is not the case. As far as I'm concerned, significance is always phenomenal.[20]

A profound critique of Lévi-Strauss' Structuralism came, not from Existentialism, but from an independent Marxist anthropologist-dialectician, Stanley Diamond:

The ethnologist is actually saying that he is not interested in meaning (significance), which he regards as merely (and always) phenomenal. For him, the primary phenomenon is not meaning, but the non-meaning which lies behind meaning and to which, he believes, meaning is reducible.[§]

The point is that the life-blood of the Hegelian dialectic—when it is not diluted by Existentialism but seen in its essence as a ceaseless movement of becoming, disclosing the meaning of history—is exactly what saved Hegel from the Kantian, impenetrable "Thing-in-itself" and its absolute idealism. Though Hegel may have wanted to confine history to history of thought, the single dialectic which characterizes both objectivity and subjectivity moved Hegel to objective idealism. That single dialectic became the ground for Marx's dialectic of revolution.

It was this, *just this*, which led proletarians to accept dialectical development, not alone for its "dynamism" but for its meaning in historic confrontation. Contrast the non-Marxist, intellectualistic, abstract approach to dialectics with that of a Marxist-Humanist proletarian attitude—and consider that it was precisely on the question of phenomenology. That does not mean phenomenal but the science of phenomena, of experience. I am referring to Charles Denby, the editor of *News & Letters* and his favorite quotation from Hegel:[21]

> Enlightenment upsets the household arrangements, which spirit carries out in the house of faith, by bringing in the goods and furnishings belonging to the world of the Here and Now. [PhGB, p. 512; PhGM, p. 296]

The whole point of Denby's interest in the Hegelian quotation was this: What does philosophy have to say on the relationship between reality and revolution? It was because he saw Hegel introducing reality into the critique of the Enlightenment that Denby's attraction to Hegelian dialectics deepened. He could then see that dialectical development signified the *transformation* of reality.

It is true that revolutionaries like Mao also tried to escape confrontation with actual social revolutions aimed against his state-capitalist regime which he called Communist. But the Chinese youth saw how empty was the word "Proletarian" before "Cultural Revolution." At the very height of the Cultural Revolution, the dissident, revolutionary youth in Sheng Wu-lian hit out against their rulers by calling them "the red capitalist class." They concretized the kind of commune they aimed to have as against what existed in China by calling for one like the Paris Commune of Marx's day: "Let the new bureau-

---

[§]See "Anthropology in Question" in section 6, "The Root is Man: Critical Traditions," of *Reinventing Anthropology*, edited by Dell Hymes (Vintage Books, Random House, 1972), p. 427.

cratic bourgeoisie tremble before the true socialist revolution that shakes the world," declared their Manifesto. "What the proletariat can lose in this revolution is only their chains, what they gain will be the whole world!"[22]

Here was Mao, who had declared himself to be a Marxist-Communist and in 1949 led a great national revolution. If he was aware of how deep the uprooting of the old had to be as he openly declared the revolution to be bourgeois-democratic and the society itself to be state-capitalist, he revealed none of it to the masses.[23] He assured them they had nothing to fear from the "Chinese who stood up," a regime that was headed by the Communist Party. By 1966, when he launched the "Great Proletarian Cultural Revolution," he not only declared his land to be "socialist" but designated it the "storm center of *world* revolution." The Chinese youth failed to be impressed as they felt his rule to be that of any capitalist (private or state) totalitarian ruler-exploiter.

The revolutionary youth of the Sheng Wu-lien themselves caught the historic link to *Marx's* Marxism and the Paris Commune of Marx's day as the decentralized political form to work out the economic-political-social emancipation which would keep the power in the hands of the masses.

The Sheng Wu-lien statement I quoted here can be found in chapter 5 of *Philosophy and Revolution*.[24] Please remember, dear Youth, as I appeal to you to engage in this battle of ideas, that it is not only the post-Marx Marxists we challenge but *all* alternatives to Marx's Marxism. *Philosophy and Revolution* critiqued not only revolutionaries like Mao and Trotsky, but also Jean-Paul Sartre, the "Outsider Looking In." It is true that I deal with him there as Existentialist and I deal with the structuralist Communist intellectual guru, Althusser, all too briefly, very nearly dismissing him in a few footnotes.[25] I do not mention Lévi-Strauss at all. Nevertheless, they represent the very same subject—Alternatives—that I began this letter with. Later I will contrast that to a true recreation of Marxism for one's age. For us that began in 1953 with the breakthrough on the Absolute Idea. It will be easier, I believe, to dig deep into that if we look first at what we are familiar with—the Youth revolt in this country, the Free Speech Movement burdened by American pragmatism.** Revolutionaries though they were, they certainly resisted philosophy of revolution. Though they had asked me to address them on Marx's Humanism, the interest was more on the subject of alienation than on philosophy of revolution.[26]

**See *The Free Speech Movement and the Negro Revolution*, by Mario Savio, Raya Dunayevskaya, and Eugene Walker [Detroit: News and Letters, 1965]. Philosophically, the Black dimension, especially Frantz Fanon, far from being pragmatist, worked out its critique of Hegel's concept of reciprocity in a revolutionary-dialectical manner. See both *Black Skin, White Masks* and my "Revolutions and Philosophies" of Aug. 1, 1983.

It was all most exciting when Mario Savio was released from jail at mid-night and arrived at 2 a.m. in a spot several miles outside of Berkeley to hear me speak on Marx's Humanism. Though they were very interested in Human-ism, and, indeed, related it to their own new lifestyles, Mario was the next day also going to meet Bettina Aptheker, because he had promised Bettina, who was also part of the Free Speech Movement, and he was open to "all ideas" and was not the least bit interested in any Party or organization.[27] In a word, the supposedly non-partyist, non-elitist, non-organizational person who was only for activism, activism, activism, did not see the contradiction in organi-zational form that lacked a philosophy of freedom and that form that was inseparable from a struggle for freedom, for revolution.

Permit me here to go back to 1953 to reexamine the process of working out, or seeing the emergence of, a new philosophic dimension. It is the year I first broke through on the Absolute Idea, removing its abstract, mystical veil and seeing it as not only a unity of theory and practice, but a totally new rela-tionship of the two *because* a new historic beginning had been reached with this live movement *from practice*. This was the period we completely rejected both the designation of the youth as "the beat generation" and the pragmatic view of the epoch itself as "an end of ideology."[28]

The breakthrough on the Absolute Idea helped us to perceive a new gener-ation of revolutionaries in that so-called "beat generation" who were rejecting a world they never made; and to see in the revolts in Latin America and Africa the emergence of a Third World. Indeed, toward the end of the 1950s, retro-gression and McCarthyism in the United States notwithstanding, we declared it to be a totally new epoch: in production (with *Workers Battle Automation*)[29]; in political freedom battles, whether that be the new Black dimension in the Montgomery Bus Boycott or in the East European Freedom Fighters against Russian state-capitalism calling itself Communism; a new stage of cognition as the Hungarian Revolution highlighted it by bringing Marx's Humanist Essays onto the historic stage. The breakthrough on the Absolute Idea was not only on the *movements* from practice and from theory but also on *organization*, as we held that its dialectic would illuminate also the dialectic of the Party, as we had long since rejected "the party to lead" concept. We were here driven to go also to Hegel's *Philosophy of Mind,* and there, as we approached the three final syl-logisms in Absolute Mind and trod on ground none had ever walked before, we felt that in place of a "dialectic of the party" we were, with Hegel's Self-Thinking Idea, with the masses' Self-Bringing Forth of Liberty, face to face with a new society. After all, Marx had unchained the dialectic as he had recre-ated the Absolute Method as a "revolution in permanence."

What has made this appeal to the youth appear so urgent to me is that, at one and the same time, we not only confront the objective situation of a nuclear world filled with economic recession and political retrogression as well as altogether too many aborted, unfinished revolutions turned into their very opposite, but also the fact that Marx's all-encompassing revolution in permanence, which desires to become ground also of organization, has, until *Rosa Luxemburg, Women's Liberation, and Marx's Philosophy of Revolution*, been left at the implicit stage.

Let's briefly, very briefly, trace and parallel the last 30-year[s of] movements from practice and from theory with our own philosophic development through the same period. What we call a trilogy of revolution—*Marxism and Freedom; Philosophy and Revolution; Rosa Luxemburg, Women's Liberation, and Marx's Philosophy of Revolution*—has, in each period, singled out what was most urgent as measured by the objective crisis for that period. Though the dialectics of liberation, the philosophy of revolution, permeates them all, the particular, concrete need in each period is what determines the focus. Thus, our first comprehensive theoretic work, *Marxism and Freedom*, which, of course, was structured around our first original historic contribution—the movement from practice to theory—had its focus not only on Marx's American and Humanist roots, but also on Lenin's break with his philosophic past so that the fact that he had not extended it to reexamination of his vanguardist party concept meant it was left unfinished. Here what is important is to watch the method and style of presentation as an indication of what should be further developed. Take the sharp break in style on philosophy and on organization. In the case of organization, I dismiss the whole period of so-called classical Marxism—the Second International, 1889–1914—as a mere Interlude, an Organizational Interlude that doesn't deserve classification as a Part; while in the case of the concept of a new relationship of worker and intellectual at a turning point in history, 1848–61, that is made a whole Part though it occupies but a single chapter.[30] Did anyone ask why? Well, the Iranian youth did single out that chapter to translate along with the Humanist Essays as necessary to their participation in that revolution.[31]

But the new generation of revolutionaries in the United States were so preoccupied with decentralization that the fatal contradiction between that and their failure to pay attention to the state-capitalist *class* nature of the Communist elitist party meant that very nearly everything was subordinated to activism. It wasn't until the 1970s, when the Women's Liberation movement also kept stressing decentralization and, at the same time, refused to disregard the male chauvinism in the Left, that it became clear that the new form of organization could not be kept in a separate compartment from that of philosophy. It was then that we turned to *Philosophy and Revolution*, beginning with "Why Hegel? Why Now?"—a Part which, at one and the same time, considered the Hegelian dialectic "in and for itself" not separate from both Marx's philosophy of revolution and Lenin's philosophic ambivalence. The youth, Women's Liberationists, as well as the Black dimension, however, appreciated chapter 9, "New Passions and New Forces" rather than chapter 1, "Absolute Negativity as New Beginning," which did get down to those three final syllogisms in depth.[††]

In the mid-1970s we finally got to know Marx's *Ethnological Notebooks* which let us hear him think.[32] By not being a work finished for the press, it compels us to work out, to labor at what Marx has only in notes. This is what we must all work at for our age. Here is why we so urgently need . . . to continue the development . . . in completing [what] the trilogy of revolution has begun. In the process, let us not forget what that great revolutionary, Rosa Luxemburg, did for us, not only in letting us discover her unknown feminist dimension, but in posing the question of the relationship of spontaneity to organization so insightfully that, though she had not worked out the answers, she helped create an atmosphere that makes it impossible any longer to ignore all the ramifications of spontaneity.

Marx's *Critique of the Gotha Program*, when reread with the totality of Marx's Marxism—where we found the "new moments" Marx experienced on what we now call the Third World and the new forces of revolution as Reason, be it Women's Liberation, Black or youth—demanded a reexamination of all the great revolutionaries, especially Lenin and Luxemburg, who seemed to be so deeply divided on the question of organization. It was that reexamination in this year of the Marx centenary, in this nuclear world, in the imperative nature of the challenge to post-Marx Marxists, which would not let revolutionaries off scot-free of the organizational question.

The youth need also to dig into the first chapter of part III[33] to grapple with the Promethean vision of the young Marx before he was a Marxist, when he was still a Prometheus Bound, when he was still a young Hegelian (1839–41) just filling in some minor gaps in Hegel's monumental *History of Philosophy*— and asking himself that imperative question: "where to begin." When we talk about "thought-divers" we can see that Marx was the greatest of all.

That's what I'm really appealing to the youth to do. Becoming a thought-diver and an activist in this period demands nothing short of *practicing* the challenge to all post-Marx Marxists, and thereby creating such new ground

---

[††]Peter Hudis, in his discussion article on "Organizational Growth and the Dialectics of 'Revolution in Permanence'" has made a truly original contribution in seeing more than any of us before had seen in the actual text of the 1953 Letters on the Absolute Idea. [For the text of this article, see *The Raya Dunayevskaya Collection*, p. 7809.]

for organization, such concretization of Marx's revolution in permanence, as to find a new way to let the actual revolution *be*.

Dialectics of Revolution and of Women's Liberation

In the fall of 1984 Dunayevskaya compiled a collection of her writings over the course of the previous 35 years on women's liberation, which was published, in 1985, as Women's Liberation and the Dialectics of Revolution: Reaching for the Future. *This work took up such topics as women, labor, and the Black dimension, as well as international developments from Latin America to China and from Poland to Iran. Its concluding section, entitled "The Trail to the 1980s: The Missing Link—Philosophy—in the Relationship of Revolution to Organization," discussed differences between Marx and Engels on women and the philosophical foundations of Dunayevskaya's earlier book,* Rosa Luxemburg, Women's Liberation, and Marx's Philosophy of Revolution. *The publication of* Women's Liberation and the Dialectics of Revolution *led to a new appreciation of Dunayevskaya's work by feminist thinkers.[34] On February 3, 1985, shortly after submitting the manuscript to the publisher, she delivered the following lecture in which she reversed the title of the book in order to emphasize the centrality of the dialectic. It was first published in the pamphlet* Dialectics of Revolution: American Roots and Marx's World Humanist Concepts *(1985).*

Introduction and Part I: *Marx's Marxism;* Lenin's Marxism

Let's go adventuring to some historic turning points that have unchained the dialectic in Marx's age, in Lenin's, and in our post–World War II age.

Let's begin with 1843–44 when Marx broke with capitalism, having discovered a whole new continent of thought and of revolution that he called "a new Humanism."

Hegel's dialectic methodology had created a revolution in philosophy. Marx criticized it precisely because the structure of Hegel's *Phenomenology of Mind* was everywhere interpreted as a revolution in thought only. Marx's "Critique of the Hegelian Dialectic" took issue with Hegel also for holding that a philosopher can know the dialectic of revolution (the French Revolution in Hegel's case) only after the revolution has taken place.[35] Marx recreated it as a dialectic of reality in need of transformation. He named the Subject—the revolutionary force who could achieve this—as the proletariat.

Put briefly, Marx transformed Hegel's revolution *in* philosophy into a philosophy *of* revolution. This will be further developed throughout this talk. For the moment, our focus must develop Marx's first "new moment"—i.e., the discovery [and] birth of what he called "a new Humanism."

It is that which characterized Marx's whole life from his break with capitalism until the day of his death, 1843–83. It included two actual revolutions—1848 and 1871. The defeat of the 1848 revolutions produced a new need for a continuing revolution, a "revolution in permanence"; and Marx concluded from 1871, which created the Paris Commune, that the bourgeois state needs to be *totally* destroyed, and he called for a *non*-state form of workers' rule like the Paris Commune.

A 31-year lapse followed before a single post-Marx Marxist—Lenin—felt compelled to have a revolutionary encounter with the Hegelian dialectic. That historic turning point followed when, in the objective world, the Second International collapsed at the outbreak of World War I. The shocking betrayal by the Second International served as the compulsion to Lenin to return to Marx's origin in the Hegelian dialectic with his own study of Hegel's *Science of Logic*. This marked the great divide in post-Marx Marxism. Lenin's grappling with the Hegelian-Marxian dialectic continued through the final decade of his life, from 1914 to 1924.

What resulted from this revolutionary encounter was a reunification of philosophy with revolution. We must see what Lenin specifically singled out to help him answer the historic task facing him, and how he reconnected with Marx's Marxism. The dialectical principle he singled out from Hegel was transformation into opposite.[36] Everything he worked out from then on— from *Imperialism* to *State and Revolution*—demonstrates that.

The main focus here is on the significance of what a revolutionary concretizes to answer the challenge of a new age. In the case of Lenin it was the dialectic principle of *transformation into opposite* that he held to characterize both capitalism's development into imperialism and a section of the proletariat being transformed into "the aristocracy of labor."[37]

Nearly two decades elapsed after Lenin died—during which would come the actual outbreak of World War II, which caused Trotskyism to split into several different tendencies—before there was the first serious grappling with the new reality that characterized the objective world. It was the outbreak of World War II which compelled me to study Russia's three Five Year Plans and to come to the conclusion that Russia was a state-capitalist society.[38] The shocker to Trotsky, to which he never reconciled himself, was that outright *counter*-revolution came, not from the outside, from imperialism, but from [within] the Russian Revolution itself. With the transformation of the first workers' state into a state-capitalist society it became clear that Stalin represented not just the bureaucrat, Stalin, but *Stalinism*, a Russian form of the new *world* stage in production.

Before, however, the dialectics of revolution could be fully unchained *philosophically* for our age, we had to experience *both* the new phenomenon in the miners general strike of 1949–50, living masses in motion posing new questions, *and* a serious grappling, philosophically, with the Hegelian-Marxian dialectic.[39] This resulted in the philosophy of Marxist-Humanism. It was this philosophy which characterized those masses in motion as a *movement from practice that is itself a form of theory*. Since we are Marxist-Humanists, what we will examine today is that whole body of ideas—taking up both what we call the "trilogy of revolution" and the new fourth book we will soon have off the press: *Women's Liberation and the Dialectics of Revolution: Reaching for the Future*.

Marx's Marxism

Let's first examine Marx himself, from 1843 to 1883, in both his relationship to, and the break from, Hegel. So far as I am concerned, the "new moments" in Marx mark not merely the last decade of his life—which became, for us, the trail to the 1980s—but begin with the very first moment in Marx, the moment of his break with capitalism, *its* production, *its* culture, *its* immediate contenders from Lassalle on. From that encounter there came the birth of a new continent of thought *and* of revolution.

There was no time for popularization; that had to be left to his closest collaborator, Engels—who was no Marx—so that the founder of this new continent of thought and of revolution could give his whole time to the concretization of that new Universal—Marx's "new Humanism."

Note how painstakingly and in what interrelationships Marx's 1844 "Critique of the Hegelian Dialectic" shows all the new elements. Though he had already designated the proletariat as the revolutionary force, it was at that moment that he also singled out the man/woman relationship and pointed to the fact that it is that which discloses how *alienating* is the nature of this capitalist society.[40] And though he had already separated himself from petty-bourgeois idealism, the power of negativity separated him also from Feuerbachian materialism.

The "new Humanism," in a word, was not just a matter of counterposing materialism to idealism; it was the *unity* of the two. By introducing practice as the very source of philosophy, Marx completely transformed the Hegelian dialectic as related only to thought and made it the dialectics of revolution. It was not only capitalism and its idealism Marx rejected, but what he called "vulgar communism"—which he stressed was *not* the goal of the overthrow of capitalism.[41] What concretized his "new Humanism" was that the revolution must be continuous *after* the overthrow of capitalism.

When the real revolutions came in 1848—and he, himself, participated in them—he called, after their defeat, for a "revolution in permanence," in his 1850 *Address to the Communist League*. And after the 1875 French edition of *Capital*, after 40 hard years of labor in economics, he projected the possibility that a revolution could occur first in a technologically backward country (what we now see as the Third World)—ahead, that is, of the so-called advanced countries—though that was the opposite of what it *seemed* he had predicted in the [section on the] "Accumulation of Capital."[42] In a word, there was nothing that was concretely spelled out in Marx's very last decade that was not first seen in the Promethean vision which he had unfolded at the very beginning, in the breaking up of the capitalist world.

Take even the one question—organization—on which the so-called orthodox claim was never touched seriously by anyone, not even a Marx, until Lenin worked it out in *What Is To Be Done?* in 1902–03. The truth is that Marx was always an "organization man." He no sooner got to Paris and finished his 1844 *Humanist Essays* (which never were published in his lifetime) than he searched out workers' meetings, created his own International Communist Correspondence Committees, and then joined the League of the Just, which became the Communist League. He tried to get everyone from Feuerbach to Proudhon to join, calling on them to be as enthusiastic about the workers' voices as he was.

What *was* true was that only with the 1875 "Marginal Notes" we know as the *Critique of the Gotha Program* did he express his views directly on the "program" of a workers' party. Those "Marginal Notes" stressed the impossibility for serious revolutionaries ever to separate philosophy of revolution from the actual organization; when a principle of philosophy *and* revolution is not in the "program," one should never join that organization, though one could participate in individual joint action against capitalism.

Did this *Critique* mean anything to any of those who called themselves Marxists? Clearly, not to the whole leadership of the Second International. That historic turning point had not meant anything to any of the German leaders—and not only not to the Lassalleans but also not to the Eisenachists, who considered themselves Marxists.

And what of the Internationalists? It took nothing short of the outbreak of World War I to have *anyone* turn to the *Critique*. The single one who did—Lenin—learned a great deal on the necessary destruction of the capitalist *state*, as *State and Revolution* shows, but he left the whole question of organization completely alone.

It took our age, specifically Marxist-Humanists, before there was a serious grappling with the type of organization Marx was calling for, and a reconnection of organization with his philosophy of "revolution in permanence." We did it publicly only when the transcription of Marx's *Ethnological Notebooks* became available in the 1970s, and were analyzed philosophically for our age in *Rosa Luxemburg, Women's Liberation, and Marx's Philosophy of Revolution*. It was there that we challenged all post-Marx Marxists on this question.

Lenin's Marxism

> The difference of the ideal from the material is also not unconditional, not excessive. . . .
> At the end of Book II of the Logic, before the transition to the Notion, the definition is given: "the Notion, the realm of Subjectivity or of Freedom":
>
> $$NB \text{ Freedom} = \text{subjectivity}$$
> $$(\text{"or"})$$
> $$\text{goal, consciousness, striving } NB$$
>
> —Lenin, "Abstract of Hegel's *Science of Logic*"
> [LCW 38, pp. 114, 164]

Lenin did not know the 1844 *Humanist Essays*. What predominated in the mind of the first generation of post-Marx Marxists was organization, and that without grappling with Marx's *Critique of the Gotha Program*: that was totally ignored. What was not only not ignored but actually became the great divide in Marxism was the dialectic, the relationship between materialism and idealism, the dialectic methodology. The only divide acknowledged by Marxists was that between reform and revolution. Put differently, though the inseparability of revolution from organization's *goal* was acknowledged, philosophy remained the missing link. That was not just in general. Specifically, it meant reducing methodology as if it were a mere "tool." It is this which shows what the true great divide was—the dialectic—which Lenin alone understood, although he kept his *What Is To Be Done?* where it was in 1902–03.

The very fact that the great divide continued within the Bolshevik movement—in great revolutionaries like Bukharin and Rosa Luxemburg—speaks volumes about the unacknowledged missing link of philosophy. Thus, the one who was accepted as the greatest theoretician—Bukharin—sharply disagreed with Lenin on his relationship to the national liberation movements, specifically the Irish Revolution. It led Lenin to use as divisive a *class* designation of Bukharin's position as "imperialist economism"![43] Lenin did not sum up his attitude to Bukharin, directly relating it to dialectics, until his *Will*. There Lenin (who by then had Bukharin's *Economics of the Transition Period*) wrote that Bukharin's views could "only with the very greatest doubt be regarded as fully Marxian, for . . . he never fully understood the dialectic" [LCW 36, p. 595].

The principle Lenin singled out in the dialectic, as we noted, was the transformation into opposite, which he related both to capitalism and to a section of the proletariat, but not to his concept of the "party-to-lead." But while he failed to submit "the party" to the Absolute Method of the dialectic of second negativity—that remained his untouchable "private enclave," the one that remains the noose around us all—Lenin did unstintingly hold to the dialectic principle that the imperative to retransform the opposite into the positive cannot be done without the creativity of a new revolutionary force. The fact that you could prove betrayal would amount to nothing unless you could point to a new force like the Irish revolution.

It was this which led him to attack what he called Luxemburg's "half-way dialectic."[44] Here was a revolutionary who, before anyone else, including Lenin, had called attention to the opportunism of the Second International and had pinpointed, *before* the actual outbreak of World War I, the International's opportunistic attitude to German capitalism's plunge into imperialism, and to the suffering of the colonial masses. Unfortunately, however, she saw the "root cause" not in the Second International alone, but in the defects of Marx's theory of the accumulation of capital. This resulted in her developing one more form of underconsumptionism.[45] Her failure to recognize the colonial mass opposition as what Lenin called "the bacillus of proletarian revolution" led her to continue her opposition to Lenin's position on the "National Question." That is what Lenin called the "half-way dialectic."

He, on the contrary, related the dialectic to everything he wrote from then on—from *Imperialism* and *State and Revolution* to his letter to the editors of *Under the Banner of Marxism* about the need to study the Hegelian dialectic in Hegel's own words [LCW 33, p. 234]. His death created a philosophic void none of his co-leaders, Trotsky included, could fill. That remained the task for a new age.

Part II: Reestablishing the Link of Continuity with Marx's Marxism and the Development of the Body of Ideas of Marxist-Humanism

After a decade of world depression and the rise of fascism came the greatest shocker, the Hitler-Stalin Pact, that signaled the timing of World War II. It was high time to recognize the startling fact that, though November 1917 was the greatest revolution, the *counter*-revolution came, not from an outside imperialism, *but from within.* Trotsky could not, did not, face that reality, much less work out the new dialectic.

It took a whole decade of digging into *what happened after* the revolution had conquered power to discover how it was transformed into its opposite—a workers' state into a state-capitalist society—through the Five Year Plans as well as the objective situation in the private capitalist world. Let's look into the two stages of that decade: first, straight state-capitalist theory; and finally, the birth of Marxist-Humanism.

A. Vicissitudes of State-Capitalism, the Black Dimension, and the Birth of Marxist-Humanism: Marxism and Freedom: From 1776 until Today: The Voices from Below of the 1960s.

Marxism and Freedom: From 1776 until Today is the first of the three books which Marxist-Humanism refers to as our "trilogy of revolution." The first edition contained two appendices. One is the first published English translation of Marx's "Private Property and Communism" and "Critique of the Hegelian Dialectic" from what has come to be called Marx's 1844 *Humanist Essays.* The second is the first English translation of Lenin's "Abstract of Hegel's *Science of Logic.*"

Some elements of humanism were present in our development as early as 1941 in the essay on "Labor and Society," which was the very first section of my analysis of "The Nature of the Russian Economy." That essay was rejected for publication by the Trotskyists (the Workers Party) when they accepted the strictly economic analysis of the Five Year Plans from Russian sources.[46]

The vicissitudes of state-capitalism would show that only when the philosophic structure is fully developed can one present the theory of state-capitalism in a way that would answer the quest for universality and what Marxist-Humanism called "the movement from practice." Which is why I prefer the way my 1941 study of the nature of the Russian economy was presented in *Marxism and Freedom: From 1776 until Today* in 1957, in part V, "The Problem of our Age: State-Capitalism vs. Freedom."

Marxists[47] and non-Marxists alike have always rejected even the attempt to give a philosophic structure to concrete events. Take the question of the Black Dimension. No one could deny that a new stage had been reached in the 1960s, and whether you called it a revolution or just a new stage of the struggle for civil rights, there was no denying the stormy nature of the 1960s. But the truth is that this could be seen not only in the '60s, but beginning with the Montgomery Bus Boycott—and not only as a new beginning but in terms of the whole philosophic structure for the following decade. Here is what I singled out from that event in *Marxism and Freedom:* 1) The daily meetings; 2) the way in which the Black rank-and-file organized their own transportation (indeed, Rev. King admitted that the whole movement started without him);

3) the fact that, whether it was the meetings or the transportation that the masses took into their own hands, the Boycott's greatest achievement was "its own working existence"—the very phrase *Marxism and Freedom* had also pointed to in another section, as Marx had written of the Paris Commune [M&F, pp. 97, 281].

We could take the same 35 years we have taken in our new, fourth book where we show the [impact of the] development of the dialectics of revolution on Women's Liberation, and show that development on the Black Dimension. The same is true for youth, as when we take the three new pages of freedom in *Marxism and Freedom* on the Hungarian Revolution, where I point to the revolutionary youth getting ever younger, as witness the 12-year-old Hungarian freedom fighters. And of course the same would be true of labor. That, indeed, begins in the French Revolution of 1789–93, when there was no industrial proletariat and the *enragés*, the *sans culottes*, the artisans, were the great revolutionaries who spelled out the same *masses in motion*.

Masses in motion have marked every historic turning point. This is articulated by going beyond every national boundary. In our age it can be seen whether we are looking at the Afro-Asian Revolutions or the Latin American Revolutions, and it is reflected both in our activity and in our publications.

The three-fold goal of *Marxism and Freedom* was: 1) To establish the American roots of Marxism, *not* where the orthodox [Marxists] cite it (if they cite it at all) in the General Congress of Labor at Baltimore (1866), but in the Abolitionist Movement and the slave revolts which led to the Civil War; 2) to establish the *world* Humanist concept which Marx had, in his very first new moment, called "a new Humanism," and which became so alive in our age and led to Marxist-Humanism; and 3) to reestablish the revolutionary nature of the Hegelian dialectic as Marx recreated it and as it became compulsory for Lenin at the outbreak of the First World War, gaining a still newer life in our post-World War II age.

The contemporaneity as well as specificity of the deep-rootedness of the Hegelian dialectic permeates the whole of *Marxism and Freedom*. Please note the book's dialectical structure and see that from the very first chapter ("The Age of Revolutions: Industrial, Social-Political, Intellectual") it discloses no division between the objectivity of the period and the subjectivity of revolutionary Marxism. And note as well its todayness as it ends the chapter with the section entitled "Hegel's Absolutes and Our Age of Absolutes." Let me read you the last paragraph of that chapter:

> To declare, in our day and age, that Hegel's Absolute means nothing but the "knowing" of the whole past of human culture is to make a mockery of the dialectical de-

velopment of the world and of thought, and absolutely to bar a rational approach to Hegel. What is far worse, such sophistry is a self-paralyzing barrier against a sober theoretical approach to the world itself. It is necessary to divest Hegelian philosophy of the dead-weight of academic tradition as well as of radical intellectual snobbery and cynicism or we will lay ourselves wide open to the putrescent smog of Communism. [M&F, p. 43]

From the very start of News and Letters Committees in 1955 we made two decisions simultaneously. At our Convention in 1956, our Constitution established our newspaper, *News & Letters*, as a unique combination of workers and intellectuals, with a Black production worker, Charles Denby, as our editor and with Raya Dunayevskaya as Chairwoman of the National Editorial Board; and we assigned the National Chairwoman to set forth our own interpretation of Marxism in what became *Marxism and Freedom: From 1776 until Today*. All of the new pamphlets we produced through the turbulent 1960s flowed out of the structure of *Marxism and Freedom: Workers Battle Automation, The Free Speech Movement and the Negro Revolution, Notes on Women's Liberation*—all written by the new voices from below; as well as my pamphlet on *Nationalism, Communism, Marxist-Humanism and the Afro-Asian Revolutions* and the [pamphlet covering the] whole history of the United States, *American Civilization on Trial*, signed by the entire National Editorial Board of *News & Letters*. These and all the others we produced you must read for yourselves.

The whole question of the unity of Theory/Practice is seen especially clearly in the difference between part I of Charles Denby's *Indignant Heart*, written when the Johnson-Forest Tendency was still a single State-Capitalist Tendency, and part II, written after Marxist-Humanism had been openly practiced for more than two decades and brought all those developments in Charles Denby.[48]

In 1969 Marxist-Humanism called a Black/Red Conference,[49] and [in 1971] Marxist-Humanist women also held their conference and decided to establish an autonomous organization. Not only did both conferences have many non-Marxist-Humanists present, but in the Black/Red Conference, they were the majority present. That year, 1969, was also the year we donated our Archives to Wayne State University. The unfinished 1968 Paris Revolt had finally made us realize that Marxist-Humanism, projected in the 1950s and spelled out comprehensively in 1957 in our first major theoretical work, cried out for concretizing Marxism as philosophy. Not only was 1969 not 1968; 1969 was high time to realize that theory, including state-capitalist theory, is not—*is not*—yet philosophy.

B. Return to Hegel and Our Dialectical Discoveries: Philosophy and Revolution: From Hegel to Sartre and from Marx to Mao

By the end of the 1960s, when the climax of all the activity had resulted only in an aborted revolution, we could no longer avoid the strictly philosophic new digging into Hegel to see what concretely related to our age. The return to all of Hegel's major works—especially the final syllogism Hegel had added to the *Philosophy of Mind*—finally resulted in our second major philosophic-theoretical work, *Philosophy and Revolution*. That new return and concentration on those final syllogisms was comprehensive in the way it reexamined not only Hegel and Marx and Lenin (which constituted part I, "Why Hegel? Why Now?"), but the alternatives that considered themselves revolutionary—Trotsky, Mao and one "outsider looking in," Sartre (which constituted part II). This time the vicissitudes of state-capitalism were not restricted to those who called themselves Communists, but included altogether new lands, new struggles, as well as a new African, Asian, Third World socialism. (Part III dealt with East Europe, Africa, and the new passions and forces.)

But it doesn't stop there. What finally summed up the new challenges, new passions, new forces—all those new relations against the objective situation—was the return to Hegel "in and for himself," by which I mean his major philosophic works: *Phenomenology of Mind; Science of Logic;* and *Philosophy of Mind* from the *Encyclopedia of the Philosophical Sciences*.

Let's begin at the end of chapter 1 of *Philosophy and Revolution*, "Absolute Negativity as New Beginning: The Ceaseless Movement of Ideas and of History," where I concentrate on the three final syllogisms of Hegel's *Philosophy of Mind*, ¶575, ¶576, ¶577. The very listing of the books of the *Encyclopedia*—Logic, Nature, Mind (¶575)—discloses a new reality and that is that Logic is *not* as important as nature, since Nature is the middle which is the mediation, which is of the essence. The second syllogism (¶576) discloses that the mediation comes from Mind itself and Logic becomes less crucial. What is Absolute is Absolute Negativity, and it is that which replaces Logic altogether. What Hegel is saying is that the movement is ceaseless and therefore he can no longer limit himself to a syllogism. The "Self-Thinking Idea" has replaced the syllogistic presentation in ¶577.

When I jammed up this conclusion of Hegel's from my first chapter of *Philosophy and Revolution* with what I worked out when I summed up the final chapter 9 on what flowed from the movement from practice (what I called "New Passions and New Forces"), here is how I expressed it:

> The reality is stifling. The transformation of reality has a dialectic all its own. It demands a unity of the struggles for freedom with a philosophy of liberation. Only then

does the elemental revolt release new sensibilities, new passions, and new forces—a whole new human dimension. Ours is the age that can meet the challenge of the times when we work out so new a relationship of theory to practice that the proof of the unity is in the Subject's own self-development. Philosophy and revolution will first then liberate the innate talents of men and women who will become whole. Whether or not we recognize that this is the task history has "assigned" to our epoch, it is a task that remains to be done. [P&R, p. 292]

C. The Marx Centenary: Rosa Luxemburg, Women's Liberation, and Marx's Philosophy of Revolution

The Marx Centenary [in 1983] created the opportunity for us, when we also had a third major philosophic work, *Rosa Luxemburg, Women's Liberation, and Marx's Philosophy of Revolution* (which completed what we call the "trilogy of revolution"), to stress how total the uprooting of the system must be. It is not only that there can be no "private enclaves" that are free from the dialectics of revolution—that which Hegel called "second negativity" and what we consider the Absolute Method, the road to the Absolute Idea. It is that the crucial thing for us, now that we had Marx's *Ethnological Notebooks*, was more than just singling out the Man/Woman relationship, because we could see that the critique of all post-Marx Marxists begins with Frederick Engels. This last work of Marx disclosed Marx's multilinear view of all of human history vs. Engels' unilinear view.

It is that which prompted us to create the category of "post-Marx Marxism," and it was precisely when we dealt with other revolutionaries like Rosa Luxemburg that it became necessary to focus on Marx's concept of "revolution in permanence."

All these new points of departure led to the new study where I reexamined Marx's Marxism *as a totality*. I cannot here go into that, which was central to the third book. I will have to limit myself simply to quoting the last paragraph of the work:

> What is needed is a new unifying principle, on Marx's ground of humanism, that truly alters both human thought and human experience. Marx's *Ethnological Notebooks* are a historic happening that proves, one hundred years after he wrote them, that Marx's legacy is no mere heirloom, but a live body of ideas and perspectives that is in need of concretization. Every moment of Marx's development, as well as the totality of his works, spells out the need for "revolution in permanence." This is the absolute challenge to our age. [RLWLKM, p. 195]

D. Unchaining the Dialectic Through 35 Years of Marxist-Humanist Writings, Which Trace the Dialectics of Revolution in a New Work on Women's Liberation

The title for my lecture today has reversed the title of our new fourth book into "Dialectics of Revolution and of Women's Liberation," not just as something needed for this lecture, but as what is the actual focus of the whole "trilogy of revolution" as well as this latest philosophic work. Indeed, the Introduction to it—and an introduction is really always also the conclusion—is called "Introduction and Overview." It is that which I will try to summarize here as the unchaining of the dialectic for the post-World War II period, whether that is expressed in activities or books, in pamphlets or *News & Letters*, or as it is implicit throughout the Archives, as well.

It is this which reveals that, no matter what specific revolutionary force turns out to be the main one in any ongoing revolution, no one can know before time who it will be. Nothing proves this more sharply than Women's Liberation, because it has been an unrecognized and degraded force, rather than seen as a force that is simultaneously Reason. It is this which has made women question: "What happens after?"

In the main, Women's Liberationists refuse to accept anything which shows that "a man" decides. In actuality, what they are thereby rejecting is the dialectics of revolution. It is this burning question of our age which led me to subtitle this final section of my lecture: Unchaining the Dialectic.

First, let us look at the unchaining of the dialectic for our age by Marxist-Humanists. Our original contributions to Marx's Marxism can be seen in our first book, *Marxism and Freedom*, as the structure of the whole—the movement from practice. It is seen in our second work, *Philosophy and Revolution*, as the working out of the Absolute Idea for our age—Absolute Idea as New Beginning. In the third work, *Rosa Luxemburg, Women's Liberation, and Marx's Philosophy of Revolution*, it is seen as the challenge to all post-Marx Marxists.

Secondly, let's see how Marx explained his return to the Hegelian dialectic in his very last decade: "My relationship with Hegel is very simple. I am a disciple of Hegel, and the presumptuous chatter of the epigones who think they have buried this great thinker appear frankly ridiculous to me. Nevertheless, I have taken the liberty of adopting . . . a critical attitude, disencumbering his dialectic of its mysticism and thus putting it through a profound change." This is from the manuscripts for Volume II of *Capital* that Marx left, and that Engels left out [of the published version].[50]

Now let's look at the structure of our fourth book, still on the press, *Women's Liberation and the Dialectics of Revolution: Reaching for the Future*. What became obvious to me was that the four parts of this book turned out to be actual moments of revolution. Thus part I, "Women, Labor and the Black Dimension," actually also includes youth, as the four forces of revolution. I insisted in my Introduction that I was not presenting my writings chronologically because I wanted each topic to reflect, even if only implicitly, the totality of my views. Even that aspect does not tell the whole story about the relationship of the forces of revolution to the Reason of any revolution—i.e., how each one of the forces "reaches for the future." This was most clearly shown not only by the forces that actually made the revolution in Russia, but by those in Persia where the women in the revolution of 1906–11 had gone beyond even what they did in Russia, itself, by establishing a new form of organization, the women's *anjumen* (soviet). Today we spell this out as committee-form in place of "party-to-lead."

Part II, "Revolutionaries All," again shows the activists, the actual participants in revolutions. Whether or not they were conscious of actually being the history-makers, they were exactly that. And that section has the footnote which returns us to *Marxism and Freedom*, choosing the section that describes the milkmaids initiating the Paris Commune of 1871.

Part III, "Sexism, Politics and Revolution—Japan, Portugal, Poland, China, Latin America, the United States—Is there an Organizational Answer?" clearly illustrates both the positive internationalism and the very negative sexism in each country, whether East or West. Yet what the Introduction and Overview made clear was that the forces of revolution had to show their actual *presence* before the concretization of the dialectics of revolution would manifest itself.

Put differently, what the very first sentence of the first paragraph of the first page of the Introduction establishes is that first there must be a definition that is a concretization of the specific nature of your epoch.[51] We had designated that as the movement from practice that is itself a form of theory, and we had arrived at that conclusion from the encounter with the Absolute Idea as being not just a *unity* of practice and theory, but a very *new relationship of practice to theory*. It is this which determined the whole structure of our very first major theoretical work, *Marxism and Freedom*. Only *after* this specific epoch and its historic content was grasped do we speak, in the second paragraph of the Introduction and Overview, about the uniqueness of one of the forces of revolution, Women's Liberation.

We now come to part IV on "The Trail to the 1980s"—which is naturally the one that is key to any concretization of the present period. Our task is two-fold: we have to catch the link of continuity with *Marx's* Marxism; and then make our own original contributions, which only the epoch in question can work out for itself. Marx opened the gates for us. Look at the way he treated his relationship to Hegel after he discovered his own new continent of thought and yet felt it important to return to the Hegelian dialectic. That was *not* to deny anything new. On the contrary—and contrary especially to all those who try to use the final decade of Marx's life to turn him into no more than a populist—the full 40 years of Marx's work, which saw the critic of the

Hegelian dialectic become the philosopher of revolution and the author of *Capital*, prove that he continued his own very original development throughout his life, including the final decade, and that the new moments were no break with his very first new discovery.

Follow the dialectics of the development of women as the new revolutionary force *and Reason*. Concretization, when it expresses a Universal that becomes concrete, shows what Absolute Idea is *as New Beginning*. All the emphasis on "New Beginnings" pinpoints the task of an age. Absolute Idea is total, but it cannot be total as a quantitative measure. That is where the new in any epoch requires the *living presence* of that revolutionary force and not just a Promethean vision. That is not because Promethean vision and reaching for the future doesn't help the next generation to see its task. Quite the contrary. That is when discontinuity is not a revision of, but a continuation with, the original new moment *when* there are all sorts of new voices and listening to them is quintessential.

It is only after the new world stage of practice is recognized that we get to that new revolutionary force of Women's Liberation, which has named the culprit—male chauvinism—as characterizing the revolutionary movement itself. That is to say, it is not only characteristic of capitalism, and not only of this epoch, but has existed throughout history. The point is not to stop there. But in order not to stop there, you have to recognize Women's Liberation as a force that is Reason and not just force—and that means a total uprooting of this society, and the creation of totally new human relations. Which is why Marx was not exclusively a feminist but a "new Humanist." The fact that feminism is part of Humanism and not the other way around does not mean that Women's Liberation becomes subordinate. It means only that philosophy will not again be separated from revolution, or Reason separated from force. Even Absolute Method becomes only the "road to" Absolute Idea, Absolute Mind.

Let me end, then, with the final paragraphs from the Introduction and Overview of our new, fourth book:

> The Absolute Method allows for no "private enclaves"—i.e., exceptions to the principle of Marx's Dialectics, whether on the theoretical or the organizational questions. As Marx insisted from the very beginning, nothing can be a private enclave: neither any part of life, nor organization, nor even science. In his *Economic-Philosophic Manuscripts*, he proclaimed that: "To have one basis for life and another for science is *a priori* a lie."[52]

And now that we have both the *Ethnological Notebooks* and the *Mathematical Manuscripts* from Marx's last years, where he singled out the expression "negation of the negation,"[53] we can see that that is the very same expression he used in 1844 to explain why Feuerbach was a vulgar materialist in rejecting it, and Hegel was the creative philosopher. As we concluded in the Introduction and Overview to *Women's Liberation and the Dialectics of Revolution*, on Marx's 1844 declaration on science and life:

> The truth of this statement has never been more immediate and urgent than in our nuclear world, over which hangs nothing short of the threat to the very survival of civilization as we have known it.

The Power of Abstraction

At the end of 1984, Dunayevskaya began to work on a new book, first entitled "Dialectics of the Party" and subsequently "Dialectics of Organization and Philosophy."[54] Her exploration of this subject led her to delve anew into the dialectic in philosophy, and especially Hegel's Absolutes. A key moment in this process was the following material, delivered as part of a presentation to a plenary gathering of News and Letters Committees in August, 1985. It was entitled "The Self-Thinking Idea in a New Concept of and Relationship to the Dialectics of Leadership, as well as the Self-Bringing Forth of Liberty." The full text can be found in The Raya Dunayevskaya Collection, *p. 10348.*

> ". . . philosophy appears as a subjective cognition, of which liberty is the aim, and which is itself the way to produce it."
>
> ". . . it is the nature of the fact, the notion, which causes the movement and development, yet this same movement is equally the action of cognition."
>
> —Hegel, *Philosophy of Mind*, ¶576, ¶577
>
> ". . . after labor, from a mere means of life, has itself become the prime necessity of life; after the productive forces have also increased with the all-round development of the individual . . . only then can the narrow horizon of bourgeois right be fully left behind and society inscribe on its banner: from each according to his ability, to each according to his needs."
>
> —Marx, *Critique of the Gotha Program*
> [MECW 24, p. 87]

It is not only the title that is abstract and strange but the whole context of what I will present here—long, long before I come to the concrete question of the dialectics of leadership—is going to be abstract. In fact, I'm going to make the "pure" abstraction of the Self-Thinking Idea a veritable Universal, because I wanted, first of all, to firmly establish that the Self-Thinking idea does not—I repeat, does not—mean *you* thinking.

Forget what I never stop repeating in the critique of Hegel, that it's not Ideas floating in the upper regions of the philosopher's heavens that "think"; it is people who think.[55] That is totally wrong if you are serious about tracing the *Logic* of an Idea to *its* logical conclusion. Therefore, instead of any person (including what was primary to Hegel—philosophers) thinking, I want you to face the Idea itself thinking, i.e., developing it to its ultimate.

At this point, remember how rarely you think something through to the end. Indeed, if you do follow an abstract thought to the end, and if your Idea is the wrong one, you will wind up sounding like an idiot. That is, thinking "in and for itself" will end up by proving that the Idea is no Universal. But if your Idea was correct, the concretization will prove you a genius. Ideas "think," not sequentially, but *con*sequentially, related to other Ideas that emerge out of *historic* ground, and do not care where all this might lead to, including transformation into opposite.

And yet, it is precisely because it is abstract, it's precisely because it goes to the ultimate without caring where this leads, that we can see what Logic does to a concrete Idea. It is this type of Absolute Method that Hegel had in mind as he was reaching the conclusion of the Absolute Idea, and said all truth is Subjectivity and Subjectivity alone.[56] It is philosophy and not philosoph*er;* and if that philosophy is revolutionary and if that Idea is the Idea of Freedom, then a new Humanism will first arise. Then the end will result in the Self-Bringing Forth of Liberty.

But it took a Marx to see that, and only then could we talk about the whole person who is not just personality but Subjectivity—body, emotion, thought as a totality that is bound for a new journey: the absolute movement of becoming. It is this "power of abstraction" (that is Marx's phrase, not mine) that Marx introduced early in the very Preface of *Capital* on the most concrete thing of all, a commodity.[57] After introducing the "power of abstraction" in the very Preface of *Capital,* before ever the reader had plunged into that most difficult chapter I, he kept developing it further all the way to his very last decade.

Dialectics of Leadership
Our problem today is what is new in our concept of leadership? And what does it mean that this subjectivity alone contains the truth and with it subjectivity has absorbed objectivity? It is this new sense of objectivity—"Human

activity itself as *objective* (*gegenständliche*) activity," as Marx put it[58]—that our age is the first to understand fully; that is, the first to understand Marx's meaning in distinction from Hegel's. Just try to concretize that in *historic* terms and you will see what a hard and very nearly impossible task that is.

For example, when I first tackled the question of Hegel's meaning of subjectivity in that sentence,[59] I hardly went further than *class*, class distinction. I refer to the section on "Two Kinds of Subjectivity" in the new chapter on Mao added to *Marxism and Freedom* [in 1964].[60] Since that wasn't exactly what I meant, since what I was trying to bring in which was new was the distinction between two kinds of Marxism—Lenin's and Mao's—I didn't really "prove" [the idea] that you could consider yourself a Marxist and yet be so near the cliff that, by just the slightest deviation, you would fall right into the abyss of a new void.

I tried again in 1969 in ["The Newness of our Philosophic-Historic Contribution"], a letter to [a friend] who did not see the very deep gulf that existed between Herbert Marcuse and me.[61] That was good, but not yet good enough, as I was only on the threshold of Absolute Idea as *new* beginning . . .[62]

The double edge of the dialectic is that the very new birth which contains a new stage of production means the *perishing* of all previous stages, so that the new dialectic can start from new beginnings, new passions, new forces, new Reason. Do not follow any post-Marx Marxists. It is true that Lenin did return to Hegel on the dialectics of revolution. None can compare to him. But he stopped short on the question of the Party, and did not let us in on the process of his thinking . . . [63]

The Process—Becoming Practicing Dialecticians as One Projects Marxist-Humanism; New Type of Collectivities; New Concept of Leadership; the Absolute Method

> Absolute Method . . . [means] objectively universal . . . every beginning must be made from the Absolute. . . . The progress is therefore not a kind of overflow.
>
> —Hegel, *Science of Logic* [SLII, p. 471; SLM, p. 829]

> The concrete totality . . . is the beginning . . . for the transcendence of the opposition between the Notion and Reality, and that unity which is the truth, rest upon this subjectivity alone.
>
> —Hegel, *Science of Logic* [SLII, p. 477; SLM, p. 835]

The concrete problem today is organization and leadership; what you have to work out is how, at one and the same time, you cannot deviate from the principle and yet be open to all new, objective and subjective developments.

Consider Marx's "new moments" in his last decade along with the new moments grasped at turning points in his life, and here is what you will find when you think of Marx's Archives: 1) When Marx decides that the accumulation of capital is not the universal, he doesn't mean that it is not the universal in capitalism. He does mean that it is no universal for the *world*, and that the underdeveloped, non-capitalist countries can experience other forms of development. But even then he qualifies it by saying that they must do it together with what the advanced capitalist countries do.[64]

2) Marx's second conclusion in his final decade was that the revolution could actually take place first in backward Russia rather than in advanced Germany.

3) The *gens* form of development, he further concluded, is higher as a form of human life than class society, although the former, too, showed that, in embryo, class relations started right there.[65] And, most important of all, is that the multilinear human development demonstrates no straight line—i.e., no *fixed* stages of development. The Iroquois women, the Irish women before British imperialism, the aborigines in Australia, the Arabs in Africa, have displayed greater intelligence, more equality between men and women, than the intellectuals from England, or the United States or Australia, or France and Germany.

Interrupt yourself for a conference with Marx on the *Critique of the Gotha Program*, which includes the sentence that was so alive and worrisome to Marcuse in his last decade that he asked me what I made of that sentence on labor being "the prime necessity of life."[66] Here is Marx's whole paragraph:

> In a higher phase of communist society, after the enslaving subordination of the individual under the division of labor, and therewith also the antithesis between mental and physical labor, has vanished; after labor, from a mere means of life, has itself become the prime necessity of life; after the productive forces have also increased with the all-round development of the individual, and all the springs of cooperative wealth flow more abundantly—only then can the narrow horizon of bourgeois right be fully left behind and society inscribe on its banners: from each according to his ability, to each according to his needs. [MECW 24, p. 87]

Now let's look at the same *type* of new moments at other turning points of Marx's life, which opened new doors for him and which he, in turn, opened for a new generation. Take the artisans that Marx, in the *Grundrisse*, considered as having experienced a greater self-development and initiative, by working manually as well as mentally, than even those considered geniuses, like the artists.

Or turn back to when Marx first discovered that new continent of thought and of revolution and broke with capitalism in 1843 and called for "revolution in permanence," not only in order to uproot the old society, but to undergo a "revolution in permanence" in every facet, including self-development.

When it comes to taking responsibility for the philosophy of Marxist-Humanism in this age, when we are aiming for nothing short of actually helping to transform the objective international situation, here are the problems we face:

Why was it that the 1905 [Russian] Revolution, which certainly had international impact, made Lenin most conscious of Asia, but "Africa," at best, was thought of as "India"? All was the "Orient." If anyone thought of Egypt at all it was only because the Greeks were there and it was half "Mediterranean."

Why was it that Rosa Luxemburg, so far in advance of all other Marxists, so movingly described the [imperialist subjugation of the masses] in the Kalahari Desert, Morocco, Namibia, Martinique[67] but couldn't see them as Reason? Could it possibly be that all her love for, and dependence upon, the spontaneous unorganized masses who could "push" the leadership to act in a revolutionary way meant that even in that new love the vanguard concept was predominant for leadership?

Philosophy is both more than, and at the same time totally different from, "decision-making," in the crucial sense that decision-making, too, is a first negativity *unless* self-development of the individual means *all* individuals.

The sharpest expression of theory is *methodology*—and let's never forget that methodology is the result of a complex interaction of 1) social base; 2) theoretical analysis and practical activity; and 3) the struggles with rival tendencies and rival methodologies.

The point about all [the] concrete tasks outlined for this year (and some for next) is that they must be tested against the Absolute dialectical method. The question of the new book-to-be on "The Dialectics of the Party"[68] and, most important of all, the real historic-philosophic outline Marx sketched for future generations in his *Critique of the Gotha Program*, must be tested by the Absolute Method. Then we will be actually expressing what the dialectics of "the Party" as well as the dialectics of the revolution are leading to—a new, truly human society.

The interpenetration of philosophy, organization, self-development would result in humanity itself developing its full potential. The development of *all* human faculties assures the birth of a new man, a new woman, new youth, and of the classless, non-racist, non-sexist society.

NOTES

1. This essay was reprinted in *The Marxist-Humanist Theory of State-Capitalism*, pp. 109–13.

2. See "Where are the 1980s Going? The Imperative Need for a Totally New Direction in Uprooting Capitalism-Imperialism" (April 26, 1984), in *The Raya Dunayevskaya Collection*, p. 8174.

3. Followers of C. L. R. James.

4. "Labor and Society" was reprinted in *The Marxist-Humanist Theory of State-Capitalism*, pp. 17–24.

5. See Phillips and Dunayevskaya, *The Coal Miners' General Strike of 1949–50 and the Birth of Marxist-Humanism in the U. S.*

6. See "War and Peace" (September 1960), in *The Raya Dunayevskaya Collection*, p. 2789.

7. P.J. Posadas (Homero Cristali) was an Argentinean Trotskyist. For background on him, see Robert Alexander, *Trotskyism in Latin America* (Stanford: Hoover University Press, 1973), pp. 25–30.

8. See Luxemburg's "Stagnation and Progress in Marxism," *Gesammelte Werke* 1 (2) (Berlin: Dietz Verlag, 1974), pp. 363–68. Dunayevskaya discusses this essay in *Rosa Luxemburg, Women's Liberation, and Marx's Philosophy of Revolution*, pp. 118–19.

9. Mao Zedong, "Report on an Investigation of the Peasant Movement in Hunan" (February 1927), included in Brandt, Schwartz and Fairchild, *A Documentary History of Chinese Communism* (Cambridge: Harvard University Press, 1952).

10. For Dunayevskaya's writings on women in the Iranian Revolution, see especially "Iran: Unfoldment of and Contradictions in Revolution," in *Women's Liberation and the Dialectics of Revolution*, chapter 9.

11. *State-Capitalism and World Revolution*, by C. L. R. James, in collaboration with Raya Dunayevskaya and Grace Lee.

12. Antonio Gramsci, *Selections from the Prison Notebooks* (New York: International Publishers, 1971), p. 465.

13. Silvio Frondizi was an Argentinean Marxist theorist who corresponded with Dunayevskaya in the early 1960s while helping to translate *Marxism and Freedom*. He was murdered by Argentine fascists on September 27, 1974. For their correspondence, see *Women's Liberation and the Dialectics of Revolution*, pp. 163–72 and *The Raya Dunayevskaya Collection*, p. 10064.

14. See *The Raya Dunayevskaya Collection*, p. 2184.

15. This is quoted from the first Constitution of News and Letters Committees (1956). It can be found in *The Raya Dunayevskaya Collection*, p. 2587. Other examples of her writings on youth include *The Free Speech Movement and the Negro Revolution* (1965), by Mario Savio, Eugene Walker, and Dunayevskaya.

16. Galena, Illinois, which Melville visited, was famous for its lead mines.

17. *The Letters of Herman Melville*, edited by Merrell R. Davis and William H. Gilman (New Haven: Yale University Press, 1960), p. 79.

18. These points are developed in more detail in chapter 9 of *Philosophy and Revolution*.

19. In Sartre's *Critique of Dialectical Reason* (1960).

20. Claude Lévi-Strauss, "A Confrontation," *New Left Review* no. 62 (July-August 1970, orig. French edition 1963), p. 64. This statement was a response to a critique by Paul Ricoeur.

21. For an example of Dunayevskaya's philosophic correspondence with Denby, author of *Indignant Heart: a Black Workers' Journal*, see her letter to him, in chapter 6, above.

22. Sheng Wu-Lien is the Chinese acronym for "Hunan Provisional Proletarian Revolutionary Great Alliance Committee," a collection of some 20 organizations which arose in opposition to Mao's regime during the Cultural Revolution. Its manifesto "Whither China?" can be found in *The Revolution is Dead, Long Live the Revolution* (Hong Kong: The Seventies Group, n.d.).

23. The first Constitution adopted by the Chinese Communists after coming to power in 1949 designated China as "state-capitalist." The phrase was dropped in subsequent revisions of the Constitution. For Dunayevskaya's further discussion of this, see chapter 17 of *Marxism and Freedom*, "The Challenge of Mao Zedong."

24. The chapter is entitled "The Thought of Mao Zedong."

25. See also Dunayevskaya's "Critique of Althusser's Anti-Hegelianism," *News & Letters*, October 1969.

26. Dunayevskaya's speech on Marx's theory of alienation, given in Berkeley at the height of the Free Speech Movement and entitled "Marx's Debt to Hegel," can be found in *The Free Speech Movement and the Negro Revolution*.

27. Bettina Aptheker was at the time a member of the Communist Party USA.

28. A reference to Daniel Bell, *The End of Ideology* (Glencoe: The Free Press, 1960).

29. See Charles Denby, *Workers Battle Automation* (Detroit: News and Letters, 1960).

30. Chapter 9 of *Marxism and Freedom*, which deals with the Second International, is entitled "Organizational Interlude," and does not occupy a specific part of the book, coming in between parts 3 and 4. Chapter 4, "Worker and Intellectual at a Turning Point in History: 1848 to 1861," which deals with Marx's activity during and after the 1848 revolutions, constitutes the whole of part 2 of the book.

31. In the midst of the 1979 Iranian revolution, a group of youth issued a translation of chapter 4 of *Marxism and Freedom*.

32. The remainder of this essay discusses themes from Dunayevskaya's *Rosa Luxemburg, Women's Liberation, and Marx's Philosophy of Revolution*.

33. Part III of *Rosa Luxemburg, Women's Liberation, and Marx's Philosophy of Revolution* is entitled "Karl Marx—From Critic of Hegel to Author of *Capital* and Theorist of Revolution in Permanence." It contains a section of a chapter on the young Marx, "Prometheus Bound, 1841–43" (pp. 122–24).

34. See especially Adrienne Rich's review essay on this work and Dunayevskaya's other books, "Living the Revolution," *Women's Review of Books*, Vol. 3:12 (Sept. 1986), pp. 1, 3–4.

35. In the Preface to his *Elements of the Philosophy of Right* (Cambridge: Cambridge University Press, 1991, orig. 1820), Hegel wrote that "the owl of Minerva begins its flight only with the onset of dusk" (p. 23).

36. In his 1914–15 "Abstract of Hegel's *Science of Logic*," Lenin wrote: "Dialectics is the doctrine of the identity of opposites—how they can be and how they become identical, transforming one into the other—why the human mind must not take these opposites for dead, but for living, conditioned, mobile, transforming one into the other" [LCW 38, p. 109].

37. In his 1916 article "Imperialism and the Split in Socialism," Lenin wrote that part of the working class of the wealthy nations, the "labor aristocracy," was "bribed and corrupted" into loyalty to the capitalist system because it received a small part of the proceeds of the exploitation in the colonies "of Negroes, Indians, etc." [LCW 23, pp. 115–16].

38. Dunayevskaya's original 1940s analysis of the state-capitalist character of the Russian economy can be found in *The Marxist-Humanist Theory of State-Capitalism*.

39. See Phillips and Dunayevskaya, *The Miners' General Strike of 1949–50 and the Birth of Marxist-Humanism in the U.S.*

40. See p. 232, note 5.

41. In his 1844 "Private Property and Communism," Marx attacked "vulgar and unthinking communism" which "completely negates the human personality" and which "is only the logical expression of private property" [MECW 3, p. 295]. In *Marxism and Freedom* (1958), Dunayevskaya analyzes these writings, considering their vantage point to be sharply different from that of Russian Communist Party ideologues who "spend an incredible amount of time and energy and vigilance to imprison Marx within the bounds of the private property vs. state property concept" (p. 63).

42. In his 1882 Preface to a new Russian edition of the *Communist Manifesto*, Marx wrote: "If the Russian revolution becomes the signal for a proletarian revolution in the West, so that the two complement each other, then Russia's peasant communal land-ownership may serve as the point of departure for a communist development" [MECW 24, p. 426]. Dunayevskaya discussed Marx's last writings frequently in the 1980s. See especially chapter 12 of *Rosa Luxemburg, Women's Liberation, and Marx's Philosophy of Revolution*, "The Last Writings of Marx Point a Trail to the 1980s."

43. See especially Lenin's 1916 article, "A Caricature of Marxism and Imperialist Economism" [LCW 23, pp. 28–76].

44. Lenin used the formulation "half-way dialectic" to describe Luxemburg's position in his 1916 critique of her antiwar *Junius Pamphlet*. See LCW 19, p. 210.

45. Underconsumptionism holds that the root of capitalist crises is the lack of effective demand to buy the surplus product. For Dunayevskaya's critique of Luxemburg on this point, see chapter 3 of *Rosa Luxemburg, Women's Liberation, and Marx's Philosophy of Revolution*, "Marx's and Luxemburg's Theories of Accumulation of Capital, Its Crises and Its Inevitable Downfall."

46. The 1942 essay "Labor and Society" was reprinted in *The Marxist-Humanist Theory of State-Capitalism*. It was rejected for publication by the Trotskyist *The New International*.

47. In the sense of "post-Marx Marxists," not Marx's own writings.

48. This new edition of Denby's *Indignant Heart: A Black Workers' Journal* was first pub-

lished in 1978. The latest edition (Detroit: Wayne State University Press, 1989), contains an "In Memoriam" to Denby written by Dunayevskaya in 1983.

49. For Dunayevskaya's speech at this conference, see part IV, above.

50. See p. 233, note 15.

51. The sentence reads, "What distinguishes the newness and uniqueness of Women's Liberation in our age is the very nature of our epoch, which signified, at one and the same time, a new stage of production—Automation—and a new stage of cognition" (*Women's Liberation and the Dialectics of Revolution*, p. 1).

52. *Women's Liberation and the Dialectics of Revolution*, p. 15.

53. See *The Mathematical Manuscripts of Karl Marx*, trans. by C. Aronson and M. Meo (London: New Park, 1983) and also *The Fetish of High Tech and Karl Marx's Unknown Mathematical Manuscripts*.

54. For the reasons for this change of title, see her "Talking to Myself" of May 19, 1987, in *Supplement to the Raya Dunayevskaya Collection*, p. 10942.

55. See for example *Marxism and Freedom*, where Dunayevskaya wrote: "Marx attacks Hegel, not for seeing development *through* contradiction, but for seeing this process of development *and yet* making it a question of 'Absolute knowledge' instead of a question of the new society which the revolutionary practice of the proletariat—not some abstract absolute negativity—would bring about" (p. 57).

56. In the *Science of Logic*, Hegel writes of the negation of the negation: "the transcendence of the opposition between Notion and reality, and that unity which is the truth, rest upon this subjectivity alone" [SLII, p. 477; SLM, p. 835].

57. Marx's phrase reads, "In the analysis of economic forms neither microscopes nor chemical reagents are of assistance. The power of abstraction must replace both" [MCIF, p. 90, MCIK, p. 12].

58. See Marx's "Theses on Feuerbach" [MECW 5, p. 3].

59. See note 56, above.

60. See p. 157, note 9.

61. Reprinted in part III, above.

62. Ellipsis in original.

63. Ellipsis in original.

64. See p. 316, note 42.

65. In "primitive" societies such as the Iroquois, as discussed in Marx's *Ethnological Notebooks* (1880–82).

66. Dunayevskaya recounts this 1978 conversation with Marcuse in her "In Memoriam" article, "Herbert Marcuse, Marxist Philosopher," *International Society for the Sociology of Knowledge Newsletter*, Vol. 5:2 (1979), pp. 10–11, included in *The Raya Dunayevskaya Collection*, pp. 5985–5997.

67. In her *Accumulation of Capital* (1913) and elsewhere.

68. Dunayevskaya subsequently changed the title of her planned book to "Dialectics of Organization and Philosophy." See also note 54, above.

~

CHAPTER SIXTEEN

Another Look at Hegel's
Phenomenology of Mind

As Dunayevskaya continued her exploration of the dialectic in the course of working on her planned book on "Dialectics of Organization and Philosophy," she turned, in the summer and fall of 1986, to a reexamination of Hegel's Phenomenology of Mind. *Though her work on this was cut short by her death on June 9, 1987, the following two selections indicate the direction of her reexamination of Hegel's Phenomenology. The first was a letter written to an Iranian colleague on June 26, 1986, excerpts of which appear here;[1] the original can be found in the* Supplement to the Raya Dunayevskaya Collection, *p. 10769. The second is an Introduction to a republication in* News & Letters, *May 8, 1987, of her 1960 Notes on Hegel's Phenomenology, the text of which appears in part II of this volume.*

Letter on Hegel's *Phenomenology of Mind*
(June 26, 1986)

Let me tell you some of the past from a faraway age—and I'm not talking so much about Marx (much less Marxist-Humanism), but about Hegel. Why do you suppose academics to this day refer to *Phenomenology of Mind* as "chaotic," "very brilliant and profound in spots," but definitely "Hegel didn't know where he was headed"; that he didn't even have subheads once he came to "Spirit"?

It was because he didn't have the categories worked out systematically as they were in *Science of Logic*, where it was nice and smooth and they took for granted they understood it; they certainly could repeat the categories; indeed, though it took them all the way until 1929 (having rejected the translation that was done in America by the Hegelians in St. Louis) before they published an English translation, they then appended a long and precise list of categories—128 to be exact—so that anyone can repeat them if they can memorize 128 names.[2]

We have yet to get any *serious*, full explanation of why there has been no reference to the fact that the year before Hegel died, he felt that he should add the three final syllogisms to the Absolute Mind. Do you know why that is? I'll tell you why. It is *because* we haven't understood that *Phenomenology of Mind* (1807, not 1830) projected *ground* for the Absolutes, and they haven't understood that *ground* because it was the *French Revolution*. And Hegel was saying very passionately: "Look at what happened in France, and we haven't even developed a single dialectical category, and we are talking philosophy time and time again."[3] The whole philosophy of 2,500 years has to find a new language, and here it is. Academics had no vision then and they have no vision now. The whole truth is that between 1807 and 1831 (death) it was a matter of developing that movement, *historic* movement, and that vision Marx alone saw. And he saw it because he was in a new age and needed a new language to express the forces and the Reason of Revolution [as] both *continuity* and *discontinuity* of the dialectic and of the new European Revolutions (1840s). That is why a serious Introduction is really always written at the end and is at the same time an Overview, which is what Marx was doing from 1843 to 1883.

Introduction to "Why Hegel's *Phenomenology*? Why Now?"

> The Spirit of the time, growing slowly and quietly ripe for the new form it is to assume, disintegrates one fragment after another of the structure of its previous world. That it is tottering to fall is indicated only by symptoms here and there. Frivolity and again ennui, which are spreading in the established order of things, the undefined foreboding of something unknown—all these betoken that there is something else approaching. This gradual crumbling to pieces, which did not alter the general look and aspect of the whole, is interrupted by the sunrise, which, in a flash and at a single stroke, brings to view the form and structure of the new world.
>
> —Hegel, Preface to the *Phenomenology of Mind*
> [PhGB, p. 75; PhGM, pp. 6–7]

The most difficult of all tasks that have confronted every generation of Marxists is to work out Marx's Marxism for its age; the task has never been more difficult than the one that confronts the decade of the 1980s. We often like to quote that creatively great statement of Hegel about the "birth-time of History" [PhGB, p. 75; PhGM, p. 6]. What is important to see is that the same paragraph that talks of the birth-time of history and a period of transition is likewise one that speaks about the period of darkness before the dawn.

That is what we all have had to suffer through—the darkness before the dawn. Hegel articulated both the darkness and the dawn in the very same paragraph lucidly enough. Yet, because this appears in the Preface to the *Phenomenology of Mind*, it looks as if it were written in anticipation of the book, whereas, in truth, the Preface was written *after* the whole work was completed; thus, we do not realize that the contradictory unity first became that translucent *after* the work was completed.

It never fails that, at momentous world historic turning points, it is very difficult to tell the difference between two types of twilight—whether one is first plunging into utter darkness or whether one has reached the end of a long night and is just at the moment before the dawn of a new day. In either case, the challenge to find the meaning—what Hegel called "the undefined foreboding of something unknown"—becomes a compulsion to dig for new beginnings, for a philosophy that would try to answer the question "where to begin?" This was the reason for a new revolutionary philosophy—the birth of the Hegelian dialectic—at the time the great French Revolution did not produce totally new beginnings in philosophy. It caused Hegel's break with romanticism. His deep digging went, at one and the same time, backward to the origins of philosophy in Greece around 500 BC and forward as the French Revolution was followed by the Napoleonic era trying to dominate all of Europe.

In a word, the crucible of history shows that the forces of actual revolution producing revolutions in philosophy recur at historic turning points. Thus in the 1840s, with the rise of a totally new revolutionary class—the "wretched of the earth,"[4] the proletariat—Marx transformed Hegel's revolution in philosophy into a philosophy *of* revolution. This founding of a new continent of thought and of revolution unchained the Hegelian dialectic, which Marx called "revolution in permanence."

Just as the shock of the simultaneity of the outbreak of World War I, and the collapse of established Marxism (the Second International) compelled Lenin to turn to Marx's deep-rootedness in the Hegelian Dialectic,* so it has become imperative to find that missing link of a philosophy of revolution in the post-World War II world.

A whole new world—a Third World—has been born. Just as the East European revolutionaries rose up against Communist totalitarianism from within

---

*See "Lenin and the Dialectic: A Mind in Action" and "The Irish Revolution and the Dialectic of History" in Part IV—"World War I and the Great Divide in Marxism"—of my *Marxism and Freedom, from 1776 until Today*.

that orbit, so the Third World arose against Western imperialism. This movement from practice that is itself a form of theory has been digging for ways to put an end to the separation between theory and practice. It is this movement that has rediscovered Marx's early Humanist Essays, as well as the work of his final decade where Marx predicted, in his studies of pre-capitalist societies, that a revolution could come first in a technologically backward land rather than in the technologically advanced West. It has had to struggle under the whip of counter-revolution in a nuclearly-armed world.

Nowhere has this been more onerous than in the 1980s under the Reagan retrogressionism, which has been bent on turning the clock backward—whether that be on civil rights, labor, women's liberation, youth and education, or children. At the same time that there is this ideological pollution and the revolutionary struggle against it, even some bourgeois Hegel scholars who opposed the "subversion" of Hegel by Marx and by today's Marxist-Humanists have had to admit: "If Hegel has not literally been to the barricades of strife-ridden cities, or explosive rural focos, he has been in the thick of current ideological combat."[†]

In its way, this, too, will help illuminate why we are publishing "Why Hegel's *Phenomenology*? Why Now?" It will have two parts. What follows, as part I, is a study of Hegel's first (and what Marx considered his most creative) work, *Phenomenology of Mind* (*Geist*), written as Lecture Notes for a class I gave on the *Phenomenology* in the 1960s.[5] Part II, which will follow in the near future, will be an essay on the Hegelian Dialectic as Marx critiqued it in his *Humanist Essays* in 1844 and continued to develop it throughout his life.[6] This is seen most clearly in Marx's greatest theoretical work, *Capital*, especially in the final section of chapter 1, which Marx expanded on the "Fetishism of Commodities," in his last decade. It is there that a citation of what first appeared in Marx's 1841 Doctoral Thesis reveals Marx's continued deep-rootedness in Hegel.[7]

NOTES

1. This letter was written to the historian Janet Afary, author of *The Iranian Constitutional Revolution, 1906–11* (New York: Columbia University Press, 1996).

2. This "Table of Categories" is found in the Johnston and Struthers translation of the *Science of Logic* (New York: Macmillan, 1929).

3. See p. 209, note 7.

[†]See George Armstrong Kelly's *Hegel's Retreat from Eleusis* [Princeton: Princeton University Press, 1978], p. 224, and my answer to his critique of my *Philosophy and Revolution: From Hegel to Sartre and from Marx to Mao* in the new Introduction I wrote for the 1982 edition.

4. This phrase is taken from the revolutionary hymn, "The Internationale," composed in 1871 by the Paris Communard Eugène Pottier.

5. For this study, see part II, above.

6. Dunayevskaya did not live to complete her part II of "Why *Phenomenology*? Why Now?" She did write a rough draft of it, entitled "Why *Phenomenology*? Why Now? What is the Relationship either to Organization, or to Philosophy, not Party, 1984–87?" It can be found in the *Supplement to the Raya Dunayevskaya Collection*, pp. 10883–90.

7. In the section on the "Fetishism of Commodities" in chapter 1 of *Capital*, Marx refers to Epicurus, the subject of his doctoral dissertation of 1841.

~

CHAPTER SEVENTEEN

Reconsidering the Dialectic: Critiquing Lenin . . . and the Dialectics of Philosophy and Organization

The following letters, written to two non-Marxist Hegel scholars—Louis Dupré and George Armstrong Kelly¹—were considered by Dunayevskaya to be of central importance for the work she had by then entitled,"Dialectics of Organization and Philosophy: The 'Party' and Forms of Organization Born out of Spontaneity." The first letter, written on July 3, 1986 to Dupré, projects a "changed perception" of Lenin's Philosophical Notebooks of 1914–15, in light of her rereading of the chapters on the "Idea of Cognition" and the "Absolute Idea" in Hegel's Science of Logic. The second letter, written on December 8, 1986 to George Armstrong Kelly, focuses on the chapter on "The Third Attitude of Thought Toward Objectivity" in Hegel's Smaller Logic in light of the problem of organization. In other writings during this period Dunayevskaya indicated that it was important to consider these two letters as a unit. The originals can be found in the Supplement to the Raya Dunayevskaya Collection, pp. 11216 and 11228.

As Dunayevskaya continued her work on "Dialectics of Organization and Philosophy," she turned anew to her 1953 "Letters on Hegel's Absolutes" and found that they spoke very directly to what she was then trying to work out concerning the dialectical relation between philosophy and organization. The following selection, which she called "Talking to Myself," represents a reexamination of her letter of May 12, 1953, on Hegel's Science of Logic, as well as a consideration of how differences over the question of "dialectics of organization" and developments in the political situation led, ultimately, to the breakup of the Johnson-Forest Tendency in

1955. It was circulated among her colleagues shortly after it was written. The original can be found in the Supplement to the Raya Dunayevskaya Collection, *p. 10848.*

Her essay, "On Political Divides and Philosophic New Beginnings," written on June 5, 1987, is the last writing from the pen of Dunayevskaya, who died on June 9. Written as one of her regular "Theory/Practice" columns, it further develops her new perceptions on Lenin's philosophic ambivalence in terms of its impact on the dialectics of organization. It also returns to discuss, on new ground, many of the philosophic themes addressed by her in the early 1980s, following the publication of Rosa Luxemburg, Women's Liberation, and Marx's Philosophy of Revolution. *It was first published in the In Memoriam special issue of* News & Letters, *on July 25, 1987.*

Letter to Louis Dupré

Dear Louis Dupré:

Suddenly I remembered when we first met at Yale University, where I talked on *Philosophy and Revolution*. We continued the dialogue after the formal talk. I believe it set the ground for my paper on "Hegel's Absolute Idea as New Beginning," which was accepted for the 1974 Hegel Society of America conference.[2] Don't you think that in a way we have had a continuing dialogue since? At any rate, I consider you a *very* good friend. I hope you agree. Or do you think that the sharpness of my critique of Hegel scholars who are non-Marxists goes beyond their critique of Marxism? I seem always to get friends—Marxist as well as non-Marxist—who consider me a friendly enemy rather than a friend. That friendly enemy relationship continued, for example, with Herbert Marcuse for three long decades, and we still never agreed, specifically on the Absolutes. That's where I want to appeal to you, even though we do not have the same interpretation either.

Along with the battle I'm currently having with myself on the Absolutes (and I've had this battle ever since 1953, when I first "defined" the Absolute as the new society),[3] I am now changing my attitude to Lenin—specifically on chapter 2 of section 3 of [the Doctrine of the Notion in] the *Science of Logic*, "The Idea of Cognition." The debate I'm having with myself centers on the different ways Hegel writes on the Idea of Cognition in the *Science of Logic* (hereafter referred to as *Science*), and the way it is expressed in his *Encyclopedia* (Smaller *Logic*), ¶225–35, with focus on ¶233–35. The fact that the smaller *Logic* does the same type of abbreviation with the Absolute Idea as it does with the Idea of Cognition, turning that magnificent and most profound chapter of the *Science* into ¶236–44, and that ¶244 in the Smaller Logic was the one Lenin preferred* to the final paragraph of the Absolute Idea in the *Science*, has had me "debating" Lenin ever since 1953. That year may seem far away, but its essence, without the polemics, you actually heard at the 1974 Hegel Society of America conference.

Whether or not Lenin had a right to "misread" the difference in Hegel's two articulations in the *Science* and in the smaller *Logic*, isn't it true that Hegel, by creating the subsection β, "Volition," which does not appear in the *Science*, left open the door for a future generation of Marxists to become so enthralled with chapter 2, "The Idea of Cognition"—which ended with the pronouncement that Practice was higher than Theory—that they saw an identity of the two versions? These Marxists weren't Kantians believing that all contradictions will be solved by actions of "men of good will."

There is no reason, I think, for introducing a new subheading which lets Marxists think that now that practice is "higher" than theory, and that "will," not as willfulness, but as action, is their province, they do not need to study Hegel further.

Please bear with me as I go through Lenin's interpretation of that chapter with focus on this subsection, so that we know precisely what is at issue. Indeed, when I began my talking to myself in 1953, objecting to Lenin's dismissal of the last half of the final paragraph of the Absolute Idea in the *Science* as "unimportant," preferring ¶244 of the smaller *Logic*—"go forth freely as Nature"—I explained that Lenin could have said that because he hadn't suffered through Stalinism. I was happy that there was one Marxist revolutionary who had dug into Hegel's Absolute Idea.

Now then, when Lenin seemed to have completed his *Abstract*, and writes "End of the *Logic*. 12/17/1914" [LCW 38, p. 233], he doesn't really end. At the end of that he refers you to the fact that he ended his study of the *Science* with ¶244 of the smaller *Logic*—and he means it. Clearly, it wasn't only the last half of a paragraph of the Absolute Idea in the *Science of Logic* that Lenin dismissed. The truth is that Lenin had begun seriously to consult the Smaller *Logic* at the section on the Idea, which begins in the Smaller *Logic* with ¶213. When Lenin completed chapter 2, the "Idea of Cognition," he didn't really go to chapter 3, "The Absolute Idea," but first proceeded for seven pages with his own "translation" (interpretation). This is on pp. 212–19 of Vol. 38 of his *Collected Works*.

---

*All the references to Lenin are to his "Abstract of Hegel's *Science of Logic*," as included in Vol. 38 of his *Collected Works*, pp. 87–238. Concretely the subject under dispute here is on the Doctrine of the Notion, Section Three, chaps. 2 and 3, "The Idea of Cognition" and the "Absolute Idea."

Lenin there divided each page into two. One side, he called "Practice in the theory of Knowledge"; on the other side, he wrote: "Alias, Man's consciousness not only reflects the objective world, but creates it." I was so enamored with his "Hegelianism" that I never stopped repeating it. Presently, however, I'm paying a great deal more attention to what he did in that division of the page into two, with these "translations." Thus: 1) "Notion=Man"; 2) "Otherness which is in itself=Nature independent of man"; 3) "Absolute Idea=objective truth." When Lenin reaches the final section of chapter 2, "The Idea of the Good," he writes, "end of chapter 2, transition to chapter 3, 'The Absolute Idea.'" But I consider that he is still only on the *threshold* of the Absolute Idea. Indeed, all that follows p. 219 in his Notes shows that to be true, and explains why Lenin proceeded on his own after the end of his Notes on the Absolute Idea, and returned to the Smaller Logic.

Thus when Lenin writes that he had reached the end of the Absolute Idea and quotes ¶244 as the true end, because it is "objective," he proceeds to the Smaller *Logic* and reaches ¶244, to which he had already referred.

Although he continued his commentaries as he was reading and quoting Absolute Idea from the *Science*, it was not either Absolute Idea or Absolute Method that his 16-point definition of the dialectic ends on: "15) the struggle of content with form and conversely. The throwing off of the form, the transformation of the content. 16) the transition of quantity into quality and vice versa. (15 and 16 are examples of 9)" [LCW 38, p. 222]. No wonder the preceding point 14 referred to absolute negativity as if it were only "the apparent return to the old (negation of the negation)."

Outside of Marx himself, the whole question of the negation of the negation was ignored by all "orthodox Marxists." Or worse, it was made into a vulgar materialism, as with Stalin, who denied that it was a fundamental law of dialectics. Here, specifically, we see the case of Lenin, who *had* gone back to Hegel, and *had* stressed that it was impossible to understand *Capital*, especially its first chapter, without reading the *whole* of the *Science*, and yet the whole point that Hegel was developing on unresolved contradiction, of "two worlds in opposition, one a realm of subjectivity in the pure regions of transparent thought, the other a realm of objectivity in the element of an externally manifold actuality that is an undisclosed realm of darkness" (SLII, p. 462; SLM, p. 820), did not faze Lenin because he felt that the objective, the Practical Idea, is that resolution. Nor was he fazed by the fact that Hegel had said that "the complete elaboration of the unresolved contradiction between the *absolute* end and the limitation of this actuality that *insuperably* opposes it has been considered in detail in the *Phenomenology of Mind*" (The reference is to pp. 611ff. of the *Phenomenology*, Baillie translation [pp. 363 ff. in the Miller translation].)

In the original German the above sentence reads: "Die vollständige Aus-bildung des unaufgelösten Widerspruchs, jenes *absoluten* Zwecks, dem die Schranke dieser Wirklichkeit unüberwindlich gegenübersteht, ist in der *Phänomenologie des Geistes* (2 Aufl., S. 453ff)."

Nothing, in fact, led Lenin back to the Idea of Theory and away from dependence on the Practical Idea, not even when Hegel writes: "The practi-cal Idea still lacks the moment of the Theoretical Idea. . . . For the practical Idea, on the contrary, this actuality, which at the same time confronts it as an insuperable limitation, ranks as something intrinsically worthless that must first receive its true determination and sole worth through the end of the good. Hence it is only the will itself that stands in the way of the attainment of its goal, for it separates itself from cognition, and external reality for the will does not receive the form of a true being; the Idea of the good therefore finds its integration only in the Idea of the true" [SLII, p. 463; SLM, p. 821].

In German this sentence reads: "Der praktischen Idee dagegen gilt diese Wirklichkeit, die ihr zugleich als unüberwindliche Schranke gegenübersteht, als das an und für sich Nichtige, das erst seine wahrhafte Bestimmung und einzigen Wert durch die Zwecke das Guten erhalten solle. Der Wille steht daher der Erreichung seines Ziels nur selbst im Wege dadurch, dass er sich von dem Erkennen trennt und die aüsserliche Wirklichkeit für ihn nicht die Form das wahrhaft Seienden erhält: die Idee des Guten kann daher ihre Ergänzung allein in der Idee des Wahren finden."

I'm certainly not blaming Hegel for what "orthodox Marxists" have done to Hegel's dialectic, but I still want to know a non-Marxist Hegelian's view-point on the difference of the two articulations on the Idea of Cognition and the Absolute Idea in the *Science* and in the smaller *Logic*. What is your view?

To follow out this question we need, in one respect, another journey back in time—to 1953 when, in parting from Lenin on the vanguard party, I had delved into the three final syllogisms of the *Philosophy of Mind*. You may remember that in my paper to the Hegel Society of America in 1974, where I critique Adorno's *Negative Dialectics*—which I called "one-dimensionality of thought"—I said that he had substituted "a permanent critique not alone for absolute negativity, but also for 'permanent revolution' itself." I had become so enamored with Hegel's three final syllogisms [to his *Philosophy of Mind*] that I was searching all over the "West" for dialogue on them.

Finally, in the 1970s, after Reinhart Klemens Maurer had published his *Hegel und das Ende der Geschichte*, which took up those final syllogisms, I tried to get him involved, his sharp critique of Marcuse notwithstanding.[4] Maurer was anxious to establish the fact, however, that he was not only non-Marxist, but not wholly "Hegelian." In any case, he clearly was not interested in any dialogue with me, and he told a young colleague of mine[5] who went to see him that "I am not married to Hegel." But as I made clear at the 1974 Hegel Society of America conference, I do not think it important whether someone has written a serious new study of those final three syllogisms because of a new stage of scholarship, or because the "movement of freedom surged up from below and was followed by new cognition studies."

The point is that as late as the late 1970s, A. V. Miller wrote me calling my attention to the fact that he had not corrected an error in [William] Wallace's translation of ¶575 of the *Philosophy of Mind*.[6] He pointed out that Wallace had translated *sie* as if it were *sich*, whereas in fact it should have read "sunders" not *itself*, but *them*.[7] That, however, was not my problem. The sundering was what was crucial to me; the fact that Nature turns out to be the mediation was certainly no problem to any "materialist"; the form of the transition which was departing from the course of necessity was the exciting part.

In introducing those three syllogisms in 1830, Hegel first (¶575) poses the structure of the *Encyclopedia* merely factually—Logic-Nature-Mind. It should have been obvious (but obviously was not) that it is not Logic but Nature which is the mediation.

¶576 was the real leap as the syllogism was the standpoint of Mind itself. In the early 1950s I had never stopped quoting the end of that paragraph: "Philosophy appears as subjective cognition, of which liberty is the aim, and which is itself the way to produce it." It justified my happiness at Hegel's magnificent critique of the concept of One in the Hindu religion, which he called both "featureless unity of abstract thought," and its extreme opposite, "long-winded weary story of its particular detail" (¶573). In the following ¶574 we face Hegel's counterposition of what I consider his most profound historic concept—and by history I mean not only past, or even history-in-the-making, the present, but as future—"SELF-THINKING IDEA."

My "labor, patience, and suffering of the negative"[8] those 33 years hasn't exactly earned me applause either from the post-Marx Marxists, or from the Hegelians, who are busy calling to my attention that the final syllogism (¶577) speaks about the "eternal Idea," "eternally setting itself to work, engenders and enjoys itself as absolute mind," fairly disregarding what is just a phrase in that sentence: "It is the nature of the fact, which causes the movement and development, yet this same movement is equally the action of cognition."

It is here that I'm in need of your commentary both on Absolute Idea in the *Science of Logic* and on Absolute Mind in the *Philosophy of Mind*. The "eternal Idea" to me is not eternality, but ceaseless motion, the movement itself. Far from me "subverting" Hegel, it is Hegel who made Absolute Method the "self-thinking Idea." George Armstrong Kelly, in his book *Hegel's Retreat from Eleusis*, said that "for the complex linkage of culture, politics and philosophy within the matrix of the 'Absolute Idea,' Mme. Dunayevskaya proposes to substitute an unchained dialectic which she baptizes 'Absolute Method,' a method that 'becomes irresistible . . . because our hunger for theory arises from the totality of the present global crisis'" [p. 239].[9]

The "eternal Idea" in the *Philosophy of Mind* not only reinforced my view of Absolute Method in the *Science of Logic*, but now that I am digging into another subject for my work on "Dialectics of Organization," which will take sharp issue with Lenin, both on the Idea of Cognition and on the Absolute Idea, I consider that Marx's concept of "revolution in permanence" is the "eternal Idea."

Letter to George Armstrong Kelly

Dear GAK:

Despite the acknowledged gulf between us on the Absolute Method, may I discuss with you (and may I hope for a comment from you?) my latest self-critique on organization? On that question I also see Hegel in a new way. That is to say, the dialectical relationship of principles (in this case the Christian doctrine) and the organization (the Church) are analyzed as if they were inseparables. All this occurs not in the context of a philosophy of religion as much as in the context of the great dividing line between himself and all other philosophers that he initiated with the *Phenomenology of Mind*, on the relationship of objectivity/subjectivity, immediacy/mediation, particular/universal, history, and the "Eternal." This addition to the [Smaller] *Logic*—the Third Attitude to Objectivity—I see in a totally new way.

I can't hide, of course, that though it's not the Absolute, I'm enamored with that early section of the *Encyclopedia* outline of the *Logic*, because it was written *after* Hegel had already developed Absolute Knowledge, Absolute Idea, Absolute Method.

Here history makes its presence felt, by no accident after the Absolutes both in the *Phenomenology* and in the *Science of Logic*, as well as in anticipation that he is finally developing the *Philosophy of Nature* and the *Philosophy of Mind*. Indeed, that to me is what made possible the very form of compression of those innumerable polemical observations on other philosophers and philosophies into just three attitudes to objectivity.

This time, as we know, a single attitude, the First [Attitude], embraces everything preceding the modern age. Further emphasis on this compression is evident when Hegel comes to the modern age and includes both empiricism and criticism in the Second Attitude.

My attraction to the Third Attitude was not due to the fact that it was directed against those who placed faith above philosophy—the Intuitionalists. (I'm not renewing our old debate, just because I'm an atheist; atheism, to me, is one more form of godliness, without God.) Rather, the attraction for me continued to be the dialectic. Far from expressing a sequence of never-ending progression, the Hegelian dialectic lets retrogression appear as translucent as progression and indeed makes it very nearly inevitable *if* one ever tries to escape regression by mere faith.

Here again, history enters, this time to let Hegel create varying views of Intuitionalism, depending on which historic period is at issue. Intuitionalism is "progressive" in the period of Descartes because then empiricism opened the doors wide to science. On the other hand, it became regressive in the period of Jacobi.

It is here that I saw a different concept of organization when it comes to the Church than in all of Hegel's many oppositions to the clergy's dominance in academia. Do please follow my strange journeys that I identify as the self-determination of the Idea.

The Third Attitude begins (¶61) with a critique of Kant, whose universality was abstract so that Reason appeared hardly more than a conclusion with "the categories left out of account." Equally wrong, Hegel continues, is the "extreme theory on the opposite side, which holds thought to be an act of the *particular* only, and on that ground declares it incapable of apprehending the Truth."

In praising Descartes, Hegel points not only to the fact that empiricism opened the door to science, but that Descartes clearly knew that his famous "Cogito ergo sum" wasn't a syllogism, simply because it had the word "therefore" in it.[10] This becomes important because Hegel's critique could then be directed against the one-sidedness of the Intuitionalists, for equating mind to mere consciousness, and thus "what I discover in my consciousness is thus exaggerated into a fact of consciousness of all, and even passed off for the very nature of mind" (¶71). That too is by no means the whole of the critique. What excited me most about this attitude to objectivity is the manner in which Hegel brings in organization. As early as ¶63 Hegel had lashed out against Jacobi's faith, in contrast to Faith: "The two things are radically distinct. Firstly, the Christian faith comprises in it an authority of the Church; but the faith of Jacobi's philosophy has no other authority than that of personal revelation." As we see, Hegel now has suddenly equated organization to principle, doctrine: "And secondly, the Christian faith is a copious body of objective truth, a system of knowledge and doctrine; while the scope of the philosophic faith is so utterly indefinite, that, while it has room for faith of the Christian, it equally admits belief in the divinity of the Dalai Lama, the ox, or the monkey."

Hegel proceeds (¶75) "And to show that in point of fact there is a knowledge which advances neither by unmixed immediacy nor unmixed mediation, we can point to the example of the Logic and the whole of philosophy."

In a word, we're back at the Dialectic and it's only after that (¶76) that Hegel uses the word "reactionary" in relationship to the whole school of Jacobi, that is to the historic period, "The Recent German Philosophy." "Philosophy of course tolerates no mere assertions or conceits, and checks the free play of argumentative see-saw" (¶77). Freedom and Revolution (which word I "borrowed" from Hegel's very first sentence on "The Recent German Philosophy")[11] will hew out a new path. In this way I see the dialectic flow in the third attitude to objectivity from a critique of the one-sidedness of the Intuitionalists to organizational responsibility.

Talking to Myself

The above title may sound strange but it is one way in which I make notes for future development, not only on the book-to-be on organization, but in all of my works when I have not yet worked out a definitive form in which to present the issue. The focus is on the May 12, 1953, Letter on the Absolute Idea. The point is to catch the dialectical flow of the self-determination of the Idea, paragraph by paragraph.

Page 21[12] [of the Letter of May 12, 1953] calls attention to p. 483 of the *Science of Logic* [SLII, p. 483; SLM, pp. 840–41], which shows how the stage of "exteriorization" is also that of intensification, i.e., "interiorization," i.e., *objective* manifestation makes the inward extension more intense.

The paragraph on p. 21, which attacks impatience in "*an absolutely uncompromising Bolshevik*" manner, I attribute to Hegel, after which I quote from p. 484 of the *Science of Logic* [SLII, p. 484; SLM, pp. 841–42]:

> That impatience whose only wish is to go beyond the determinant . . . to be immediately in the absolute, has nothing before it as object of its cognition but the empty negative . . . or else would-be absolute, which is imaginary because it is neither posited nor comprehended.

The dialectic flow of this quotation is in no way related to the two names quoted in the preceding paragraph of the letter, but even if said unconsciously, has everything to do with what I follow the Hegel quotation with:

> I am shaking all over for we have come to *where we part from Lenin*. I mentioned that, although in the *approach* to the Absolute Idea Lenin had mentioned that man's cognition not only reflects the objective world but creates it, but that *within*

the chapter he never developed it. Objective world connections, materialism, dialectical materialism, it is true, but not the object and subject as one fully developed.

Stop for a moment. Hold tightly to the fact that ever since 1948–49, when I first translated Lenin's Abstract of the *Science of Logic,* I have done nothing less than extol Lenin philosophically, specifically on the *Science of Logic.* There is no question about the fact that it was Lenin who created the great divide in Marxism in 1914–17. Our present *changed* perception of Lenin's philosophic ambivalence shows here that I actually did have some philosophic differences as far back as the early 1950s.

The fact is that it was not only Lenin who, by keeping the *Philosophic Notebooks* to himself, separated philosophy from politics. When we broke politically with the concept of the vanguard party, we kept philosophy and politics in two separate compartments.[13] What this 1953 Letter shows now is that embedded in it was a sharper critique of Lenin's philosophic ambivalence than shown in *Marxism and Freedom.* In 1953, on the other hand, as we saw above, I had stressed that in the chapter on The Idea of Cognition Lenin had not concretized the *objectivity* of cognition.

Here I wish to introduce something totally new . . . a letter to me from Grace Lee dated August 31, 1952. With her usual hyperbole, here is part of what she wrote me:

> You have mastered Hegel. You write in your letter of August 29 as you have never written before. Instead of that one-to-one correspondence where you impose a movement on the *Logic,* you are now inside the movement of the *Logic,* caught up in its rhythms. The number of people in the world who can do that can probably be counted on the fingers of one hand. You are absolutely right in characterizing Herman's (Johnny Zupan)[14] search for the party as the Logic of the "Idea of the Good"—which stands in its own way and hence must in the end turn against itself.

We haven't found my letter of August 29, 1952, which produced that enthusiasm a year before I broke through on the Absolute, but it is clear from what she said on August 31 that I had evidently been writing on the penultimate chapter from the *Science of Logic,* "The Idea of Cognition." She further points to that specific chapter because, very clearly, I had been relating the [chapter on the] Idea of Cognition to the concept of organization. What was facing the Johnson-Forest Tendency now that it finally broke fully with Trotskyism was the question: What kind of organization now? This took a most ominous turn as I was coming to a break with Johnsonism, 1950–53.

The specific objective event that precipitated the crisis in 1953 was Stalin's death.[†]

In March 1953 I felt very strongly that an incubus had been lifted from the heads of the Russian and East European masses (evidently also from my head) and that revolts were sure to happen. It was a very exciting day in Detroit, both because the Black production worker Charles Denby, and the head of the Youth, Ben, had independently thought that, no doubt, I wished to write a political estimate of that world-shaking event; they volunteered to work with me all night. When Denby appeared after his day at Chrysler he concretized this further, laughing jubilantly and saying that what all the workers were talking about, as the radio blared forth the news of Stalin's death, was: "I've got just the person to take his place—my foreman." Denby asked if I had that article I was always talking about on the great trade union debate between Lenin and Trotsky in 1920 (on which I had been working since the 1940s). Denby felt that the workers would now welcome such a revelation; he wished to distribute it to them.[15]

Think of the unpleasant shock that then occurred when Grace, who was in California and the responsible editor for the issue of the mimeographed *Correspondence*, felt that the Lead article could not be on Stalin's death, but on the "new" women around Selma [James] who disregarded the blare from the radio announcing Stalin's death. Instead, they were exchanging recipes for hamburgers. Not only was that idiotic suggestion floated, but she undertook to censor my analysis on the significance of Stalin's death, so that it too sounded not so world-shaking. Such an attitude toward a world event produced such a struggle between me and Grace, that it actually affected the whole Johnson-Forest Tendency.[16]

What was C. L. R. James's "solution" to the crisis created by the different attitudes, both to Stalin's death and to the tasks of a Marxist newspaper? It was typically Jamesian: I was judged to be "politically" right, but nevertheless totally wrong because of my sharp attack on Grace. Grace was judged to be "politically" wrong, but absolutely right because she listened to the "new." After two months of this type of meaningless, diversionary, empty "solution"

[†]The same type of crisis as occurred in March-April 1953 over the Johnson-Forest Tendency's attitude to Stalin's death recurred with the first issue of *Correspondence* on October 3, 1953, for which I had written the lead on the Beria Purge. Reexamining this in 1987, I realize that what looks like the "Russian Question"—that same old "Russian Question" which caused the first break with Trotskyism at the approach of World War II and reoccurred in 1950 on the Korean War—far from being on the "Russian Question," was actually on the decisive question of war and revolution which has always marked that new continent of thought and revolution of Marxism from its birth. 1917 designated its move to the twentieth century. It was Stalin's counter-revolution that gave it a narrow nationalist stamp. Why the hell have all of us been caught in that linguistic web?

to both things happening in the objective world and attitudes to what are the tasks of a Marxist newspaper to objective events, I asked for a week off, left Detroit for Ann Arbor, and out of me poured those Letters of May 12 and 20 on the Absolute Idea.

Now then, because the dialectic flow in the present singling out of p. 21[17] of the May 12, 1953, Letter points also to the relevance of looking at it with eyes of 1987, let me examine the new find, the 1952 letter which shows I had made a plunge into the Idea of Cognition, especially on the section "The Idea of the Good." Clearly, I definitely had organization in mind. This was not on the level of James and Grace and their dialectic of the "Party," but on the question of dialectic "in and of itself." While I do not remember where I raised the question that I wasn't quite happy with Lenin's 16-point definition of the dialectic, I had called attention to the fact that Lenin says its final two points (15 and 16) are *examples of point 9.*"[18] This, I felt, was a step back from proceeding with the Absolute Idea and returning to the Doctrine of Essence, Form, and Content specifically.

At the same time—and that's when I did get brave and started arguing with Lenin as if he were right there—I began arguing with Lenin because he had asked the readers to disregard the last half paragraph of the chapter on the Absolute Idea while I insisted that had he suffered from Stalinism for three long decades he would have seen the relevance of following Hegel's Absolutes to the end. (This of course is taken up in the May 20, 1953, Letter, where I deal with the three final syllogisms [of Hegel's *Philosophy of Mind*], but for the present what is compelling is to trace the many ways of the development of the Self-Determination of the Idea.)

Here is how the May 12, 1953 Letter manifested the dialectical flow on p. 21[19] *from* exteriorization/interiorization it lapsed into a would-be "absolute" which led Lenin to remain at the "approach to," i.e., on the threshold of the Absolute Idea. This is the reason why Lenin preferred to let the Absolute Idea stop at *Nature* (Practice), crediting Hegel with "stretching a hand to materialism," instead of following Hegel to the last part of that paragraph when Hegel insists that the Absolutes had not been completed with the Absolute Idea, and must still go through the *Philosophy of Nature* and *Philosophy of Mind* before completion is reached with Absolute Mind. Put another way, in place of any *self-criticism,* or *objectivity,* Lenin left future generations without full illumination of what may befall them—Stalinism. It is the generation that followed, our age that suffered through those three decades of Stalinism, that had to face the reality of what happens after. It is *this* point, *this* objectivity, *this* concreteness, that emboldened me not to stop where Lenin stopped at the approach to the Absolute Idea, but to follow Hegel to the *Philosophy of Mind.*

The Absolute Method opened new doors already in the Absolute Idea, which Hegel defined as:

> The pure Idea, in which the determinateness or reality of the Notion is itself raised to the level of Notion, is an absolute *liberation*, having no further immediate determination which is not equally *posited* and equally Notion. Consequently there is no transition in this freedom. . . . The transition here therefore must rather be taken to mean that the Idea freely releases itself. [SLII, pp. 485–86; SLM, p. 843]

Now stand up and shout: "The Idea freely releases itself." Shout this while a flashing light illuminates Reality and its meaning, philosophy and revolution.

Instead of placing a "No Entrance" sign over organization as "pure politics," we finally are in the process of working out dialectics of philosophy *and* organization.

On Political Divides and Philosophic New Beginnings

The abysmal lower depths that the Reagan retrogression has sunk the world into throughout the seven years of this decade have polluted the ideological air, not only of the ruling class, but have penetrated the Left itself. Such a deep retrogression urgently demands that, along with the economic and political tasks facing us, we look for philosophic new beginnings.

In the midst of the work I am doing on my new book, "Dialectics of Organization and Philosophy," I have been digging into research on two opposed forms of organization—that is, our opposition to the vanguard party-to-lead, and our support of forms of organization born out of the spontaneous activity of the masses. Suddenly I realized that the relationship between these two opposed forms was exactly what I had posed back in 1982, on the eve of the publication of my third book, *Rosa Luxemburg, Women's Liberation, and Marx's Philosophy of Revolution*. I then (September 1982) added a paragraph to chapter 12 of that just-completed work. It was this articulation, which I reached only after the book was completed, that made me feel that the process of working out such questions demanded a book unto themselves.

This became even clearer when I realized that though [*Rosa Luxemburg, Women's Liberation, and Marx's Philosophy of Revolution*] was already at the printer, and had dealt with forms of organization both in Marx's day and in the early 20th century—with Lenin, Luxemburg, and the council communists—I nevertheless felt compelled to write a Philosophic-Political Letter to my colleagues on this subject. I called it: "On the Battle of Ideas: Philosophic-Theoretic Points of Departure as Political Tendencies Respond to the Objective Situation" (October 1982).[20] Here I would like to take up two points from the Letter, which begins:

> I am taking advantage of the fact that we do not yet have the new book in hand, which will plunge us into so many activities that we will have a tendency to forget "abstract" philosophic points of departure.

I returned to the final chapter 12 of *Rosa Luxemburg, Women's Liberation, and Marx's Philosophy of Revolution*. Its penultimate paragraph read:

> It isn't because we are any "smarter" that we can see so much more than other post-Marx Marxists. Rather, it is because of the maturity of our age. It is true that other post-Marx Marxists have rested on a truncated Marxism; it is equally true that no other generation could have seen the problematic of our age, much less solve our problems. Only live human beings can recreate the revolutionary dialectic forever anew. And these live human beings must do so in theory as well as in practice. It is not a question only of meeting the challenge from practice, but of being able to meet the challenge from the self-development of the Idea, and of deepening theory to the point where it reaches Marx's concept of the philosophy of "revolution in permanence."

It was at that point that I asked that the following paragraph be added [to that book]:

> There is a further challenge to the form of organization which we have worked out as the committee-form rather than the "party-to-lead." But, though committee-form and "party-to-lead" are opposites, they are not absolute opposites. At the point when the theoretic-form reaches philosophy, the challenge demands that we synthesize not only the new relations of theory to practice, and all the forces of revolution, but philosophy's "suffering, patience and labor of the negative," i.e., experiencing absolute negativity. *Then and only then* will we succeed in a revolution that will achieve a class-less, non-racist, non-sexist, truly human, truly new society. That which Hegel judged to be the synthesis of the "Self-Thinking Idea" and the "Self-Bringing-Forth of Liberty," Marxist-Humanism holds, is what Marx had called the new society. The many paths to get there are not easy to work out.[21]

I also suggested an addition to the Introduction of the book, to be added directly after I pointed out that "just as the young Marx, in first turning to what he called 'Economics,' had discovered the proletariat as the Subject who would be the "gravedigger of capitalism" and the leader of the proletarian revolution, so, at the end of his life, Marx made still newer discoveries as he turned to new, empirical anthropological studies like Morgan's *Ancient Society* as well as to the imperial incursions into the Orient and the carving up of Africa.

Here is what I proposed to add at that point:

> That seems to have been the first point so misunderstood by post-Marx Marxists, beginning with Frederick Engels, who, without having known of the massive *Ethnological Notebooks* Marx had left behind, undertook to write his own version of Morgan's work—his *Origin of the Family*—as a "bequest" of Marx. When Ryazanov discovered these notebooks, he rushed, before he ever had a chance to decipher them, to characterize them as "inexcusable pedantry."[22] If an Engels, who was a close collaborator of Marx and without whom we could not have had Volumes II and III of *Capital*, could nevertheless suddenly have gotten so overconfident about his own prowess of interpreting Marx as to assume he was speaking for Marx; if an archivist-scholar like Ryazanov could, at a time when he was actually publishing those magnificent early essays of Marx (the 1844 *Economic and Philosophical Manuscripts*), spend a good deal of his first report on the Archives of Marx in asking for 20 to 30 people to help him sort these manuscripts out, and yet pass judgment before he dug into them—it says a great deal about literary heirs but nothing whatsoever about so great an historic phenomenon as *Marx's* Marxism. Isn't it time to challenge all of the post-Marx Marxists when even those who have achieved great revolutions—and none was greater than the 1917 Russian Revolution—did not, in thought, measure up to Marx? Isn't it time to dig into what Marx, who had discovered a whole new continent of thought, had to say for himself?

My letter to my colleagues then concluded:

> The fact that in my latest work, *Rosa Luxemburg, Women's Liberation, and Marx's Philosophy of Revolution*, I focus on Marx's "translation" of absolute negativity as the revolution in permanence, calling that the absolute challenge to our age, will draw greater criticism from academia and outright attacks from post-Marx Marxists. This makes it necessary to be prepared, not only for that encounter, but for further concretizing that challenge. With this in mind, I decided to add that paragraph quoted earlier directly to the Introduction. For while it is true that the actual events of the 1970s—Women's Liberation on the one hand, and the publication of Marx's *Ethnological Notebooks* on the other—are what first led to a renewed interest in Rosa Luxemburg; and while it is true also that the Women's Liberation movement helped disclose the feminist dimension in Luxemburg never before recognized; it is not true that that is the goal of the new book.
>
> The need to see all post-Marx Marxists in strict relationship to *Marx's* Marxism is what revealed that even so great and independent a revolutionary as Rosa Luxemburg did not fully comprehend Marx's dialectic of liberation and thereby committed her biggest error—disregard of the revolutionary nature of Polish desire

for national self-determination. Put simply, the determinant of the new book is Marx's philosophy of revolution. This is not for any academic reason, or any sort of orthodoxy, but the fact that his works disclosed a trail to the 1980s and revealed the problematic of this age. The totally new question that Luxemburg posed—socialist democracy *after* gaining power—pointed to a new aspect of Marxism itself.

The new moments in Marx that the book discloses and that center around what we now call a Third World are not limited to the manner in which Marx revealed an "Asiatic mode of production" in the *Grundrisse*. Rather, this is extended to the 1880s as Marx was commenting on Morgan's *Ancient Society* and other then-new anthropological works on India, on the Australian aborigines, as well as his letters both on his visit to Algeria and his correspondence with revolutionaries in Russia on the ancient commune there and its possible transformation into an altogether new type of revolution. In a word, it is to revolution in permanence that the book keeps returning, whether the subject is Luxemburg, or Lenin, or Women's Liberation, or the Hegelian dialectic. At the same time, we must keep in mind that, whereas it is Marx who transformed Hegel into a contemporary, and transformed the Hegelian dialectic into the Marxian dialectic of liberation, the revolution is also present *in Hegel*. Hard as Hegel tried to confine this to a revolution in thought alone, he made his presence felt in history, even as he spoke of the *Philosophy of Mind* and *History of Philosophy*. As Hegel put it:

"All revolutions, in the sciences no less than in general history, originate only in this, that the spirit of man, for the understanding and comprehension of himself, for the possessing of himself, has now altered his categories, uniting himself in a truer, deeper, more intrinsic relation with himself."[23]

Now return to our own situation, and think of the attacks that we will be facing in 1987, when we state openly that even the one post-Marx Marxist revolutionary who did reach deeply into philosophy—Lenin—nevertheless did not do so on the question of organization. In truth, he never renounced his position on the vanguard party set out in 1902 in *What Is To Be Done?*, though he often critiqued it himself. He profoundly extended his new breakthrough in philosophy to a concretization of the dialectics of revolution, and yet never changed his position on the need for the "thin layer of Bolsheviks" [LCW 33, p. 257] as a vanguard party organization. In 1982 in *Rosa Luxemburg, Women's Liberation, and Marx's Philosophy of Revolution*, we critiqued Lenin politically. To fully work out the dialectics of philosophy and organization for our age, it is now clear that that critique must dig deep philosophically.

The whole truth is that even Marx's *Critique of the Gotha Program*, which remains the ground for organization today, was written 112 years ago. What is demanded is not mere "updating," after all the aborted revolutions of the post World War II world. "Ground" will not suffice alone; we have to finish the building—the roof and its contents. This is what I am working on now in the "Dialectics of Organization and Philosophy"—I would appreciate hearing from our readers on their thoughts on this.

NOTES

1. Louis Dupré, a leading scholar on Hegel, Marx, and Western philosophy, is the author of *The Philosophical Foundations of Marxism* (New York: Harcourt Brace, 1966), *Marx's Social Critique of Culture* (New Haven: Yale University Press, 1984), and *Passage to Modernity* (New Haven: Yale University Press, 1993). George Armstrong Kelly (1932–87) was a noted scholar of Hegel and Enlightenment thought, and the author of *Idealism, Politics, and History: Sources of Hegelian Thought* (Cambridge: Cambridge University Press, 1969) and *Hegel's Retreat from Eleusis* (Princeton: Princeton University Press, 1978). Dunayevskaya carried on an extensive correspondence with both Dupré and Kelly, who reviewed and commented on her work, as did she on theirs.

2. For the text of the talk, see part IV, above.

3. In her 1953 "Letters on Hegel's Absolutes," published in chapter 2 of this volume.

4. Dunayevskaya discussed Maurer's book in her *Philosophy and Revolution*, pp. 300–01, as well as in her Hegel Society lecture, "Hegel's Absolute as New Beginning," in this volume, part IV.

5. This is a reference to Kevin Anderson.

6. A.V. Miller translated the *Zusätze* (additional comments) for the republication of Wallace's translation of the *Philosophy of Mind*, which remains the only available English translation of that work. Miller's correspondence with Dunayevskaya as well as the text of his version of the final three syllogisms of the *Philosophy of Mind* can be found in the *Supplement to the Raya Dunayevskaya Collection*, pp. 11239-47.

7. The sentence from ¶575 of the *Philosophy of Mind*, as translated by Wallace, reads: "Nature, standing between the Mind and its essence, sunders itself, not indeed, to extremes of finite abstraction, nor to something away from them and independent."

8. A reference to the Preface to Hegel's *Phenomenology* [PhGB, p. 81; PhGM, p. 10].

9. The passage from Dunayevskaya—quoted by Kelly—is from her *Philosophy and Revolution*, p. 6.

10. In ¶64, Hegel writes, "And yet it was as self-evident or immediate truth that the *cogito, ergo sum* of Descartes, the maxim on which may be said to hinge the whole interest of Modern Philosophy, was first stated by its author. The man who calls this a syllogism, must know little more about a syllogism than that the word '*ergo*' occurs in it. Where shall we look for the middle term? And a middle term is a much more essential point of a syllogism than the word '*ergo*.'"

11. Hegel's discussion of "The Recent German Philosophy" constitutes the third and final section of the concluding volume of his *History of Philosophy*. Its first sentence reads, "In the philosophy of Kant, Fichte, and Schelling, the revolution to which in Germany mind has in these latter days advanced, was formally thought out and expressed; the se-

quence of these philosophies shows the course which thought has taken" [*History of Philosophy*, Vol. III (New York: The Humanities Press, 1974), p. 409].

12. This corresponds to the page number of the May 12th Letter as found in this work, in chapter 2, above.

13. By 1950, James and Dunayevskaya had broken with the concept of the vanguard party. Her view that the break stayed on a political level, and did not reach directly into philosophy itself, is illustrated by *State-Capitalism and World Revolution* (1950), written by James in collaboration with Dunayevskaya and Grace Lee. The chapter on philosophy presents Hegel merely as a critic of rationalism, and does not go into detail on the serious discussions on Hegel and dialectics found in their correspondence of 1949–50.

14. Johnny Zupan, a Detroit auto worker, became the editor of the tendency's newspaper, *Correspondence* in 1953.

15. The article on the 1920 trade union debate in Russia, "Then and Now," was published in the mimeographed *Correspondence* in 1952, and can be found in *The Raya Dunayevskaya Collection*, 2181–92. This article became the basis of the chapter on the 1920 trade union debate in *Marxism and Freedom*.

16. The debate around Dunayeskaya's analysis of Stalin's death occupied the first several printed issues of *Correspondence*, in October and November 1953.

17. In this volume.

18. Points 15 and 16 of Lenin's 16-point definition of dialectic were "the struggle of content with form and conversely. The throwing off of the form, the transformation of the content" and "The transition of quantity into quality and vice versa." Point 9 was "not only the unity of opposites, but the transition of every determination, quality, feature, side, property, into every other (into its opposite)?" [LCW 38, p. 222]. In point 14 Lenin had gone further than this, in singling out "the negation of the negation."

19. In this volume.

20. See this volume, pp. 237–49.

21. See p. 267, note 13.

22. See p. 267, note 16.

23. Hegel, *Philosophy of Nature* , trans. by A.V. Miller (Oxford: Oxford University Press, 1970), p. 11.

EXCERPTS FROM 1949–51 PHILOSOPHIC CORRESPONDENCE WITH C. L. R. JAMES AND GRACE LEE BOGGS

~

Letters to C. L. R. James

The following three letters to C. L. R. James are among Dunayevskaya's earliest writings on Hegel and dialectics. From January through March of 1949, Dunayevskaya translated from the Russian Lenin's 1914–15 "Abstract of Hegel's Science of Logic*" as well as his "Abstract of Hegel's* History of Philosophy*." She shared the typescript of this translation with her two close colleagues at the time, C. L. R. James and Grace Lee Boggs. During the years 1949–51, they carried out an intensive three-way correspondence in which copies of letters addressed individually were shared by all of them. This correspondence was related to a never-completed joint work on Marxist theory. Dunayevskaya's three letters to James published below were written to accompany each of the three parts of her translation of Lenin's notes on Hegel's* Science of Logic*—those on Being, Essence, and Notion. In them, she began the close and extensive analysis of Lenin's writings on Hegel which was to have an important place in her work for the next 40 years, right up until her death. One can also see here the beginnings of Dunayevskaya's direct study not only of Lenin on Hegel, but also of key categories in Hegel's* Logic *in and for themselves. Finally, some early differences with C. L. R. James, including an implicit critique of his emphasis on Essence rather than Notion, can be discerned. Dunayevskaya deposited her copy of the three-way correspondence between James, Lee, and herself in the* Raya Duna-yevskaya Collection, *where it comprises over 150 closely typed pages. Inside the text of the three letters to James printed below, we have given bracketed references to the text of Lenin's notes on Hegel as they appear in the 1961 edition of Lenin's* Collected Works. *However, Dunayevskaya's translation differs from the Moscow one, in part because she is often more sensitive to dialectical language.[1] Her 1949 translation, which she is quoting here, also differs in some respects from her own subsequently published version in the appendix to the 1958 edition of* Marxism and Freedom. *The typescript of the 1949 translation from which she was working in these letters can also be found in* The Raya Dunayevskaya Collection, *p. 1492.*

345

Letter to James of February 18, 1949

Dear J:

I decided to translate the *Philosophic Notebooks* on the *Science of Logic* in toto as excerpts cannot avoid the appearance and actuality of being forced. Here is the first section, dealing with the Prefaces, Introduction, and Doctrine of Being. Note that the Leap (translated by Hegel's translators as Jump) you made so famous in your *Notes [on Dialectics* (1948)] is not in Quality but in Measure. It is the climax, that is, to entire first volume.[2] He begins by objecting to the pedantry which listed the title of the Observation to the Nodal Line of Measure-Relations: (Examples of Such Nodal Lines; *natura non facit saltum* [nature makes no leaps]) in the contents pages but not in the text itself.[3] He then proceeds to introduce his conclusions with "gradualness explains nothing without leaps," then he repeats the title of the Observation "as if Nature did not make jumps" which he emphasizes further by repeating the word "Leaps!" at a side, then softly emphasizes "Interruptions to gradualness" [LCW 38, p. 123] and ends with quoting pages 389–90, "It is said, *natura non facit saltum*" [SLI, p. 389; SLM, p. 370] and two more Leaps! follow that. You would think at this point that he feels gaily and can transit to Essence easily. No, he complains here that the end of Vol. I, "Transition of Being to Essence is analyzed doubly obscurely" [LCW 38, p. 125]. How much that man knew and how much more he was searching for!

You will enjoy the notes on Being which you practically skipped over in your hurry to get to Essence. It seemed to me one of the reasons was the necessity to begin with simplest categories, because both in philosophy, economics, politics and what have you those simple categories "contain in germ the whole."[4] An excellent example of this firm grasp of the dialectic at its simplest is his remark, after complaining that Hegel is unclear, or rather he is unclear about Hegel's full meaning in "*Die Objektivität des Scheins, die Notwendigkeit des Widerspruchs* [The Objectivity of Appearance, the Necessity of Contradiction]" (inherent negativity) [SLI, p. 67; SLM, p. 56; LCW 38, p. 98]:

> Is not this the thought, that appearance is also objective, since it is *one of the sides* of the objective world? Not only *Wesen* [Essence], but also *Schein* [Appearance] are objective. Even the distinction between subjective and objective has its limits. [LCW 38, p. 98]

No wonder that man could write of *appearance* so profoundly! *Imperialism: A Popular Outline*.[5] Need I harp on my favorite peeve: compare this analysis of appearance to Rosa's analysis of essence in her *Accumulation [of Capital]*.[6]

Another thing that struck me anew was emphasis on Method, Method,

Method, "the dialectic which it has [comprises] in itself": The first reference to *Capital* occurs here when he quotes Hegel, "not a mere abstract Universal, but as a Universal which comprises in itself the full wealth of Particulars" [SLI, p. 69; SLM, p. 58; LCW 38, p. 99]. When you add to his emphasis on the development of thinking through "its own necessary laws," his attack against "using" forms of thought "as a means," the attacks both on Kantianism and his "thing-in-itself" and Transcendental Idealism and its "subjectivism," you can see that the concretes which Lenin had in mind when he was reading Logic were both the economic conditions—*Capital* plus the *Imperialism* he was going to work out—and Ideology of the Bernsteins, Kautskys, and, yes, Rosa Luxemburg since in that very period he also made notes on her book. What rich years were 1914–16 for Lenin in his "study room"!

Evidently for the first time he was struck also by the fact that in the back of Hegel's mind when he worked out the "self-development of concepts" was the whole history of philosophy. (He had made these notes before those on Hegel's *History of Philosophy*.)[7] Along with this was the emphasis on how "materialistic" rang the sound of Hegel's statement, "What is first in science has had to show itself first historically" [SLI, p. 101; SLM, p. 88; LCW 38, p. 106]. Lenin gave a very, rather truly materialistic interpretation of history as it meant to him also the *economic* foundations of society. At the same time he contrasts "Sophistry and Dialectic" in general when he quotes Hegel: "For sophistry is an argument proceeding from a baseless supposition which is allowed without criticism or reflection; while we term dialectic that higher movement of Reason where terms appearing absolutely distinct pass into one another because they are what they are, where the assumption of their sepa-rateness cancels itself" [SLI, p. 117; SLM, p. 105; LCW 38, p. 107]. Both Hegel and Lenin hit at "baseless assumptions"; this is very important for our work, of course.

Among the "baseless assumptions" are those that divide finite from infinite by an impassable barrier, or, as Hegel would put it, by making one "a this-sid-edness" and then establishing an "other-sidedness," a beyond. It is at this point that he deals with "Ought and Barrier as moments of the finite" [SLI, pp. 144–45; SLM, pp. 131–32], but very briefly; I went back to Hegel very care-fully on that, and the correspondence with G [Grace Lee Boggs] on the rela-tion of this to the general contradiction of capitalism you are acquainted with.[8] I will return to that again at another time.

No one reading Lenin can resist temptation to quote him on the dialectic, although they know the reader is all too anxious to stop reading this to get to Hegel himself, so here goes: This comes after Hegel's "The things are, but the truth of this being is their end" [SLI, p. 142; SLM, p. 129].

Thoughts of dialectic *en lisant* [in reading] Hegel. NB. Sharp and wise! Hegel analyzes concepts which usually appear dead and he shows that there *is* movement in them. The finite? That means *movement* has come to an end! Something. That means not what Other is. Being in general? That means such indeterminateness that being=Not-Being.

    All-sided universal flexibility of concepts—flexibility reaching to the identity of opposites. This flexibility, subjectively applied=eclecticism and sophistry. When this flexibility is *objectively* applied, i.e., reflecting the all-sidedness of the material process and its unity, then it is dialectic, it is the correct reflection of the eternal development of the world. [LCW 38, p. 110]

Have fun with Lenin and be patient about his Notes on Essence since this is a very large section and I do this between many other activities.

Yours,
R

Letter to James of February 25, 1949

Dear J:

    Herewith Lenin's Notes on Essence; I am moving faster with the translation than I had counted upon mainly because I had thought it would take time "to find" the quotations but now find that as I myself internalize Hegel I nearly always flip open the right page.

    The deep richness of Lenin's Notes would overwhelm me if it were not for their utter simplicity. As if you did not believe me, let me cite but one instance. He is talking about a "purely logical" working out of the dialectic and continues "*Das fällt zusammen* [It coincides]. It *must* coincide as does induction and deduction in *Capital*" [LCW 38, p. 146]. Not for one instant does he permit you to think that to compare the dialectic "merely" to the deductive and inductive method of *Capital* is "narrow," for the comment occurred as an addition to: "The continuation of the work of Hegel and Marx must consist in the *dialectic* working out of the history of human thought, science and technique" [LCW 38, pp. 146–47]. Moreover, "technique," or the technology which sets the ground for our mode of production, production relation[s], and generally the whole intellectual development, is nowhere here so overpowering that you think of the mind's development as a *mere* reflection of the economic relations; that too not only has its own laws but "works upon," so to speak, the economic material and the result is not any one of these things *alone* but *all* of them together. This can be seen, for example, in the three dates that he sets down for universal development: 1) 1813—*Science of Logic*, or the theory of development, 2) 1847—the *Communist Man-*

ifesto, or the application of dialectic to society, 3) 1859—[Darwin's] *Origin of Species*, or "application" of dialectics to man [LCW 38, p. 141]. Whoever is still so foolhardy as to look for a "primary cause" may do so if he has enough time to waste; Lenin will have none of that—he will have only totality and movement and break-up and movement.

If the three sections of the Doctrine of Essence had to be summarized in three words, I'd say *Manifoldness* for Show (Reflection), *Law* for Appearance, and *Totality* for Actuality. Manifoldness is particularly important if you consider that Lenin wrote his Notes when the world was being rent asunder. Lenin, in quoting Hegel on the fact that both Skepticism and Idealism admitted manifoldness and yet the one dared not "affirm 'it is'" and the other dared not "regard cognition as knowledge of the thing-in-itself" [SLII, p. 22; SLM, p. 396], comments:

> "You include all the manifold riches of the world in *Schein* and you reject the objectivity of *Schein*!!" [LCW 38, p. 131]

Lenin notes, further, not only that Essence must appear (rather he comments on this statement of Hegel's, thus: "The little philosophers dispute whether one should take as basis the essence *or* the immediately given. . . . Hegel substitutes 'and' for 'or' and explains the concrete content of this 'and'" [LCW 38, p. 134]) but he emphasizes that even more, [it] is "*one* of the determinations of essence" [LCW 38, p. 133]. Naturally, he does not fail to underline that one-sided determinateness of Essence has no truth, but he emphasizes also (permit me to skip here): "Causality is ordinarily understood by us as only a small part of the universal connection, but (a materialistic addition) the small part is not subjective but the objectively real connection" [LCW 38, p. 160]. I could not help but feel that these "small parts" which had "objectively real connection" were the elements of the phenomena about him which became the book *Imperialism*.

May I be permitted to linger a moment on Law of Contradiction, seeing that both Lenin and you[9] considered [it] so much the essence of the book as to quote it in toto? I however wish to limit myself only to its relationship to the general contradiction of capitalism. I began to harp on the applicability of parts of the dialectic to that general contradiction even when I was in the Doctrine of Being (Section on Ought and Barrier in relation to infinite production—production for production's sake, that is[10]) and now I find that Hegel notes (p. 67): "Infinity, which is contradiction as it appears in the sphere of Being," and then moves rapidly on to demonstrate that "the principle of self-movement . . . consists of nothing else but the exhibition of contradiction" [SLII, p. 67; SLM,

p. 440]. Having moved that rapidly, he concludes, "Motion is *existent* contradiction." The emphasis is Lenin's and suit[s] me perfectly for grappling with the law of motion of capitalist society in philosophic rather than in value terms. If [I] am wrong, I can always return home—to the law of value[11]—but something bids me continue with it.

Some time back I wrote to Grace about the fact that "kingdom of laws" in *Phenomenology*[12] had me baffled since there seemed to be a contradiction between that analysis which fitted the primitive conception of the Stalinists and the economic laws to which Marx refers as dominating over society regardless of the consciousness of men. I was on the point of considering myself still as a mere "Woman of understanding"[13] when I met with Lenin's notes on the Law of Appearance, where he not only sends himself back to the very same section in the *Phenomenology*,[14] but after listing no less than 10 definitions of law in Hegel, he concludes that all these definitely differ from the final conclusion, p. 135 [SLII, p. 135; SLM, pp. 505–6]. Allow me to take these summations step by step as they will help me transit to totality. Law is, says Lenin, paraphrasing Hegel:

1) unity of show and existence; 2) *one* of the steps of the cognition of unity and connection of reciprocal dependence and totality of the world process; 3) the enduring and persistent in appearance; 4) the identity of appearance in its reflection; 5) the *quiescent* reflection in appearance; 6) narrow, incomplete, approximate; 7) essential appearance; 8) law and essence of concept are homogeneous . . . expressing the deepening of man's knowledge of appearance; 9) reflection of essential; 10) a part; appearance, totality, wholeness is richer than law.[15]

But here Lenin stops himself to note: "But further, although it is not clear, it is acknowledged, it seems (p. 135 especially), that law can overcome this inadequacy and grasp also the negative side, and *Totalität der Erscheinung* [totality of appearance]. Must return here!" [LCW 38, p. 152]. Now pp. 135ff has what appears to me the key sentence: "The determination of Law has thus changed [in] Law itself" [SLII, p. 135; SLM, p. 506]. At which Hegel proceeds to show what it was "at first," what it became as "negative intro-Reflection" developed it, and concludes "Thus Law is *Essential Relation*" [SLII, p. 141; SLM, p. 511]. The emphasis is Lenin's and brings us precisely to the comprehension of law in the sense in which Marx uses "absolute general law,"[16] which can only be abrogated by the mediation of the proletariat establishing different social relations.

What a dialectician that Hegel was; nothing else can explain the sheer genius of that man's language which defines identity as "unseparated difference,"[17] and now as he enters Actuality and *Totalität* [totality], asserts that totality is found as "*sundered completeness*" [SLII, p. 170; SLM, p. 539]. The emphasis is Lenin's [LCW 38, p. 156], which shows he was not going to be outdone by a man who lived and died long before WWI. You will like the way Lenin weaves in the Smaller Logic to clarify the essence of the dialectic. He underlines Hegel's "*The sum total of the elements* which, as it opens itself out, discloses itself to be necessity" [EL, ¶143]. And then translates: "The unfoldment of the whole totality of moments of actuality NB=essence of dialectic knowledge" [LCW 38, p. 158]. He also asks himself whether by "moments of concept" Hegel does not mean "moments of transition." He is full of "all-sidedness and all-embracing character of world connection" [LCW 38, p. 159]. Always it is: Connection, relation, mediation, necessity, motion, unity of opposites, break-up of identity, transition and motion, motion and transition, and that is totality. I believe I am ready to follow him into Notion.

Yours,

Raya

Letter to James of March 12, 1949

Dear J:

I am extremely happy in being able to send you the conclusion of Lenin's *Notes* on the *Logic*. If you wrote your *Notes on the Dialectic* [1948] for me, then I translated Lenin for you. Surely you who have gone into a regular "conspiracy" with Lenin on the analysis of Hegel deserved seeing Lenin's notes in their entirety, and not merely in extracts. Being the only Russian, it was my duty to have done this long ago. The only reason (and it is the real ground, not a mere excuse) I have for not doing so is that I could not have without first having digested your Notes; so now we are "quits." Perhaps I'll even be conceited enough to say that when you come to rewriting your Notes I can be of service.

Let me say at the start that, although you have entered into this "conspiracy" with Lenin, the outstanding difference between the two "versions" is striking. You will note that Lenin's notes on the Notion are as lengthy as those on the Introduction and Doctrines of Being and Essence combined. Yours were too—but in your notes on the Notion you included the actual application of it, both insofar as a balance sheet of Trotskyism is concerned as well as in outlining our own leap, but Lenin's Notes on the Notion are that bulky *in and for themselves*, with bare indications as to how to apply. The difference is not accidental. Lenin was looking for a new Universal. He found Hegel's Idea, and said, if I may steal an expression from Marx who stole it from someone else: *hic Rhodus, hic salta*.[18] And even then Lenin couldn't fashion his new universal—revolutions to a man—until there appeared the Soviets, 1917 version. The Idea had him pose the question correctly; the Russian masses supplied the practice; and then Lenin arrived and unified the two and called it: *State and Revolution*. We, on the other hand, although we are looking for our (this age's, that is) universal, have something to go by as Lenin had not. Hence, although you spent that much time on Notion, and included its practice, the thing you chose most to stop at and say: *hic Rhodus, hic salta* to was the Law of Contradiction in Essence. That too is not accidental since what we are confronted with is not a "betrayal" (like that of the Second International) but the *contradictions* of Trotskyism which still passes for Leninism and in which we too have our roots and being, so much so that even when you come to the Notion (in your Synthetic Cognition) you return back to Essence, contradiction of form and content, cause and effect, etc., in order once and for all not only [to] do away with, but overcome, transcend Trotskyism.[19]

Just as the LEAP characterized Lenin's comprehension of the Doctrine of Being, LAW as Essential Relation his grasp of the Doctrine of Essence, so PRACTICE characterizes his very profound analysis of The Doctrine of the Notion, and why he chooses to single out the section on the Idea as you had Observation.[20]

Lenin begins with the fact that "The dialectic road to cognition of truth is from living observation to abstract thinking and from this to practice" [LCW 38, p. 171] and never lets go of this for a single second. He insists that the laws of logical cognition reflect objectivity in the subjective consciousness of man, but he does not stop at reflection. No, he states categorically, "Man's cognition not only reflects the objective world, but *creates* it" [LCW 38, p. 212]. (My emphasis.) But if you think for a moment that that means you can get off into the high clouds of the land beyond, he brings you right back to earth and practice, practice, practice:

> "Conclusion (Syllogism) of action" . . . For Hegel *action*, practice is the *logical 'conclusion'* of the figure of logic. And this is true! Of course, not in the sense that the figure of logic has by its otherness the practice of man (=absolute idealism) but vice versa: the practice of man repeating itself billions of times, fastens itself in consciousness of man by the figures of logic. These figures have the solidity of a prejudice, an axiomatic character precisely (and only) because of this billion-timed repetition." [LCW 38, p. 217]

And again:

> The activity of man, composing for itself an objective picture of the world *changes* the external activity, transcends its determinateness (=changes these or other of its

aspects, qualities) and thus takes away from it the traits of appearance, externality and nullity and gives it being in-itself and for-itself (=objective truth). [LCW 38, p. 218]

And before that:

undoubtedly practice in Hegel stands as a link in the analysis of the process of cognition and precisely as a transition to objective ("absolute" according to Hegel) truth. Marx, consequently, clings to Hegel, introducing the criteria of practice into the theory of knowledge: cf. Theses on Feuerbach.[21] [LCW 38, p. 212].

And before that: he had traced the embryo of historical materialism in Hegel, quoting and emphasizing (in caps) the following from Hegel:

In his tools man possesses power over external nature even though according to his ends, he frequently is subjected to it. [SLII, p. 388; SLM, p. 747; LCW 38, p. 189]

His *whole* emphasis on the *End*, and *Subjective* notion is that the aims of man are generated by the objective world but that he changes, subjectively desires change and acts; there he goes so far as to call the objective world non-actual and the desires of man *actual,* and the reason he hangs on so to the Idea is that "it not only has the dignity of a universal, but also the simply actual" [LCW 38, p. 213]. Let me see whether I can do with The Idea, what I tried to do with the Law, listing it in detail, for Lenin has no less than seventeen definitions— more correctly, manifoldednesses: (What a word I just made up!)

1) Notion *and* objectivity; 2) *relations* of subjectivity to objectivity; 3) *impulse* to transcend; 4) *process* and subordination of thought and object; 5) contains strongest *contradiction in itself* since notion reaches freedom and *eternally* creates, *eternally* overcomes; 6) is *Truth* (only as *totality* and relation does it realize itself; 7) is *Reason* (Subjective and Objective; 8) is objective *activity;* 9) *develops* through a) Life, b) process of knowledge, *including practice,* c) reaches the Absolute Idea or complete truth; 10) *logical* notion, which= nature AND concreteness AND abstractness AND phenomena AND essence AND motion AND relation; 11) not only dignity of universal but also simple *actual;* the richest *is* the *most concrete;* 12) *unity* of cognition and practice; 13) three postulates summarize it: a) *good End* (subjective End) vs. *actuality* ("external actuality"); b) external *means* (weapon) (objective), c) correspondence of subject and object, the verification of subjective ideas, which are (14) criteria of objective truth; 15) Absolute Idea as unity of theoretical and practical idea; 16) *method* of absolute cognition, after which is 17) the summation of the *dialectic.*[22]

For that Lenin gives seventeen other aspects which constantly develop through relations, objectivity, contradiction, struggle, transition, unfolding of new sides which seem to be a return to old (negation of the negation), motion, practice. He sums up science which he considers, after Hegel, "*a circle of circles*" [LCW 38, p. 233] as the movement from "subjective Idea to objective truth *through* practice" [LCW 38, p. 191], with no end of emphasis on technique *and* the objective world *and* subjective aims: "*Technique, mechanical and chemical, thus serves the aims of man, in that its character (essence) consists in its determination by external conditions (by the laws of nature)*" [LCW 38, p. 188]. Finally concluding that the only verification of all these dialectical laws is the application to *individual* sciences and hence the emphasis on our restudying Marx's *Capital*, which *none* of the Marxists of the 20th century understood [LCW 38, p. 180], and a remark against himself: "Marxists criticized the Kantians and Humists at the beginning of the 20th century more in the Feuerbachian (and Buchnerian) than in a Hegelian manner" [LCW 38, p. 179]. The emphasis on the plural (Marxists) is Lenin's; it follows the remark against Plekhanov; and has an additional remark: "The question of the criticism of contemporary Kantianism, Machism, etc." [LCW 38, p. 179]. In other words, the emphasis on the plural includes himself as he is the only one in addition to Plekhanov who had bothered much with Machism.

It is a masterly understatement to say that I am immensely impressed. A better way to express it is that I am dying to get down to apply all this to two things: 1) the American economy to which I hope to get to seriously this summer; 2) to Marx's *Capital* on which I hope Grace will collaborate; I have written on some of the aspects already and will tomorrow send off another letter on other aspects.

Because I have been very anxious to finish this (Novack's[23] visit took a week out) I have not read either the notes on the Puritan Revolution or the one on the Negro question;[24] I hope I can keep both till next week and will let you have my reactions then.

My love to Connie.[25]

NOTES

1. The Moscow edition translates everything from the Russian and German anew. Unlike Dunayevskaya's 1949 translation, it does not even give page references to current English or German editions of Hegel's writings.

2. The Doctrine of Being, Book I of Hegel's *Science of Logic*, contains three sections: Determinateness (Quality), Magnitude (Quantity), and Measure.

3. The table of contents of the *Science of Logic* lists the title of the three-page section

Lenin is here discussing as "Observation: Examples of Such Nodal Lines; *natura non facit saltum* [nature makes no leaps]," but in the actual text [SLI, p. 388; SLM, p. 368], it is simply entitled "Observation." In his notebooks, Lenin objects to this failure by Hegel's German editors to remedy an apparent gap in the original edition, calling this omission "pedantry" [LCW 38, p. 123]. This discrepancy still exists in the most widely printed recent German edition of the *Wissenschaft der Logik* (Frankfurt: Sührkamp Verlag, 1969).

4. In Lenin's 1915 essay fragment, "On the Question of Dialectics," he writes, referring to Marx's introduction to the first edition of *Capital,* of the "commodity" as revealing "the germs of *all* the contradictions" of capitalism [LCW 38, pp. 360–61].

5. The full title of Lenin's book was *Imperialism, the Highest Stage of Capitalism: A Popular Outline* (1916).

6. In a letter to James of October 14, 1948, Dunayevskaya had discussed what she considered to be Luxemburg's "failure 'to see' the monopolization of capital and thus [her] falling prey to the glitter of imperialism" (*The Raya Dunayevskaya Collection,* p. 1329). See also Dunayevskaya's article, "Luxemburg's Theory of Accumulation. How It Differed with Marx and Lenin," *New International* (April and May 1946)—included in *The Raya Dunayevskaya Collection,* pp. 436–47.

7. In 1915, Lenin made lengthy notes on Hegel's *History of Philosophy* [LCW 38, pp. 247–304]. Dunayevskaya reflects on her work translating them in a letter to James of January 27, 1949 (*The Raya Dunayevskaya Collection,* pp. 9213–14).

8. See Dunayevskaya's letters to Lee of January 5, February 1, February 10, and February 17, 1949, and Lee's to Dunayevskaya of February 14, in *The Raya Dunayevskaya Collection,* pp. 9210–9223.

9. In *Notes on Dialectics* (1948).

10. Dunayevskaya did so in a letter to Lee of February 1, 1949. The Johnson-Forest Tendency referred frequently to Marx's statement in *Capital* that in the formula "production for production's sake . . . classical political economy expressed the historical mission of the bourgeoisie" [MCIK, p. 65; MCIF, p. 742].

11. In the Johnson-Forest Tendency, Dunayevskaya was considered to be more an economist than a philosopher, while Lee was the designated specialist in philosophy.

12. We have not been able to locate this letter. "Kingdom of laws" apparently refers to part of Hegel's discussion on Reason in the *Phenomenology of Mind.*

13. In his *Notes on Dialectics* (1948) and elsewhere, C. L. R. James frequently used Hegel's critique of "the understanding" to attack other Marxists, especially other Trotskyists. James considered "men of understanding" to be stuck in empiricist, common sense thinking and thus unable to grasp issues such as the Johnson-Forest Tendency's notion that Stalinism was a Leninism which "has been corrupted, turned into its opposite" (p. 47).

14. In a note in her translation of Lenin's Abstract, Dunayevskaya suggests that this refers to the sections of the *Phenomenology,* including Force and Understanding, the discussion of Appearance in the chapter on Consciousness, and then the first parts of the chapter on Self-Consciousness, including the discussion of Lordship and Bondage (*The Raya Dunayevskaya Collection,* p. 1528).

15. These ten points are drawn from Lenin's discussion in LCW 38, pp. 150–52.

16. See p. 31, note 3.

17. Hegel does not actually use this phrase in this section, but its sense is conveyed by his discussion of how "the Absolute contains every distinction and form-determination whatever, or is itself Absolute Form and Reflection, and therefore variety of content too must emerge in it. . . . The Absolute is Absolute only because it is not abstract identity, but the identity of Being and Essence, or of Inner and Outer" [SLII, p. 162, 164; SLM, p. 531, 533].

18. "Here is Rhodes, leap here!" In one of Aesop's fables, this is addressed to a braggart who claimed to have made a great leap in Rhodes. It more generally means "now show us what you can do." In *The Eighteenth Brumaire of Louis Bonaparte* (1852), Marx uses this expression to illustrate what he termed the way in which, unlike "bourgeois revolutions," which "storm swiftly from success to success . . . proletarian revolutions . . . criticize themselves constantly . . . recoil again and again from the indefinite prodigiousness of their own aims, until a situation has been created which makes all turning back impossible, and the conditions themselves cry out: *Hic Rhodus, hic salta!*" [MECW 11, p. 106–7]. Earlier, Hegel referred to this expression in the Preface to his *Philosophy of Right* (1820).

19. In his *Notes on Dialectics*, James devoted considerable space to Hegel's critique of synthetic cognition in "The Idea of Cognition," the penultimate chapter of the *Science of Logic*. James argued that Trotskyism was trapped in synthetic cognition. In this work, James also stressed many of Hegel's categories in the Doctrine of Essence such as contradiction.

20. The section on "The Law of Contradiction" in the Doctrine of Essence.

21. In the first of his "Theses on Feuerbach" (1845), Marx wrote that "all materialism up to now" had failed to grasp human experience "subjectively": "Hence the *active side* was developed abstractly in opposition to materialism by idealism." Feuerbach "therefore does not comprehend the significance of 'revolutionary,' practical-critical activity" (MECW 5, p. 3).

22. These seventeen points are drawn from Lenin's discussion in LCW 38, pp. 214–21.

23. George Novack, the Trotskyist thinker and a leader of the Socialist Workers' Party.

24. During the late 1940s, James wrote a number of articles and drafts which discussed both the English Puritan Revolution of the seventeenth century and what was then termed the "Negro question." However, we have not been able to locate the specific notes referred to here, presumably from February or March 1949. They are not listed in the various published bibliographies of James' writings.

25. Constance Webb, James' wife at that time.

~

Select Bibliography

Works by Raya Dunayevskaya

Note: Numerous additional writings by Dunayevskaya and related materials, many of them published in mimeographed form or in the Chicago-based newspaper she founded in 1955, *News & Letters* (www.newsandletters.org), can be found in *The Raya Dunayevskaya Collection: Marxist-Humanism—A Half Century of Its World Development* and in the *Supplement to the Raya Dunayevskaya Collection* (Detroit: Walter Reuther Archives of Labor and Urban Affairs, microfilm).

Books

Dunayevskaya, Raya. *Marxism and Freedom, from 1776 until Today*, with a preface by Herbert Marcuse, contains first English translation of Marx's 1844 Essays and Lenin's Hegel Notebooks (New York: Bookman, 1958); second edition, with a new introduction by the author and an added chapter on China (New York: Twayne, 1964); third edition, with another added chapter on China and a new preface by Harry McShane: London: Pluto Press, 1971); fourth edition, with a new introduction by the author (New Jersey: Humanities Press, 1982); reprint, with new material by the author (New York: Columbia University Press, 1988); reprint, with a new foreword by Joel Kovel (Amherst, New York: Humanity Books, 2000); translations: Italian (Florence: La Nuova Italia, 1962); Japanese (Tokyo: Modern Thought, 1964); French, with a new introduction by the author (Paris: Champ Libre, 1971); Spanish, with a new introduction by the author (Mexico: Juan Pablos, 1976); Chinese, with a new preface by Wang Ruoshui (Shenyang: Liaoning Education Press, 1999).

———. *Philosophy and Revolution, from Hegel to Sartre and from Marx to Mao* (New York: Delacorte, 1973); second edition, with a new introduction by the author (New Jersey: Humanities Press, 1982); reprint, with new prefaces by Erich Fromm and Louis Dupré (New York: Columbia University Press, 1989); translations: Spanish (Mexico, D. F.: Siglo Veintiuno, 1977); Italian, with a new preface by Mariachiara Figazza and Amedeo Vigorelli (Milan: Feltrinelli, 1977); German (Vienna: Europa Verlag, 1981); Slovak, with a new epilogue by Peter Hudis (Bratislava: Iris, 1995); Chinese (Shenyang: Liaoning Education Press, 1999).

―――. *Rosa Luxemburg, Women's Liberation, and Marx's Philosophy of Revolution* (New York: Humanities Press, 1982); second edition, with a new foreword by Adrienne Rich (Champaign-Urbana: University of Illinois Press, 1991); translations: Spanish, (Mexico, D. F.: Fonda de Cultura Economica, 1985); German, with a new foreword by Frigga Haug (Berlin: Argument Verlag, 1998).

―――. *Women's Liberation and the Dialectics of Revolution* (New Jersey: Humanities Press, 1985); reprint, with a new preface by Olga Domanski (Detroit: Wayne State University Press, 1996); translation: Spanish (Mexico, D. F. Fontamara, 1993).

―――. *The Marxist-Humanist Theory of State-Capitalism*, with an introduction by Peter Hudis (Chicago: News and Letters, 1992).

Pamphlets and Articles

Dunayevskaya, Raya, "A New Revision of Marxian Economics," *American Economic Review*, Vol. 34: 3 (1944), pp. 531–37.

―――. "Revision or Reaffirmation of Marxism? A Rejoinder," *American Economic Review*, Vol. 35:3 (1945), pp. 660–64.

―――. *Nationalism, Communism, Marxist Humanism, and the Afro-Asian Revolutions* (Chicago: News and Letters, 1984 [orig. 1959]).

―――. *American Civilization on Trial* (Detroit: News and Letters, 1983 [orig. 1963]).

―――. "Marxist-Humanism," *Présence Africaine*, Vol. 20, No. 48 (1963), pp. 58–70; see also the French version, "Socialismes africains et problèmes nègres," published in No. 48 of the French edition of the journal, pp. 49–64.

―――, Eugene Walker, and Mario Savio. *The Free Speech Movement and the Negro Revolution* (Detroit: News and Letters, 1965).

―――. "Marx's Humanism Today," pp. 63–76 in *Socialist Humanism*, ed. by Erich Fromm (New York: Doubleday, 1965).

―――. *State-Capitalism and Marx's Humanism, or Philosophy and Revolution* (Detroit: News & Letters, 1967).

―――. "The Shock of Recognition and the Philosophic Ambivalence of Lenin," *Telos*, No. 5 (1970), pp. 45–57.

―――. "Humanism and Marxism," pp. 151–58 in Paul Kurtz, ed., *The Humanist Alternative* (Buffalo: Prometheus, 1973).

―――. "Hegelian Leninism," pp. 159–75 in *Towards a New Marxism*, ed. by Bart Grahl and Paul Piccone (St. Louis: Telos Press, 1973).

―――. "Leon Trotsky as Man and as Theoretician," with a Comment by Ernest Mandel, *Studies in Comparative Communism*, Vol. X: nos. 1 and 2 (Spring/Summer 1977), pp. 166–83.

―――. *New Essays* (Detroit: News & Letters, 1977).

―――. *Political-Philosophic Letters*, Vol. I (Detroit: News & Letters, 1977).

―――. *Marx's Capital and Today's Global Crisis* (Detroit: News & Letters, 1978).

―――. "Herbert Marcuse, Marxist Philosopher," *International Society for the Sociology of Knowledge Newsletter*, Vol. 5:2 (1979), pp. 10–11.

———. *Outline of Marx's Capital, Volume One* (Detroit: News & Letters, 1979).

———. *Political-Philosophic Letters*, Vol. II (Detroit: News & Letters, 1979).

———. *Woman as Reason and as Force of Revolution* (Detroit: News & Letters, 1980).

———. *25 Years of Marxist-Humanism in the U.S.* (Detroit: News and Letters, 1980).

———. *Iran: Revolution and Counter-Revolution* (Detroit: News & Letters, 1982).

———. *Grenada: Revolution, Counter-Revolution, Imperialist Invasion* (Detroit: News & Letters, 1983).

———. and Andy Phillips. *The Coal Miners' General Strike of 1949–50 and the Birth of Marxist-Humanism in the U.S.* (Chicago: News and Letters, 1984).

———. "Marx's 'New Humanism' and the Dialectics of Women's Liberation in Primitive and Modern Societies," *Praxis International*, Vol. 3:4 (1984), pp. 369–81.

———. "Marxist-Humanism, an Interview with Raya Dunayevskaya," *Chicago Literary Review*, Vol. 94:41 (1985), pp. 16–19.

———. *The Myriad Global Crises of the 1980s and the Nuclear World Since World War II* (Chicago: News & Letters, 1986).

———. "A Post-World War II View of Marx's Humanism: 1843–83. Marxist Humanism in the 1950s and 1980s," *Praxis International*, Vol. 8:3 (1988), pp. 360–71.

———.*The Philosophic Moment of Marxist-Humanism*, with a preface by Peter Hudis and Olga Domanski (Chicago: News & Letters, 1989).

———. "Afterword: Charles Denby, 1907–83," pp. 295–303 in Denby, *Indignant Heart: A Black Worker's Journal* (Detroit: Wayne State University Press, 1989).

———. *China in Revolt and the Idea of Freedom* (Chicago: News & Letters, 1989).

———. *Selections from Raya Dunayevskaya's Writings on the Middle East* (Chicago: News & Letters, 1990).

Recent Writings That Discuss Dunayevskaya

Note: See also the prefaces and introductions to the various editions of Dunayevskaya's books and pamphlets, listed above, as well as other reviews and discussions in the *Raya Dunayevskaya Collection* or *News & Letters*.

Afary, Janet, "The Contribution of Raya Dunayevskaya: A Study in Hegelian Marxist Feminism," *Extramares*, Vol. 1:1 (1989), pp. 35–55.

Alan, John, and Lou Turner, *Frantz Fanon, Soweto, and American Black Thought* (Chicago: News & Letters, 1986).

Alexander, Robert, *International Trotskyism* (Durham: Duke University Press, 1991).

Anderson, Kevin B., "Sources of Marxist-Humanism: Fanon, Kosík, Dunayevskaya," *Quarterly Journal of Ideology*, Vol. 10:4 (1986), pp. 9–13.

———. "Rosa Luxemburg: Feministe et révolutionnaire," pp. 107–110 in *Rosa Luxemburg Aujourd'hui*), edited by Claudie Weill and Gilbert Badia (France: Presses Universitaires de Vincennes, 1986).

———. "Raya Dunayevskaya, 1910 to 1987, Marxist Economist and Philosopher," *Review of Radical Political Economics*, Vol. 20:1 (1988), pp. 62–74.

————. "A Preliminary Exploration of the Dunayevskaya-Marcuse Dialogue, 1954–79," with a comment by Douglas Kellner, *Quarterly Journal of Ideology*, Vol. 13:4 (1989), pp. 21–33.

————. "The Marcuse-Dunayevskaya Dialogue," *Studies in Soviet Thought*, Vol. 39:2 (1990), pp. 89–109.

————. *Lenin, Hegel, and Western Marxism: A Critical Study* (Urbana: University of Illinois Press, 1995).

Beilharz, Peter, *Trotsky, Trotskyism and the Transition to Socialism* (London and Sidney: Croom Helm, 1987).

Brokmeyer, Ron, et al. *The Fetish of High Tech and Karl Marx's Unknown Mathematical Notebooks* (Oakland: News and Letters, 1985).

Buhle, Paul. C. L. R. James. *The Artist as Revolutionary* (London: Verso, 1988).

Chattopadhyay, Paresh, *The Marxian Concept of Capital and the Soviet Experience* (Westport, CT: Praeger, 1994).

Cleaver, Harry, *Reading Capital Politically* (Austin: University of Texas Press, 1979).

Dietrich, Gabriele, "Raya Dunayevskaya: Rosa Luxemburg, Women's Liberation and Marx's Philosophy of Revolution," *The Marxist Review* (Calcutta), Vol. 18: 2 (1985), pp. 155–76.

Domanski, Olga, "Dunayevskaya on Rosa Luxemburg, Women, and Revolution: A Response to Peter Beilharz," *Thesis Eleven*, Nos. 10/11 (1984–85), pp. 216–21.

Dupré, Louis, "Recent Literature on Marx and Marxism," *Journal of the History of Ideas* (April 1974), pp. 703–14.

Easton, Susan, "Raya Dunayevskaya, 1910–1987," *Bulletin of the Hegel Society of Great Britain*, No. 16 (1987), pp. 7–12.

Edmondson, Linda, "Lives of Rosa Luxemburg," *Revolutionary Russia*, Vol. 2:2 (1989), pp. 35–44.

Franklin, Stephen, "Portrait of a Revolutionary," with photographs by David C. Turnley, *Detroit Free Press Sunday Magazine*, June 12, 1983, pp. 6–9.

Fraser, Ian, "Hegel, Marxism and Mysticism," *Bulletin of the Hegel Society of Great Britain* Nos. 41/42 (2000), pp. 18–30.

Greeman, Richard, "Raya Dunayevskaya: Thinker, Fighter, Revolutionary," *Against the Current*, Nos. 12–13 (1988), pp. 55–57.

Haug, Frigga, *Beyond Female Masochism: Memory-Work and Politics* (New York: Verso, 1992).

Hudis, Peter, *Marx and the Third World* (Detroit: News & Letters, 1983).

————. "Toward Philosophic New Beginnings in Marxist Humanism," *Quarterly Journal of Ideology*, Vol. 13:4 (1989), pp. 87–94.

————. *Harry McShane and the Scottish Roots of Marxist-Humanism* (Glasgow: The John MacLean Society, 1993).

————. "Dialectics, 'the Party' and the Problem of the New Society," *Historical Materialism*, No. 3 (1998), pp. 95–117.

Ito, Narihiko, "Raya Dunayevskaya on Rosa Luxemburg" [in Japanese], *Gekkan Forum* (May 1992).

Jeannot, Thomas M., "Raya Dunayevskaya's Concept of Ultimate Reality and Meaning," *Journal of Ultimate Reality and Meaning*, Vol. 22:4 (1999), pp. 276–93.

Johnson, Patricia Altenbernd, "Women's Liberation: Following Dunayevskaya in Practic-ing Dialectics," *Quarterly Journal of Ideology*, Vol. 13:4 (1989), pp. 65–74.

Kellner, Douglas, *Herbert Marcuse and the Crisis of Marxism* (Berkeley: University of California Press, 1984).

———. "Raya Dunayevskaya," *Encyclopedia of the American Left* (Urbana: University of Illinois Press, 1992).

Kelly, George Armstrong, *Hegel's Retreat from Eleusis* (New Jersey: Princeton University Press, 1978).

Kliman, Andrew and Ted McGlone, "The Transformation Non-Problem and the Non-Transformation Problem," *Capital & Class* No. 35 (1988), pp. 56–83.

Le Blanc, Paul, ed., *Rosa Luxemburg: Reflections and Writings* (Amherst, NY: Humanity Books, 1999).

Linden, Marcel van der, *Von der Oktoberrevolution zur Perestroika: Der westliche Marxismus und die Sowjetunion* [From the October Revolution to Perestroika: Western Marxism and the Soviet Union] (Frankfurt: dipa-Verlag, 1992).

McGlone, Ted, *A Study of Raya Dunayevskaya's Marxist-Humanism* (Ph.D. Dissertation: University of Utah, 1994).

Mondolfo, Rodolfo, *El Humanismo de Marx* (Mexico, D.F.: Fondo de Cultura Economica, 1973).

Moon, Terry. "Raya Dunayevskaya," *Women Building Chicago 1790–1990: A Biographical Dictionary*, ed. Rima Lunin Schultz and Adele Hast (Bloomington: Indiana University Press, 2001).

Nielsen, Aldon Lynn, *C.L.R. James: A Critical Introduction* (Jackson: University Press of Mississippi, 1997).

Plaut, Eric and Kevin Anderson, eds., *Marx on Suicide* (Evanston, IL: Northwestern University Press, 1999).

Portales, Gonzalo, "Raya Dunayevskaya: Ein humanistische Tradition des Marxismus in Amerika," *Hegel-Studien*, Vol. 25, Sonderdruck (1990), pp. 135–37.

Randall, Margaret, *Gathering Rage: The Failure of 20th Century Revolutions to Develop a Feminist Agenda* (New York: Monthly Review, 1992).

Rich, Adrienne, "Living the Revolution," *Women's Review of Books*, Vol. 3:12 (1986), pp. 1, 3–4.

———. *What Is Found There, Notebooks on Poetry and Politics* (New York: Norton, 1993).

———. *Arts of the Possible: Essays and Conversations* (New York: Norton, 2001).

Turner, Lou, "Frantz Fanon's Journey into Hegel's 'Night of the Absolute'," *Quarterly Journal of Ideology*, Vol. 13:4 (1989), pp. 47–63.

Worcester, Kent. *C.L.R. James: A Political Biography* (Albany: SUNY Press, 1995).

Other Works

Adorno, Theodor. "Aspects of Hegel's Philosophy," in *Hegel: Three Studies*, trans. Shierry Weber Nicholsen (Cambridge: The MIT Press, 1994).

Alexander, Robert. *Trotskyism in Latin America* (Stanford: Hoover University Press, 1973).

Althusser, Louis. *For Marx* (New York: Vintage Books, 1970).

Anderson, Kevin B. "On Hegel and the Rise of Social Theory: A Critical Appreciation of Herbert Marcuse's *Reason and Revolution*, Fifty Years Later," in *Sociological Theory*, Vol. 11:3 (Nov. 1993).

———. "The 'Unknown' Marx's *Capital*, Vol. I: The French edition of 1872–75, 100 Years Later," in *Review of Radical Political Economics*, Vol. 15:4 (1983), pp. 71–80.

Buber, Martin. *I and Thou*, trans. by Walter Kaufmann (New York: Scribner's, 1970).

Bukharin, Nikolai. *Historical Materialism: A System of Sociology* (New York: International Publishers, 1925).

Cohn-Bendit, Daniel. *Obsolete Communism: The Left-Wing Alternative* (New York: McGraw Hill, 1968).

Cruse, Harold. *The Crisis of the Negro Intellectual* (New York: William Morrow & Co., 1967).

Denby, Charles. *Indignant Heart: A Black Worker's Journal* (Detroit: Wayne State University Press, 1989 [orig. 1978, with Part I first published in 1952]).

———. *Workers Battle Automation* (Detroit: News and Letters, 1960).

Diamond, Stanley. "Anthropology in Question," in *Reinventing Anthropology*, ed. by Dell Hymes (New York: Vintage Books, 1972).

Djilas, Milovan. *The New Class: An Analysis of the Communist System* (New York: Praeger, 1957).

Dupré, Louis. *Marx's Social Critique of Culture* (New Haven: Yale University Press, 1984).

———. *The Philosophical Foundations of Marxism* (New York: Harcourt Brace, 1966).

———. *Passage to Modernity* (New Haven: Yale University Press, 1993).

Fanon, Frantz. *Black Skin, White Masks* (New York: Grove Press, 1967).

———. *The Wretched of the Earth* (New York: Grove Press, 1973).

Findlay, J. N. *Hegel: A Reexamination* (New York: Collier, 1958).

Gramsci, Antonio. *Selections from the Prison Notebooks* (New York: International Publishers, 1971).

Hegel, G. W. F. *Early Theological Writings* (Chicago: University of Chicago Press, 1948).

———. *The Encyclopedia Logic*, trans. by T.F. Geraets et al. (Indianapolis: Hackett, 1991).

———. *Hegel's Logic*, trans. by William Wallace (Oxford, Clarendon Press, 1975).

———. *Hegel's Philosophy of Mind*, trans. by William Wallace (Oxford: Clarendon Press, 1971).

———. *Hegel's Philosophy of Nature*, trans. by Michael John Petry (London: Unwin Brothers, 1970).

———. *History of Philosophy* (New York: The Humanities Press, 1974).

———. *Lectures on the History of Philosophy*, Vol. III (Berkeley: University of California Press, 1990).

———. *Hegel on Tragedy*, ed. with an Introduction by Anne and Henry Paolucci (New York: Harper & Row, 1962).

———. *Phenomenology of Mind*, trans. by J.B. Baillie (London: Allen & Unwin, 1931).

———. *Phenomenology of Spirit*, trans. by A.V. Miller (Oxford: Oxford University Press, 1977).

———. *The Philosophy of Right*, trans. by T. M. Knox (Oxford: Clarendon Press, 1942)

———. *Elements of the Philosophy of Right*, edited by Allen Wood (Cambridge: Cambridge University Press, 1991).

———. *Science of Logic*, trans. by Johnston and Struthers (New York: MacMillan, 1929).

———. *Science of Logic*, trans. by A. V. Miller (New Jersey: Humanities Press, 1969).

———. *System of Ethical Life and First Philosophy of Spirit*, ed. and trans. H. S. Harris and T. M. Knox (Albany: SUNY Press, 1979).

Hudis, Peter, "Labor, High-Tech Capitalism, and the Crisis of the Subject: A Critique of Recent Developments in Critical Theory," *Humanity and Society*, Vol. 19, no. 4 (1995), pp. 4–20.

———. "Conceptualizing an Emancipatory Alternative: István Mészáros' *Beyond Capital*," *Socialism and Democracy*, Vol. 11:1 (1997), pp. 37–55.

James, C. L. R. *The Black Jacobins: Toussaint L'Ouverture and the San Domingo Revolution* (London: Secker and Warburg, 1938).

———. *Notes on Dialectics, Hegel, Marx, Lenin* (Westport, Connecticut: Lawrence Hill & Co., 1980, orig. 1948).

———. *Nkrumah: The Ghana Revolution* (Westport: Lawrence Hill, 1977).

———, Grace Lee and Raya Dunayevskaya. *State-Capitalism and World Revolution* (Chicago: Charles Kerr, 1986, orig. 1950).

Joravsky, David. *Soviet Marxism and Natural Science* (London: Routledge and Kegan Paul, 1961).

Kelly, George Armstrong, *Idealism, Politics, and History: Sources of Hegelian Thought* (Cambridge: Cambridge University Press, 1969).

King, Martin Luther, Jr. *Why We Can't Wait* (New York: Harper and Row, 1963).

Koinange, Mbiyu. *The People of Kenya Speak for Themselves* (Detroit: Kenya Publication Fund, 1955).

Kosík, Karel. *Dialectics of the Concrete*, trans. Karel Kovanda and James Schmidt (Boston and Dordrecht: D. Reidel, 1976).

Korsch, Karl. *Marxism and Philosophy* (London: New Left Books, 1970).

Lenin, V. I. "Abstract of Hegel's 'Science of Logic'" in *Collected Works*, Vol. 38 (London: Lawrence & Wishart, 1961).

———. *Collected Works*, Vols. 1–45 (Moscow: Foreign Languages Publishing House, 1968).

———. *Selected Works*, Vols. 1–12 (New York: International Publishers, 1943).

Lévi-Strauss, Claude. "A Confrontation," *New Left Review* no. 62 (July-August 1970).

Löwith, Karl. *From Hegel to Nietzsche: The Revolution in Nineteenth Century Thought* (New York: Holt, Rinehart and Winston, 1964).

———. "Mediation and Immediacy in Hegel, Marx and Feuerbach" in W. E. Steinkraus, ed., *New Studies in Hegel's Philosophy* (New York: Holt, Rinehart & Winston, Inc., 1971).

Lukács, Georg. *Existentialisme ou Marxisme?* (Paris: Éditions Nagel, 1948).

———. *History and Class Consciousness* (Cambridge: MIT Press, 1971 [orig. 1923]).

———. *The Young Hegel*, trans. Rodney Livingstone (Cambridge: MIT Press, 1975).

———. *The Ontology of Social Being. 1. Hegel*, trans. by David Fernbach (London: Merlin Press, 1978).

————. *The Ontology of Social Being. 2. Marx*, trans. by David Fernbach (London: Merlin Press, 1978).

————. *The Ontology of Social Being. 3. Labour*, trans. by David Fernbach (London: Merlin Press, 1980).

————. *The Destruction of Reason* (New Jersey: Humanities Press, 1981 [orig. 1954]).

————. *The Process of Democratization* (New York: SUNY press, 1991).

Luxemburg, Rosa. *The Accumulation of Capital* (London: Routledge, 1951, orig. 1913).

————. "Stagnation and Progress in Marxism," *Gesammelte Werke* 1 (2) (Berlin: Dietz Verlag, 1974), pp. 363–68.

Mao Zedong. "On Contradiction," in *Selected Works of Mao Zedong*. Five Volumes (Beijing: Foreign Languages Publishing House, 1960–65).

————. "On the Correct Handling of Contradictions Among the People," in *Selected Works of Mao Zedong*.

————. "Report on an Investigation of the Peasant Movement in Hunan," in Brandt, Schwartz and Fairchild, *A Documentary History of Chinese Communism* (Cambridge: Harvard University Press, 1952).

Marcuse, Herbert. *Reason and Revolution* (New York: Oxford, 1941).

————. *Soviet Marxism* (New York: Columbia University Press, 1958).

————. *One-Dimensional Man* (Boston: Beacon Press, 1964).

————. *An Essay on Liberation* (Boston: Beacon Press, 1969).

Marx, Karl. *Capital*, Vol. I, trans. by Ben Fowkes (London: Pelican, 1976).

————. *Capital*, Vol. I, trans. by Samuel Moore and Edward Aveling (Chicago: Charles Kerr, 1932).

————. "Contribution to the Critique of Hegel's *Philosophy of Right*" (1843), in *Marx-Engels Collected Works*, Vol. 3 (New York: International Publishers, 1975).

————. *Critique of the Gotha Program*, in *Marx-Engels Collected Works*, Vol. 24 (New York: International Publishers, 1989).

————. *Critique of Hegel's Philosophy of Right*, ed. with an Introduction by Joseph O'Malley (Cambridge: Cambridge University Press, 1970).

————. "Critique of the Hegelian Dialectic," in Appendix A of Raya Dunayevskaya, *Marxism and Freedom, from 1776 until Today* (New York: Bookman, 1958).

————. *The Ethnological Notebooks of Karl Marx*, transcribed and ed. by Lawrence Krader (Assen: Van Gorcum, 1972).

————. *The Holy Family*, in *Marx-Engels Collected Works*, Vol. 4 (New York: International Publishers, 1975).

————. *Marginal Notes on Adolph Wagner's Lehrbuch der politischen Ökonomie*, in *Marx-Engels Collected Works*, Vol. 24 (New York: International Publishers, 1989).

————. *The Mathematical Manuscripts of Karl Marx*, trans. by C. Aronson and M. Meo (London: New Park, 1983).

————. "Private Property and Communism," in Appendix A of Raya Dunayevskaya, *Marxism and Freedom, from 1776 until Today* (New York: Bookman, 1958).

————. "Theses on Feuerbach," in *Marx-Engels Collected Works*, Vol. 5.

————. and Frederick Engels, *Collected Works*, Vols. 1–47 (New York: International Publishers, 1975–98).

Maurer, Reinhart Klemens. *Hegel und das Ende der Geschichte: Interpretationen zur 'Phänomenologie des Geistes'* (Stuttgart: W. Kohlhammer Verlag, 1965).

Merleau-Ponty, Maurice. "Marxism and Philosophy," in *Politics*, No. 4 (1947), pp. 173–76.

Melville, Herman. *The Letters of Herman Melville*, ed. by Merrell R. Davis and William H. Gilman (New Haven: Yale University Press, 1960).

Mészáros, István. *George Lukács, The Man, his Work, and his Ideas*, ed. by G. H. R. Parkinson (New York: Vintage, 1970).

Pannekoek, Anton. *Lenin as Philosopher* (London: Merlin Press, 1975, orig. 1938).

Pöggeler, Otto. "Zur Deutung der Phänomenologie des Geistes," *Hegel-Studien*, Bd. I (Bonn: Bouvier Verlag, 1961), pp. 282–83.

Riedel, Manfred. *Theorie und Praxis im Denken Hegels* (Stuttgart: 1965).

Rosdolsky, Roman. *The Making of Marx's 'Capital'* (London: Pluto Press, 1977).

Rubel, Maximilien. *Karl Marx. Oeuvres: Economie*, Vol. II (Paris: Éditions Gallimard, 1968).

Sartre, Jean-Paul. *Critique of Dialectical Reason* (London: New Left Books, 1976 [orig. 1960]).

———. *Search For a Method* (New York: Knopf, 1963).

Styron, William. *The Confessions of Nat Turner* (New York: Random House, 1967).

Trotsky, Leon. *The Permanent Revolution.* (New York: Pathfinder, 1969, orig. 1930).

———. *The Revolution Betrayed* (New York: Pathfinder, 1972, orig. 1937).

Turner, Nat. *Nat Turner*, ed. by Eric Foner (Englewood Cliffs, NJ: Prentice Hall, 1971).

INDEX

Abern, Martin, 21, 31n15

Abolitionism. *See* Anti-slavery movement

Absolute(s), xx–xxii, xxiv, xxvii–xxviii, xxxi, xxxiii, xxxvii–xxxviii, 5, 19, 43, 65, 70–71, 80, 85, 93–97, 108, 113, 133–34, 141–42, 155, 165–66, 172, 180, 185, 199, 207, 209n9, 210n20, 237, 239, 246, 248, 266, 283, 288, 302, 309, 311, 326, 331, 333, 336, 353, 356n17; Idea, xix, xxi, xvi–xxvii, xxxii, xxxiii, 6–8, 15–25, 27, 49, 56, 58, 62, 65, 68, 70–72, 87–88, 91–94, 96–101, 103–6, 109, 112–18, 123n30, 129, 133, 136n15, 141–44, 156, 157n8, 162, 171, 177–85, 188, 239–40, 248, 264–66, 274–75, 281, 283–84, 292, 305–8, 310, 325–33, 336–37, 353; Idea as new beginning, xxiv, 177–78, 189, 196, 203, 207, 227, 232, 249, 306, 308, 311, 326; Knowledge, xix–xx, xxiii–xxiv, 17, 35–36, 43, 45–47, 52–53, 96, 103, 138–42, 170, 174n20, 196, 198m, 239, 283, 317n55, 331; liberation, xix, xxviii, 22, 97, 102, 109, 184, 188, 204, 337; Marx, in, 171, 174n22, 180, 188, 209n9, 288; method, 6, 21, 51, 72, 94–95, 100–101, 108, 114, 117, 132–34, 178–79, 181, 183–84, 190n3, 191, 246, 282–84, 292, 305, 308, 310–11, 313, 328, 330–31, 337; Mind (Spirit), xix–xx, xxviii, 6, 26–30, 95–96, 98, 103–4, 133, 141, 170, 185, 196, 239–41, 248, 283, 292, 308, 330, 336; movement of becoming, 232, 260, 263, 283, 310; negativity, xviii–xxv, xxviii–xxx, xxxii, xxxvii, 8, 104, 106, 134, 154, 167, 179, 181, 183–87, 208, 239–40, 243, 246, 264, 304, 317n55, 328, 338–39; negativity as new beginning, xxxiii–xxxiv, 164, 166, 177, 246, 294, 304; new beginning, as, 179, 184, 188–89, 192, 209; unity of theory and practice, as, xxviii, 5, 50, 87, 113, 123n25, 132, 169–70, 178–79, 194, 196, 227–28, 265–66, 307, 353. *See also* Dialectic; Dunayevskaya, Raya; Hegel, Georg Wilhelm Friedrich; Marx, Karl

Adorno, Theodor, xvii, xxi–xxiii, xxxiii, xln18, xln19, 186–87, 190n7, 191, 207, 211n47

Afary, Janet, 322n1

Africa, xxxiii, 27, 73, 100, 102–3, 113, 149, 152–53, 165, 173n15, 188, 192, 242–43, 245, 264, 277, 292, 304, 312–13, 339. *See also* Egypt; Ghana; Guinea; Kenya; Madagascar; Morocco; Namibia; Revolution; Senegal

CPSIA information can be obtained at www.ICGtesting.com
Printed in the USA
LVOW01s1432100715

445774LV00002B/316/P

9 780739 102671